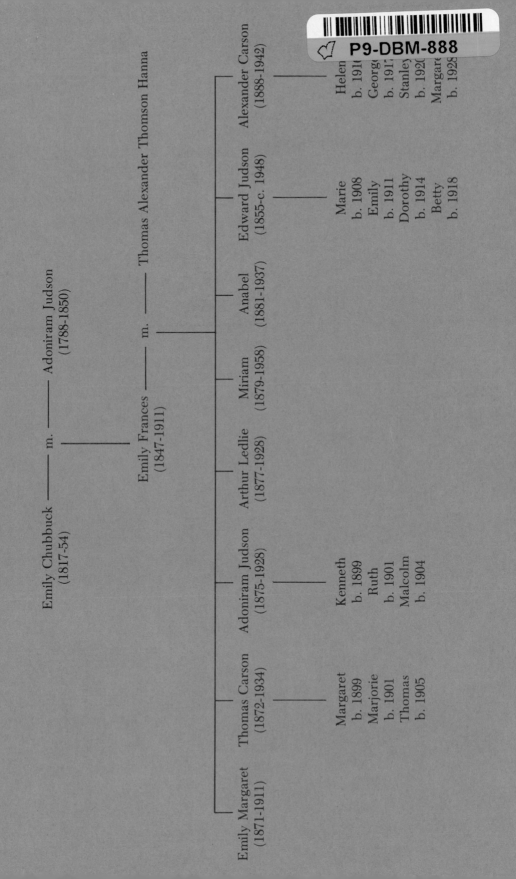

Mission for Life

Mission for Life

The story of the family of Adoniram Judson,
the dramatic events of the first American foreign
mission, and the course of evangelical religion
in the nineteenth century

Joan Jacobs Brumberg

THE FREE PRESS
A Division of Macmillan Publishing Co., Inc.
NEW YORK

Collier Macmillan Publishers
LONDON

For
David Brumberg
and
Adam Brumberg

The Free Press
A Division of Macmillan Publishing Co., Inc.
866 Third Avenue, New York, N.Y. 10022

Collier Macmillan Canada, Ltd.

Library of Congress Catalog Card Number: 79–54667

Printed in the United States of America

printing number
1 2 3 4 5 6 7 8 9 10

Library of Congress Cataloging in Publication Data

Brumberg, Joan Jacobs.
   Mission for life.

   Includes index.
    1. Baptists--United States--Biography. 2. Judson
family. 3. Missions, American--History. 4. Evan-
gelicalism--United States--History. I. Title.
BX6493.B73 1980   286'.1'0922   79-54667
ISBN 0-02-905100-2

Contents

Acknowledgments

In the creation of this book I owe my primary intellectual debts to Joseph F. Kett. Throughout my graduate education, in the writing of my Ph.D. dissertation, and in the preparation of this book, Joseph Kett has given generously of his time and his acute historical insights.

I am also indebted to Robert D. Cross of the University of Virginia for his careful and evaluative reading of earlier versions of this book. Michael Kammen and R. Laurence Moore, both of Cornell University, and Fay Dudden of The University of Rochester have also provided me with important and provocative commentary. My editor Colin Jones at The Free Press has proven to be a valuable and perceptive critic of my work.

Because of my commitment to making American history intelligible to those beyond the professional historical community, I have considered family and friends as important barometers of the viability of this manuscript. I wish to thank Ellen Richardson Grebinger, Frances and Sidney Jacobs, Midge Wiggins Kerlan, and Marjorie Moore for their comments, support, and good-humored tolerance of my never-ending stream of Judson stories. Bea Goldman has been a helpful reader and critic of my prose style; Mildred O'Connell located some interesting visual accompaniments to the manuscript. I am indebted also to Stanley Hanna, the great grandson of Adoniram Judson, for genealogical information provided in the notes to Chapter 6.

A number of archivists and librarians were essential to this project. Herbert Finch, Assistant University Librarian for Special Collections, Cornell University, deserves special thanks. William Brackney, American Baptist Historical Society; Joseph Ernst, Curtis Clow, and Walter Hovious, Rockefeller Archives Center; Howard Williams, Colgate University; Mary Huth, The University of Rochester; Martha Mitchell, Brown University; Gerald Hamm, Wisconsin State Historical Society; and Pat Harpole, Minnesota Historical Society, were also helpful. Gould P. Colman and the staffs of the Department of Manuscripts and University Archives and the Wason Collection, Olin Library, Cornell University, were also important. In the early stages of this project, Don Thompson and Nancy Heiser, Hobart-William Smith College Library, provided valuable reference advice.

I also wish to acknowledge the research assistance of Deborah Paddock (on Chapter 6) and the support and friendship of Carol Stevenson, who, in my year as visiting faculty at the State University of New York at Binghamton, helped to sustain both my teaching and writing efforts. I am also grateful to Veronica Stackonis, Gloria Gaumer, Ella Kalinich, and Ida Williams at SUNY-Binghamton, who have been more than helpful in taking care of the typing and correspondence that ensued in my effort to reconstruct the Judson genealogy. Roberta Ludgate typed the original version with remarkable precision; John Crispin of Ithaca and Pat Sommers of Rochester did much of the photographic work.

Finally, my work has benefited from the kind of day-to-day interchange that comes from living with another historian. To David Brumberg I am profoundly grateful for his dispassionate criticism and his patient, loving support.

Ithaca, N.Y.
August 1979

Introduction

The book you are about to read is a cultural biography of an important Protestant American family, abstaining for the most part from their internal, psychological dynamics and concentrating on their relationship to the world at large. The patriarch of the family, Adoniram Judson (1788–1850), was born at Malden, Massachusetts, and reared in Plymouth by orthodox parents. Adoniram Judson was an heir to the Congregationalist traditions of New England. At twenty, after graduating from Brown, he entered Andover Theological Seminary where he came in contact with other young men whose piety and religious energies were, increasingly, directed abroad, to the evangelization of the heathen. Largely as a result of the efforts of a small band of Andover seminarians, the American Board of Commissioners for Foreign Missions was formed in 1810, constituting the first official American support organization for the work of foreign evangelization. In 1812, when he was twenty-four years old, Adoniram Judson left the United States for the East in the employ of that Congregational board.

Before reaching India, Judson and his young wife, Ann Hasseltine (1789–1826), became convinced that there was no scriptural authority for their own baptism, as infants, in the Congregational church. Both Judsons were rebaptized in Calcutta, joining the Baptist denomination. Within months of the receipt of this news, American Baptists responded with the formation of the Baptist Society for Propagating the Gospel in India, a precursor of their Triennial Convention. The Judsons' adoption by the Baptists was the beginning of a significant relationship for the denomination, a relationship that may, in part, explain the denomination's tremendous success in the antebellum period.

During the thirty-eight years he spent abroad, Adoniram Judson was regarded by Baptists as the showpiece of American evangelicalism. Judson and the Baptist mission in Burma were the focal point of a wide variety of denominational activities. From his post at Maulmain, Judson wrote often, and at length, to denominational officers explaining and defining the nature of foreign mission work. With the completion of his Bible translation in 1834, Judson became distinguished as "the man who gave the word of God" to nineteen million heathen. Admired for his skills as a translator and lexicographer, Judson was lionized at home by his fellow Baptists who, in turn, promoted the family's accomplishments and reputation in both the religious and secular press. Biographies of Judson's wives, particularly the sainted Ann Hasseltine and Sarah Hall Boardman (1803–1845), were included in countless nineteenth-century anthologies of famous women, indicating their significance as models for female religious behavior. Thus, I have chosen to use the Judsons as their nineteenth-century constituency did: as demonstration and symbol of the workings of evangelical religious culture.

Traditionally, the term "evangelical" is used to signify specific groups of Protestants, especially Methodists and Baptists, who made proselytizing, conversion, and the revival basic procedural tenets. While this definition still applies, throughout this study I use the designation in a larger context, including those Congregationalist-Presbyterians, and even Episcopalians, who, although repudiating the "excesses" of the revival, adopted the notion of a "mission for life."[1] In nineteenth-century America, there were groups like the Universalists, Episcopalians, and Spiritualists who, while opposed to enthusiastic religion, came to adopt some of the organizational and promotional techniques of the strictly evangelical denominations. Thus, I shall use the uncapitalized term "evangelical" to denote those values and forms associated with the Protestant denominations that laid special stress on the Gospel as a basis for their belief and social practice.

The religious and social imperative to create a Protestant "empire" under the cultural jurisdiction of the evangelical churches has been described by Martin Marty in *The Righteous Empire*.[2] Generally, the effort to evangelize their fellow Americans led the popular Gospel churches away from both ponderous debate over doctrinal points and theological tests of faith. While some of the better educated clergy built their professional reputations on their ability to defend various aspects of orthodox doctrine, the evangelicalism embraced by most nineteenth-century Americans was first and foremost a religion of the heart. On this point, the story of the Judson family is particularly illustrative. Adoniram Judson was not, in fact, a theologian, and the examination of his life and work does little to explicate where antebellum evangelicals stood on doctrinal questions of free will, the Trinity, predestination, or vicarious atonement. Instead, his biography stands as testimony to the romantic spirit of the movement and to the persistent evangelical belief in a divinely inspired Bible. It was within the context of their faith in Biblical infallibility that evangelical religionists argued with one another over which denomination was apostolically pure.

My assumptions throughout this work are: that despite the fact that fifty percent of the antebellum population was simply "unchurched," evangelicals were the largest and most influential group within American Protestantism, and that they articulated a set of values which they were able to transmit to successive generations. I have characterized evangelicalism as a culture because it was, effectively, a whole system of living, based on a common set of assumptions about parenting, education, reading, sex roles, and behavior. I am very much aware, however, that it does not meet the anthropological specifications for a culture, and that evangelicalism cannot be seen apart from the larger American cultural context, having no independent viability.[3] I use terms like "the culture of evangelicalism" or "evangelical culture" to indicate that complex of values, behaviors, and institutions that were deliberately promoted by antebellum evangelicals as an alternative to secular culture.

Evangelicals, regardless of denominational affiliation, shaped their personal and organizational lives according to Scripture, and specifically, Christ's final invocation at Mt. Olivet: "Go Ye into all the world, and preach the Gospel to every creature" (Mark 16:15). Whether the Gospel was to be preached at home or abroad, in public by ordained clergymen, or in private by pious women, the rationale was the same: true Christians dedicated their lives to the work of evangelization. To do otherwise was to misread the Scriptures, to insult both God and Jesus.

"The motto of every missionary, whether preacher, printer or schoolmaster, ought to be 'Devoted for Life,'" wrote Adoniram Judson in 1833.[4] The evangelical was by definition a missionary, one whose assignment, in effect, was lifelong and unchanging. Throughout his years in the field, Judson never condoned what he called the "limited term" system whereby foreign missionaries might return home after a time. From the beginning, Judson envisioned his work as a "mission for life," an expression of the evangelical's tremendous faith in the power of individual action and behavior.

In John 10:16, evangelicals found another maxim of their faith: "There shall be one fold." Congregationalist Timothy Dwight envisioned a "single church, one in character, life and destination." Dwight's 1813 plea for unity did not, of course, encompass "Catholicism . . . or Latitudinarian Protestantism."[5] In fact, the pervasive cry for Christian unity was never more than a lofty ideal, for the world of nineteenth-century evangelicalism allowed full play for a competitive, sectarian spirit. Sharing a common hostility to "sacramentalism," evangelicals were able to cooperate in interdenominational agencies like the American Bible Society, but they were plagued by discord. Ultimately, most of the collaborative efforts degenerated, as each denomination came to support its own structure for doing the work of evangelization. Paradoxically, individuals moved comfortably from one evangelical denomination to another, in the equivalent of a religious buyer's market.

Despite the competition implicit in American denominationalism, evangelicals clung tenaciously to their ideal of a universal Christendom that would be biblical in orientation. The "work" was similar whether one was surrounded by heathens, infidels, or retrograde Christians. Subscribing to a religious "domino theory," evangelicals everywhere toiled for conversions, those "decisions of character" that insured a modicum of Christian behavior and promised the further spread of the Gospel. The process was, by Christian definition, laborious and constant, terminating only in death or in the coming of the millennium. Adoniram Judson's thirty-eight-year career as a foreign missionary illustrated how an exemplary Christian was tenacious and enduring as well as humble and pious.

In the nineteenth century, the Judsons were popular exemplars of the "mission for life" concept. The number of biographies generated by their lives and the amount of honorific prose and poetry dedicated to their memory confirms the extent to which their biographies penetrated the popular consciousness. In order to illustrate the pervasive nature of the Judson phenomenon, I have exhumed, in Chapter 1, the literary tributes to them. Throughout, I use these sources as a point of reference, for this study is as much concerned with the way in which the Judsons were portrayed as with what they actually did. The fact that their lives were so carefully documented by Baptist publicists reveals the magnitude of the Judsons' reputation and the denomination's faith in propagating the evangelical mission through printed sources.

The Judson story is also a convenient and dramatic demonstration of what evangelicals valued and how they transmitted their values. In Chapter 2, I describe the evangelical interest in youth and the social and intellectual background that contributed to Adoniram and Ann Hasseltine Judson's decisions for a "mission for life." Family piety, orthodox education, and revivalistic fervor explain the nature of their early dedication to the foreign missionary cause. That antebellum evangelicals had a compelling interest in the circumstances that made for Christian commitment is evident in their support of organizations and institutions for youth, many of which became the catalyst for adolescent and young adult conversions. The fact that the lives of so many antebellum men and women took shape in the process of religious conversion suggests that the Judsons' experience was more typical than anomalous.

In Chapter 3, I address the question: how did evangelicalism work? In addition to the enlistment of young converts, evangelicals were zealous in their efforts to create a Christian literature for America and for the world. Adoniram Judson's career as the man "who gave the Bible to the Burmese" was a demonstration of the evangelical Protestant's faith in the regenerative power of a Christian literature, epitomized by the Bible in its various translations. This interest on the part of orthodox religion was related both to Protestant dogma and the movement's need to keep pace with secular developments in the nation at large. It appears that evangelicals were more than able to accommodate their traditional simplicity of behavior to modern opportunities in the field of publishing.

Because women were the mainstay of both evangelicalism and the burgeoning national cultural industry, I have used Chapter 4 to explore the nature of evangelical womanhood.[6] In the mission of Ann Hasseltine Judson, evangelical women found a plausible identity and a program for its achievement, validating their interest and claim to activity in the religious sphere. Their feminist concerns were expressed in their support of foreign missions, which promised the social elevation of heathen women through Christianity, rather than the political feminism that put a knife to the heart of "True Womanhood." Ann Hasseltine Judson was enshrined in the annals of nineteenth-century female hagiography for the very reason that she represented an activist, but religious, alternative to the social revolution implicitly threatened by the women at Seneca Falls.

In Chapter 5, I turn to the career of Emily Chubbuck Judson, the third wife of Adoniram, who made her own considerable success as a popular fiction writer in the 1840s. Chubbuck's career as "Fanny Forester" made her a pariah among the intensely orthodox, who lamented the growth of secular culture which, coincidentally, was providing young women like Chubbuck with the opportunity to earn their livings writing sentimental fiction. In Emily Chubbuck, Adoniram Judson saw the opportunity to expropriate to the cause of religion a publicist skilled in the techniques for which the public clamored. Judson's effort to enlist popular cultural forms in the cause of Gospel Christianity indicated his consummate dedication to disseminating the Truth in whatever vernacular language was required. His willingness to utilize popular media foreshadowed the development of evangelicalism in the twentieth century, a movement which, in our own time, is characterized by the exploitation of modern communication techniques and the recruitment of celebrities drawn from the world of popular culture.

Without negating the missionary efforts of other Protestant evangelical denominations, the Judsons undoubtedly still stand as the foremost exemplars of the foreign mission movement. With the possible exception of the Beechers, no nineteenth-century American family was so closely tied in the public mind to the cause of evangelical Christianity. I have used the story of the Judsons' lives and labors as a device for exploring a number of significant and related themes in the cultural history of the nineteenth century. By preserving a narrative framework, I hope to involve the reader with the major protagonists and with the dramatic events of their lives; in considering the making of the Judsons' contemporaneous reputation as well as their actual missionary work, this study ultimately moves beyond collective biography and traditional religious history into the realm of popular culture. The focus on two generations has also served my basic concern: the description of the dynamics of a nineteenth-century religious culture.

Each of the Judson children drew different measures from the wellspring of evangelicalism, although none pursued careers in the foreign mission field. In Chapters 6 and 7, I turn to an examination of the careers of several of the Judson children, emphasizing their lives and careers and describing their responses to the changes wrought by industrialization, urbanization, immigration, and Darwinian Science. In this way, the biographies of George Dana Boardman (1828–1903), Abby Ann Judson (1835–1902), and Edward Judson (1844–1914) are used to explore the nature of evangelical religious culture at the turn of the century. While both of the men retained their essential orthodoxy, the material success of the evangelical movement implied new directions and associations, culminating in the creation of the Judson Memorial Church at Washington Square, New York City. Abby Ann Judson, who favored the pseudo-scientific vocabulary of Spiritualism, rejected the religious tenets of Christian orthodoxy but invoked the presence and reputation of her parents in doing so. In fact, the generational transitions illustrated by these biographies reveal the persistent pattern of an evangelical inheritance and foreshadow the course and spirit of the movement in the twentieth century.

In our own time, there are approximately 45.5 million American evangelicals, outnumbered only by Roman Catholics. Without doubt, evangelicalism in the 1970s is active and expansive, drawing its primary strength and vitality from the demographic and economic resources available within the rapidly growing Sun Belt and old "Bible Belt" areas of the United States. While the traditional Protestant establishment lost 2.7 million members over the past decade, the Southern Baptist Convention has grown by over 2 million, becoming the nation's largest Protestant denomination.[7] Surely, the balance of power within American Protestantism has shifted out of the Northeast and back to the zealous, oldtime, emotional faith that mainline, socially prominent Protestants regard with some distaste.

Although this study of nineteenth-century evangelicalism has been generally confined to New England and the Middle Atlantic States, the story of the Judson family is part of the heritage of southern as well as northern Baptists. While I have been restricted by circumstance to a historical investigation in archival repositories of the Northeast, there is certainly evidence to suggest that interest in and support of the Judson mission penetrated into the American South.

Adoniram Judson's missionary colleague, Luther Rice, included southern cities on his early fund-raising tour on behalf of the Burman enterprise; in 1839, a Judson Female Institute was established at Marion, Alabama. That school was named for Ann Hasseltine Judson, allegedly at the suggestion of Mrs. E.D. King, the wife of a prominent local Baptist, who reportedly kept Ann Hasseltine's portrait in her home. A Marietta (Ohio) college professor, Milo P. Jewett, who went to Alabama to establish the school, later became the first president of Vassar College. A Judson University was chartered at Judsonia, White County, Arkansas, in 1871.[8]

Adoniram Judson himself paid no homage to the sectional divisions that split the Baptist Church in the mid-1840s. When he returned to the United States from Burma in 1846, he visited Baltimore and Richmond where he paid his respects to the newly formed southern convention and uttered not a single public word on the divisive question of American slavery. Anxious for financial support from all quarters, Judson seemed to intentionally avoid exclusive identification with the Northern Baptist Convention. During 1913 and 1914, when Baptists throughout the United States celebrated the centennial of the Judson mission to Burma, separate but equally important observances were sponsored by both the Northern and Southern Baptist Conventions.

This longstanding veneration of the Judsons by Baptist Americans should not be taken to mean that the Judsons are purely denominational figures. The fact that their names are virtually unknown to those outside the denomination reflects the biases of much of our traditional historical writing which has been consistently preoccupied in the antebellum period with the story of the liberal Congregationalist and Unitarian churches. This continual focus on developments within the "elite" churches tends to overplay the way in which liberal religious ideologies have shaped American life and letters. In addition, it obfuscates the single most important fact of religious history in the nineteenth century: that, by 1850, Catholics, Methodists, and Baptists had become the three largest organized religious groups. The concentration on "good religion," like "good literature," ultimately obscures the social and cultural history of the mass of American men and women. It is my hope that, in rescuing the Judsons from the relative obscurity of denominational history, this study makes some contribution to a more inclusive social history of American religion. It has been both rewarding and exciting to breathe new life into these once-mythic figures.

Chapter 1

Christian Hagiography

By 1845, in those homes where Protestant evangelical religion predominated, it was unlikely that any individual—adult or child, male or female—had not at least heard the names of Adoniram and Ann Hasseltine Judson.

"For more than thirty years his name had been a household word," wrote Hannah Chaplin Conant from Rochester, New York, after Adoniram's death. "A whole generation had grown up, familiar with the story of his labors and sufferings, not one of whom had ever seen his face." Conant was describing her own generation, those Americans born after 1800, who regarded Judson as "a sort of Christian Paladin, who had experienced wonderful fortunes, and achieved wonderful exploits of philanthropy, in that far off almost mythical land of heathenism."[1]

Hannah Chaplin Conant's father, Jeremiah Chaplin, the first president of the college at Waterville, Maine, may well have told his daughter what he remembered about the February 1812 departure of Adoniram and Ann Hasseltine Judson for missionary work in India. Dr. Chaplin, like many older Baptists, probably followed

1

the Judsons' career closely. Such persons remembered that the young and newly married Judsons had gone out as the first American missionaries to the heathen, as representatives of the Congregationalists' American Board of Commissioners for Foreign Missions (ABCFM).[2] In January 1813, American Protestants received their first word, through personal communications directed to certain New England clergymen, that Mr. and Mrs. Judson had become Baptists, that they had severed their ties to the Congregationalist ABCFM, and that they were now dependent on American Baptists for their future support.[3]

The news of the Judson decision was transmitted beyond the circle of men and women who had known them in Plymouth, Bradford, Boston, and Salem to a larger community through the pages of the *Massachusetts Baptist Missionary Magazine*. A collection of Judson's letters explaining why he had abandoned pedobaptism appeared in the March 1813 issue of the *Magazine*, just two months after the first news had arrived.[4] Ann Hasseltine's letter to a friend, a very personal explanation of her new belief, was published the following May: "Can you, my dear Nancy, still love me, still desire to hear from me, when I tell you I have become a Baptist?" The young woman explained carefully that she and Adoniram became Baptists "not because they wished to be, but because the truth compelled" them.[5] Adoniram and Ann Hasseltine Judson had, according to their letters, independently come to the conclusion that the word "baptism" denotes "immersion" rather than "sprinkling," so that the order of New Testament baptisms (in rivers) must therefore be followed. Because there was no apostolic model for the administration of any church ordinance to the children of professors, Adoniram Judson, who had been baptized in infancy, was baptized again. Ann Hasseltine and Judson's colleague, Luther Rice, who was also under ABCFM sponsorship, followed suit.

For Jeremiah Chaplin's generation of Baptists, the Judsons' new denominational identification had a number of meanings, not the least of which was financial. The news of the decision, which spread throughout the country "like the sound of a trumpet,"[6] required careful attention from Baptists, who virtually had the Judsons and Luther Rice dropped in their laps. It was an event that the then relatively unorganized and impoverished denomination had not anticipated. Should and could this minority of 173,000 coreligionists adopt and support the runaway children of New England orthodoxy?[7]

The Baptists answered in the affirmative, and denominational missionary societies multiplied. The Baptist Society for Propagating the Gospel in India and Other Parts was formed at Boston almost immediately. In the spring of 1813, Luther Rice arrived from the East; he and Judson had decided that they needed an agent at home to insure support for the mission. Rice, with his "trumpet voice," roused "churches still sleeping" and "intensified the enthusiasm of those already awake."[8] In October 1813, Baptists in Richmond, Virginia, organized to support the foreign missionary enterprise; in December, Philadelphia and Savannah were organized. By May of 1814, Baptist foreign missionary societies had been realized in New York, Baltimore, Fredericksburg, and Washington, D.C., and a national organization had been created: the General Missionary Convention of the Baptist Denomination in the United States of America for Foreign Missions, generally called the Triennial Convention. There were twenty-two auxiliaries by the close of 1814; by the end of the following year there were almost six times as many.[9]

The Baptist response to the Judsons' predicament reveals a great deal about antebellum religious life and, specifically, relationships between the denominations. First, there seems to have been general agreement among Baptists that the Judsons must be adopted and supported. God, in His Divine Providence, had led the couple to the missionary cause and, from there, to the Baptists. This belief was maintained despite the presence of some legitimate questions about the entire undertaking. There was, for example, a period of time when no one knew for certain where the Judsons would do the work. In fact, the Judsons did not commit themselves to a sphere of activity until the summer of 1813, when they landed in Burma. When Luther Rice left them on the Isle of France in early 1813, in order to return to the United States to create interest in foreign missions among the Baptists, he did not know where the work was to be done. Rice reportedly had "nothing really to tell" of Mr. and Mrs. Judson except wanderings and loneliness, and he was also ill-equipped to provide any detailed information about the costs of operating an American Baptist mission. From the perspective of 1888, it all seemed incredibly unbusinesslike and naive:

> When it is considered that the motive to missionary effort was to be sustained without a syllable of fact from the field, such as we now depend upon for the kindling of the missionary flame, the churches of that day must be credited with a high type of benevolence.[10]

Judson's legitimacy as a Baptist preacher was, however, an important consideration. The neophyte Baptist had his credentials established early by William Carey, a veteran British Baptist missionary to India, who wrote to William Staughton in Philadelphia: "Judson has . . . preached the best sermon on Baptism that I ever heard on the subject." It was so good Carey announced he would print it; in turn, Carey's letter to Staughton was published in the *Massachusetts Baptist Missionary Magazine* in September 1813.[11] Indeed, Judson's "Christian Baptism, a sermon preached in the Lal Bazar Chapel, Calcutta, September 27, 1812," was subsequently printed at Calcutta in that year, and in London a year later, before going through five American editions between 1817 and 1846.[12]

The Congregationalist response to Judson's change of heart also contributed to the Baptists' perception of Judson as a reliable and authentic figure. On receiving the news, the ABCFM dissolved their relationship with the Judsons and voted that their Prudential Committee examine future missionary candidates more closely.[13] There was no doubt, then, that Judson had in fact clearly severed his ties with the Congregationalists and that he and Ann were on their own. This did much to dispel assertions that Judson was insincere. After all, why give up all means of worldly support for a cause that is less than true?

Congregational criticism of Judson's action never directly confronted what was at the heart of Judson's reasoning: that pedobaptism was not consistent with the Scriptures. Rather, Judson was compelled to defend himself against the charge that he had received a "reprimand" from the ABCFM which prompted him to connive some seemingly honorable way to escape from the Board's jurisdiction. He had become a Baptist, it was implied, by deceit, not conviction.[14] This accusation appeared again in an 1819 pamphlet by Enoch Pond, pastor of the Congregational Church at Ward, Massachusetts. Pond's version was more embroidered; he alleged that Judson had never discussed his "change of heart" with his fellow missionaries (because "the change" had not really occurred) and that Judson had no new arguments for becoming a Baptist (because he hadn't really labored over the decision).[15] The testimony of Samuel Nott, former missionary with Judson, and, most importantly, a Congregationalist, helped to dispel the Pond story. Nott attested that Judson had never received a "reprimand" and that they had discussed Judson's views on Baptism "within three hours" of Nott's arrival in Calcutta.[16]

While some Congregationalists looked for a rope with which to hang Judson, they were simultaneously keeping him alive with debates within their own circle. The most characteristically evangelical view of the affair was expressed by Gordon Hall, a Congregationalist missionary to India, from the vantage point of 1836: "After the lapse of more than twenty years, it may now be confidently said, that the apparent hindrance has undoubtedly promoted the furtherance of the gospel. By the division of the mission [between Congregationalists and Baptists] a large evangelical body of Christians was called into the missionary field."[17]

The controversy over Judson's change of sect was a precursor of things to come in the course of the Second Awakening. A conspicuous feature of the evangelicalism that absorbed New England and upstate New York in the period 1790 to 1850 was denominational mobility. Individuals and family groups were able to change their denominational affiliation with apparent ease. This may have been an institutional response to the geographic mobility that characterized the lives of so many in the antebellum period.[18] Individuals arriving in newer regions might have to worship with different denominations if they were to worship at all. In the history of the area of New York State that was "burned over" by revivalism, Whitney Cross observed that "it mattered little whether [an individual] was nominally Congregational, Baptist or Methodist." They might "change affiliation several times as one sect or another . . . seemed to enjoy particular manifestations of heaven born agitation."[19]

The biographical literature of the antebellum period is replete with examples of men and women who changed their denominational affiliation. Alexander Beebee, reared a Presbyterian, educated at Columbia College, and a friend of Washington Irving, became a Baptist in his thirties after the death of a child. He went on to become the editor of the influential *New York Baptist Register* in 1824.[20] Milo P. Jewett, an Andover graduate and promoter of common schools in New England and Ohio, became a Baptist in 1839 after a Congregationalist upbringing. Jewett was later involved with Matthew Vassar in the formation of the college at Poughkeepsie.[21] At the age of twenty-one, Angelina Grimke explained her conversion from Episcopalianism to Presbyterianism: "The Presbyterians, I think, enjoy so many privileges that on this account, I would wish to be one. They have their monthly prayer-meetings, Bible classes, weekly prayer-meetings, morning and evening, and

many more which spring from different circumstances."[22] Augusta
Jane Chapin, who became a Universalist minister, had been reared
and educated in the Congregational tradition; Horace Greeley had
come to Universalism by way of Presbyterian beginnings.[23] In her
later years, Catharine Beecher, who labored most of her life with
her father's evangelical Calvinism, put aside Presbyterianism and
joined the Episcopal Church.[24]

The circumstances surrounding a denominational change were
highly personal and probably dependent upon the religious and social situation in each peculiar locale. Lyman Eddy, a young clerk in
a Geneva, New York, leather goods establishment, was caught up
in the 1831 revival there. Eddy, a Presbyterian, wrote in his journal
that he was simultaneously desirous and fearful of becoming a
Methodist. That church, he wrote, was "composed of people of the
lowest class. I could not bear the idea of making known my wants
to a class of people who were so lightly esteemed by the community
in general."[25] In conservative Geneva, where Presbyterians and
Episcopalians had a firm hold on the town's social and economic
life, a switch to Methodism may not have been an astute move for a
young man on the rise, like Lyman Eddy.[26] Had Eddy been in
another central New York town, his predilection for Methodism
might not have presented such difficulties.

Denominational mobility, a fact of life in antebellum America,
was related to a number of factors: physical accessibility to a
church; the social composition of individual communities; the influence of denominational figures (settled pastors, itinerant revivalists, missionaries, writers), revivals, and sectarian controversy.
The way in which Judson's "switch" was hailed in the Baptist press
and derided by Congregationalists was part of the evangelical order
of things. A free marketplace for religion, or a healthy tension between the denominations, particularly in the competition to bring
in converts, was the best, and uniquely American way, to produce
their common goal: the Kingdom of God on earth. "However we
may wish all men to become Baptists, we will all to become evangelical Christians," wrote a contributor to *The Columbian Star*.[27]

Sect changing, then, was neither uncommon nor irreversible. So
long as one stayed within the evangelical camp and eschewed the
Universalists and the Catholics, it constituted no breach of evangelical protocol. At any given time, all denominational constituencies were in flux. Some individuals were former members of a
church, others were current members in good standing. And an

even larger group were always potential members. With this fluid state of affairs, it is no wonder that Judson's name traversed the boundaries of his original Congregational and Baptist constituencies.

And, indeed, all indications are that when Adoniram Judson returned to the United States in 1845, after almost thirty-four years in Burma, his name was a "household word," and that his triumphant reception was built on the existence of an evangelical community that had vicariously shared his experiences through the religious press. The very sight of the now middle-aged missionary appears to have evoked a whole set of images and events. William Gammell, a professor at Brown University, recalled the presentation of the venerated Judson to a Baptist audience in November 1845:

> Hundreds were gazing for the first time upon one, the story of whose labors and sorrows and sufferings had been familiar to them from childhood, and whose name they had been accustomed to utter with reverence and affection as that of the pioneer and father of American missions to the heathen. They recalled the scenes of toil and privation through which he had passed, they remembered the loved ones with whom he had been connected, and their bosoms swelled with irrepressible emotions of gratitude and delight.[28]

J.H. Raymond, who was later to become the president of Vassar College, wrote that as he looked at Judson, "all the startling and romantic incidents of his wonderful life passed in review [before him]."[29] Knowledge of his exploits and accomplishments created the desire to see Judson "in the flesh." "Throughout the Union," wrote one biographer, "there was a desire to see him, which was so earnest that there seemed no other course open than for him to visit some, at least, of the chief cities."[30] Judson's tour took him to New York, Providence, Albany, Utica, Philadelphia, Washington, D.C., Baltimore, and Richmond, where "thousands who had been born since he had left . . . hastened to grasp his hand, and addressed him as one whose name," and hence exploits, "had always been familiar to their lips."[31]

Judson's "triumphal march" through the nation's urban centers was supplemented in November 1845 by a two-day sojourn at a smaller Baptist enclave in Hamilton, New York, where Judson stayed in the home of Rev. Nathaniel Clark Kendrick, Professor of Systematic and Pastoral Theology and President of Hamilton Lit-

8

erary and Theological Institution. Baptist biographers were fond of recalling that Kendrick was reared by Congregational parents in Hanover, New Hampshire. At about age twenty, he left the family farm and began dividing his time between academy studies and common school teaching. As a participant in local revivals, he was prompted to ask both Baptist and Congregationalist pastors to state their views. Finding this method unsatisfactory, Kendrick "resolved to examine the New Testament," demonstrating the evangelical imperative for apostolic purity. Nine months of direct personal experience with scripture convinced Kendrick that the Baptists' "peculiarities" were "derived from and supported by the New Testament."[32]

At the Hamilton Literary and Theological Seminary, Judson cautioned Kendrick's students against "an impulsive and transient missionary zeal." On his first full day in Hamilton, he attended services in the village and on the hill at the Seminary and met with the Eastern Association, a student home missionary group, in a private room for about ten minutes. The following morning he was moved to tears by the sight of the seminarians in the galleries before him, many of whom were to be his successors in the great work of evangelizing the heathen.

Hezekiah Harvey, who was in the Hamilton audience, wrote to Lucy Loomis, his fiancee and a student at the Utica Female Seminary, in November 1845 describing Judson's visit to Hamilton. Harvey's letter provides the personal voice that much of the Judson reportage lacks. Additionally, his letter suggests that the writer had already absorbed the story of Judson's travails and work in the East, that the venerable missionary's visit was an opportunity to recall familiar history:

> I feel that I can hardly pass this Sabbath evening more profitably than in recalling to my own mind and seeking to convey to yours the hallowed scenes of the past day. It is a day I shall never forget—one of those days that make an indelible imprint on the memory, [because it is] associated with the deepest and richest emotions of the heart. Judson has been here. Though he could speak but few words with his lips, the man spoke volumes. What a world of associations cluster around him.[33]

Harvey could hardly resist the opportunity to retell the Judson story: how Adoniram had gone out "in the dark hour of the American Church," how "he had toiled for years in Burma without a convert," how his life had been imperiled in "loathsome dungeons"—all for the love of Christ. He eulogized his faithful wives—one "beneath the shade of the green Hopia" and the other in "the rock of the ocean"—and he thought about Judson's work in translating the Bible into Burmese. He repeated it all like a liturgy, crediting Judson with the conversion of 5,000. "And here before me," he wrote to his future wife, "was the man who had been the pioneer and presiding genius in this great moral enterprise. It seemed like a dream—yet it was reality."[34]

That Judson was a role model for Hezekiah Harvey is evident in the remainder of his letter to Lucy, which casts their future life together in a distinctly Judsonian framework. Harvey expresses to the young woman his desire to go out and do foreign missionary work and includes her in this life plan. "I look forward with pleasing anticipation to our union," he writes. "With the presence of Christ, and with you by my side I can but be useful and happy." Cautioning her that she "must not go to the heathen for [his] sake only," he suggests the development of those characteristics which distinguished Adoniram Judson's wives. Aware of the Judsons' difficulty in mastering Burmese, and the wives' assistance in this matter, he concludes his projection: "I'll trust your patience and sagacity for learning any language that men have ever spoken—should think you'd make a first rate missionary to translate Chinese."[35]

Other young men of serious purpose would have reason to emulate Judson's character and piety. Communicants of the Baptist Church in Trumansburg, Tompkins County, New York, formed a missionary society in May 1832 expressly for the purpose of educating one Adam Cleghorn at Hamilton Literary and Theological Seminary, "with the view of preparing him with the necessary intellectual cultivation for a Missionary to Burmah."[36] The fact that these Trumansburg Baptists sought to sponsor a missionary with some degree of education is probably a reflection of both their recognition of and esteem for Judson (who had received formal training at Brown University and Andover Theological Seminary) and the presence of a Baptist training institution in upstate New York.

For Cleghorn, whom the community saw as its own contribution to the work, piety and competent performance at Hamilton must have been essential. He was under a serious mandate. His attendance at services, while at home in between seminary terms, is noted in the church records; reports are made by Cleghorn on his spiritual condition. The Trumansburg Baptists supported Adam

Cleghorn's education for at least three years; during this time they were visited by missionary Jonathan Wade, one of Judson's co-workers in the Burman field. This contact with Burma, and the sponsorship of one of their own, brought them close to the mission-ary cause and to Judson. If we can generalize from the Trumans-burg experience, it is not surprising that some families named their sons for the venerable missionary, hoping that his namesakes might "bear a like character."[37]

Because they read their own denominational history correctly, the Baptists saw Judson's potential both as an "energizer" of young men and as a way to fill up the denominational coffers. The *New York Baptist Register* reported on January 16, 1846, that Judson's visit to Philadelphia had raised $14,200 for support of their mission-ary work. Lest they be accused of "using" Judson for their own sec-tarian purposes, the correspondent reminded the reader that it was all to a larger, evangelical end: "thousands in this city will love the cause of missions more from having become so intimately ac-quainted with Judson. . . ."[38] The fact that Judson suffered from a respiratory ailment throughout the tour and that he was almost al-ways unable to address his audience is truly "mute testimony" to his reputation and to the power of the associations he evoked.

That Judson's presence was used to generate funds within Bap-tist communities should not obscure the interdenominational na-ture of his 1845–1846 reception. The "joy in the land" was "not con-fined to the denomination with which he was identified; but in it members of every religious community participated, and even those who took no interest in the cause of missions. . . ."[39] "The feelings were not confined to Baptists. Thousands ranged under a different standard . . . welcomed him with the catholic fellowship of Chris-tian love. . . . So general a feeling of enthusiasm towards an indi-vidual, simply on the ground that he was a GOOD MAN, had never before been awakened in the country." [40] "These manifestations of regard were not confined to the religious denomination to which he belongs; members of every Christian communion and citizens of every rank were eager to . . . honor [him]. . . . It was no sectarian adulation."[41]

Evangelical protocol and belief shaped the nature of Judson's reception. It was Baptist publicists, in the Baptist press, who docu-mented his movements about the East coast.[42] Judson was received cordially by non-Baptist evangelicals. He was accorded the respect and admiration that his record in Burma deserved; he was, after all, part of the world mission to the heathen of which they, too, were a part. Judson's official biographer, Francis Wayland, observed that by 1845 and 1846 "the momentary irritation" of Judson's denominational change had evaporated, Baptists and pedobaptists gave freely to one another's treasuries, and "at their monthly concerts they communicat[ed] the missionary intelligence from both societies." Adoniram Judson was, in fact, received by the officers of the ABCFM as a "brother beloved."[43] A letter from soap manufacturer William Colgate in January 1846 indicates that Judson was accorded some secular honors. "Senator [William] Marcy introduced him to . . . President [Polk] as the Greatest Ecclesiastical Character now living," wrote Colgate to his daughter Mary. He continued: "Mr. [Daniel] Webster offered to introduce him to the Senate but by some oversight it was not done."[44] When secular papers such as the *Utica Daily Gazette* noted Judson's arrival, it was usually done with respect and care not to offend any of its readership:

The distinguished Baptist Missionary has recently returned to this country . . . the noble, self-devoted man desires to go back instantly to Burma. Well do we honor this missionary. Right or wrong in his religious views he certainly gives great evidence of sincerity.[45]

Sincerity may, in fact, be a key to understanding the popularity of the biographies that followed Judson's death in 1850. His perseverance in the face of trials and tribulations with the Burmese, with British officialdom, and with ailing wives and children provided the perfect ingredients for the kind of inspirational biography that was central to evangelical notions of education. Biography, particularly the biography of the trials of sincere individuals, regardless of denomination, had unlimited potential as a molder of character, a socializing agent. "The influences which flow from acquaintance with the history of great men's lives are powerful and abiding," wrote an evangelical minister in the preface to his biography of Judson. "Religious biographical literature," he continued, "is highly appreciated by Christians of every name. . . . It would be difficult to indicate any means separate from its issues of the inspired volume, by which the press has done more efficient service in quickening spiritual life and promoting Christian usefulness."[46] The Bible, in fact, consists of biographies of "the enemies and friends of God . . . recorded to teach mankind," wrote another evangelical.[47] Biography was for Susan Huntington the dividing line between civilization and savagery. Savages "live and die unimproved by the experiences of others"; they have no biography.[48]

Biographies of Judson were numerous and often competitive. After his death, his third wife, Emily Chubbuck, returned to the United States with the intention of assisting Dr. Francis Wayland, President of Brown University, in the preparation of an authorized version of Judson's life. The proceeds of this official biography were to go to Emily Chubbuck Judson and the Judson children. Upon her arrival in Boston in October 1851, Judson's widow was met with the first indication that the official biography would be facing some competition. A New York publishing house, not united to the Judsons by any denominational tie, had printed a memoir of Adoniram; its publishers proposed to pay Mrs. Judson $50 for each thousand copies sold. Careful not "to sanction this as a final and authoritative memoir," Emily Chubbuck declined the income from the sale of this memoir.[49]

In October 1853, just as Wayland's two-volume authorized biography was coming before the public, E.H. Fletcher, a New York publisher with Baptist connections, advertised an inexpensive memoir of Adoniram Judson in a single volume. Wayland's "authoritative version" cost two dollars; Fletcher's less than half that. Judson's widow, who refused to consider lowering her volume's price, wrote the offending publisher requesting that he consider the financial harm he was doing to her and "the orphans of [her] sainted husband. . . . "[50] She implored him to stop publication of the cheaper memorial.

Fletcher was recalcitrant. He argued that his version of Judson's life, *Burmah's Great Missionary,* by Robert Middleditch, was designed for a different audience, less affluent and educated, than the Wayland volumes.[51] "No provision is made or proposed," he wrote, for providing "the thousands of little country Sabbath schools and poor families" with a life of Judson. Fletcher basically was accusing Mrs. Judson of an elitism that obscured larger evangelical goals. He believed that "each work will find a place for which it is adapted." He claimed the support of a number of unidentified Baptist clergy and discredited Emily Chubbuck's assertion that the Judson family was "strapped" financially. Finally, Fletcher asserted that "the public life of a public man is public property." Adoniram Judson's life, like that of statesman Daniel Webster, had entered the public domain. [52]

There is further evidence that Judson family and friends tried to halt the publication of another memorial entitled *Grace and Apostleship: Illustrated in the Life of Judson,* by Robert Woodward Cushman.[53] Cushman wrote in the preface to his volume that publication was initially declined by the American Baptist Publication Society, "from fear that its publication would be adverse to the interests and wishes of the family of Dr. Judson, such publications being considered as calculated to interfere with the [Wayland] Memoir."[54] What the Baptist Publication Society had failed to anticipate, according to Cushman, was the market for Judson material.

Wayland and Cushman were to share this audience with the following antebellum Baptist publicists: Edgar Harkness Gray, pastor of the First Baptist Church in Shelburne Falls, Massachusetts;[55] Abram Dunn Gillette, pastor of the Eleventh Baptist Church in Philadelphia;[56] Rufus Babcock, editor of *The American Baptist Memorial* and author of *Tales of Truth for the Young* (1846);[57] William Hague, author of *Home Life: Twelve Lectures*;[58] Hannah Chaplin Conant, editor of the *Mother's Journal*;[59] and Daniel C. Eddy, pastor of the Harvard Street (Baptist) Church.[60] Wayland's authorized biography, the premier purchase for Judsonphiles, sold at least 26,000 copies within its first year, despite Baptist fears that the market would be co-opted by other biographies and tracts.[61]

Further literary evidence of contemporary recognition of the Judsons permeates antebellum culture. These tributes were not confined to Baptist circles, nor did they recognize Adoniram only. In fact, the literary remains suggest that the women named Judson (particularly the first wife, Ann Hasseltine) were established figures in the female hagiography of the nineteenth century. "If she had lived," wrote one biographer, "in legendary instead of historical times, she would have ranked with Saint Agnes and Saint Cecilia; but as plain truth is now spoken of the good, the devoted, and the martyrs, she will be remembered for ages, as one deserving of high praises in the churches."[62] Because "good" women's actions were supposed to be tied to an admirable quality called "disinterest," it would follow that women were less sectarian than men. This may explain why so many more non-Baptists wrote about the Judson women than about Adoniram. The patriarch still had the power to evoke sectarian feelings; the women were simply outside or above denominational politics.

Ann Hasseltine Judson's biography is included in at least the following antebellum collections: An American Lady, *Sketches of the Lives of Distinguished Females, written for Girls with a View to their Mental and Moral Improvement* (New York, 1833); Lydia Maria Child, *Good Wives* (Boston, 1833); J. Clement, *Noble Deeds of American Women; with biographical sketches of Some of the More Prominent* (Buffalo, 1851); Frank B. Goodrich, *World-Famous Women. A Portrait Gallery of Female Loveliness, Achievement and Influence* (New York, 1858); Sarah Josepha Hale, *Woman's Record; or Sketches of All Distinguished Women* (New York, 1855); and Samuel Lorenzo Knapp, *Female Biography, Containing Notices of Distinguished Women, in different nations and ages* (New York, 1834).

In post-Civil War anthologies of famous American women, Ann Hasseltine was still prominent. In fact, her biography is uniformly given throughout the century. The story of her missionary exploits was retold by Sarah K. Bolton, *Famous Types of Womanhood* (New York, 1892); by Phebe Hanaford, *Daughters of America, or Women of the Century* (Boston, 1883); and by Emma R. Pitman, *Heroines of the Missionary Field* (New York, 1880). Collections of ninteenth-century "women worthies" were popular throughout the post-Civil War period because they were, generally, a distinctly conservative and religious means of explicating the "woman question."

Some of the collections in which Ann Hasseltine was included were a response to nationalist feeling. In 1851, Jesse Clement stated that "a failure to do justice to American women" was the motivation for his book. In Cecil B. Hartley's *The Three Mrs. Judsons, the Celebrated Female Missionaries*, the author compared the English Florence Nightingale to "our heroine," Ann Hasseltine Judson. "Can we not, in America," he asked, "point out our bright stars in the galaxy of heroines?"[63]

These comments suggest that, to a certain extent, interest in Ann Hasseltine and Adoniram Judson may be explained in terms of cultural nationalism—that the Judsons were simply the first Americans to do what they did. On the other hand, Congregationalist Samuel Mills, often described as "The Father of Modern Missions," was never lionized in the same way. Ann Hasseltine's presence may, in fact, have been the Judsons' "drawing card." American women, who formed an increasingly large part of the reading public, were interested in how one of their own would fare in the non-Christian East.[64]

Interest was so high that in the 1850s Daniel C. Eddy, a biographer of Adoniram, made something of a second career writing about Judson's wives. He produced three volumes on female missionaries in 1850, 1855, and 1859. The text was basically the same, however, in each edition; only the titles changed. In 1850 and 1855, he gave his books these generic titles: *Heroines of the Missionary Enterprise, or Sketches of Prominent Female Missionaries* and *Daughters of the Cross; or Women's Mission*. By 1859, probably in response to a persistent market for Judson material and the popularity of the name, Eddy's title had evolved to *The Three Mrs. Judsons, and Other Daughters of the Cross*.[65] Ann Hasseltine and Emily Chubbuck were included in a mezzotint portrait series of five religious females offered in *Godey's* in August 1848. [66] The fact that the second Mrs. Judson (Sarah Boardman) was not included in the series prompted the reviewer at Geneva, New York, to write: "the plates should have contained one figure more— the portrait of Judson's other wife. . . ."[67]

Some readers and writers tended to "embalm in one urn" all of Judson's wives. The most popular antebellum collection of the three biographies was done by Arabella Stuart Willson.[68] *The Lives of the Three Mrs. Judsons*, as the book was known colloquially, was first published at Auburn in 1851, after the death of Adoniram Judson., Emily Chubbuck Judson, who was still alive at that time and living in Hamilton, New York, was included in a brief sketch at the end. Engravings of Ann Hasseltine and Emily Chubbuck by J. C. Butte were popular attractions of the editions issued at Auburn which sold at least 26,000 copies by 1856. The book was also printed in New York City by C. M. Saxton in 1858, 1859, and 1860, and in Boston by Lee and Shepard in 1855, 1869, and 1875.[69] According to Arabella Stuart Willson, her memoir was intended to be "more attractive to youthful readers than the excellent biography [of Ann Hasseltine] by Mr. Knowles."[70]

Knowles' biography of Ann Hasseltine Judson had been published by Gould, Kendall, and Lincoln, a Boston printing house with Baptist connections, in 1829; the 1830 edition was under the sponsorship of the interdenominational American Sunday School Union. It was the Boston firm, however, that reaped the profits from this highly successful book by reissuing it for the next three decades and as late as 1875. Knowles' *Life of Mrs. Ann Hasseltine Judson, late missionary to Burma* went through ten editions by 1838; after that it was reissued in editions of undetermined size on an almost yearly basis until 1856.[71] Knowles' biography is included in Harvey Newcomb's 1833 list of recommended reading for young women.[72] Unitarian Lydia Maria Child referred to Knowles' biography as "a book so universally known that it scarcely need be mentioned."[73]

A letter from the young wife of a paymaster in the Union army suggests why the Knowles memoir was popular throughout the Civil War period. Writing from upstate New York in July 1861, Elizabeth Camp told a woman friend that she was reading "the life and letters of Mrs. Judson." She said of Ann Hasseltine: "her mission with Mr. Judson seemed so perfect—and her married life so short—and with her such a sad termination. I could sympathize with her intense love for her husband and her experience made me . fear that mine might be the same."[74] One can only speculate on how many wives of fighting men saw in the story of Ann Hasseltine Judson something akin to their own experience.

Despite its Boston origins, Knowles' biography obviously made its way westward to newly settled regions. It was available at Van Brunt and Sons, a central New York bookstore in January 1842, and it was published at Cincinnati by Anderson & Knox in 1847.[75] A year later, in 1848, the reading public got the opportunity to gather even more information and inspiration from the Judsons. The *Memoir of Sarah B. Judson, member of the American mission to Burma*, written by Emily Chubbuck Judson, sold at least 15,000 copies within the year.[76] In the United States, 30,000 had been printed by 1855. In that year, a professor at the University of Rochester, Asahel Clark Kendrick, who had known Adoniram and Emily Chubbuck personally, brought out *The Life and Letters of Mrs. Emily C. Judson*.[77] Ten thousand copies of Kendrick's biography were in print a year later.

Tributes to Ann Hasseltine were also presented to the American reading public by two of the period's foremost literary personages, Sarah Josepha Hale and Lydia Huntley Sigourney, both of whom were Episcopalians.[78] Hale, editor of the popular *Godey's Lady's Book*, wrote that Ann Hasseltine, as "the first American woman . . . to leave her friends and country to bear the gospel to the heathen," merited "the reverence and love of all Christians. . . ." She considered Sarah Hall Boardman a "less distinguished figure than her predecessor . . . but not inferior in loveliness of character."[79] Sigourney's inevitable poetic tribute evoked all the associations that were part of the saga of Ann Hasseltine: the departure to an unknown land; brutality at the hands of the Burmese; and, eventually, death, alone, with "dark Burman faces around her bed."[80] When Judson's second wife died at St. Helena in 1845, Sigourney wrote a poem in her honor also.[81] H.B.H., identified as an "esteemed professor" at the Newton Theological Seminary, described the same event "for the public" after hearing "the particulars" from "a friend who was present."[82]

Poetic effusions about the Judsons were popular. John Dowling, editor of *The Judson Offering* (1846), chose selected poems by H. S. Washburn, S. Dryden Phelps, Stephen P. Hill, Mrs. H.L.C., Mrs. T. P. Smith, Charles Thurber, S. Wallace Cone, and James D. Knowles to grace his elaborate commemorative volume.

There were other aspiring poets who tried their hands at a Judson verse. Some, like Pamela S. Vining, were published locally or in the religious press. Vining's "Judson's Grave" focuses on the missionary's anonymous grave at sea:

> No shroud is around him,
>   no flowers bloom above,
> No mourners surround him
>   With grief drops of love.[83]

Other poems about the Judsons remained obscure in personal diaries and journals. A poem, "For Mrs. Judson," written by Mary H. Day, probably a student, was copied into an album belonging to Maria Mansfield, a student at Castle Hall Seminary in Catskill, New York, in April 1827.[84]

The dissemination of the Judson story beyond the formal bounds of the evangelical sects has been documented through the adulatory prose and poetry of Unitarian Lydia Maria Child, as well as Episcopalians Hale and Sigourney. A fourth antebellum woman, with another set of associations, suggests that we can extend the perimeters of the Judsons' notoriety and influence even further.

Charlotte Newcomb was born in 1823 and named for a family friend, Charlotte Ellery Channing, mother of William Ellery. Charlotte Newcomb's mother, Rhoda Mardenborough Newcomb, was a member of the Providence Athenaeum and was involved, as a writer, with the *literati* of that city. She was well versed in eighteenth-century literature, was fond of Johnson and Addison, and

probably introduced her daughter to her ninteenth-century favor-
ites: Goethe, Schiller, Carlyle, and Coleridge. Charlotte studied for
a time at Margaret Fuller's school, receiving, it seems, especially
close attention, because her brother, Charles King Newcomb, was
a friend of Fuller's. In 1839, two years before he began his "residen-
cy" at Brook Farm, Fuller wrote to Charles about his sixteen-year-
old sister Charlotte: "I hope she will be your friend and companion,
since I cannot be myself. I flatter myself," she continued, "[that]
she will be more to you for having been with me."[85]

It is unclear how the young Charlotte Newcomb grew intellec-
tually from her relationship with Margaret Fuller, or through her
brother's close association with men like Ralph Waldo Emerson,
Bronson Alcott, and other Transcendentalists. The fact that she
was nurtured in the bosom of that American tradition and that she
was exposed, through mother and brother, to the German and English Romantics, may be a partial explanation of her predilection
for the pseudo-literary religious sentimentality that was often associated with evangelicalism and with the Judsons.[86] The great Romantic convention of her own life was her marriage to a tubercular
poet, John Matthewson.

Among the possessions she left to her posterity is a collection of
music that she either sang or accompanied in her passage through
Rhode Island society. Of particular interest is a quartet for voices
and piano entitled "The Burial of Mrs. Judson at St. Helena, September 1, 1845." Charlotte Newcomb was probably familiar with
the Romantic conventions of this dirge-like song:

> Mournfully, tenderly, Bear on the dead.
> Where the Warrior lain, Let the Christian be laid;
> No place more befitting—O Rock of the Sea
> Never such treasure was hidden by Thee
> Never such treasure was hidden by Thee

The warrior also buried at St. Helena is Napoleon, a figure of great
interest to the Romantics. The lyrics here are typical of descriptions
of Sarah Boardman Judson's death; most writers used the common
burial ground at St. Helena as an opportunity to contrast worldly
(Napoleon) and religious (Judson) forces. The personification of the
natural world ("Tears are bedewing the path as you go") and the
emphasis on the struggle that is life ("Mournfully, tenderly, gaze on
that brow, / Beautiful is it In quietude now")[87] were typical of popular Romantic writing.

The song was made specific to the Judsons by its evocation of the memory of "precious dust . . . laid by the Hopia tree" (Ann Hasseltine) and an "equally precious treasure" in "The Rock of the Sea" (Sarah Boardman). Filled with praise for Judson, "Thou servant of God," Charlotte identified herself as part of a community of mourners. "Kindred and strangers / Are mourners to-day,"[88] the lyrics went. Charlotte Newcomb, educated at the knee of Margaret Fuller, was participating in an evangelical-cultural exercise. Her case illustrates that evangelical-cultural experiences were not alien territory to Transcendentalism's extended family. In fact, the women of these two discrete groups, Protestant evangelicals and Transcendentalists, were mutually comfortable with a restrained, but decidedly Romantic, vocabulary.

If the Judson story can be used as any measure, and there is reason to think it can, evangelical-cultural forms were diffused far beyond the confines of those churches commonly considered evangelical, embracing all of American Protestantism. Consequently, the popularity of their story helps to explain how "the first half-century of [our] national life saw the development of evangelicalism as a kind of national church or national religion."[89] While evangelical religious practices remained distasteful to some, it was hard to contain the cultural implications of the evangelical movement.

A cursory look at the young nation's institutions of higher learning in 1850 confirms the point: Protestant evangelicalism was enthroned everywhere. Unitarian Harvard, a solitary general in the struggle with orthodox religion, had almost no troops outside of New England.[90] Colleges and academies were falling largely to the orthodox camp, reflecting a widening control by evangelical sects at the local level.[91] Native support troops, in the form of printers and publishers, appeared everywhere but capitulated to evangelicalism because it was, by its very nature, a growing and therefore profitable business. It is no wonder then that the lives of so many antebellum Americans have a pattern and quality that conform to the world as described by practitioners of evangelical religion.

Chapter 2

In the Bloom of Life,
with
the Sentiments of Old Age

Because the evangelicals were passionately interested in the circumstances that made for Christian commitment, they paid close attention to the Judsons' youth. Descriptions of Adoniram Judson and Ann Hasseltine in the years before the departure for Burma became a standard but important component of their posthumous biographies.

What the biographers found and what they described were fairly ordinary: two young people whose lives took on evangelical shape as a consequence of their family backgrounds and their own youthful participation in the orthodox religious currents that were part of the Second Great Awakening in New England. The biographies reveal that the Judsons were not unique among young people at all and that, until their departure for Burma in 1812, their experiences did not differentiate them from thousands of other sons and daughters of New England and New York whose commitment to an evangelical life coalesced in the intensity of the revival or in the "moral incubator" of the denominational college or academy. It was a simple fact of antebellum life that the youth of America provided the raw material for the Second Awakening.[1]

Adoniram Judson was born at Malden, Massachusetts, in 1788, the son of a family with impeccable Congregationalist credentials. His father, Adoniram Judson, Sr., was the pastor of Malden's Third Church. Ann Hasseltine, born a year later in Bradford, was the daughter of a Congregational deacon. Above and beyond the contributions of their pious families, the Judsons' mature Christian convictions were born of their individual conversion experiences. In the case of seventeen-year-old Ann, the "change from sin to holiness" came after a period of protracted anxiety about the state of her soul while a student in the academy in her revival- struck home town. Conversion was followed by the urge "to be useful" and subsequent employment as a teacher in nearby Salem, Haverhill, and Newbury. For Adoniram, conversion came at age twenty, at the Andover Theological Seminary, after graduation from Brown (1807) and a short, conventional bout with infidelity. His devotion to a "mission for life" among the heathens can be dated from the Andover period.

Experiences like these were so predictable and so pervasive that they became an integral part of evangelical culture. Throughout the ninteenth century, evangelicals of every denomination collaborated in the creation of a literature that contributed to the expectation of religious conversion in youth. Judson biographers, for example, found in the young couple's preparation for missionary work the perfect materials for developing the scenario of early piety, adolescent conversion, and youthful religious voluntarism. Because their childhood and adolescent experiences were so commonplace, the Judsons were among the finest exemplars of the potentiality of converted youth.

The nature of their biographical literature demonstrates that the evangelical orthodox were moving in the direction of a modified Calvinism that made salvation a possibility for every person who sought it. However, in the effort to stave off the implications of strictly environmental thinking, Knowles prefaced his biography of Ann Hasseltine in this way:

> It has been said, that the character of men is formed by the education they receive; the companions among whom they are placed; the pursuits to which they are led by inclination or necessity; and the general circumstance of the situation into which accident or choice may have guided them. This opinion, though doubtless it derives some plausibility from the undeniable effects of education, of example, and of the numberless other influences which affect

the minds and hearts of men, is yet untrue, in regard both to the
intellectual and moral character. Neither the reason nor the affections are so obsequious to the power of external circumstances, as
readily to take any new shape or direction.

Knowles then went on to suggest a combination of "factors" in human development.

There exist, without doubt, in the original structure of every
mind, the distinctive elements of the future character. Favorable
opportunities may be needed, to develop their character, *but they*
cannot alone create it.[2]

Biographers who looked at the Judsons' early years for internal
indicators of saving grace found nothing remarkable. "His father
early and anxiously strove to imbue his mind with the principles of
the divine work and to develop his moral sensibilities," reported one
author, "but as is frequently the case, the seed seasonably sown did
not take root immediately, nor show any promise for years."[3] Francis Wayland, Judson's foremost biographer, did attribute a certain
amount of intellectual precocity to Adoniram. According to Wayland, Adoniram Judson read very early and asked penetrating questions.[4] While Ann's posthumous admirers gave her similar credit for
early "activity of the mind," they revealed that she too lacked
Christian commitment in childhood. In fact, one biographer stated
at the outset her failure to identify in Ann Hasseltine's early history
any of the distinguishing signs of her later "resplendent lustre."[5]

Since neither of the Judsons had been precocious Christians,
their adult lives underlined all the more heavily the redemptive
power of a Christian environment. Judson commentary generally
focused on external and environmental circumstances hospitable to
the production of American Christian martyrs: family piety, a supportive ministry, earnest peers, orthodox education, and serious
reading.

Not surprisingly, evangelical writers depicted family piety as a
sine qua non. Evangelicals were staunch supporters of family
prayer and parental monitoring of childhood spirituality. Philip
Doddridge's *Family Worship*, published in New York in the last
decade of the eighteenth century, was an evangelical classic. During the first sixteen years of his life, Adoniram received from his
parents a heavy dose of orthodoxy and Christian nurture. At twenty, when he embarked on an adventure in infidelity, it was the leg-

acy of his pious parents that acted as his conscience, saving him from disaster: "his mother's tears and warnings followed him now wherever he went. He knew that he was on the verge of such a life as he (and they) despised."[6]

A measure of the piety of Ann Hasseltine's father was his willingness to sacrifice his daughter by giving his consent to the missionary marriage. Judson biographers were fond of recalling that Adoniram confronted Deacon Hasseltine with the hard fact that if he and Ann were married, the father would see Ann "no more in this world." The young man allegedly raised the possibility of her "degradation, insult, persecution, and perhaps violent death" abroad, and put this question:

> Can you consent to all this for the sake of Him who left his heavenly home and died for her and for you; for the sake of perishing immortal souls; for the sake of Zion and the glory of God?[7]

From the evangelical perspective, this ritualistic exchange between the prospective son-in-law and the father had but one answer. Had Judson and Hasseltine acted in any other way their religious legitimacy would have been destroyed.

While the "impressions of an early religious education"[8] were credited with setting the Judsons on the proper path, the biographers were imprecise as to the content and form of that education. As a result, any description of the Judsons' youth has to be approached on two levels. First, there is the information, scanty and predictable though it is, contained in the biographies. Second, there is information culled from our understanding of the social and intellectual currents in New England in the first decade of the nineteenth century. When we put these two components together, we get a clearer, but admittedly only suggestive, picture of the Judsons in their formative years. Taking as a cue the biographers' emphasis on family piety and on fathers generally, we may begin with a consideration of the New England tradition of which Adoniram Judson, Sr., and Deacon Hasseltine were a part.[9]

Neither Adoniram Judson nor Ann Hasseltine were strangers to the concept of a Christian mission. Their fathers had assured their children's education through the example of their own religious lives. When Adoniram was fourteen and living at home in Plymouth, Massachusetts, his father delivered a sermon offered in praise of the "wonder working providences of Puritan history in the New

World." The pastor's purpose was "to commemorate the spirit of self-denial, boldness and perseverance in the cause of religion," which was the heritage of his neo-Puritan audience.[10]

Judson, Sr., took his text from 2 Cor. 6:17: "Come out from among them, and be ye separate, saith the Lord, and touch not the unclean thing; and I will receive you." The Puritan story, of coming out on an "errand into the wilderness," was retold and the inevitable question asked, "Do we live as righteously as our fathers?" Like many orthodox clergy of the post-Revolutionary period, Judson's response moved to the convention of the Jeremiad:

> We have observed, that Babylon, in scripture is used to represent all the sin and moral evil in this world of apostasy. And do not facts testify that there is sin enough at the present day, to justify an application of the text to us? Has not vice, infidelity, and a neglect of duty, become prevalent? Have we not departed from the example of our fathers?[11]

At the same time that he perceived a New World Babylon, the elder Judson saw special workings of Divine Providence in the history of the American nation. Of the separation from England, he said: "How remarkably did God appear for us, in our American Revolution!"[12] Having settled the Americans in independence and peace, God was responsible for the present "increase in the light." Despite his injunctions against rampant infidelity, Judson concluded with an affirmation: "there is more Christian knowledge at the present, than in any past age."[13]

The father's reverence for his New England forbears was based on his application of their apostolic creed. Good men, said Pastor Judson, follow "the example of the primitive Christians."[14] In cataloging the achievements of New England heroes, Judson laid heavy emphasis on the apostolic models of men like pioneer missionaries John Eliot and David Brainerd. As had Cotton Mather, Judson marveled at Eliot's accomplishment, the translation of the Bible into Mohawk. Mather wrote of that work in *Magnalia Christi Americana*: "Behold, ye Americans, the greatest honor that ever you were partakers of. The Bible was printed here at our Cambridge, and is the only Bible that ever was printed in all America, from the very foundation of the world."[15]

The elder Judson surely knew Jonathan Edwards' 1749 biography of David Brainerd, the most famous missionary in eighteenth-century New England. In it, Edwards testified to his own spiritual indebtedness to Brainerd. The young missionary's journal of work among the Indians and soul searching in a "lonesome wilderness" was a model of missionary zeal and Puritan practice. The story was made more poignant by the fact that Jerusha Edwards, the biographer's daughter, nursed Brainerd through his final illness. She died soon after and was buried at his side. "All my desire was the conversion of the heathen," Brainerd wrote; for an example of Christian self-denial, his life was exemplary.[16]

Stories of Eliot and Brainerd were part of the Christian lore passed from parents to children and from pastor to congregant. In a culture that consistently harkened back to the accomplishments of its fathers, there was little likelihood that luminaries like Eliot or Brainerd would be forgotten or ignored. We do know that Ann Hasseltine, along with her reading of Edwards, Hopkins, Bellamy, and Doddridge, read the life of Brainerd.[17] Leonard Woods, a professor at the theological school that Adoniram Judson would attend, wrote that Brainerd's life was the kind of reading that could not be neglected "without experiencing an essential loss both as to the present advancement in holiness, and . . . future usefulness in the ministry."[18] To get through Andover without reading Brainerd was virtually unthinkable.

In addition to Eliot and Brainerd, Judson also knew about the foreign missionary work of the British Baptists, which began in 1792 at Serampore, India.[19] The names of William Carey, Joshua Marshman, and William Ward were known to religious communities on both sides of the Atlantic.[20] In 1806, a circular letter to all the American churches had gone forth from Philadelphia, under interdenominational sponsorship, to urge support for Carey's translation of the Bible into Hindu dialects. The effort was supported by the orthodox Calvinist journal *The Panoplist* and by the *Connecticut Evangelical Magazine*.[21]

In response to the British effort, or in anticipation of their own, American missionary organizations were formed in New England and New York in increasing numbers. The New York Missionary Society, the first interdenominational agency for this purpose, was begun in 1796. It was soon followed by other denominational and state groups. The Baptists organized associations in New York (1796), Massachusetts (1802), Connecticut (1809), and New Jersey (1811). The Congregationalists formed associations in Connecticut (1798) and Massachusetts (1799). A host of auxiliary organizations were formed, some of them interdenominational mite and cent

societies of Congregationalists and Baptists, such as the Boston
Female Society for Missionary Purposes (1800).[22] All of the organizations were domestic in orientation except the Massachusetts Missionary Society, which modified its constitution in 1804 to allow for
the possibility of diffusing the gospel in "more distant regions of the
earth, as circumstances shall invite."[23]

A knowledge of the British effort and the formation of these
support groups made American participation in the foreign missionary enterprise inevitable. While there is some evidence that
there were advocates of foreign evangelization within the professional religious community before 1810,[24] the moving force behind
American foreign missions was a small cadre of zealous young men,
students at Williams College and the theological seminary at Andover. The convergence at Andover of Adoniram Judson and Samuel J. Mills provides a striking demonstration of the dynamics of
youthful voluntarism; the additional presence of the Hawaiian native, Henry Obookiah, helps to explain, in part, the young men's
enthusiasm for the work of foreign evangelization.

Obookiah was a youth of about seventeen when he came to New
Haven in 1809. The memory of his parents' slaughter in a tribal war
compelled him to leave Hawaii. "I thought to myself," he later
wrote, "that if I should get away, and go to some other country,
probably I may find some comfort, more than to live there [in Ha-
waii] without father and mother."[25] A Captain Brintnall brought
him to New York and to New Haven, where he mixed with students
at Yale College and began to study English with Edwin Dwight.
His spiritual awareness, by Christian definition, was only rudimentary in this period. However, he showed himself to be quickly "impressed with the ludicrous nature of idol worship." "Hawaii gods!
they *wood, burn*. Me go home, put'em in a fire, burn'em up. They
no see, no hear, no anything," Obookiah is reported to have said.[26]
The young Hawaiian's eagerness to stand against his native iconola-
try must have warmed the hearts of the Christians who took him in.

In 1810, Obookiah met Samuel J. Mills, who had graduated
from Williams College in the previous year. While a student at Williams, Mills had been influential in founding a secret society, the
Brethren, to undertake the work of foreign missions.[27] Obookiah
was of obvious interest to a young man planning a career as a foreign missionary. The Mills family welcomed the young Hawaiian
into their Torringford, Connecticut, home where he contributed to

the family's support by cutting wood and mowing and pulling flax, all the while studying English and learning to read in the Bible. When Samuel J. Mills removed to Andover, Massachusetts, in the winter of 1810 to study at the theological institution there, Henry Obookiah went with him. "I took much satisfaction in conversing with many students in the institution at Andover," Obookiah later wrote.[28]

Adoniram Judson had entered the institution at Andover two years before, in the first year of the school's operation. The theological seminary was founded as a counter against further liberal, or Unitarian, intrusions into Calvinist territory. The appointment in 1805 of the Unitarian minister, Henry Ware, Sr., to the Hollis Professorship of Divinity and the curricular substitution of French for Hebrew were evidence enough to the orthodox that Harvard had succumbed to the forces of apostasy and infidelity. Thus, parties within the orthodox ranks put aside their differences in order to found Andover, an institution for the training of "learned and able defenders of the gospel of Christ, as well as orthodox, pious, and zealous ministers of the New Testament." The faculty was under a Calvinist mandate, to be affirmed every five years in the presence of the trustees, to inculcate the Christian faith "in opposition not only to Atheists and Infidels, but to Jews, Mahommetans, Arians, Pelgians, Antinomians, Arminians, Socinians, Unitarians, and Universalists, and to all other heresies and errors, ancient or modern, which may be opposed to the Gospel of Christ, or hazardous to the souls of men."[29]

In the setting of Andover's orthodoxy, Judson, Mills, and Obookiah met. Judson and Mills were to have close association as members of the Brethren Society, which Mills transferred to Andover when he entered there. Obookiah's relationship to the Brethren Society is unclear. Its members, however, like much of the community, were interested in Obookiah's spiritual progress. Gordon Hall, a society member, Williams graduate (1808), and Andover seminarian who went out with Judson in 1812, reported meeting Obookiah in 1810. "I saw the Hawaiian youth," he recalled, "and heard him read and spell and say his lessons—I could not but think of the poor heathen."[30] Obookiah's presence in the Andover community was a visible reminder of the work to be done in foreign fields. At Andover he made his first attempts to pray in the presence of Christians. "Tell folks in Hawaii no more to pray to stone god," Obookiah requested of the Divine Father. His prayers stated specifically: "Make some good man go with me to Hawaii, tell folks in Hawaii about heaven—about hell. . . ."[31]

Because the curriculum at Andover was unsuited to his needs, Obookiah left Andover in late 1810 for the academy at Bradford where Ann Hasseltine and her sisters were students. There he boarded with the family of Deacon Hasseltine, an important coincidence that went uniformly unreported in the biographical literature on Ann Hasseltine Judson.[32] Obookiah spent the next five years in New England, living, working, and studying Christianity in a variety of locales including Hollis, New Hampshire, and Torringford, Litchfield, and Goshen, Connecticut. It is not known if he attended either the 1812 ordination or embarkation ceremonies for the first American foreign mission enterprise. Certainly he knew the Andover men who petitioned the Congregational General Association in 1810 for support to begin the first American evangelization effort: Adoniram Judson, Samuel J. Mills, Samuel Newell, and Samuel Nott.[33]

In 1816, as a result of "the veritable rage for heathen education" that swept pious communities in New England after the 1812 departure, the Congregationalists established a Foreign Mission School at Cornwall, Connecticut, where Obookiah and a few other Hawaiian youths formed the nucleus of the student body.[34] Obookiah died a Christian, at Cornwall, in 1818 at the age of twenty-six. Lyman Beecher, who eulogized him, noted that his death would do much to advance the cause, bringing "notoriety" to the school and "awaken[ing] a tender sympathy for Owhyhee [Hawaii]."[35] Undoubtedly, Obookiah became a symbol of Congregationalist foreign mission activity and his memoir, which went through twelve editions, was the first of a long line of biographical and autobiographical accounts of converted heathens.[36]

The convergence at Andover of Obookiah, Mills, and Judson was not strictly fortuitous. Rather, it was the result of the emerging evangelical interest in providing the young people of each denomination with a sympathetic host environment for the nurture and maturation of proper religious sentiments. To that end, prospective Congregational clergymen were shaped by Andover's controlled environment, with its regulated pattern of prayer, study, and useful work, including the production of coffins and wheelbarrows and seasonal agricultural labor. In addition to the seminary's well-known function as an orthodox arsenal for the war against the liberals, it provided the means for directing youthful evangelism, like that of Mills and Judson, into the appropriate conduits.

The denominationally sponsored college and academy were both an institutional cause and effect of the harvest of youth wrought by the revivals. In the effort to harness the energies of susceptible young people and, in some cases, to assure the quality and continuity of the denominational clergy, evangelical Protestant sects spawned their own educational institutions in New England, New York, and Ohio throughout the antebellum period.[37] Denominationally sponsored colleges and academies proliferated, providing fertile ground for the germination of conversions and lives of Christian activism.

It is not surprising that conversion became a significant, if not always official, part of the educational program at colleges and academies. Since the extension of church membership through the recruitment of converts was the guiding principle of the Second Awakening, it was incumbent upon educational institutions to do their part in pushing out the perimeters of Christendom. As a result, in communities where there were colleges or academies under evangelical aegis, they generally became an integral part of the communities' religious machinery, particularly with respect to the inception of the revival. Ann Hasseltine's home town, Bradford, is one case in point, but there were countless others throughout the duration of the Awakening.

Students at Mrs. Ricord's school in Geneva, Ontario County, New York, were the first in that town to be struck by the revival fires of 1831.[38] Even within this upstate enclave of Episcopalianism, the academy, which had a Presbyterian preceptress, took on the function of a revival agency. One young woman, who was boarding in the town and soon to be converted, wrote to a friend: "It is a solemn time here. There is a revival in the school. Many of the young ladies have given themselves to Christ."[39] Another commented on the inclusiveness of the revival in the life of the school: "Nearly all in the Seminary have found Christ, even to the youngest in the school are affected."[40] Of the 270 converts reported by the Geneva Presbytery in 1831, at least fifty were said to be students at the female seminary.[41] "The great object of [the female seminary]," wrote an academy teacher many years later, "was to train pupils for eternity as well as time."[42]

Ann Hasseltine and her friend Harriet Atwood were students at Bradford Academy during the revival of 1806. As a hopeful student convert, Ann Hasseltine fought off the attractions of her former "gay associates," many of whom were her fellow students. For Ann Hasseltine, Bradford Academy was both a spur and a deterrent to religiosity. "I was exposed to many more temptations than before," she wrote of her attendance at the school. In the spring of 1806, she attended village conference meetings but returned home in the company of "light companions" with whom she "assumed an air of gayety [sic] very foreign to her heart."[43] Her social persona was actually masking a pious conformity to the revival's influence:

> The spirit of God was now evidently operating on my mind; I lost all relish for amusements; felt melancholy and dejected; and the solemn truth that I must obtain a new heart, or perish forever, lay with weight on my mind.[44]

Within six months of the onset of the revival, seventeen-year-old Ann Hasseltine made public profession of her faith in the Congregational Church to which her parents belonged.[45]

If Hasseltine's conversion narrative is accurate, her academy preceptor, an unidentified male, was a "significant other" in guiding her towards grace. On a number of occasions when she was confused by her inability to extricate herself from sin, Ann turned to the preceptor: "I had been unaccustomed to discriminating preaching; I had not been in the habit of reading religious books; I could not understand the Bible," she wrote, "and felt myself as perfectly ignorant of true religion as the very heathen. In this extremity, the next morning, I ventured to ask the preceptor what I should do. He told me to pray for mercy, and submit myself to God."[46] To help her along the way, the preceptor gave her religious magazines which she read, confining herself to her room and denying herself "every innocent gratification; such as eating fruit . . . not absolutely necessary to support life." "[I] spent my days reading and crying for mercy," she later wrote.[47] The fact that Ann's asceticism was both voluntary and temporary suggests its artificiality. Like the counterculture homesteader of the 1960s who attempted to recover the ecological purity of a lost age, Ann Hasseltine was simply imitating the lonely travails of the apostles and David Brainerd.

In the Second Awakening, youthful Christian commitment grew primarily out of the social milieu of revivals, groups organized for piety and benevolence, and schools. Hasseltine's case exemplifies the manner in which conversion and academy attendance converged, as well as the managerial role of the anonymous preceptor.

The experiences of Fanny Kingman (1814–1868), also an adolescent convert, not only mirror Ann Hasseltine's early life but reflect on the academy as a conversion agency, only this time from the perspective of the teacher.

Fanny Kingman was converted at age nineteen in Berkeley, Massachusetts, during the winter of 1833, after intermittent attendance at the Bridgewater Academy and a stint of teaching in the town's common schools. Like Hasseltine, she kept a journal; typically, Kingman's begins at the time of consecration to the "new life."[48] The Kingman diary, like that of Ann Hasseltine nearly twenty years before, is characteristic of so many written by anonymous American women in that it is primarily a vehicle for recording religious progress, for the articulation of spiritual hope and of self-doubt. All of the perceptions, decisions, and events of these young women's lives were cast in religious terms, creating the kind of autobiographical record that has prompted a historian of American youth to observe: "In America between 1790 and 1840, evangelical Protestantism was the context in which the moral and intellectual conflicts of young people often received their primary expression."[49]

When she was twenty-one, Fanny Kingman moved to Fall River to begin a school for young women.[50] Her journal is filled with indications of her own daily religious activity and notations of "dear pupils who have been able to submit to the Saviour." In fact, during the school year of 1836, the young teacher proudly recorded at least a dozen conversions among her seminary students. Although she continued to worry about the state of her own soul, as a teacher she regarded her students' progress toward Christ as a reflection of her spiritual condition. As a consequence, teachers like Fanny Kingman had a very heavy investment in the religious lives of their students.

Letters written to a former class, months after she left, made specific inquiries about the spiritual condition of each young woman: "To Anne R. what can I say? Often have I felt, dear girl, that you were just ready to enter the fold of our Great Shepherd and I have seemed ready to welcome you as a sister in Christ." "E. Swift . . . I rejoice in the hope that you dear girl, will endeavor to live in the Church of God, not as a mere idler, but as one who has much to do."[51] Another academy teacher, Clarissa Thurston, assistant to Elizabeth Ricord in the school at Geneva, orchestrated the conversion of Mary Mortimer in 1837.[52] Forty years later, Thurston would still be able to describe Mortimer's move toward grace in great detail.[53] This was the nature of the evangelical teacher. It is no wonder that so many who wrote about growing up in the antebellum period recalled specific teachers who were "professors of religion."

Pedagogical efforts were paralleled and supported by the students themselves. Evangelical teachers and clergy understood that young converts, by articulating the effects of the conversion experience, exerted pressure on their peers. The state of the soul was a legitimate and interesting source of conversation and concern. Friends were apt to discuss who was under conviction, who had professed, whose behavior indicated a loss of resolve. A friend wrote of Ann Hasseltine's behavior in the period prior to her conversion: "Redeeming Love was now her theme. One might spend days with her, without hearing any other subject reverted to."[54]

As ministers, preceptors, teachers, and parents urged an early decision of character through conversion, friends marveled at its effects. In the 1830s, Kingman wrote to her friend Mehitable: "I found that at God's right hand there flows a stream of happiness, exhaustless as the source from whence it issues. And the more deeply we drink of this stream, the more abundantly does it flow."[55] Two decades earlier an optimistic Ann Hasseltine told a friend:

> I find more solid happiness in one evening meeting, when divine truths are impressed on my heart by the powerful influences of the Holy Spirit, than I ever enjoyed in all the balls and assemblies I have attended during the seventeen years of my life. Thus when I compare my present views of divine things, with what they were, at this time last year, I cannot but hope I am a new creature, and have begun a new life.[56]

Peer testimonials like these were probably one of the evangelical movement's greatest persuasion techniques. Strategically, what they meant for the antebellum girl was that she was receiving unambiguous and parallel support for conversion from figures of authority and from her peer group.[57]

For males the situation was more complex because the behavioral options were wider. Young women, however, had no monopoly on religious enthusiasm or activity, despite their participation in disproportionate numbers. A majority of the young male volunteers for foreign mission work were fueled by the revival fires which struck the small towns and villages of central and western New England and upstate New York.[58] The circumstances surrounding the founding of the Brethren Society in 1808 at Williams illustrate how college revivalism promoted missionary zeal. Although the actual story of the Brethren's initial meeting has been obscured by layers of filiopietistic history, it is agreed that the so-called "Haystack Prayer Meeting" occurred during or following a revival at the college. The young foreign missionary enthusiasts, who were all converts, had a constitution written in cipher to insure secrecy. "Let us be more cautious in the admission of members than even the Illuminati," wrote Samuel J. Mills. "We shall do well to examine their every look, their every action. . . ." The test of membership for a host of missionary and moral societies spawned by college revivalism was an "experiential acquaintance with the religion of the gospel."[59]

College revivalism became a part of the academic calendar at denominational colleges throughout New England and New York.[60] As a result, conversion came to be associated with the college years, and, in the case of Andover, a theological training school, it was a prerequisite for admission. When Adoniram Judson applied to Andover in the autumn of 1808, he could not provide evidence of saving grace. In fact, he entered the institution through a special "compensatory education" provision. Leonard Woods, a seminary instructor at the time, recalled: "When Mr. Judson came to Andover, he was not a professor of religion and gave no evidence of being a Christian. We consented to his staying in the Seminary for a time, but did not then admit him as a member.[61]

That Judson experienced the darkness of "gloomy skepticism" and walked through "the valley of humiliation" made his conversion, and his subsequent life of exemplary evangelical practice, all the more affecting. All of his biographers would relate how he graduated with the class of 1807 from Brown, where he was valedictorian but not a convert. "In the years which Mr. Judson spent at Providence, French infidelity was extremely popular," wrote one biographer.[62] In reality, Brown was a pious place that had revivals while Judson was a student; he was obviously not engaged by the one in 1805 which promoted "the general piety" of the college rather than specific "doctrinal practices."[63] Adoniram Judson's collegiate disinterest in religious matters was attributed to the deistic spirit of the day and to the tendencies of young men "to favor novel and extreme views."[64] Thus, Judson embarked upon the voyage of life unfortified by personal religious conviction.

Two weeks after his Brown graduation, Judson opened a private academy in his home town, Plymouth, which he maintained for about twelve months. During this time he published two respectable school texts, *The Elements of English Grammar* and *The Young Lady's Arithmetic*, but he was not converted[65]—despite the proximity and probable influence of his father, a local pastor, and his pious mother. In August 1808, for reasons never articulated by the man or his biographers, Judson headed out on a "tour of the Northeast," a euphemism for the proverbial male bout with infidelity. According to the evangelical *volksgeist*, Judson would ultimately be a better Christian, and more steadfast in his conviction, because of this experience.

What the twenty-year-old former school teacher did during the two months between his departure from Plymouth and his arrival at divinity school is difficult to uncover. His biographers suggest that in this unsupervised and unstructured situation, the skepticism he was exposed to in his collegiate days inevitably surfaced. Some say he rode Robert Fulton's steamboat down the Hudson River and landed at New York, where he was tempted by "fashionable amusements"; he allegedly tried his hand at playwriting and joined a New York theater company.[66] His dalliances, however, were short-lived. By October 1808, "destitute of the proper qualifications," he was seeking admission not only to Andover, but to the Kingdom of God.

What happened to turn Judson's attention from the stage to the state of his soul? For evangelical writers this was the most important part of a Christian life. Since conversion would determine the future course of the individual and, by implication, the world, evangelical literature was conversion-centered. In fact, there was an intriguing variety of ninteenth-century literature produced by evangelicals which focused on conversion in one way or another. In addition to spiritual autobiography and conversion narratives, evangelicals wrote advice books, childrearing literature, memoirs of missionaries and converted heathens, temperance tales, and domestic and sentimental fiction.[67]

Austin Phelps of Andover explained the meaning of the conversion process:

> Conversion is the change from sin to Holiness. It is a change from absolute sin to the first dawn of holiness in the soul. It is that unique change which has no parallel and no adequate similitude, in which an intelligent mind, a free mind, a self-acting mind, a mind which has intelligently, freely, of its own will abandoned

God, is led for the first time in its moral history by almighty grace
to return and give itself to God. For the first time, then, a sinner
appreciates God. For the first time he loves God. For the first time
he chooses God. For the first time he enjoys God. For the first time
he is born of God. For the first time his life is hid with Christ in
God. God, God, GOD, is the one being to whom his soul mounts
up and in whom he enters into rest. He may be flooded with joy
unspeakable, because he is engulphed in the blessedness of God.[68]

The doctrine of "the change of heart" would be basic to writing
about Judson's life and work. Though he was "unsettled in his opin-
ions and tending to a habit of skepticism, . . . he still retained the
impressions of an early religious education, and wished for a better
state of mind."[69] Using his childhood experiences as a storehouse
from which he could draw spiritual supplies, Judson, in the late
summer of 1808, reoriented himself towards Christianity. Two
events were responsible for the "energizing" of his latent Christian
talents and the direction of his postconversion life.

The first of these occurred in an unidentified inn in an unnamed
location. Judson was, according to his biographers, returning home
to New England. He spent the night at the inn aware of the fact
that a man in an adjoining room was struggling for his life. In the
morning, he discovered not only that the gentleman had died, but
that he was, in fact, a young man who had been a friend during his
days at Brown. Impressed by the loss of his classmate, whom he
knew to be like himself, unconverted, Judson faced the possibility
and consequence of his own early demise in an unrepentent state.
The story of the discovery at the inn is probably apocryphal; on the
other hand, conversion—or steps toward it—were often precipitated by the death of a friend or loved one. In later years, Judson
never mentioned the incident. He did, however confirm the intent
of the story. "I was then a wretched infidel," he told Leonard
Woods, of those early years.[70]

The second event that had a determining effect on Adoniram
Judson was his preliminary reading of Thomas Boston's treatise,
The Fourfold State, and his subsequent encounter with Claudius
Buchanan's *The Star in the East.*[71] In looking for the circumstances
that made great modern Christians, evangelical writers put heavy
emphasis on empathetic reading and on the role of literature as an
energizer. A large number of the heroes and heroines of evangelicalism were awakened by a specific piece of literature other than
Scriptures. In the case of Judson, the Boston treatise was especially

appropriate to his preconversion state because it caused him to become anxious about the condition of his soul. Apparently, he read the work before coming to Andover, where he found the necessary correctives for his former impiety: vigorous religious leadership on the part of the faculty and pious companionship among the student body. While there is no conversion narrative detailing his change of heart, we can get some idea of the intensity of his convictions from a description of the effects of reading Buchanan's *The Star in the East*:

> For some days I was unable to attend to the studies of my class, and spent my time in considering my past stupidity, depicting the romantic scenes in missionary life, and roving about the college rooms, declaiming on the subject of missions. My views were very incorrect, and my feelings extravagant; but yet I have always felt thankful to God for bringing me into that state of excitement.[72]

It was not surprising that Judson's conversion came less than two months after his entry to Andover.[73] As was the practice, Adoniram professed his faith publicly in his father's church in May 1809—approximately six months after his conversion.

Where conversions occurred, meetings and organizations followed, making them both cause and consequence of the evangelical offensive. During a revival, the denominations would sponsor a complete program of religious activities for youths and for adults. In Bradford, Ann Hasseltine attended conference meetings and prayer groups organized in support of the revival of 1806. Those associated with, or interested in, Presbyterianism in Geneva during the revival of 1831 could attend meetings for inquiry (unconverted) or prayer (converted) on Monday nights, a service for the "unawakened" on Tuesday evening, and "social prayer meetings in different sections of the village and lectures in the more distant neighborhoods" on Wednesday. On Thursday there were Bible classes for youths and, on Friday night, a meeting for the special instruction of young converts, followed by a meeting for prayer. On Saturday, all of the pious were asked to convene to request a special blessing for the next day's labor. On Sunday, there were three regularly scheduled and distinct services to attend.[74]

From the ad hoc groups that were organized in support of specific bursts of revivalistic energy, the evangelical denominations moved to a more permanent regional and local network of voluntary associations for religious endeavor.[75] Obituaries in religious newspapers indicate that antebellum religious life was extremely well organized and that few pious men and women stood outside the network of voluntary associations. The record of Susan Huntington, a wealthy Episcopalian widow who died at the age of thirty-two, demonstrates how much Christian benevolence could be packed into even a relatively short life.

At the time of her death in 1823, Huntington had borne six children. She was a life member of the Female Orphan Asylum and of the Fragment Society; a life member and vice president of the Graham Society;[76] a life member and director of the Corban Society[77] and of the Female Society of Boston and vicinity for promoting Christianity among the Jews; a life member, the corresponding secretary, and one of the visiting and distributing committee of the Female Bible Society; an annual subscriber to the Widow's Society and the Boston Female Education Society; an annual subscriber and vice president of the Old South Charity School Society; an annual subscriber and a director of the Boston Female Tract Society; and a member of the Boston Maternal Association.[78] Although Huntington had domestic help, women of lesser means—namely Baptist and Methodist women—exhibited the same pattern of organizational involvement.

What obituaries like this suggest is that evangelicals valued collective rather than individual, or anarchic, religious practice. In the case of the Judsons, their adolescent religious anxieties were ultimately assuaged in the arena of social intercourse, in a revival, at an academy and college, in proximity to people—teachers, preceptors, pious peers, even infidels. Throughout the ninteenth century, the youthful conversion narratives that were typical of evangelical culture set the experience against the backdrop of a collective Christian setting rather than in the spiritual wilderness.[79]

While much of the associative activity was initiated by the institutional churches, a goodly proportion was carried off by youth itself, functioning always as collective entities, under the watchful eye of denominational elders. Typically, adolescent evangelicals were involved in prayer societies and in youthful auxiliaries of adult groups such as the Young Men's Bible Society established in 1823 in New York City.[80] So too, young women at academies were proverbially organizing for benevolence. In 1830, young converts at a female seminary in upstate New York formed their own Infant School Association, hired a teacher, rented a room, and raised half the operating budget from subscriptions within the school.[81]

The single most dramatic incident of this youth-initiated evangelicalism was certainly the foreign missionary movement. In fact, to a certain extent, the Andover Brethren looked to their Congregational elders simply for financial support. By and large, the conception and actual execution of this project was left to the young men.[82] Judson, Mills, and others from the secret society formed the Society for Inquiry—a public group for those interested but not necessarily "called" to the missionary life. Organization of the Andover Society led to the formation of similar societies at other seminaries, beginning with the establishment of one at Princeton in 1814.[83] At Andover, they began a missionary library and published the memoirs of the "electrifying" Buchanan and an answer by Englishman David Bogue to the critics of foreign missions.[84] In June 1810, four Andover men went to Bradford to petition a meeting of the Congregational General Association for support to begin the first American foreign mission.

Samuel Newell, Samuel Nott, and Samuel J. Mills joined Adoniram Judson in putting the following questions to their elders at Bradford:

> Whether, with their present views and feelings, they ought to renounce the object of missions, as either visionary or impracticable; if not, whether they ought to direct their attention to the eastern or western world; whether they may expect patronage and support from a Missionary Society in this country, or must commit themselves to the direction of a European Society;—what preparatory measures they ought to take, previous to actual engagement.[85]

In fact, the Andover men announced that if they were denied support in the United States, they would go anyway and solicit assistance among the British religious community. In 1811, Adoniram Judson actually went to England, as a representative of the ABCFM, to confer with the London Missionary Society about a joint venture.[86] The willingness of the English to employ the young men, without a cooperative scheme, provoked the Americans to action.

Samuel Hopkins' theory of "disinterested benevolence" was the New England seasoning that made this activist scheme palatable to the Congregational elders. Judson and his colleagues had been schooled at Andover in a new humanitarian Calvinism. Hopkinsianism taught that total devotion to God is not in the least inconsistent with the practice of benevolence to humanity. Hopkinsianism appeared to open the Calvinist door to a wide variety of human "betterment" projects.[87] Support for evangelization of the heathen came also from the most orthodox of Trinitarians. Jedidiah Morse, editor of the *Panoplist*, took up his pen in support of the cause, as part of an all-out campaign against Unitarian liberalism.[88]

Nationalism should not be totally discounted as an additional motive for the foreign mission undertaking. The British had been engaged in world evangelization for almost two decades, a fact which the young Andover men did not neglect to call to the attention of the General Association. This, plus the realization that American missions to the Indians were nearly moribund, contributed to the acceptance of the idea. In 1811, Congregationalist Samuel Worcester virtually wrote off the western hemisphere as a scene of evangelization because of the Amerindians' general resistance to cultural and religious assimilation. "The attempts which have been made to evangelize the aboriginal tribes of the North American Wilderness, have been attended with so many discouragements," he observed, "and South America is yet in so unpromising a state, that the opinion very generally prevalent is that for the Pagans on this continent little can be immediately done."[89] For all these reasons, the Congregational General Association approved the student plan in the form of a resolution creating the American Board of Commissioners for Foreign Missions. In the months ahead, the Prudential Committee of the ABCFM would begin to develop the organizational supports which would be necessary to send the young men to India. Appeals went forth from pastors before their congregations and in the form of letters from members of the Board. Missionary candidates visited the churches of surrounding communities in order to solicit funds.[90]

When there was opposition to the foreign mission plan, it came largely from liberal Unitarians who were hostile to anything emanating from Andover—"an institution which would have disgraced the bigotry of the Middle Ages."[91] Those with latitudinarian views who asked, "What right do American Christians have to interfere with the religion of other nations?" got this response:

> Some think it enough, if people have a religion; and if they be sincere in it, they conclude, that they shall certainly be saved; no matter what kind the religion is. This discovers the lowest abyss of mental stupidity, and an utter ignorance of the nature of God and virtue.[92]

For evangelicals who were tied to parochial notions of a Christian salvation and a Christian God there was virtually no consideration

of the ethics and morality of other religious systems.[93] If humans
were social beings, they lived best with Christian ethics, none
other. Confronted with the morality of any other religion, the
evangelical answered, 'Will poison nourish like wholesome food?'[94]
God, after all, had enjoined them to interfere in other religions:
"Go ye and preach the Gospel to every creature."

Proponents of foreign evangelization preferred to deal with the
kinds of questions that came from within the evangelical family.
They liked to, and repeatedly did, field objections such as: "the
time has not come," "the work is too difficult to be done by man,"
"foreign governments will interfere in the work," "the heathen are
so bad, there is no hope for success," "there is neither money nor the
proper people to do the work." Evangelicals argued that, were the
heathen world not bad, it would not require help and that God,
through technological developments like the compass, had already
opened up the globe for the gospel invasion. Admittedly, good men
were hard to find, but Christ, after all, found the apostles in obscure places. Then they were trained and "outfitted by God." Pro-
fessing Christians had unlimited economic potential to do the work.
It was simply a question of giving up luxuries: "When folly and
vanity call for support, no lack of money is observed. When an
opera house or a theatre is to be erected, is it found impossible to
provide funds?"[95]

As foreign missionary history was being made, another avenue
of criticism was opened. By the close of 1812, before even reaching
the field, nineteen-year-old Harriet Newell was dead.[96] Within the
decade, the foreign missionary cause lost James Colman and Edward Wheelock as well. Colman died a natural death; Wheelock
apparently threw himself into the sea in a fit of despondency.[97] In
early 1827, American Christians received the news that Ann Hasseltine Judson had fallen victim to the alien climate and the aftereffects of Burmese brutality. Missionary successes were everywhere
muted by the deaths of missionaries of every denomination.

Those who were opposed to foreign evangelization viewed the
mounting missionary death toll as both a needless sacrifice and a
demonstration of the zealotry of the orthodox. An 1829 review of
Knowles' biographical memoir of Ann Hasseltine, in the Unitarian
Christian Examiner, articulated what would become a common
objection by 1850:

> What has been the fruit, or what may reasonably be expected to
> be the fruit, of all these labors, and sufferings; of all these priva-

tions, sacrifices, sickness, and deaths? The answer is, as yet, the
conversion, real or only external, of a few native heathens . . . it is
our deliberate conviction, that the whole enterprise was uncalled
for, and that these immense labors, expenses, and sufferings . . .
might have been spared.[98]

If the results of missionary work were questionable, so was the
practice of sending off naive and idealistic young people. A critic,
identified only as the Reverend D.B., wrote that he could not support a crusade that operated on the principle that with "12-1/2
cents-a-piece, and a parcel of crazy boys and romantic girls, you
[can expect] to see the world converted."[99]

Adoniram Judson's third wife, who lived to return to the United
States, addressed an entire book, *The Kathayan Slave and Other
Papers Connected with Missionary Life* (1853), to dispelling the
idea of "missionary madness." Her essays attempted to counter the
idea that female foreign mission work was especially romantic,
deadly, and should be outlawed.[100] Mrs. Judson claimed that the
hostile criticism came from "a set of petty philosophers, of whom
every country village can furnish its quota—physiognomists, phre-
nologists, psychologists, and professors of other dreamy nonsense,
suddenly . . . aware of a new object for the exercise of their philanthropic vocation."[101] In reality, the critics were centered in Boston,
still a Unitarian outpost. The *Boston Evening Transcript* had this to
say about Mrs. Judson's own departure in 1846:

> This is another case of *infatuation* which would almost seem to be
> for an untimely death. We really think there should be a law
> against the wholesale sacrifice of life which is continually chron-
> icled amongst those who imagine they are "called" to labor in
> unhealthy climes as the wives of missionaries. . . .[102]

According to one estimate, at least half the number of those in
the service of foreign mission boards, prior to 1860, were women.[103]
Most of the women who "went out" were, like Ann Hasseltine and
Harriet Atwood, newly married and in their peak childbearing
years. Therefore, their first exposure to a foreign culture was complicated by adjustments to both marriage and parenting. It is no
wonder that women suffered greater mortality than men; the danger of childbirth in alien climates was undoubtedly a physical as
well as an emotional burden.

What critics of foreign missions failed to understand, however,
was the evangelical sensibility—which was touched, rather than

angered, by youthful death in the cause of religion. In fact, the martyrology of foreign missions included small children as well as youthful missionaries.[104] To see youth be pious, to see them organize for religious action, to witness even their early deaths in a holy cause—these were the experiences that evangelicals would immortalize. "Youthful piety," wrote a Methodist editor, "though not so venerable as aged virtue, is certainly more attractive and lovely."[105] Pious youth was a popular subject for the antebellum engraver, as well as the writer of sentimental didactic fiction. In addition to their beauty, evangelicals had some definite adolescent behavior in view:

> To see good principles governing the whole conduct; to see them prevail over all youthful levitie [sic] and follies; to see passions, at a season of life when usually most ungovernable, subjected to reason and conscience; to see spirit and vanities of the world despised and trampelled under foot; to see constancy, uniformity, and steadiness, at a period when irresolution and the caprice of fancy are apt to prevail; to see persons in the bloom of life, with the sentiments of old age—is certainly a most delightful spectacle.[106]

Youthful decision of character, or adolescent conversion, was the guarantor that this process of early emotional and intellectual maturation would occur. With character assured, the physical energies of youth could be harnessed to the difficult work of world evangelization.

The role of youth is central to an understanding of the workings of antebellum America's distinctly evangelical religious culture. Evangelical ministers, writers, and practitioners understood the potential of their investment in youth—church membership might grow, organizations and audiences certainly multiplied, and more funds were available to do the work. In 1860, shortly before his death, Theodore Parker remarked on the Unitarians' failure to recognize just this:

> No sect had ever a finer opportunity than the Unitarians to advance the religious development of a people. But they let it slide, and now they must slide with it. In 1838 the Unitarians were the controlling party in Boston: the railroads were just getting opened and it was plain the Protestant population of the town would soon double. Young men with no fortune but their character would come in from the country and settle and grow rich; the Unitarians ought to have welcomed such to their churches; to have provided

helps for them and secured them to the Unitarian fold. . . . But they did no such thing. . . . They were aristocrats and exclusive in their tastes, not democratic and inclusive.

Failing to "seize the main chance," the Unitarians virtually surrendered a generation of American youth to the evangelical denominations.

Evangelical religionists were, in contrast to the Unitarians, tactically adroit. In the undistinguished story of the Judsons' early years, the movement demonstrated its capacity to engage, to educate, and to convert the youth of America. By the second decade of the century, it was apparent that pious youth like the Judsons, who were sacrificing both the prospect of worldly gain and possibly their lives, had the capacity to draw the attention of the American reading audience. That youthful voluntarism could be directed to powerful ends was evident in the history of the foreign missionary movement. Andover students did, after all, provoke New England's orthodoxy into involving itself in a foreign sphere; a young married couple in India could be responsible for the organization of a major new arm of that Christian crusade. Increasingly throughout the century, evangelicals coupled the actual experience of youthful voluntarism with a literature supportive to it.

Chapter 3

Does the Bibliomania Rage at Tavoy?

Adoniram Judson's preoccupation with words had already led him from the Congregationalist to the Baptist fount. In Burma, the same exacting concern for language, and the recognition of its power, were controlling elements in his missionary career. The great accomplishment of his life was the translation of the Bible into Burmese, a work that he completed in 1834[1] and continued to revise up until his death, in the field, in 1850. By 1849, he had also completed an English-Burmese dictionary.[2] While Judson never denied the effectiveness of gospel preaching, his single-minded perseverance in the work of translation, as well as his early involvement in printing activities, demonstrated his living faith in the transforming power of personal experience with the Scriptures.

Although his translation work took him on many excursions into the world of Burmese literature, Judson felt that these enjoyable literary adventures must be kept under control.[3] Whatever his personal proclivities for Burmese poetry and folk tales, he became, for the home audience, a living symbol of a basic evangelical axiom: that knowledge of the Bible can and will change your life. Indeed,

44

Adoniram Judson's public life was a testimony to the way in which evangelical Protestantism was a veritable "religion of the book."[4]

The Baptists lionized Judson for his biblical translation, which was the preliminary and all-important step in the creation of a Christian literature for Burma. He was the man who made the Burmese a gift of "the authoritative guide book of God Himself," who provided an entire people with "a correct transcript of God's word." It was only incidental that his work provided the means for commercial intercourse with the Burmese. What Judson and the mission press were providing was permanent accessibility to the truths of Scriptures for nineteen million heathen.

The evangelicals saw in the history of the Nestorians, a fifth-century Christian sect, what could happen if Christianity relied solely on verbal dissemination for its transmission. The Nestorian churches failed, according to Isaac Shepard, editor of the *Christian Souvenir*, because they "did not possess a self-preserving and propagating power. The Gospel in its purity they had not. The press . . . they knew not of. As a consequence they had no printed scriptures, and could not give their converts the word of God. . . . They were compelled to leave them, without the word of life, without a Christian literature, and with barely enough of truth to avail for their first conversion."[5] This perception, which overlooked the startling success of the apostles and other great Christians before the sixteenth century, explains why the evangelical churches had, by the 1840s at least, begun the commercial merchandising of religious books. The *New York Baptist Register* (1843) wrote that in antiquity the truths were "powerless and inert," with "no transforming influence," because there was no press as in the present age.[6] By 1850, the charity publication societies of the Protestant churches—in the form of the American Tract Society, the American Sunday School Union, the American Bible Society, the Presbyterian Publication Society, the American Baptist Publication Society, the Methodist Book Concern, the Episcopal Sunday School, and the Evangelical Knowledge Society—were in serious competition with private publishers and booksellers for the market in religious and quasi-religious books.

The missionary career of Adoniram Judson and the home audience's knowledge of him were closely tied to the evangelical's perception that the cause of Gospel Christianity required the deployment of modern publishing and merchandising techniques. The popularization in magazines and biographies of Judson's thirty-eight-year career made him significant for all the evangelical denominations. The pattern he established—of codification of the vernacular language, the translation of the Scriptures, and the distribution of tracts and Bibles—became more than just a foreign missionary formula. In his commitment to the transforming power of the Bible and a Christian literature, Judson made his life a metaphor for the whole of evangelical culture.

———◆◆———

The home audience did not have to wait for the posthumous biographies to read tales of the Judsons' Christian adventure in Burma. The day-to-day work of foreign evangelization and the stunning events of the British-Burmese War (1824–1825) were conveyed to the American reading audience through denominational periodicals like the *Massachusetts Baptist Missionary Magazine* and the *Western New York Baptist Missionary Magazine* (later the New York Baptist *Register*) which published missionary letters and journal extracts from Burma. In addition to the Massachusetts and New York journals, communiques were printed in other early Baptist periodicals that span the first dozen years of the Judsons' tenure in Burma: *Christian Watchman, Columbian Star*, and the *Latter Day Luminary*. These communications, written to family, friends, and their new denominational sponsors, provided readers with firsthand accounts of their labors and their emotional responses to life among a non-Christian people.[7]

The Judsons were given prominent attention in the *Massachusetts Baptist Missionary Magazine* and the *Western New York Baptist Missionary Magazine*. Judson letters and journal extracts usually appeared in the Massachusetts journal about three times a year from 1812 to 1850.[8] Generally, publication of the letters came anywhere from twelve to eighteen months after they were written. Given the distance the letters had to travel and the fact that prior to publication they were probably passed among the Judsons' close associates, the time lag was to be expected. Under the heading of "Religious Intelligence," the Judsons were news, even when the information was a year old.

Judson reportage did not present a neat chronological narrative of the progress of the Burmese mission. In fact, from a reading of the magazine, it is difficult to ascertain the exact chronological order of events. This is probably explained by the fact that the Judsons' friends in America contributed to the press only those letters that they felt were exemplary and merited public attention. Additional letters must have been withheld or lost in transit, leaving substantial gaps in the developing story. Skewed by these factors, the published commentary created an enticing, but fragmentary, record of their activities in Burma. (In the case of the Judsons' New England followers, information culled from the magazines was probably augmented by some word-of-mouth reporting derived from unpublished letters the missionaries wrote to intimates in the area.) In any case, readers of periodicals probably created a basic market for the later biographies described in the first chapter of this work.

In their correspondence from Burma, the Judsons mapped out a pattern for an evangelical life and marriage. As we shall see later, in Chapter 4, Ann's letters focused on her emotional reactions to Burmese culture and on the care and management of her family and the Burmese she employed and taught. Adoniram's published accounts addressed questions of how best to do the work of evangelization. Because he had no preliminary conversations with his Baptist sponsors, correspondence must have been peculiarly important. Almost all of Judson's published papers were, in this sense, professional rather than personal.

This mission, which was to prove so pivotal for American evangelical culture, began inauspiciously. After a four-month voyage, the Judsons and the Newells landed in Calcutta in June 1812, at the very time that the United States and Great Britain declared a state of hostility. People within the Judsons' inner circle, that is, their family and friends, must have known about their difficulties with the British, although the story of this "pre-Burmese" stage of the mission was not published until 1823.[9] The young missionaries did indeed receive a hostile reception from local authorities, as both the government of Bengal and the British East India Company were, in any case, opposed to American evangelization efforts among the Hindus. Thus, within two weeks of their arrival, they were ordered to leave the country and return to America. Rather than face that prospect, they sought to go, temporarily, to the Isle of France, a British possession in the Indian Ocean.

The first available ship had only two berths which were taken by the Newells, now expectant parents, who hoped to reach the island before Harriet's "confinement." Unable to book passage, the Judsons and Luther Rice, who had arrived from Philadelphia, remained behind in Calcutta for over two months before receiving a

Bengali government order to proceed to England in a ship belonging to the East India Company. Within a few days, the missionaries found their names among a list of passengers about to embark for England.

Refusing to be diverted from their goal, the Judsons found a vessel, the *Creole*, that was bound for the Isle of France. Although they were officially forbidden to embark on the ship, the sympathetic captain allowed the young people to board surreptitiously. However, as they were proceeding downriver into the Bay of Bengal, the *Creole* was overtaken by a government dispatch ordering them not to continue. Stymied again, the Judsons left the ship and spent the next few days attempting to avoid what was becoming, it seemed, inevitable: passage to England.

With hope evaporating, the missionaries were ultimately saved by an unsolicited pass, written by an unknown Bengali magistrate, which allowed them to proceed on board the *Creole*, bound for the Isle of France. Most biographers considered this *deus ex machina* ample evidence that the Supreme Being was chaperoning the expedition. The missionary party was then rowed seventy miles downstream where, by another stroke of good fortune, the *Creole* lay at anchor, as if she were expecting them.

The Judsons' arrival in January 1813 at Port Louis, in the Isle of France, might have been an occasion for a joyous reunion had not the intervening months brought the death of Harriet Newell and her infant daughter.[10] For Ann Hasseltine it was an enormous loss: "Harriet is dead. Harriet, my dear friend, my earliest associate in the Mission, is no more. O death, thou destroyer of domestic felicity, could not this wide world afford victims sufficient to satisfy their cravings, without entering the family of a solitary few, whose comfort and happiness depended much on the society of each other?" Soon Luther Rice would depart for the United States on account of a liver ailment and the need to enlist Baptist support for the foreign mission. "Mr. J. and I are now entirely alone," wrote Ann Hasseltine after Rice's departure in March. "[There is] not one remaining friend in this part of the world."[11]

In May 1813, Adoniram and Ann Judson left Port Louis for Madras, even though a sympathetic governor would have had them remain to serve the spiritual needs of the island's British soldiers. But Judson's vision of a "mission for life" did not include ministrations to a British military outpost. He sought a larger field among an indigenous heathen population. Because Madras was also under the jurisdiction of the East India Company, the couple again faced the possibility of imminent deportation to England. When Judson could find no ship to take them to Penang (Prince of Wales Island), he and Ann took the next best thing, the *Georgianna* to Rangoon, only somewhat accidentally fulfilling ABCFM instructions which directed its missionaries to the Burman empire "unless circumstances should render it inexpedient."[12]

Portents of hardship were everywhere. The Burmese government was known for its despotic character. Previous evangelization attempts by British missionaries had failed. A European woman engaged as a companion and nurse for the ailing Ann dropped dead on the deck of the ship shortly before embarkation. The sea was tempestuous, Mrs. Judson came close to death, and the ship's crew were infidels. "There are no bread, potatoes, and butter and very little animal food," Ann Hasseltine wrote her family about Burma before she arrived. "The natives live principally on rice and fish." It was on July 13, 1813, that the Judsons reached Burma. They made their new home, their first alone together, in a house deserted by Baptist missionaries from Serampore. Ann wrote of the future: "I should have no society at all, except Mr. J for there is not an English female in all Rangoon."[13]

For Judson, the work of evangelization began with personal mastery of the written forms of the vernacular tongue of Burma. A letter from his wife gave a graphic description of Judson at his work: "Could you look into a large room . . . you would see Mr. Judson bent over his table, covered with Burman books, with his teacher at his side, a venerable looking man in his sixtieth year, with a cloth wrapped around his middle, and a handkerchief round his head. They talk and chatter all day long, with hardly any cessation."[14] That Burmese was difficult there is no doubt; Judson and his wife commented on the problem of learning this second language. "For a European or American to acquire a living oriental language, root and branch, and make it his own, is quite a different thing," wrote Adoniram, "from his acquiring a cognate language of the West, or any of the dead languages. . . ."[15] Ann, who attempted to describe the sounds of Burmese, also posited that religion was the most difficult subject to talk about "because of the want of religious terms in the [Burmese] language."[16] Judson spent at least the first three years in Burma in the business of mastering the structure of the tongue. Ann wrote that she took upon herself the entire management of the family "for the sake of Mr. Judson's attending more closely to the study of the language." What happened was predictable. "I am frequently obliged to speak Burman all day," she wrote. "I can talk and understand others better than Mr. Judson, though he knows more about the nature and construction of the language."[17] By 1824, Ann would write to her family, "We feel it an inestimable privilege, that amid all our discouragements we have the language, and are able to constantly communicate truths which save the soul."[18]

That Judson was trying to acquire more than verbal skills is apparent in this January 1816 letter:

> The greater part of my time, for the last six months, has been occupied in studying and transcribing, in alphabetical arrangement, the Pali Abigdan, or dictionary of the Pali language, affixing to the Pali terms the interpretation in Burman, and again transferring the Burman words to a dictionary, Burman and English. With the close of the year, I have brought this tedious work to a close, and find that the number of Pali words collected amounts to about four thousand. It has grieved me to spend so much time on the Pali, but the constant occurrence of Pali terms in every Burman book makes it absolutely necessary.[19]

Pali was, in actuality, a dead language, a language of scholars. Judson spent his time on it because he believed it was essential to the successful completion of his ultimate goal: the translation of the Bible into Burmese. In this work he was exacting; aware of the earlier works of translation, he judged them unacceptable. "The Portuguese missionaries," he wrote, "left a version of some extracts of Scripture not very badly executed, in regard to language but full of Romish errors."[20] Three years after his arrival he was able to report: "I am beginning now to translate a little. I am extremely anxious to get some parts of Scripture into an intelligible state, fit to read to Burmans that I meet with."[21]

Judson was not content with the efficacy of reading the Bible aloud. "I am more and more convinced that Burmah is to be evangelized by tracts and portions of Scripture," Judson wrote. "The press is the grand engine for Burmah. Every pull of the press throws another ray of light through the empire."[22] Evangelization depended not only on the preaching of the Gospel, but on the dissemination of it in printed form. Mindful of this evangelical axiom, missionaries had to take an active role in developing, for every heathen nation, a Christian literature, in the vernacular, with the Bible at its heart.[23] To this end, Judson worked continually on Scriptural translations and revisions throughout his thirty-seven years in Burma. In an address before the American and Foreign Bible Society, the Burmese veteran vindicated his own career as a missionary-translator and lexicographer. "All missionary operations to be permanently successful," Judson theorized, "must be based on the written word."[24]

In 1815 the Baptist Board of Foreign Missions appointed to Burma the printer, George H. Hough, and his wife to go out equipped with a press.[25] In so doing, the Baptists believed they were significantly swelling Christian ranks among the heathen. Two thousand dollars was appropriated for support of the Houghs and the Judsons, and one thousand for printing expenditures. The agreement signed by Judson and Hough, after the latter's arrival in 1816, conveys the intent of the new collaboration. "We agree," affirmed the missionary and the printer, ". . . that our sole object on earth is to introduce the religion of Jesus Christ into the Empire of Burmah; and that the means by which we hope to affect this are translating, printing, and distributing the Holy Scriptures; preaching the Gospel; circulating religious tracts, and promoting the instruction of native children."[26] The fact that preaching and teaching had not as yet won a single native convert created intense interest in the potentiality of other evangelization techniques.

By November 1817, the editors of the *American Baptist Magazine* were able to announce an important preliminary step in their campaign to create a Christian literature for Burma. A tract by Adoniram and a children's catechism by Ann, both in Burmese, were issued by the mission press at Rangoon.[27] In the same year, Judson completed his translation of Matthew, and 500 copies were distributed among the natives;[28] 3,000 copies of Ann's Burmese catechism were printed.[29] Massachusetts Baptists responded enthusiastically: "Thus, the PRESS, that powerful engine employed by Providence in the propagation of the truth, has been put in motion in this land of darkness. We confidently hope that these first fruits of the mission . . . will be succeeded by a rich harvest of immortal souls."[30]

In one year alone (1829), the press of the American Baptist Mission in Burma issued a dozen separate publications, a number in Siamese and Talain, as well as Burmese.[31] Judson claimed to have distributed nearly 10,000 tracts, only to those who asked, during the annual Burmese holiday of Shway Dagon. "I should have given away double the number," he wrote home to America, "if I could have obtained sufficient supplies."[32] In 1830, his statements to the effect that he and printer Cephas Bennett could not meet the demand for tracts resulted in the assignment of two more mission printers, Oliver Cutter and Royal Hancock. To Bennett's press and Burman type, Cutter added an additional press in the spring of 1832. The following January, Hancock arrived with two more presses, a standing press, a large font of types, and all the materials for a stereotype foundry, making possible the production of reusable metal printing plates. By April 1833, the Burman mission press reported having issued 6,237,800 pages.[33] After the arrival of the presses, the preparation and distribution of tracts and catechisms were always a major focus of Burman mission activity.[34]

"The Burmese," Judson observed, were "a reading people beyond any in India."[35] By "reading people" Judson probably meant that the Burmese had an extensive literature all their own, not that literacy was widespread. Of his biographers, Wayland alone described the personal battle of conscience that developed from Judson's exposure to Burmese literature as part of his program of mastering the tongue:

> He had become fully aware of the temptations to which missionaries are exposed when the treasures of a new language and of a peculiar form of literature are presented before them, and he therefore guarded himself with peculiar strictness. At one time, he had found the literature of Burmah exceedingly fascinating, especially its poetry; and he had sundry pleasant visions of enriching the world of English literature from its curious stores.[36]

According to Wayland, Judson "flattered himself" for a time in thinking that by interesting the Christian world in Burmese literature, the "flood gates of sympathy" would be opened and Christians would unite to bring about Burmese emancipation from "pagan thraldom." Fortunately, according to Wayland, Judson realized that all his work should be in the service of God, and to but one end: the production of a Bible for the Burmese. Missionary translation work, then, was not intended to provide access to foreign literature. Wayland praised Judson for his refusal to translate the Life of Gaudama (Buddha) for a Calcutta literary society. The Christian world needed to acquire the Burmese language in order to present the great truths of its own literature, not to garner information about another culture. "Though perfectly familiar with more than a hundred Burman tales, and able to repeat Burman poetry by the hour," Wayland attested, "he never committed a line to paper." Judson "resisted his own natural tendencies [and] took care never to excite in the minds of others an interest in things of this sort." According to Wayland, "Mr. Judson disapproved of missionary contributions made either to literature or science, even as a recreation; for he insisted they could not be made with safety, and that nothing reliable could be accomplished without a draught on those energies which should be devoted to higher objects."[37]

The *magnum opus* of Judson's life was his translation of the Old and New Testaments, a project that commenced in late 1815. The nature of the work was solitary and less than dramatic. Furthermore, it was difficult to describe to people at home exactly what he was doing. "I long to write something more interesting and encouraging to the friends of the mission," wrote Judson from Rangoon in January 1816, "but it must not yet be expected. It unavoidably takes several years to acquire such a language, in order to write intelligibly on the great truths of the Gospel."[38] On another occasion he wrote to Dr. Bolles of Salem hoping to show "to the friends of Missions . . . the impropriety of expecting FRUIT before the way is prepared to sow the seed."[39] To Luther Rice he directed,

> If any ask what success I meet with among the natives?—tell them to look at Otaheite, where the missionaries labored nearly twenty years, and not meeting with slightest success, began to be neglected by all the Christian world . . . and how the blessing begins to come. Tell them to look at Bengal also, where Dr. Thomas has been laboring seventeen years, that is from 1783 to 1800, before the first convert, Krishno, was Baptized. When a few converts are made, things move on. But it requires a much longer time than I have been here, to make an impression on a heathen people.[40]

The problem for Judson was that his codification of the language and translation of the Bible were very slow going. He had been in Burma for five years without a single convert. The continual publication of his and Ann's letters and journal extracts had created a situation in which the religious reading audience was "awake" and expecting some quantitative gratifications—namely, converts they could count. In early 1818, Judson began the building of a zayat, or wayside preaching station, away from the more "retired" mission house, on a main road. The zayat, which cost American Baptists about two hundred dollars, would add an additional moral ingredient to the religious pot that was brewing in Burma. A combination of preaching, teaching, and publication efforts finally brought in the first convert, a Burmese male called Moung Nau, in July 1819. Judson's letter about the baptism described the scene: "after the usual Burman [Christian] worship . . . we proceeded to a large tank [artificial pond] in the vicinity, and there by an enormous image of Gaudama, which seemed to scowl on the dead, we administered the ordinance of Christian baptism to the first Burman convert."[41] "Let the people of God in America take comfort," wrote the editors of the *American Baptist Magazine*. "They have not prayed and wept in vain."[42]

By December 1819, Judson was able to report the beginnings of a small flock of converts. A young man in his twenties, Moung Thalah, and a middle-aged man, Moung Byaa, were baptized. Potential converts numbers four and five were already "lined-up." Number five was particularly noteworthy because he was a "learned man" who was being pressured by a Burmese viceroy to abandon his interest in Christianity.[43] The question of number five's conversion raised the spectre of religious repression, a theme that developed increasing concern for the safety of the Judsons and the future of the Burmese mission. In a November 1820 magazine, Judson ominously reported that, after an interview with the King at Ava, he was convinced that it was standing policy of the Burmese not to extend toleration to any foreign religion.[44]

Ann and Adoniram Judson continued their ministrations to the Burmese in the early 1820s despite foreshadowings of trouble with the government. Adoniram continued preaching in the zayat while nearing completion of the New Testament translation; Ann continued her teaching among the women, and her Siamese translating. Their personal lives were marked by short-lived happiness and, then, sorrow. The infant son born to them in the late summer of 1815 was dead by early May of the following year. Ann wrote to her parents: "Death, regardless of our lonely situation, has entered our dwelling, and made one of the happiest families wretched. Our little Roger Williams [Judson], our only little darling boy, was three days ago laid in the silent grave. Eight months we enjoyed the precious little gift, in which time he so completely entwined himself around his parents' hearts, that his existence seemed necessary to their own."[45] The lost happiness of the young parents was apparent to the reader: "When we had finished study, or the business of the day, it was our exercise and amusement to carry him round the

house or garden, and though we were alone, we felt not our soli-
tude when he was with us."[46]

Ill health plagued both Judsons almost continually. In fact, it is
difficult to reconstruct all their ailments. In 1816, Judson suffered
from an eye condition that left him unable to read.[47] For months he
sat in semidarkness, with a scribe or Mrs. Judson at his side, speaking aloud words for a Burmese dictionary for future missionaries.
During the course of this disease, he began a lifelong regimen of
daily walking and horseback riding, which he felt balanced the sed-
entary "mental exertions" which occupied so much of his time.[48]
Both had "cholera morbus" at one point and survived. Ann's 1821
illness did not respond to any therapy of diet or exercise. Although
she sought medical help in Bengal for a "chronic affection [*sic*] of
the liver," she was not cured.[49]

The mission's problems were compounded by what was now
open Burmese hostility to any form of Christian evangelization,
something which the Burmese, according to all reports, associated
with the British. Moung-Shwag nong, who was Judson's closest
Burmese associate and an important translating resource, was being
persecuted. Judson saw this kind of personal harassment as a serious
impediment to bringing individuals to Christ.[50] He wrote that he
expected the mission itself to be driven from Rangoon.[51] An editorial prepared the mission's American sponsors for that possibility:". . .
should he [Judson] . . . finally be compelled to retire to another station, . . . Christians should rejoice that on that idolatrous spot, the
seed of divine grace has been sown, and that it will there pros-
per."[52] In November 1822, the *American Baptist Magazine* reported that Judson was doing little public preaching because of the
climate of opinion in Burma. War between the Burmese and the
British was becoming increasingly likely. At the same time, Mrs.
Judson's condition worsened.

In May 1822, religious leaders learned that Ann Hasseltine Judson would be returning home because of ill health.[53] The financial
responsibility for the return of a missionary wife, for reasons of convalescence, had never before been identified.[54] Judson's published
letter to Dr. Baldwin of the Baptist Foreign Mission Board included
testimony from the doctor describing the "hopelessness" of Ann's
condition and a statement from Judson that all expenses associated
with her stay in America could be charged against his usual allowance. Judson apologized for having to use mission monies for the sea

passage but urged consideration of "the extreme necessity of the case." As it happened, Mrs. Judson would receive free passage from Calcutta to England, courtesy of a pious British family traveling with their children. "If the pain in my side is entirely removed, while on my passage to Europe," Ann wrote Dr. Baldwin, "I shall return to India in the same ship, and proceed immediately to Rangoon. But if not, I shall go over to America, and spend one winter in my dear native country."[55]

Mrs. Judson's passage to England was marked by the physical discomfort associated with her liver complaint and by demonstration of her ever-present religious zeal. Confined to her cabin by her malady, she requested that two fellow passengers, young women of "rank and influence," read to her. Even in her distress, she had the presence of mind to choose selections which she thought might have "salutary effects upon their minds"; after conversations with the pious Mrs. Judson, the young women were indeed "solemnly impressed."[56]

In England, Ann Hasseltine Judson was introduced to Joseph Butterworth, a member of Parliament and a Baptist. Butterworth invited her to make his house her home while she was in his country. Later biographers reported that, through Butterworth, Mrs. Judson came to meet a number of persons distinguished for their piety and literature—including William Wilberforce and John Sumner, the King's chaplain and, subsequently, Archibishop of Canterbury. While in Britain, she visited the spa at Cheltenham, known for its mineral waters, and then traveled to Scotland, where she received a request from the American Baptist Board of Foreign Missions to return home in the New York packet. On 16 August 1822, she embarked from Liverpool to New York, her passage again defrayed by some pious Liverpool women.[57] At a meeting of the English Baptist Missionary Society, Butterworth was alleged to have told the membership that Mrs. Judson's visit with them recalled the apostolic admonition: "Be not forgetful to entertain strangers, for thereby some have entertained angels unawares." Butterworth later donated £100 sterling for the angel's Burman mission school.[58]

The ship Amity, carrying this effective link to the American Baptist mission in the East, arrived in New York on September 25, 1822. Unable to land because of a yellow fever epidemic, the missionary took a steamboat to Philadelphia, where she was met, apparently by Dr. William Staughton. Staughton was an important senior figure in the denomination who had been elected to the presidency of Columbian College just the year before. Adoniram had paved the way for Ann's official reception in a published letter to Thomas Baldwin: "I beg leave to recommend Mrs. Judson to the kindness of the friends and patrons of the Mission, as one who has faithfully laboured many years in their service; and whose sole object in visiting her country once more, is to recover her health and strength, that she may spend the remainder of her days to the promotion of the Redeemer's Cause among the perishing Burmans."[59] Because Staughton invited her to come to Washington, Mrs. Judson delayed her return to her home in Bradford for about one week.

There are no written accounts of what the elder Staughton and the young Mrs. Judson had to say to each other. Ann's liver ailment was obviously in remission, since she was well enough to make the additional side trip to Washington. Probably, Staughton and others associated with the Baptist mission enterprise used the occasion to interview Mrs. Judson about a wide variety of topics having to do with their Burmese mission. Luther Rice, last seen by Ann Hasseltine ten years before on the Isle of France, was living in Washington at the same time, serving as treasurer and agent of Columbian College. There is no doubt that conversations between Mrs. Judson and the denominational leaders went well. Throughout her nine-month stay in America, Mrs. Judson would, at the risk of her health, be publicly associated with the Baptist missionary cause.

There was little time for quiet convalescence, even at Bradford. "My father's house was thronged with visitors day to day," Ann reported to Mrs. Chaplin of Waterville, Maine.[60] She complained that in Bradford she got no rest, that she was in a "state of constant excitement," and that her cough increased. Her husband's brother, Elnathan, suggested that she spend the winter with him in Baltimore, which held the promise of a more therapeutic climate. Despite the fact that she was in great distress and taking mercury to induce excess salivation, those who were escorting her to Baltimore made a stop in New York, a detour that was surely demanding for someone in her feeble condition. At the home of a Mr. C., "a pious and wealthy Baptist," the ailing missionary wife spent the evening at a prayer meeting among a crowd of "pious and devout Christians." A proposal to devote part of each Sabbath to prayers for the restoration of her health accompanied entreatments for Mr. Judson and the perishing Burmans. "I found much of a true missionary spirit in New York," Ann wrote to Francis Wayland, then pastor of Boston's First Baptist Church. "The intelligence of Mr. [James]

Colman's death seemed to have a proper effect. . . ."[61] Ann's attribution was naive. As she remained longer in America she would realize the effectiveness of her own presence.[62]

The "lavish attentions" of the religious community in America were problematic for Mrs. Judson's spirituality. Some claimed her health was not seriously impaired and that she "visited the South [Baltimore] with a view to excite attention and applause."[63] In her letter to Mrs. Chaplin, she assured that pious matron that all the fuss was really not affecting her:

> I am well aware that human applause has a tendency to elate the soul, and render it less anxious about spiritual enjoyments, particularly if the individual is conscious of deserving them. But I must say, that since my return to this country, I have often been affected to tears, in hearing the undeserved praises of my friends, feeling that I was far, very far, from being what they imagined. . . .[64]

It is not clear if Ann Hasseltine Judson ever realized that she and Adoniram were entering the realm of mythic figures. In Baltimore, as she took mercury and was salivated and bled, she began work on an account of the Burmese mission, a project which she said was urged on her by her British friends, who were less familiar than the Americans with the details of the story. Servants in her brother-in-law's house were instructed to tell visitors that, "Mrs. Judson did not see company."[65] She spent the winter of 1823 in her "chamber" in Baltimore working on her spirituality as well as her physical recovery. Her reaction to the many invitations she received was expressed to Mrs. Chaplin: "Strange as it may seem, I do believe there is something like religious dissipation, in a Christian's being too entirely engrossed in religious company, as to prevent . . . spiritual enjoyments."[66]

As much as she wanted to escape the demands of her notoriety, Ann Hasseltine Judson was aware of the necessity to impress American Christians with the importance of the foreign mission cause. "I want the Baptists throughout the United States to feel," she wrote in January 1823, "that Burmah *must be converted* through their instrumentality. They must do more. . . . They must pray more, they must give more. . . ."[67] She saw her account of the Burmese mission, basically a compilation of her letters from abroad, as an agency of this work. In March 1823, she was well enough to travel to Washington, where she corrected proof sheets for her "little history" and met with students at Columbian College. She noted with pleasure to her sisters that David Brown, a converted Indian, had come to call on her while she was in Washington.[68]

Mrs. Judson's American visit was a confirmed success by the spring of 1823. First, she now felt well enough to travel and to meet with those who were interested in foreign missions. In late April she decided to return to Washington from Baltimore, because the former city would soon be the site of the denomination's Triennial Convention. "The hope of exciting more attention to the *subject of missions* . . . induced me to return," she wrote to Wayland.[69] Second, her book, *A Particular Relation of the American Baptist Mission to the Burman Empire*, had been published, the copyright of which she offered to the Triennial Convention.[70]

Furthermore, the actions of the Baptist assembly indicated in a variety of ways the denomination's approbation for, and commitment to, the Judsons. A committee of the Convention met with Mrs. Judson to solicit her suggestions about the missionary enterprise. Additionally, monies were appropriated for the cost of printing 2,000 copies of Adoniram's New Testament translation and for the purchase, on behalf of the ministers of the denomination, of two handsome globes as gifts to the Burmese King.[71] The optimistic Convention reported the formation of Judson societies, as well as the receipt of £200 sterling for the female schools in Burma from the estate of Hannah More, the celebrated religious writer. Most importantly, Mrs. Judson would not be the lone American Christian returning to Burma. Two young men, Jonathan Wade, from the Theological Institute at Hamilton, and George Boardman, from Waterville College, were assigned to the missionary field.[72] On June 21, 1823, Ann Hasseltine Judson, in the company of Jonathan and Deborah Wade, left Boston for Calcutta and Rangoon. Now that they knew her, her fellow Baptists and other evangelicals would be following her movements with even greater attention.

During his wife's absence, Judson spent most of his time on his translation work. He reported to Dr. Sharp: "Indeed all the Gospels and the Acts are in a tolerable state; the Epistles are still deficient. But I never read a chapter without a pencil in my hand, and Griesbach and Parkhurst [Biblical commentaries] at my elbow." As if his reader didn't realize, he told him: "It will be an object with me through life, to bring translation into such a state that it may be a standard work."[73] The parts of his journal that Judson regularly sent to America continued to be published, only now they were given to Mrs. Judson to read beforehand.[74]

Communications between the missionary couple were highly irregular during Mrs. Judson's absence from Burma. At one point, the missionary reported that he hadn't heard from his wife in ten months.[75] Part of a letter from Adoniram to Ann, made public in March 1823, while Mrs. Judson lay in sickbed in Baltimore, conveyed their proper pious sentiments for each other:

> Your last letter lies before me, and Winchell's Collection, also; open at the hymn, "Blest be the tie that binds." Not that I cannot repeat it without the book, but I wish to refresh myself with a view of the very words. How exactly suited to our case! How it describes the manner in which we have lived together, for many years, the pain which we feel in being parted, and the glorious hopes and prospects before us![76]

Judson's hopes were high for Ann's return because he believed that together they might make religious inroads at Ava, the capital city. In October 1822, Judson traveled to Ava with Jonathan Price, a Princeton graduate and medical doctor, whose healing skills were responsible for getting the missionaries an audience with the King. Although the King proved indifferent to their Christianity, his half-brother, Prince M., a young paralytic of twenty-eight, displayed a genuine interest in foreign science, which gave Judson the opportunity to impress him with arguments in favor of the Copernican system. "If he admitted them [the arguments]," wrote Judson, "he must also admit that the Boodhist system was overthrown."[77] Eventually, over the course of a few weeks, the subject of religion was introduced. When the Prince's wife became interested in meeting the absent Mrs. Judson, and the Prince asked to see the translated Bible, Judson vowed to return with Ann to the capital, close to the seat of power.

A letter from Judson, published in July 1824, carried the happy news that Mrs. Judson and he were reunited, that she and the young Wades had arrived safely in Rangoon during the previous December.[78] "I had the inexpressible happiness of welcoming Mrs. Judson once more to the shore of Burma," wrote the grateful missionary to Dr. Baldwin.[79] If Ann's recovery and safe return were not evidence enough of God's blessing, Judson sent along additional proof: a statement, in English from the convert Moung Shwa-ba, attesting to his Christian devotion. "The doctrine of the Cross is the religion of life, of love, of faith," wrote the eloquent Burmese convert. "I am a servant of faith. Formerly I was a servant of Satan.

Now I am a servant of Christ. And a good servant cannot but follow his master."[80] Because there was the possibility of even more important converts at Ava, the Judsons removed there almost immediately.

In February 1824, Ann Judson wrote from Ava that "in consequence of war with the Bengali government, foreigners are not so much esteemed at court as formerly." "I know not," she told her parents, "what effect this war will have on our mission. . . ."[81] This was the last letter Mrs. Judson would write for two years. The Wades and other English-speaking foreigners were able to flee Rangoon for Calcutta after a brief imprisonment by the Burmese. In November 1824, a Baptist magazine urged faith rather than alarm, positing that, "as a matter of policy, the Burman government may command its subjects to suspend all communications with foreign countries, while the war between her and the British continues. . . ."[82]

By February 1825, American readers had learned more about the situation. Printer Hough wrote ominously from Rangoon: "I cannot but fear for Messrs. Judson and Price . . . at Ava."[83] An editorial explained: "The state of our Missionaries at Ava was by our latest accounts [Hough's] eminently perilous. The war seems to have been carried on with unusual ferocity. Should the exasperation against the English be extended to the Missionaries, we cannot but tremble for the result. . . ."[84] In a March 1825 magazine, Hough reported that "now all communication is cut off" with Ava.[85] In April, a letter from Mrs. Wade, in safety in Calcutta, stated that there was "every reason to believe, that Dr. Price, and Dr. and Mrs. Judson are imprisoned."[86] Other letters from the Wades reported starvation, chaos, and violence in Burma. The King and Queen were beheaded, Wade said; "we think of them [the Judsons] only with great trembling," he wrote.[87]

Throughout the fall of 1825, the religious press had no words of intelligence from Ava. There was only the familiar refrain from Wade: "what has been the fate of our friends at Ava, is still uncertain; we can obtain no information concerning them."[88] The editors, as if in preparation for the worst, urged the readership: "Should the dear missionaries at Ava fall a sacrifice to Burman cruelty, our loss would indeed be incalculable, our grief inexpressible; but we hope even in that case, the friends of missions, instead of fainting under the affliction, and leaving us to faint also, will send others to supply their place, and to strengthen our hand."[89]

As the *American Baptist Magazine* went to press in December 1825, intelligence was received that the Judsons were alive. In January 1826, the editors expressed their gratitude for this news: "Nearly two years had elapsed since a word had been heard from them; and everyone who knew the dangers to which they had been exposed, began seriously to fear that their labors on earth were ended, and that from the midst of their usefulness they had been called home, perhaps by a violent death."[90] The point of the Judsons' survival was apparent: "Let this teach us a lesson of confidence. Let us learn from it the importance of prayer."[91] The denomination, and everyone in the religious community, clearly understood the Judsons' importance: "Above all, they [are] the only Europeans, sufficiently acquainted with the language to translate the Scriptures for these 19 millions of perishing Souls. This connects an indescribable importance to the preservation of their lives."[92]

In February, the readership learned that "the information alluded to in [the] last number . . . was premature." The Judsons were, apparently, still in captivity, a fact that stimulated anew concern for their survival. Throughout the spring of 1826, the continued uncertainty of their fate was reported by other missionaries.[93]

In July, news of the termination of the Burmese War finally arrived, but it was not until October 1826, more than two years since Mrs. Judson's last letter, that foreign missionary supporters read the headline:"JOYFUL INTELLIGENCE." Two brief letters, one from Adoniram to Samuel Baldwin and another from Ann to Francis Wayland, marked out the terrain of hardships through which they had passed. "We survive a scene of suffering which, on retrospect, at the present moment, seems not a reality, but a horrid dream," wrote Adoniram.[94] Said Ann: "I can hardly, at times, believe it a reality that we have been safely conducted through so many narrow passages."[95] With the home audience appetite whetted, Ann Hasseltine Judson would describe the gory details in a letter of more than 14,000 words to Elnathan Judson, her brother-in-law in Baltimore. Of that letter, which took over two months to write, Knowles remarked: "Fiction itself has seldom invented a tale more replete with terror."[96]

———————◆●◆———————

As letters from the Judsons began appearing, those who had waited out their captivity began to piece together a compelling story of Christian fortitude in the face of heathen oppression. That the drama's major protagonist was Ann Hasseltine Judson was apparent by March 1827: "We thank God for endowing Mrs. Judson with that heroism and Christian perseverance, and unconquerable attachment, which on this occasion, so remarkably rescued the Christian prisoners from the hands of cruelty."[97]

The Judsons' adventures in Ava and at the Oung-pen-la prison made good reading. When the publication of their letters began, the *American Baptist Magazine* experienced an increase in readership. "Several hundred new subscribers from the state of Maine" were reported in the spring of 1827.[98] Commentators observed even larger positive effects of the "painful suspense" that the denomination had endured for two years. Fletcher wrote: "The long suspense in which the Christian world was held concerning the fate of the missionaries at Ava, and the intelligence subsequently received of their hardships, endurance, and deliverance, led to an interest in Christian missions which contributed to a far more efficient occupancy, than, judging by the interest previously manifested, there was any reason to hope."[99] John Dowling similarly explained that "something that was of a thrilling, striking, and excited character was needed to arouse them [American Baptists]. . . . Such a stimulus was afforded, when after two years . . . the touching recital of their unparalleled sufferings for Christ's sake, and of their wonderful deliverance . . . burst like a shock of electricity upon all the American churches."[100] Robert Cushman also wrote of the "affecting power" of the "tests of fidelity" that the Judsons had passed.[101]

Their stories of imprisonment, forced marches, physical cruelty, and material deprivation were later rehashed in all the biographies and in commemorative volumes like *The Judson Offering.* Daniel C. Eddy suggested that these stories were, in fact, becoming ritualized: "I have inserted entire the accounts given . . . [of] his [Judson's] sufferings there [at Ava] in 1824. No abridgement of these would have been allowed by the reader; and though they have been read, again and again, they will not lose their interest."[102] Joseph Parker, an upstate agent for the New York Baptist Missionary Convention, made the following report on the effect of reading about the Judsons' trials:

I called one morning at the house of a brother who took "The New York Baptist Register." The post-boy had just left the paper, and the brother's daughter was reading it in the room where I entered. After the usual salutation I took my seat and commenced conversation with the wife of the brother, who had been for several years a faithful member of the church. After spending a few moments in talking about the Kingdom of Christ, I heard a deep sigh from the young woman, which turned my attention to her. She soon returned with her cheek bathed in tears, and handing me a quarter of a dollar (all the money she had) with trembling she said, "Will you send that to Burma?" I felt anxious to know the cause of her grief and requested her to tell me. She, however, could not at that time, but taking "The Register," and pointing to a letter, turned away to weep.[103]

Parker's account of the power of mission reportage had important implications for the denomination. In the 1820s, the Judson saga had been carried by only a handful of denominational publications. However, its popularity and its effect foreshadowed the flowering of religious journalism that came in the 1830s.[104] Like many other religious newspapers, the *Baptist Register* of New York had a less than successful financial record in the early years of its operation. Despite its insolvency and a growing debt, the State Missionary Convention chose, in 1830, to continue its operation.[105] In part this decision can be explained by evidence that suggests that missionary giving was heaviest where there were religious periodicals. The 1836 report of the New York State Missionary Convention alluded to the *Register*'s "exhibitions of the field spread before the church [which] . . . have often untied the purse strings of selfishness and caused the Lord's silver and gold, which has been hoarded up, to be consecrated to the advancement of his blessed cause in the world."[106] A year before Adoniram Judson's death in 1850, the Foreign Mission Board of the Southern Baptist Convention reported that the largest donations came from those sections of the country in which Baptist periodicals had the widest circulation.[107]

While fund raising was an obvious and important consideration, it does not provide a total explanation for the evangelical interest in the creation of denominational newspapers, magazines, and publishing houses. Actually, denominational publishing was not in itself a new phenomenon. In the late eighteenth century, Methodists, Catholics, and Mennonites had operated presses in the United States.[108] By 1850, however, each of the major American Protestant denominations had a charitable publication society that did its own printing and marketing of books. Organizations like the American Baptist Publication Society, the American Tract Society, the American Sunday School Union, the American Bible Society, the Presbyterian Publication Society, and the Methodist Book Concern published long lists, advertised through denominational newspapers and pulpits, carried books by colportage to isolated communities and homes, and sold large quantities of their production to their own Sunday schools and mission enterprises.

Evangelically inspired publishing was big business, and it prompted at least one extensive critique of the industry. In 1849, an anonymous pamphlet, *An Appeal to the Christian Public on the Evil and Impolicy of the Church Engaging in Merchandise; And setting forth the wrong done to booksellers, and the extravagance, inutility and evil-working of charity publication societies*, was published at Philadelphia. The author argued that the entrance of the Protestant denominations into the book trade was destroying the livelihood of private publishers and book dealers. The charity publication societies, he maintained, had "paralyzed the enterprise of individuals lawfully engaged in publishing religious and useful books."[109] In addition, they undersold private publishers and used the charitable contributions of religious people to meet their deficits and pay large staffs. The charitable publication societies had also caused the publication and circulation of "useless and injurious" books, by driving the capital of private publishers into the only field where they could survive. The religious and quasi-religious book market had been expropriated by religious societies:

> The entire book business has undergone a change. Wholesale dealers, who supplied country booksellers, seldom got an order five years ago, which did not include religious books. Now, it is a rare thing that a single book of a religious kind is called for by houses that formerly sold thousands. They say they cannot sell them, that the demand has ceased. This is known to be true throughout the whole country, as a change in the times. They can now only sell school books, novels, picture books, and standard books, and none other pay for publishing. This is the general statement of men engaged in the trade. It is caused by the action of religious societies. . . .[110]

According to the author, who was a displaced member of the book trade, a million and a half dollars a year was given to the Protestant churches to publish and disseminate the religious word.[111]

The fact that some commercial publishers associated themselves with specific denominational interests further suggests that the religious book business was good business. According to William Charvat, a distinguished historian of American literature, the major publishers, up until the Civil War, had specific denominational connections. Harpers was allied with the Methodists, Appleton with the Episcopalians, Munroe and Frances with the Unitarians, and Ticknor with the Baptists.[112] At Boston's Gould, Kendall, and Lincoln, Charles Gould, one of the city's leading Baptists, published a list heavy with Baptist works. The firm published a number of books on the Judsons as well as works by popular Baptist writers like Daniel C. Eddy. Their publications were advertised in denominational organs, such as the *Baptist Almanac*, carried by Baptist colportage wagons, and ordered by Baptist Sunday schools, church libraries, and foreign and domestic mission societies. In Utica, two of the principals associated with a local publishing firm served as agents of the American Baptist Publication Society.[113]

Evangelical religious societies, propelled by the relationship they perceived between the reader and the printed page, were energetic in their support of all reading that was broadly defined as religious. The records of the Philomathesian Society at the Hamilton Literary and Theological Institute in the early 1820s provide some measure of the pervasiveness of religious periodical reading among upstate New York student evangelicals. From 1821 to 1823, the Hamilton students subscribed to all of the following Baptist publications: *London Baptist Magazine, American Baptist Magazine,* the *Latter Day Luminary, The Christian Watchman, The Columbian Star, The Christian Secretary, The Religious Intelligencer,* and *The Western New York Baptist Missionary Magazine.* Additionally, they took these non-Baptist periodicals: *Christian Observer, London Quarterly Review, Edinburgh Review, Eclectic Review, Portfolio,* and *North American Review.* All of these had been recommended by a committee of the Society. In addition to spending a great deal of time in setting up regulations for the equitable use of these publications, the young men began, in March 1822, to sell those periodicals that had been in the Society's reading room for at least ten days. This policy of quickly turning over the newspapers and magazines for the profit of the Society, plus the need to put locks on the reading room tables where the papers were kept, suggests that the students were regular, if not voracious, in their periodical reading habits.[114] A British Baptist visitor to New York State in the 1830s recalled that, when his wagon broke down traveling east out of Syracuse, he had simply to mention his name: " . . . we found that they [the wheelwrights] knew at once all my movements. Thus do the newspapers penetrate everywhere, and convey an immense mass of general information and knowledge through every corner of the land."[115] A Presbyterian evangelical, who grew up in Waterloo, New York, would attribute his "world outlook and missionary zeal" to his early reading of *The Missionary Herald, The Genesee Evangelist, The American Presbyterian*, and, later, *The New York Evangelist*.[116] It was that denomination, according to one student of the religious press, that aimed, and perhaps succeeded, in placing "a church paper in every Presbyterian home."[117]

By the mid-1830s, the development of denominational newspapers to disseminate such religious news as the Judsons' story was a distinguishing characteristic of the evangelical community, North and South, and on the frontier. By the close of the 1840s, most of the principal denominations had established an official or unofficial organ for each state. Some of these were privately owned and unofficially adopted by the church; others were in the possession of the institutional church or a religious body and had some official status.[118] In 1860, Baptist historian David Benedict reflected on the deluge of religious newspapers and observed that the idea of them had been "nowhere entertained" in 1800.[119] Horace Bushnell, the inveterate Congregationalist critic of evangelical religious practice, inveighed against the earnest enthusiasts for acting "as if God would offer man a mechanical engine for converting the world, . . . or as if types of lead and sheets of paper may be the light of the world."[120] Actually, the evangelicals' enthusiasm for utilizing the rapidly developing technology of the printed word was part of a national infatuation. There were newspapers and magazines of all kinds, representing the wide spectrum of antebellum reform interests as well as religious benevolence. Americans produced newspapers devoted exclusively to the cause of temperance, colonization, anti-slavery, emancipation, prison reform, and phrenology.[121] Frank Luther Mott dubbed the period beginning 1825 "The Golden Age of Periodicals."[122] From 1810 to 1828, newspaper circulation increased twice as rapidly as the population.[123]

Bushnell was probably reacting to a kind of evangelical calculus that posited an incremental relationship between the printing press and Christian conversions. Adoniram Judson's career as the man who gave the Bible to the Burmese was, after all, premised on such a connection. In an 1840 letter to a fellow missionary, Judson asked hopefully, "Does the bibliomania rage at Tavoy?"[124] At home, sponsors and editors of denominational organs extolled the possibilities of harnessing print and transportation technology to the cause of religion. Comparative considerations of the religious energy expended in "propagation through print" versus preaching led the editors of the *Religious Telescope* to conclude that "a well conducted religious periodical is like a thousand preachers, flying in almost as many directions by means of horses, mailstages, steamboats, railroad cars, ships . . . offering life and salvation to the sons of men in almost every clime."[125] The *Baptist Register* observed a decrease in the amount of mechanical labor requisite for producing their periodical, commenting "how slow must have been the circulation of knowledge [in the past]. How few comparatively [were] addressed" before the coming of modern printing devices.[126] In 1835, Dr. Samuel Bolles proudly announced to the Triennial Convention that the Baptists in that year used "2500 reams of paper" and "produced 7,000,000 pages," "about 1,000,000 more . . . than any other missionary body in the United States."[127] It is important to note that Bolles' report on the Baptists' production of printed pages did not mention missionary converts. The relationship was simply assumed.

It was the life experiences of the second generation of Baptist foreign missionaries that solidified the causal relationship between Christian reading material and evangelical Christian behavior. Young people, like George and Sarah Hall Boardman, attributed their activist commitments to their reading—particularly their reading about the Judsons and the work of Burmese evangelization. This second generation of missionary volunteers confirmed the denomination's confidence in their publications as an effective agency for engendering emotional, as well as financial, support for a wide variety of religious projects.

Attributions like those of the Boardmans were actually not uncommon among pious New England men of the late eighteenth century. Jonathan Edwards was in David Brainerd's spiritual debt; the missionary patriarch, Adoniram Judson, dated his dedication to the cause from the time of his reading Buchanan's *Star in the East*. What was new to the process of energizing through literature was the "presentist" quality, that is, the awareness of the way in which contemporary reportage, in the denominational periodicals, could function as a religious stimulant, and its effects on women, who comprised a significant portion of the American reading audience after 1820.[128]

At age seventeen, Sarah Hall wrote that she had just completed perusal of the *Life of Samuel J. Mills:*

> Never shall I forget the emotions of my heart, while following in thus the footsteps of this devoted missionary. I have almost caught his spirit, and been ready to exclaim: oh, that I, too could suffer privations, hardships and discouragements, and even find a watery grave (as did he) for the sake of bearing the news of salvation to the poor heathen.[129]

Hall checked her enthusiasm, because, as a woman, she was unable to act on her own without having the status of a missionary wife. She was, however, a conscientious reader of religious periodicals, and she distributed tracts.[130] The courtship of Sarah Hall and George Boardman, the requisite missionary husband who would take her to the East, was formed out of their common bereavement on reading about the death, in 1820, of Judson's colleague, the American Baptist missionary to Arracan,[131] James Colman.

Boardman, then nineteen and a student at Waterville College, vowed to replace Colman in the field. Sarah Hall, doomed by gender to staying home, did the next best thing. She wrote an elegy in Colman's honor which, after its publication in the *American Baptist Magazine*, "met the eyes of the young man in Maine":

> Tis the voice of deep sorrow from India's shore,
>   The flower of our churches is withered is dead,
> The gem that shone brightly will sparkle no more,
>   And the tears of the Christian profusely are shed,
> Two youths of Columbia, with hearts glowing warm
>   Embarked on the billows far distant to rove,
> To bear to the nations all wrapp'd in thick gloom,
>   The lamp of the gospel—the message of love.
> But Wheelock now slumbers beneath the cold wave,
> And Colman lies low in the dark cheerless grave.
>
> Mourn, daughters of India, mourn!
> The ray of star, clear and bright,
>   That so sweetly on Arracan shone
> Are shrouded in black clouds of night,
>   For Colman is gone![132]

Reading this elegy, Boardman was prompted to seek out its pious young author as his wife.[133]

Emily Chubbuck, who became a central figure in the Judson drama, also attributed her early interest in the missionary cause to

reading about the Burmese mission. Even families as insolvent as
the Chubbucks took the "religious papers." Chubbuck recalled that
while she was working in the woolen mills at Pratts Hollow, New
York, she one day "took up a little, dingy coarse newspaper—the
Baptist Register in its infancy":

> My eyes fell on the words: "Little Maria lies by the side of her fond
> Mother." I had read about the missionaries, and my sister had told
> me respecting them; I knew, therefore, that the letter was from
> Mr. Judson and that his little daughter was dead. How I pitied his
> loneliness! And then a new train of thought sprung up, and my
> mind expanded to a New Land of Glory. . . . Yes, I will be a mis-
> sionary.[134]

The ability of the printed page to awaken nascent Christians,
and to vitalize the faith of those already committed, was a basic axiom of evangelical communication theory. As late as 1914, a Baptist
writer, A.L. Vail, was concerned with identifying exactly what it
was that influenced Judson to become a Baptist over one hundred
years earlier. Vail reasoned, in what had become true evangelical
fashion, that Judson's behavior was a response to his knowledge of
the Bible and to his exposure to a supportive Christian literature, in
this case a specifically Baptist library in the possession of a Mr. Rolt,
identified as a founder and architect of the original Baptist church
in Calcutta. Vail wrote that Judson "might have satisfied [his] conscience while remaining a Congregationalist if [his] impressions
from the Scriptures had not been perfected and clinched by Rolt's
Library."[135] What Vail was really saying was that, whatever Judson's predispositions toward the Baptists, it was ultimately the
books he read that caused him to believe and act in a certain way.

The perception of a direct relationship between literary content
and form and human behavior made literature and the printed
page a moral and political problem. As a group, American evangelicals were so heavily imbued with this "impact theory,"[136] that they
might have become a deterrent to the spread of literacy, pointing to
the French Revolution as proof of their point.

In the case of the French, evangelical historiography did posit a
relationship between reading and radicalism. The *Baptist Register*
(1843) described the French Revolution as a "moral tornado"
brought on by the circulation of "an immense number of infidel papers, tracts and books [which] made the French people discon-
tented in the double slavery, both religious and political, under

which they had so long suffered."[137] In a ten-part series, meant for youthful readers, the upstate Baptists clarified their initial statement: the radicalism produced by reading was only a secondary cause of that tumultuous revolution. The primary source of discontent in France was absolutism and Catholicism, "twin slaveries" that spawned infidelity and turned the French people away from God. This interpretation was informed by the evangelicals' republican and Protestant biases, as well as some degree of identification with the "oppressed" of France.

Historical considerations differentiated the American case from the British, where fear of the radical and infidel implications of reading were articulated by the propertied classes in a public controversy over educating the working class poor.[138] In America the issue was not so much who should read, but what should be read. As early as 1647, the General Court of Massachusetts mandated that every township of at least fifty people designate "one within their towne to teach all such children as shall resort to him to write and reade."[139] Reading, promoted by the Puritans as a religious skill, was never the class issue in America that it was in Britain. In 1800, the Bishop of Rochester denounced the English Sunday and charity schools as "schools of Jacobinical rebellion."[140] This was an unlikely image for Americans, who, by and large, saw their Sunday school movement (beginning about 1820) as an important arm of a larger crusade to educate and Christianize the country simultaneously. The revolutionary legacy always informed American attitudes toward reading: "In a Republic, as every one hath to act a part, he should be able to write and read, at least, and to say why he will give his voice for this thing rather than any other."[141] In antebellum America, many of the people who needed or desired to learn to read were bound by denominational ties to those who wanted to Christianize all literature. The content of the books, not books themselves, was the American *ideé fixe*.

This overriding concern for the religious and moral quality of everything they read and wrote brings to mind Judson's "battle of conscience" with Burmese literature and helps to explain why there is no discernible relationship between evangelicalism and the American canonical writers.[142] The evangelicals were particularly adamant in their hostility to fiction, which, they claimed, provided inappropriate models, tended to "enervate the youthful mind," and taught nothing about preparation for a "future state."[143] The evangelicals created the stock character of a young female novel reader who inevitably lost all her reason and operated solely on the basis of romantic conventions. The evangelical description of this misguided soul was so prevalent that it was satirized by Tabitha Tenney in *Female Quixotism* (Boston, 1841). This three-volume account of the adventures of the deluded Dorcasina Sheldon was drawn from the diagnosis of evangelicals.

The American Tract Society, the great collaborative agency of Presbyterian and Congregational evangelicals, refused to have anything to do with fiction, blacklisting even the respectable works of Scott and Cooper. In 1836, the Society complained of the "injurious moral tendency" of those works of fiction that made up a major portion of the 8,000 volumes then on American trade publication lists.[144] Discursive prose was the safest literary style; religious poetry was considered admissible by most. "Infidelity has been served up in every shape that is likely to allure, surprise or beguile the imagination," warned the editor of the 1828 annual, *Moral and Religious Souvenir*. Infidelity could be found "in a fable, a novel, a poem; in interspersed and broken links; remote and oblique surmises; in books of travel, of philosophy, of natural history; in a word, in any form rather than the right one, that of a professed and regular disquisition."[145] To be sure, this was an extreme statement of the case, yet a distrust of literature that was not explicitly Christian pervaded much of the popular writing of the period.

There was a wide-ranging concern about reading in all sectors of antebellum society, reflecting a general confusion over what should be read. William Charvat describes a parallel boom in land and literature that followed the opening of the Erie Canal in 1825.[146] There is no doubt that the development of a national culture industry was made possible by both the invention of inexpensive printing machinery (in the late 1820s) and the opening in the same decade of more efficient transportation routes to the West.

This phenomenon was observed from a number of corners. The Unitarian *Christian Examiner* called the United States "the great reading country of the world," crediting the literary boom to the extension of literacy through common schools, a favorite Unitarian project.[147] Most commentators were more perplexed than analytical. "Look around you . . . and see how many hundreds every week is adding to the mass of tomes already in existence," suggested the editors of the *Southern Literary Messenger* (1836), "glance at the book-sellers catalogues . . . at the countless host of Reviews and Magazines, and of newspapers, tracts, pamphlets, speeches, addresses—effusions of ten thousand various forms and merits—craving your attention and bewildering your choice!"[148] The *American Quarterly Review* (1838) complained about the difficulty that moral and religious masterpieces had in a market characterized by "novelties" and "the mass of exciting periodical literature."[149] By 1830, Americans were exposed to what seemed to be a confusing array of affordable reading material.[150] In a poetic address in that year before the Phi Beta Kappa Society at Harvard, Grenville Mellon proclaimed:

> Home to wise and witless it must come,
> A truth that strikes all disputation dumb,
> Books by the bale proclaim it without stint,
> ERA OF PAPER, and the AGE OF PRINT.[151]

Despite all their fears about literary forms as either distractions or demonic points of contact, the American evangelicals threw their collective hat in the ring of entrepreneurial journalism and became, as a result, a contributing force in the development of a mass reading audience. In the United States, the pervasive class considerations of the British struggle for popular reading were inoperative. Orthodox religionists, with their open distaste for a number of literary forms, might have been a retrogressive force in the development of the American common reader, but they were not. While almost none of the evangelicals are remembered for a contribution to American imaginative literature, they were a literate people, the result of their neo-Puritan concern for the importance of individual experience with the Scriptures. Because many of their constituency were people who wanted to get ahead, and because the work of evangelization was increasingly tied to material prosperity, it was clearly undemocratic and impractical to wage a holy war against popular literature among a people who tied their republican virtue to the freedom of the press.

In the effort to reconstruct the evangelical mind, one senses that Christian literature and secular literature were in Manichean combat in this competitive and open literary marketplace. In the *Age of Print*, Mellon described a "Battle of the Books," in which the leading combatants are "Books of the Church and Books of the Boudoir!"[152] Actually, the lines were never as clearly drawn as Mellon and others suggest, primarily because the proponents of orthodox religion, the evangelicals, were able to make a number of successful adaptations. The aroma of the literary smorgasbord served up by

the commercial publishers penetrated everywhere, causing them
to relent on their adherence to a purist's diet of strictly religious
reading.

One option was to propagate the notion of cautious consumer-
ism, to give the appropriate product labels, and to develop techniques for limiting intake. Among the young, selection of books
required guidance rather than autonomy. "Seek the advice of judicious friends in the choice of books," was a typical refrain.[153] The
judicious friends were probably pious parents, older siblings, or
members of the religious community. As a young woman, Susan
Warner, later the author of the best-selling domestic novel of the
1850s, *Wide Wide World*, was allotted bits and pieces of Waverly
novels as a dietary supplement, but only as her father deemed it
wise.[154]

Random reading, an important tool of self-education in a democratic society, and an obvious necessity for many of the lowly born
evangelical constituency, was discouraged. Young men and women
were urged to develop a prearranged course or reading plan. In a
sense, the reading list was an approximation of a school curriculum,
helpful to those who lacked either the time or money to attend an
academy or college. Typical is Harvey Newcomb's *Letters to a Sister*, which recommended a system of reading that assigned two
days a week to history, two days to biography (which specified
Knowles' *Memoir of Mrs. Judson*), a day to doctrinal subjects, and
two to religious newspapers and periodical publications. "Pursue
this plan for ten years," suggested Newcomb, "and you will have
read 200 books containing 60,000 pages." The Bible was, of course,
to be read daily and on all occasions when other "profitable employments were unavailable."[155] "It would be unwise counsel to tell
you to read indiscriminately whatever comes to hand," wrote the
editor of the *Religious Souvenir* (1833): "The press gives circulation
not only to useful knowledge but to error dressed up plausibly in the
garb of truth. Many books are useless, others are on the whole injurious, and some are impregnated with a deadly poison."[156] One
senses that the evangelicals felt better simply by issuing their product warnings and supplying a system which differentiated the
genres.

That they came to accept a variety of literary forms which they
never publicly condoned is evident in reading the popular religious
giftbooks, or annuals, of the period 1825–1860.[157] The religious giftbook was a kind of portable academy, a potpourri of information

and sensibility which barely penetrated the surface of any subject. Selected and original pieces were brought together under a moral and religious umbrella that was not specifically sectarian, although a few denominations did try their hands at publishing their own annuals.

Religious giftbooks, such as *The Christian Offering, The Christian Keepsake and Missionary Annual, The Christian Souvenir, The Laurel Wreath, The Religious Souvenir,* and *The Remember Me,* all published some fiction throughout the 1830s. The stories were largely anonymous and always formulaic, reflecting the authors' close adherence to a common moral universe. The authors, who were generally women, often told their tales in the first person, relying on devices like deathbed confessions or chance meetings with travelers to give the story some semblance of fact rather than fiction. It was common for the author to preface her tale with the explanation that the story was "told to me," or conveyed to the author by the subject "in his/her own words."[158]

Fiction by Emma C. Embury, Hannah Gould, Lydia H. Sigourney, Harriet Beecher Stowe, Ann S. Stephens, and other anonymous women writers, as well as some clergy, became a set feature of even these explicitly moral and religious annuals. Yet, even as they contributed these formulaic tales, there were lingering doubts about their propriety. Catharine Beecher, who herself contributed the story of "Fanny Moreland, or Use and Abuse of the Risibles," to the 1838 *Christian Keepsake and Missionary Annual,* still saw the American Christian's relationship to fiction as problematic:

> Why should so much fiction pervade our lighter literature, when the annals of truth furnish such an abundant supply of all that is exciting in incident, elevated in virtue, pure in principle, and romantic in chivalry? Why should an American, who in his own history can find so much that is thrilling and wonderful turn to the pages of romance, when the realities of truth surpass them?[159]

In the mid-1840s, the controversy over the third Mrs. Judson's early life as a formulaic fiction writer (described in Chapter 5) indicated the continued uneasiness among the orthodox about the benignity of the connection between imaginative literature and the religious life. Even exemplary evangelicals like Judson and his third wife were not immune to seduction by art.

The giftbook editors, who were generally clergymen, proposed that their annuals were a safe means of combining "religious and

literary interest." By literary interest, they undoubtedly meant popular fiction, though the word is never used. The clergy's careful
perusal of the literary component of the books insured their accept-
ability among "friends of morality and religion." The preface of the
annuals became a kind of product label, or content guarantee. The
editor of *The Religious Souvenir* of 1833 wrote that he was "not unwilling to hazard his reputation as a Christian" on the morality of
his book's contents.[160] The pastor of the Houston Street Church of
New York City and editor of the 1846 *Laurel Wreath* confirmed
that "as a watchman on Zion's walls . . . he had occasion to mourn
over the sad effects of the light literature, which is scattered over
our wide extended country; hence he has carefully excluded whatever might be deemed objectionable, even by the most cautious and
considerate. The articles admitted will be seen to have a moral, and
most of them a decidely Christian tendency."[161]

This claim was unilaterally made by religious giftbook editors
who accepted the new symbiosis so long as they retained content
control. In justifying their acceptance of a less-than-explicitly-
Christian literary form, the editors almost always made some kind
of oblique reference to popular taste, to the "ERA OF PAPER" and "THE
AGE OF PRINT." "There can be no doubt," argued John Chowles, pastor of the Second Baptist Church in Newport, Rhode Island, and
editor of the *Christian Offering for 1832*, "that the wide diffusion
of the light and elegant literature of the day is exciting a powerful
influence on the community, and especially on the youthful mind;
and it is therefore incumbent on the friends of truth to aid the circulation of such works as shall produce the best moral and religious effects." In this volume, said Chowles, "an attempt had been made to
show, that literary elegance and Christian instruction may happily
coalesce."[162] Other annuals affirmed the same purpose: "ours is a
feeble effort to Christianize American literature, and hang its
choice garlands on the Cross of the Redeemer."[163] "It has long been
[the editor's] opinion that it would prove one of the happiest means
of extending a holy and regenerating influence . . . to combine as
much as possible with the literature of the land, and with all that is
ornamental, and sweet and graceful in the Fine Arts, the hallowing
and sanctifying influence of EVANGELICAL RELIGION."[164]

What was ultimately most appealing about the Judson story
was the manner in which its truth read like the dreaded fiction.
Ann Hasseltine's biographer, James D. Knowles, had alluded to the
startling, dramatic quality of the imprisonment narrative: "Fiction

itself has seldom invented a tale more replete with terror." The old lessons of religious piety, perseverance, and courage were newly animated against a colorful backdrop of exotic heathenism.[165] The context of a non-Christian culture also provided high dramatic content in the identifiable personal battles of illness, loneliness, and death that plagued the Judsons. In this setting, the possibilities of doing good were so enlarged that the eventual outcome was mind-boggling. After all, the Judsons were, according to evangelical theory, the Christian link to nineteen million possible converts.

And, because the story was being made as it was being read, there was a measure of importance and urgency to each epistolary or journal installment. The reading audience simply did not know the final outcome. Always there was the hope of seeing massive conversions among the Burmese. What is instructive for the study of evangelical culture is the way in which this early media event, which was an essentially circuitous and open-ended story, became linear and formulaic in the hands of evangelical interpreters, who valued the didactic above all else.

The Judson story was a comfortable one for evangelicals who felt at home with "religious biography" depicting the lives of individuals of eminent piety and Christian work. Harvey Newcomb's reading plan recommended religious biography as the "best kind of practical reading":

> Suppose a traveller just entering a dreary wilderness. The path which leads through it is exceedingly narrow and difficult to be kept. On each side, it is beset with thorns, briers, and miry pits. Would he not rejoice to find a book containing the experience of former travellers who had passed that way; in which every difficult spot is marked; all their contests with wild beasts and serpents, and all their falls described; a beacon, or *guide-board*, set up, wherever a beaten track turns aside from the true way? All this you find in religious biographies. There, the difficulties, trials, temptations, falls and deliverances of God's people are described.[166]

Religious biography, as a record of personal triumph over adversity and sin, reflected the evangelical interest in establishing the exact point of contact where an individual and the religious movement converged.[167] No longer content to operate as if the Holy Spirit needed no help, or as if there were only the points of contact preordained by God himself, the practitioners of evangelical religion looked to the historical record of great Christians for information about the circumstances that made for Christian commitment. The Judsons were of great value to the Baptists because their early history delineated these circumstances, and the story of their activist adult lives was a demonstrable motivational device for those in the Christian community.

The notion of points of contact, created by human agencies, became central to American evangelical communications theory. "In every company and in every situation, be on the watch for opportunities to speak a word for God," wrote Presbyterian Samuel Miller. "And where you do not find opportunities, by a little address you may *make* them."[168] The multiplication of contact points was certainly a rationale for the development and support of denominational publications; it was also a consideration in pushing the orthodox beyond a solely biblical orientation to acceptance of, and participation in, the creation of a popular American Christian literature. The evangelicals surely knew that not every reader responded in like manner to the effusions of pious pens. However, the fact that so many committed Christians ascribed their religious convictions to things they had read validated the traditional Protestant faith in the Word, and lent increasing potency to the idea that the growth of a modern religious constituency depended upon a denomination's propagative powers.

Chapter *4*
———◆———

The Apostolate of Women

Women were at the heart of American evangelical religious culture.[1] Because evangelicalism mandated initiative in the cause of Christ, evangelical women, whether in exotic Burma or in their home communities, were extended significant opportunities for self-assertion in the religious sphere. Women were involved, without equal, in every religious benevolence of the day: Bible and tract societies, ministerial education groups, charitable societies for widows and orphans, moral reform, evangelization of the Jews, and domestic and foreign missions.

There is also some evidence that revivalism promoted egalitarianism within the church itself. In 1827, at New Lebanon, New York, the "New Measures" associated with evangelical religious innovation in western New York came under attack by more conservative New Englanders like Lyman Beecher and Asahel Nettleton. The discussion centered to a large extent on the role of women in the Presbyterian evangelical movement, the eastern opposition taking issue with western evangelical practice, which was apparently

moving in the direction of equal and audible participation by
women in religious meetings.[2]

What the New Lebanon dialogues suggest is that, within Presbyterianism at least, there was some question about the participa-
tory role that the revivalism of Charles Grandison Finney seemed to
imply. The Presbyterians were reluctant, as were other evangelical
denominations, to go the complete route: to accord women their
full rights and privileges within the church. Assuming that the as-
sembled church elders surely knew women to be the largest percentage of their audience, the conference begged the real question: was
evangelicalism, and not simply Finney's revivalism, altering female
behavior by providing women with enlarged Christian opportunities?

So long as their gaze was affixed on the glory of the millennium,
the evangelical denominations legitimized a wide range of female
activities in the cause of world evangelization. Throughout the
nineteenth century, proselytizing without women was considered
incomplete, if not handicapped. As early as 1815, the ABCFM recommended that male missionaries live in a "married state." The
Congregationalists reasoned, and other denominational groups followed suit, that Christian familial and social patterns could not be
taught to heathens unless there were present, on the scene, "missionaries, who are married to well educated and pious females, who
have formed all their habits and modes of thinking in a Christian
country."[3] By 1870, the staffs of many foreign missions were pre-
dominantly female, and women had formed their own denominational foreign mission boards, independent of male organizations.[4]
Arabella Stuart Willson, a biographer of the three Mrs. Judsons, explained the attraction of foreign mission work, a crusade that absorbed the energies of large numbers of women well into the present
century:

> The missionary enterprise opens to woman a sphere of activity,
> usefulness and distinction, not, under the present constitution of
> society, to be found elsewhere. Here she may exhibit whatever she
> possesses of skill in the mastery of unknown and difficult dialects;
> of tact in dealing with the varieties of human character; of ardor
> and perseverance in the pursuit of a noble end under the most try-
> ing discouragements; and of exalted Christian heroism and forti-
> tude, that braves appalling dangers, and even death in its most
> dreadful forms. . . .[5]

An engraving of the 1812 departure of the Judsons for the East, taken from *The Judson Offering* (1846).

An engraving of the grave of Ann Hasseltine Judson and her daughter Maria, taken from *The Judson Offering* (1846), reprinted in a number of other 19th-century imprints and periodicals.

This engraving of the young Adoniram Judson was done in 1811, the year before he embarked on the first American foreign missionary enterprise. At the time he sat for this portrait, Judson was twenty-three and a student at Andover Theological Seminary. The engraving was published in the *Massachusetts Missionary Magazine* in March 1818. Portraits of the mature Judson indicate that the missionary dropped the mannered 18th-century dress and hairstyle recorded in this student picture. *(Courtesy of the American Baptist Historical Society)*

Both of these early portraits of the young Ann Hasseltine are from 19th-century imprints. The representation above, which has deteriorated badly, has an 18th-century tone and was done, presumably, before the 1812 embarkation. *(Courtesy of the American Baptist Historical Society)* Most likely, the portrait on the right was done from life in 1823 when Mrs. Judson returned to the United States. This is the most primitive of at least a dozen different engravings done of Ann Hasseltine Judson in the 19th century. *(From the collection of the author)*

Although Adoniram Judson lamented the fact that there was no portrait of his second wife, these two engravings, from 19th-century imprints, depict and interpret events in the life of Sarah Boardman Judson. Right, Sarah Judson and a nursing infant are threatened by heathen men. (*Reproduced from* Women of Worth. A Book for Girls, *n.d.*) Below, a romantic landscape, titled for a poem by Sarah, portrays the Judsons together, in 1845, before Sarah's departure for a recuperative sea voyage which ended with her death. (*Reproduced from Emily C. Judson*, Memoir of Sarah B. Judson of the American Mission to Burmah, *1850*)

SARAH JUDSON AND THE BURMESE FREEBOOTERS.
"The rounded limbs of the little infant lay motionless as their marble counterfeit; for if their rosy lips had moved but to the slightest murmur, or the tiny hand crept closer to the loved bosom in her baby dream, the chord in the mother's breast must have answered, and the death-stroke followed. Murderers stood by the bedside; regarding the tableau, and the husband and father SLEPT."—PAGE 113.

"We part on this green islet, love." Page 235.

The engraving on the left is from a collection that extolled the values and virtues of women missionaries. *(Reproduced from D.C. Eddy,* Daughters of the Cross; or Woman's Mission, *1855)* The portrait of Ann Hasseltine Judson, below, is another romantic representation of the "Apostolate of Women." *(Courtesy of the American Baptist Historical Society)*

Adoniram Judson's forced march through the Burmese jungle to the prison at Oung-pen-la
was retold in each of his biographies. This engraving shows Judson on the "Blood Tracked
March," accepting pieces of cloth to bind his torn feet from a kind-hearted Bengali servant.
(Reproduced from Robert Middleditch, Burmah's Great Missionary, *1854)*

Portraits of the mature Judson almost always show the missionary with Bible or translation work in hand. The portrait on the left appeared in a popular posthumous biography. *(Reproduced from Robert Middleditch,* Burmah's Great Missionary, *1854)* Below is a photograph of an oil painting done from life when Judson visited Hamilton Literary and Theological Seminary in 1846. The portrait was burned in a fire at Colgate University. *(Courtesy of the Colgate University Archives)*

This engraving from an 1854 biography shows the graves of the three wives (beneath the hopia tree, in the rock at St. Helena, in the village cemetery at Hamilton) and the "watery grave" of Judson who died at sea in 1850. *(Reproduced from Robert Middleditch,* Burmah's Great Missionary, *1854)*

This family portrait (taken from an ambrotype made at Hamilton, N.Y., in 1853) shows the widow of Adoniram Judson, Emily Chubbuck ("Fanny Forester") with three of the Judson children: Edward, Henry Hall, and Emily Frances. The young woman on the right is a Burmese convert cast as an American black by the unsophisticated engraver. *(Reproduced from Edward Judson,* The Life of Adoniram Judson, *1883)*

In the effort to encourage missionary giving among children, the Women's American Baptist Missionary Society published (c. 1890) this rebus for use in the Sunday Schools. *(From the collection of the author)*

Dear [children] and [boys]

Here is your new [purse] just right for

your [coin] [coin] [coin] or a big [coin]

Wouldn't that be fine?

What shall we do with the money when your box is full?

We will send some to the little [child] some to the [child]

some to the [child] and some to the [child]

It will help build a [school] buy [trowel] and

pay for food and [clothes] Poor little children, they

are often hungry, and they do wrong because they do not know

about our Saviour, and they pray to a dreadful [idol]

Do save all the money you can, send missionaries on the big

[ship] to tell them about our dear Jesus. At

night when you go to [bed] don't forget to [pray]

for them. Fill the box full.

Your friend,

LUCY W. WATERBURY.

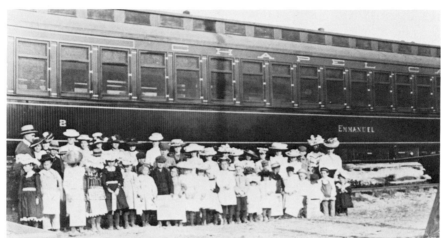

Evangelicals have carried Bibles and tracts across the country for more than 150 years. These photographs show how the work of evangelization has adapted to changing modes of transportation. On the reverse side of the Chapel Car Emmanuel is written: "God so loved the world that he gave his only begotten son so that whosoever believeth in him should not perish but have everlasting life." (*Courtesy of the American Baptist Historical Society*)

At age fifty-five, Abby Ann Judson, the eldest daughter of Adoniram and Sarah Boardman Judson, became a Spiritualist and began a public career as a Spiritualist lecturer and writer. *(Reproduced from Abby Ann Judson, The Bridge Between Two Worlds, 1894)*

In 1875, Edward Judson, the youngest son of Adoniram and Sarah Boardman Judson, left a wealthy pastorate in New Jersey to do the work of urban evangelization among the immigrants in lower New York City. *(Courtesy of the American Baptist Historical Society)*

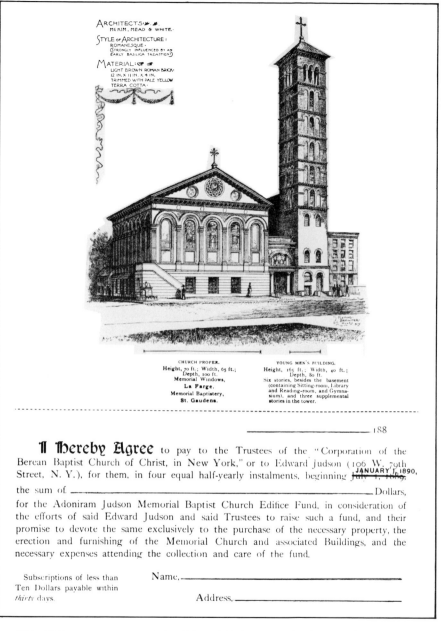

ARCHITECTS:
McKIM, MEAD & WHITE.

STYLE OF ARCHITECTURE:
ROMANESQUE.
(STRONGLY INFLUENCED BY AN
EARLY BASILICA TREATMENT)

MATERIAL:
LIGHT BROWN ROMAN BRICK.
12 IN. X 11 IN. X 4 IN.
TRIMMED WITH PALE YELLOW
TERRA COTTA.

CHURCH PROPER.
Height, 70 ft.; Width, 65 ft.;
Depth, 100 ft.
Memorial Windows,
La Farge.
Memorial Baptistery,
St. Gaudens.

YOUNG MEN'S BUILDING.
Height, 165 ft.; Width, 40 ft.;
Depth, 80 ft.
Six stories, besides the basement
(containing Sitting-room, Library
and Reading-room, and Gymnasium), and three supplemental
stories in the tower.

—————————————————— 188

¶ Ibereby Bgree to pay to the Trustees of the "Corporation of the Berean Baptist Church of Christ, in New York," or to Edward Judson (106 W. 79th Street, N. Y.), for them, in four equal half-yearly instalments, beginning ~~July 1, 1889~~ JANUARY 1, 1890,

the sum of _____ Dollars,

for the Adoniram Judson Memorial Baptist Church Edifice Fund, in consideration of the efforts of said Edward Judson and said Trustees to raise such a fund, and their promise to devote the same exclusively to the purchase of the necessary property, the erection and furnishing of the Memorial Church and associated Buildings, and the necessary expenses attending the collection and care of the fund.

Subscriptions of less than
Ten Dollars payable within
thirty days.

Name, _____

Address, _____

This 1890 contract was used by Edward Judson as a fund-raising device in the campaign to build the Judson Memorial Church at Washington Square, New York City. The Italianate style, shown here in an architectural rendering by the architects McKim, Mead, and White, was intended to act as a lure to the immigrant Italians of lower New York. *(Courtesy of the Rockefeller Archives Center, Pocantico Hills)*

In the 1890s, this logo was used to symbolize the charitable activities of the Judson Memorial Church, particularly the Memorial Fresh Air Flower and Cool Water Fund. *(Courtesy of the Rockefeller Archives Center, Pocantico Hills)*

The Rockefeller family often entertained New York guests, such as Edward Judson, at their Forest Hill estate near Cleveland, Ohio. In this photograph taken by John, Jr., in 1880 or 1881, the Rockefeller's visitors include Richard Arnold (second from right, standing), the concert master of the New York Philharmonic and John, Jr.'s, violin teacher; Mrs. Arnold (with parasol); and Mrs. J. Ellen Foster, a temperance speaker (seated between Mrs. Rockefeller, on the far left, and the standing John D. Rockefeller, Sr.) *(Courtesy of the Rockefeller Archives Center, Pocantico Hills)*

American Baptists designated 1913 the centennial year for the celebration of the founding of the foreign mission to Burma. This photograph shows the interior of Tremont Temple, Boston, where the Northern Baptist Convention held its annual meeting on June 24-25, 1914. On this occasion, Edward Judson was elected Honorary President for life of the American Baptist Foreign Missionary Society. His brother, Adoniram Brown Judson, the New York physician, and his half-sister Emily Judson Hanna, also attended the denominational festivities. *(Courtesy of the American Baptist Historical Society)*

Bridal Pictures

Somewhere in Christian America	Somewhere in Heathen India

Evangelical women continued to emphasize the degradation of their heathen sisters well into the 20th century. This brochure, published c. 1920 by the Women's American Baptist Missionary Society, makes the comparison in a visual fashion. *(Courtesy of the Department of Manuscripts and University Archives, Cornell University)*

In opportunities like these, rather than in "superior feminine susceptibility," there is the beginning of a comprehensive explanation of why women were drawn, in much larger numbers than men, to the institutional churches and to organized religion.[6] Woman's religious commitment was less an act of quiet desperation than a collective action with other women bonded together by similar social values and economic situations.[7] Neither was religion taken as pablum to resolve the problems of an increasingly isolated, domestic existence.[8] The wide-scale participation of women in antebellum evangelical religion brought more than a simple promise of a better life in the hereafter. The evangelical concept of "The Apostolate of Woman" legitimized the idea of female activity in the here-and-now and accorded women some real opportunities for demonstrating their competence, fortitude, and skills of expression. Women "got religion" in antebellum America because religion was larger than the church itself.

In the evangelical movement, women, who were by and large outside circles of affluence and high culture, found a coherent intellectual system. Through prescribed reading, evangelicalism encouraged a degree of Christian initiative and ingenuity; at the same time, it provided a historical and international context for women's lives. In Scripture, women found biblical precedents for the concept of the female apostolate.[9] In Ann Judson's epistolary reports, they were provided with a comfortable mechanism for exploring their own situations vis-à-vis the women of the heathen world.

What religious women drew from the reports of foreign missionaries was a bleak picture of female degradation in non-Christian cultures. This perception reinforced, rather than undercut, their belief in "The Cult of True Womanhood."[10] Concern for the uplift of heathen women simultaneously mitigated the nascent, domestic movement for woman's political equality. Religious women who accepted the mantle of "True Womanhood" because of its Christian underpinnings directed their attention instead to the pervasive ignobility of their heathen sisters.

The religious feminism of the American evangelical woman was a cautiously constructed and tenuous ideology: mistreatment of women was located abroad, rather than at home, and criticism of men was levied only at heathens, infidels, alcoholics, and possibly slaveholders, not at practicing Christians. In the name of woman's uplift abroad and at home, antebellum women were able to develop careers in Christian endeavor, as managers of the "benevolent empire," as teachers, and as missionaries. This, the "apostolate of women," rather than political feminism, absorbed the hearts and minds of evangelical women.

Ann Hasseltine Judson's biography became sacrosanct because it was the perfect expression of this idealized religious commitment to the moral uplift of heathen women. For her dramatic demonstration of the function and potential of American Christian womanhood, Ann Judson was enshrined as the "moral heroine of the 19th century."

———————◆◆———————

From the beginning, Ann Hasseltine Judson had her own ministry, distinct from that of her husband. On her wedding day, February 5, 1812, in the Congregational Church at Haverhill, the Rev. Jonathan Allen preached a farewell sermon, which included remarks addressed specifically to Ann and to her friend, Harriet Atwood Newell:

> It will be your business, my dear children, to teach these women, to whom your husbands can have but little or no access. Go then, and do all in your power, to enlighten their minds, and bring them to the knowledge of truth. Go, and if possible, raise their character to the dignity of rational beings, and to the rank of Christians in a christian land. Teach them to realize that they are not an inferior race of creatures; but stand upon a par with men. . . .[11]

Allen's directive was an expression of the spiritual egalitarianism which characterized the evangelical and foreign missionary movements. For all the cultural arrogance implicit in their attitude towards non-Christians, the evangelicals valued male and female souls equally. The male editor of the 1828 *Moral and Religious Souvenir* told his readership: "By the prevalence of the Gospel, it was soon understood, that the souls of your sex were of an origin as high, a value as precious, a destination as lofty, as our own."[12] Consequently, the conversion of heathen men and women had equal value in the foreign mission field.

Ann Judson's letters from Burma noted the condition of her own sex, made reference to unfamiliar social practices, and described her own efforts at explaining herself, and Christianity, to Burmese women. In one of her earliest letters to her family, Ann Judson wrote:

> I desire to no higher enjoyment in this life, than to be instrumental of leading some poor, ignorant females to the knowledge of the Saviour. To have a female praying society, consisting of those who were once in heathen darkness, is what my heart earnestly pants after, and makes a constant subject of prayer. [I am] resolved to keep this in view; as one principal object of my life.[13]

It is clear that Ann Judson took Allen's final invocation seriously: "May you live to see the fruit of your labors, in the conversion of thousands of your sisters in the east. . . ."[14]

In the minds of American evangelical Protestants, the status of women, in any given culture, was tied to the acceptance of the Bible. "The Bible is the only guarantee of woman's rights," wrote Sarah Josepha Hale in an 1855 catalogue of 2,005 women who, in her mind, deserved historical recognition. Of these women, she noted, fewer than 200 were non-Christians, although heathens made up more than seventy-five percent of the world's population.[15] The transforming power of the Gospel in relation to the condition of women was described by a returning missionary to a mixed audience of men and women members of the American Bible Society:

> Women! They are a mere blank [in India]; they are nothing, they are not even to be spoken of. If I should inquire of a respectable man in Bombay how his wife was, or his daughters, he would instantly turn his back upon me and consider himself insulted. . . . Females are things too low, too vile to be mentioned. . . . And why are things so different in this land? Why do I look upon such a company as that which now surrounds me? Oh it is this book, this divine book that has accomplished the whole.[16]

With the Gospel defined as an agency of their guardianship, evangelical women were inextricably drawn to the Bible, to stories of the New Testament, and to a consideration of the role of women marked out by Jesus himself. Stories of biblical women were often retold, complemented by engravings, in the religious giftbooks of the day. While some of these were from Old Testament sources, the majority came from the New Testament. One of the most popular was the story of Martha and Mary, the sisters of Lazarus, who, in Luke 10:38–42, met Jesus at Bethany. Martha, who according to the 1843 *Christian Souvenir* represented "abounding hospitality," had come to "exaggerate the importance of her own sphere . . . [and] in her estimation, woman's only high provenance was to *guide the house*." While Martha bustled about in domestic preparations, Mary, "oblivious of all that belonged to that occasion," sat at the feet of Jesus, in "holy trustfulness," listening to his words.[17]

When Jesus commended Mary for having "chosen the good part," he marked her for the evangelical reader as one of the most spiritually sensitive women in the New Testament. In countless sermons addressed to their female congregants on the subject of their religious responsibility, the evangelical clergy evoked the names of Martha and of Mary; of Phebe, Priscilla, and Persis; of Hannah, Dorcas, Tryphena, and Tryphosa.[18] Women were reminded that in Luke 8:1–3 certain women ministered to Christ of their substance, that in Proverbs 31:29 daughters had performed virtuously, that in Luke 21:2–4 the widow had given her two mites.[19] In fact, wherever one looks in the literature read by antebellum religious women, there is a single message: ". . . form your characters after the model of those, who are distinguished on the sacred pages by their faith and good works."[20] To make sure that women were acquainted with their biblical antecedents, evangelicals recommended anthologies like: *Women of the Bible: Historical and descriptive Sketches of the Women of the Bible as maidens, wives, and Mothers, from Eve of the Old, to the Marys of the New Testament.*[21]

What the evangelicals drew from the catalogue of female biblical experience was a decidedly conservative social position, demonstrating what literal readers they could be. Given the social message of the Pauline Epistles (Ephesians 5:22–24: "Wives, submit yourselves unto your own husbands, as unto the Lord"),[22] evangelical women never challenged the hierarchy of the marital relationship and the legal subordination it implied. In 1895, as president of the National American Woman Suffrage Association, Elizabeth Cady Stanton, who had only negative feelings about the revivalism she experienced as a young girl, published the *Woman's Bible*, which was her attempt to reinterpret those biblical texts that traditionally kept large numbers of religious women alienated from political feminism.[23] What Stanton's anticlerical and antiliteral interpretations of religion failed to assess was the degree to which evangelical women were tied to the making of a spiritual rather than a political revolution. As a result, evangelical women gave only reluctant consideration to their domestic and legal subjugation to American Christian men. In fact, the kind of woman who was drawn to the evangelical movement was almost always more interested in converting men than in achieving equality with them.

This was the female persona that evangelicals found most compatible with what the New Testament taught. However, on the basis of a literal reading of Scripture, the evangelical clergy also encouraged women to Christian endeavor, for in the life of Jesus they found testimony to Christianity's valuation of women's "deep and lively interest in Christ."[24] In the introduction to an 1834 collection of female biography, Samuel Lorenzo Knapp used women's biblical history to justify their current importance:

> Some have objected to bringing women forward, as inconsistent with female delicacy. The great writers of the Old Testament did not think so. They have given us many models of excellence in public and private life. . . . If it were not proper and just to hold the worthy woman up to notice, would the Apostles have filled their writings with the names and deeds of women, those too, not remarkable for birth, fortune, or standing in society, but those who, by their virtues and their zeal, assisted to spread the truths of the Gospel.[25]

Knapp also put this question to his readership: "Shall it be asked by our posterity, when they read of the deeds of their fathers, why were not the virtues of our primitive mothers put on record also?"[26] The same kind of information was requested by an interested young woman in the dialogue that formed the introduction to *Sketches of the Lives of Distinguished Females* (1833), who inquired, "Are there no histories of good and great women, mother?"[27]

Besides the Bible and sermons taken from Scripture, there were other sources—all largely subsumed to a Christian context—which addressed the question of women in history. Everyone knew, posited an 1828 giftbook, that Christian martyrologies were filled with the names of female sufferers. What was significant was that women "were not only pure maidens and faithful wives, but they became also thinkers and students; apologists as well as martyrs for Christianity. Where the new faith was received, they often introduced it. They established it on the thrones of the Northern nations."[28] In fact, the evangelical interpretation of the history of Christianity supplied women with lofty heroines, as well as humble sisters in the cause. "The women in the infant churches," wrote

Arabella Stuart Willson, "rivalled the brethren in attachment and fidelity to the cause; and to their ministry the new religion was indebted in no small degree for its unparalleled success."[29]

For American evangelicals, the apostolate of women was validated by traditional sources, such as the Bible and Christian history, and by the case of Ann Hasseltine Judson. By the time of her return to the United States in 1822, Ann Judson had become an expert on the subject of heathenism and heathen women. Her life in Burma, which included domestic responsiblities, as well as translation duties and the teaching of reading and Christianity, was particularly interesting to her home audience because of its context. In the United States, female religious activity operated in "the full blaze of Gospel light," an evangelical euphemism for an organized, Protestant culture. Denied all "bonds of sisterhood" and association by Harriet Newell's premature death and the accidental drowning of William Carey's wife and children, Ann Judson stood, a lone Christian woman, in an alien geographical and cultural landscape. As a result, American evangelical women were sympathetic and interested in both how she fared and what she had to report about the relative position of women in Christian and heathen societies.

From the heart of heathendom, Ann Judson reported that the elevated moral status of women was a characteristic feature of Christendom, that heathen women were in a desperate and deplorable condition. It was Ann Judson's early religious feminism, as expressed in her letters and in her personal appeals for emotional and financial support, that did much to define the nature of Christian service to heathen women. Ann described the need for education and immediate Christian conversion; like many of her fellow missionaries she would find little to value in a culture distinguished by "female wretchedness."

In an 1822 address, probably written for delivery before a group of Boston women, Ann Judson articulated the nature of her commitment to the women of Burma. It was Ann's conviction that American women would mobilize for action if they knew the truth. "Shew [sic] us the situation of our tawny sisters on the other side of the world," Ann imagined her audience to say, and "though the disgusting picture breaks our hearts, it will fill us with gratitude to Him who has made us to differ, and excite to stronger exertion in their behalf."[30]

At the outset, Ann labeled her story a "tale of woe." Among women in Bengal and Hindustan she observed female infanticide and infant marriage. Young women spent their time in "listless idleness, in mental torpor," uneducated and without benefit of social intercourse. Indian men were both authoritarian and decidedly bestial in their treatment of women:

> So far from receiving those delicate attentions which render happy the conjugal state, and which distinguish civilized from heathen nations; the wife receives the appellation of *my servant*, or *my dog*, and is allowed to partake of what her lordly husband is pleased to give at the *conclusion* of his repast![31]

Smarting from the image of married women reduced to living on the crumbs of their husbands' bread, Ann explained that the secluded lives of women in the East produced "imbecility" and "malignant passions" rather than a tranquil "culture of amiable feelings."

Ann Judson's 1822 analysis indicates that she made some effort to discriminate among national behavioral patterns in the East. She reported that in Burma, where women mixed in society, ate with their families, and displayed a "lively, inquisitive, strong and energetic character," they were only marginally better off than their Bengal and Hindustan sisters and were still victimized by the "tyrannic rod" of Burmese males. "The wife and grown daughters," she observed, "are considered by the husband and father as much the subjects of discipline, as younger children."[32] Besides being kept in a state of perpetual childhood, Burmese women were "taught nothing."

Ann's message, based on sound evangelical theory and practice, was abundantly clear: Burmese women were not taught to read; this accounted for their inferior status. If they could learn to read, which was one of her primary teaching responsibilities, they would have access to the Bible, the crucial agency of spiritual transformation and female uplift. Money for Bibles and tracts, for translation projects, and for schools was absolutely essential. Women were asked to support these projects in the name of decency, on behalf of their sex:

> Shall we, my beloved friends, suffer minds like these to lie dormant, to wither in ignorance and delusion, to grope their way to eternal ruin, without an effort on our part, to raise, to refine, to elevate, and point to that Saviour who has died equally for them as for us? . . . Let us make a united effort, let us call on all, old and young, in the circle of our acquaintance, to join us in attempting

to meliorate the situation, to instruct, to enlighten and save females in the Eastern world. . . .[33]

Writing from Maulmain in 1831, Adoniram Judson enjoined American women to forsake "the demon vanity" for the amelioration of
their sisters in the East. Judson's suggestion was the formation of
Plain Dress Societies, and the publication of his address in 1832 included "Retrenchment Rules," or guidelines for their operation.[34]
In a two-part series in the New York *Baptist Register* (1843), the
editors similarly explored "The Claims of the Heathen upon American Females." American Christian women were perceived as having a special responsibility to practice "proper economy" within the
home and in terms of their personal attire.[35] The mites they saved
by eschewing necklaces, ear ornaments, and the seductions of creative millinery were to be set aside for their heathen sisters.

The missionary's cry for female betterment abroad was one of
the chief emotional appeals for foreign missions.[36] In *Ocean
Sketches of Life in Burma* (1857), Marilla B. Ingalls encouraged
even small children to join in the crusade: "And my young lady
friends and little girls, think of the degradation of these daughters
[of Burma], and do your part in the great work."[37] In the effort to
rouse women of all ages to the support of missions, there was much
moral stereotyping of non-Christian cultures. On the most basic
level, evangelical Christians simply saw no truth in other religious
systems. Arabella Stuart Wilson, the biographer of Judson's three
wives, called Buddhism "one of the most ancient and wide-spread
superstitions existing on the face of the earth."[38] In the *Memoirs of
Ann H. Judson*, Knowles reported that "the religion of Burmah . . .
is, in effect, *atheism*. . . ."[39]

Ann Judson's accounts of the religious life of Burma laid heavy
stress on the fact that the natives were "idolaters." On her third day
in Burma, Ann recounted the following for her family:

> . . . there was a celebration of the worship of the Juggernaut. We
> went about ten in the morning. The immense multitude of natives
> assembled on the occasion, and the noise they made, answered to
> the account Buchanan gave. The idol was set on the top of a stone
> building. He is only a lump of wood, his face painted with large
> black eyes, and a large red mouth. He was taken from his temple,
> and water poured on him to bathe him. . . . After these poor de-
> luded creatures had bathed their God, they proceeded to bathe
> themselves. Poor, miserable deluded beings, they know not what
> they do.[40]

The rhetoric of Ann Judson's account of the worship of the Jugger-
naut demonstrates the way in which evangelical perceptions were
consistently informed by familiarity with both the Old and New
Testaments. Besides the obvious link to Jesus in the last line ("Poor,
miserable deluded beings, they know not what they do."), Ann's
perspective was that of the knowing observer, of Moses returning to
witness the celebration of the golden calf. Rather than smash idols,
in retributive Old Testament form, Ann's was an apostolic mission,
a labor of love, of persuasion, and of education.

Wherever she looked, Ann Judson found images of Gaudama:
in zayats, in private homes, in pagodas and temples. William Gammell described Burma as a place where marble was in short supply
because of all the images.[42] Many of the religious giftbooks of the
antebellum period recounted scenes of pagan idolatry. In the *Moral
and Religious Souvenir* (1828), there was a description of a Hindu
festival in which an anthropomorphic wooden idol, dressed in
black and gold, was carried upon a sixty-foot tower pulled by Hindu men. The procession, led by five elephants bearing towering
crimson flags, culminated in a human sacrifice. A primitive attempt at an evangelical travelogue, the author used such value-
laden terms as "obscene stanzas," "lascivious offerings," "sensual
yell," "indecent action," and "disgusting exhibition" to describe the
day's activities.[43] James Knowles aptly synthesized the evangelical
position: "The essence of idolatry is everywhere the same. It is
everywhere 'abominable' in its principles and in its rites, and everywhere the cause of indescribable and manifold wretchedness."[44]

A memorable story, illustrating the evangelical opposition to all
objects of worship, was told by Arabella Stuart Willson in an account of Sarah Hall Boardman Judson's work in Burma. Apparently, when the Boardmans came among the Karens, they heard about
a "deified book" left among the people more than ten years before.
Soon, the Boardmans were "waited on by a large deputation of Karens, bringing with them in a covered basket, the mysterious volume, wrapped in fold after fold of muslin; on removing which it
proved to be an Oxford edition of the Common Prayer Book in the
English language!" The Boardmans, of course, assured the Karens
that the book was a good one, but they were careful to note that it
"should by no means be made an object of worship."[41]

In addition to their critique of any form of worship that appeared idolatrous, the missionary-evangelicals were close observers,
and consistent reporters, of certain social practices abroad. Evan-

gelical newspapers, missionary magazines, publications for women, and giftbooks were rife with reports from "Sodom and Gomorrah," laden with stories of heathen women, victimized by a system of amorality that condoned the *zenana*,[45] the harem, and the seraglio, as well as the practices of polygamy and suttee. With few exceptions, the evangelicals reported the imposition of barbarities upon heathen women, rather than examples of sexual immodesty or intemperance among the women themselves.[46] The Rev. Eugenio Kincaid, captured by banditti in Burma and imprisoned for one week, typically reported female victimization: "Daily I saw women tied with ropes, their hands and feet bound together, and they were then beaten with ratans."[47] Lydia Maria Child posited that heathen men "reproach the objects of their tyranny with the very degradation and vices which their own contempt and oppression have produced."[48]

The evangelicals' emphasis on the degraded state of the heathen female may have been a deliberate attempt to counter the new cultural tolerance born of the rudimentary anthropological studies of the eighteenth-century *philosophes*, and the infatuation with primitivism associated with Rousseau and nineteenth-century Romanticism.[49] Certainly the evangelical world view left little room for the aesthetic or moral appreciation of non-Christian cultures. Both Ann Hasseltine Judson and, later, Emily Chubbuck Judson directly addressed the challenge of Romantic Primitivism. "Who ever heard that ignorance was favorable to the culture of amiable feelings?" queried Ann Judson, intolerant of the idea that women in a state of ignorance were both lovely and "destitute of the violent passions which are exhibited among some American females."[50] If Ann Judson was hostile to the stridency of the women's rights movement, she was equally unreceptive to the notion of the "noble savage." She found little nobility in women outside the Christian pale.

In *The Kathayan Slave*, Emily Chubbuck Judson turned her attention to the proposition, suggested by critics of the foreign mission movement, that "The Heathen [Are] Better Than Christians." In an essay so named, she directed her acerbic pen against critics of Adoniram Judson, critics who posited that "people are worse in Christendom than in heathen lands."[51] Disgusted with the Romantic veneration of primitive virtue, Emily Judson raised the spectre of infanticide, suttee, caste, and, finally, cannibalism, for her, all characteristic practices in heathendom. Of the Andamans, an Indian people of the islands in the Bay of Bengal, the third Mrs. Judson quipped that while they "dine with peculiar zest off a barbecued European," "philanthropists of a certain school may have the pleasure of knowing that the vices of Christianity will probably be slow in reaching them."[52]

Rather than accept an identification of the evangelical Christian as "narrow-minded [and] meddling," Emily Judson struck back, labeling critics of missionaries as elitist and challenging their veracity as informants:

> . . . one need but glance at the pretty pictures of American Savages and dark eyed orientals, which figure so largely in poetry and romance; and which are about as true to the original, as would be a mortal's map of fairy-land. And if the missionary's daring pencil venture upon a few of the black shadows, which in truth constitute nine-tenths of the real landscape—why, he is a poor, plodding sort of creature incapable of appreciating anything estimable beyond the pale of his own church, and quite ignorant of the world, of course. True, he may have travelled the earth over, and been conversant with men of every nation and every grade, but it is all the same. His views are so shockingly literal,—he is such an utter stranger to the rosy, refracting atmosphere surrounding men of taste, that it is evident even to persons whose observations of human nature have been necessarily bounded by the magic limits of *"our set,"* and whose travels have never extended beyond the streets of their native town, that he does not *know the world*!"[53]

In fact, the argument between Emily Judson and the rarified "men of taste" was a debate over who was really provincial. While the evangelicals stood proudly for orthodox religion and monolithic Protestant Christianity, they thought of themselves as cosmopolitan in orientation. They were, after all, involved in a global mission and stationed in at least a dozen lands, offering spiritual salvation and educational opportunities to any seeker. A generalized feeling of sympathy for the unity and suffering of humanity everywhere made the prototypical evangelical a Romantic.[54] However, when that sympathy was Christianized, it became the primary tool for defining differences in human experience, for delineating the distance between Christians and heathens.

In the Hindu practice of suttee, a widow's self-immolation on her husband's funeral pyre, American readers found the perfect symbolic representation of the moral gulf between Christianity and heathendom. Stories of suttee, reported either firsthand or indirectly, were pervasive in the periodical literature read by antebellum Christian women. In the introduction to the *Christian Keepsake and Missionary Annual* (1838), suttee figured prominently in the first two verses of editor Sigourney's poem:

> Tint the red flame, and paint the gazing throng,
>   Where sultry India rears the funeral pyre;
>   Plead for the widow, ere the thundering gong
>   Drowns the last wild shriek of her death of fire.[55]

In *The History of the Condition of Woman; In Various Ages and Nations* (1835), Lydia Maria Child reported that "it not unfrequently happens that a number of wives are burned at once with the death of their husband. . . . A Koolin Brahmin of Bagnuparu had more than a hundred wives, twenty-two of whom were consumed with his corpse. The fire was kept kindled for three days. . . . Some of them were forty years old, and others no more than sixteen. Nineteen of them had seldom ever seen the husband with whom they consented to perish."[56] Sarah Josepha Hale asked the question: "How can the heathen women, Her hopeless lot endure?"[57]

With few exceptions, there was never any real analysis by evangelicals of the economic or social circumstances that contributed to the perpetuation of the practice of suttee. Rather, the immolation of widowed women was catalogued as simply another highly dramatic example of "Horrid Pagan Customs." Under that rubric, there was a detailed account in an 1813 missionary magazine of the death of forty-seven women, wives of the Prince of Marava, who cast themselves one by one into the flames.[58] A year later, a religious magazine published in Madison and Cayuga counties, New York, reported the death by suttee of the wife of a Brahmin. The woman first took opium and then, stripping herself naked, plunged herself into a river, before running atop the funeral pyre: "as the flames reached her, she began to scream; the whole company struck up a doleful kind of hymn, and the more her screams increased, the louder they raised their voices. When the wood and bodies were reduced to ashes, each departed home; and thus ended the process of this horrid, superstitious and most unnatural ceremony."[59]

Stories of suttee continued long after it was outlawed in British India in 1829. Missionaries returning to the United States continued to evoke pagan brutality as a basis of appeals for support. Such was the case of one Reverend Reed, a Presbyterian missionary to

Bombay, who addressed the twentieth anniversary of the American Bible Society:

> Suttee, or burning of widows is not abolished beyond the limits of the British government. One [a suttee] was celebrated within five miles of me shortly before I left India; while at another, within twenty five miles of the capital city, seven wives were burnt at once with the dead body of their husband.[60]

The *Baptist Magazine* for May 1846 confirmed the continuation of this "abhorrent superstition" and asked its readers to "Imagine, then, the pile of wood, the dead body laid on it, the widow ascending the pile . . . the nearest relative setting fire to the wood; . . . the spectators shout [ing] and the drums beat[ing], to stifle the groans of the miserable victim!"[61] Some didactic juvenile works, like Maria B. Ingall's *Ocean Sketches of Life in Burma* (1857), had plates or frontispieces depicting the widow throwing herself on the pyre.

It is no wonder that a poem by the young Sarah Hall [Boardman Judson], entitled, "Come Over and Help Us," focused on suttee as an expression of the degradation of heathen women:

> By that rending shriek of horrour,
>   Issuing from the flaming pile,
> By the bursts of mirth that follow,
>   By that Brahmin's fiend like smile.[62]

At the time she wrote this, Sarah Hall was only sixteen. Although she had never witnessed the practice, she was obviously familiar with what had become an evangelical literary convention. On the basis of missionary letters and reports, religious readers were awakened to the social and sexual abuses that were, according to most reports, part of the daily life of women in the East.

Ann Judson's early years in Burma were spent cultivating friendships with heathen women. In 1813, she began a relationship with the wife of the Burmese viceroy, ostensibly because she and Adoniram might someday need the protection of a woman of influence.[63] That friendship, which came to naught in terms of a conversion, was distinguished by both women's willingness to transcend their cultural differences. Although the viceroy's wife was only one of his many wives, and although she smoked a long silver pipe, she and Ann Judson were able to share some degree of information about their families, their children, and their respective countries.[64] When little Roger Williams Judson died in 1816, the wife of the viceroy came to pay a visit of condolence. She had known the Judson child, played with him, and was intrigued by his white skin and his remarkably ample hands. "When she saw me after his death," Ann wrote, "she smote her breast, and said, 'Why did you not send me word that I might have come to his funeral?' "[65]

Like all of Ann's relationships with Burmese women, her friendship with the vicereine had, for her, a religious context. Ann wrote to Dr. Baldwin in January 1818:

> Her Highness . . . professes a particular regard for me, and I, in return have presented her with a translation of Matthew's Gospel, a tract, and Catechism, and have had two or three opportunities of conversing with her privately on the subject of religion. How much she reads in the former, or believes in the latter, I am unable to say; but neither produces any visible effect.[66]

In true apostolic fashion, Ann's mission of friendship provided her with the opportunity to persuade and to teach. She often reported having religious conversations with the local women, many of whom told her respectfully: "Your religion is good for you, ours for us. You will be rewarded for your good deeds in your way—we in our way."[67]

Ann Judson's service to heathen women often left her alone with groups of Burmese women, performing the role of teacher. In August 1817, she reported conversations that she had with a group of fifteen or twenty female Sabbath scholars, to whom she read and spoke about God.[68] She also functioned as a teacher of reading, a skill to which few Burmese women had access. In 1819, after the building of the zayat, Ann Judson reported on her classes in the new building: "all the women are seated, with their lights and black boards, much in the same position and employment as the men. The blackboard, on which all the Burmans learn to read and write, answers the same purpose as our slates. They are about a yard in length, made black with charcoal and the juice of a leaf. . . ."[69] In the 1820s, the Judson Association at Ann's alma mater, Bradford Academy, sponsored two little Burmese girls, to be known as Mary and Abby Hasseltine.[70] Ann's letters intermittently reported both the girls' progress in learning Christianity and reading and the names of Burmese women who sought her guidance in working towards a Christian conversion.[71] Before the outbreak of the Burmese-British War in 1824, Ann Judson had directly led at least four women converts to the cause of Christ.[72] Her translation efforts, like those of Adoniram, were expected to bring in even more.[73]

At the risk of minimizing Ann Judson's prewar accomplishments, her apostolate took on heightened and dramatic meaning after her husband's imprisonment by the Burmese in June of 1824. If Ann Judson was already distinguished for her service to heathen women, her performance during the war demonstrated woman's capacity for service to the Cross. Without doubt, it was Ann Judson whose perseverance, ingenuity, and initiative kept the Baptist foreign misison alive. In 1826, at the conclusion of the war, some of Judson's fellow prison veterans published a paean to Mrs. Judson in the *Calcutta Review*, lauding her for both her "benevolence and talents," and attributing their survival, and that of her husband, to her indefatigable efforts on their behalf.[74]

From the moment Adoniram Judson was imprisoned, Ann Hasseltine Judson worked arduously and creatively to seek his permanent release from his Burmese jailers. According to her recollections of that awful day, the missionary was torn from the dinner table by a cadre of Burmese officers, one of whom Ann knew to be an executioner, a man with a "spotted face." As Judson's arms were bound tightly with a cord and he was thrown to the floor, his desperate wife made the first of many offers to buy her husband's freedom. In this case, silver was no help in winning over the "normally avaricious" Burmese. By evening, the missionary translator was consigned to the death prison at Ava. His wife had the foresight to destroy all their letters, journals, and writings that disclosed any relationships to the British or indicated a critical outlook on Burmese society.[75]

Ann Judson was placed under house arrest and left to her own resources. Her household at this time was composed of herself, a few Bengali servants, and the two Burmese girls, called Mary and Abby. She was also within the first trimester of her second pregnancy. According to her later reports, her first reaction to her Burmese guards was defiance: "I obstinately refused to obey, and endeavored to intimidate them by threatening to complain of their conduct to higher authorities on the morrow."[76] When her Bengali servants were about to be tortured for information about the British, she changed her posture and offered them presents. "I endeavored to soften the feelings of the guards," Ann later wrote, "by giving them tea and segars for the night."[77]

Ann's capacity to connive with Burmese officialdom for her husband's release was demonstrated early on in his confinement. On June 10, two days after Adoniram's imprisonment, she had a personal audience with the governor of Ava, where she presented her husband's case and argued that, as an American, he had nothing to do with the war. The Governor responded that "it was not in his power to release [Judson] from prison or irons, but that he could make [his] situation more comfortable."[78] The Governor turned Mrs. Judson over to his head officer, who, in turn, informed her that the Judsons' "future comfort" must depend on her "liberality in regard to presents." He warned her that "presents" were to be made in a strictly "private way," unknown to any officer in government.[79]

It cost Mrs. Judson 200 tickals, or about $100, two pieces of cloth, and two handkerchiefs to get Adoniram released from the common interior prison and confined to an "open pen." She was allowed to send food and sleeping mats to her husband and his fellow English-speaking prisoners, but she was not allowed to see them. In the meantime, she presented her case to the Queen's sister-in-law, a woman she knew, but got no results. Her property was also seized by the Royal Treasurer. Fortunately, she had been warned of this possibility, and was able to "secrete as many little objects as possible; together with considerable silver."[80] Legend has it that at this time Ann Hasseltine Judson took her husband's biblical translation and sewed it into an inconspicuous pillow which had little value to her captors.[81]

Denied admission to the prison for nearly two weeks, Ann Judson attempted to sneak in notes. Unfortunately, the poor fellow who carried the communications was "found out, beaten and placed in the stocks."[82] Another temporary stroke of misfortune was the news that the Burmese King considered Judson a spy. However, the officers who had enumerated the Judsons' property reported to the King that "Judson is a true teacher; we found nothing in his house but what belongs to priests."[83]

The next three months brought "continual harassment," Ann Judson later wrote, "partly through my ignorance of police management, and partly through the insatiable desire of every petty officer to enrich himself through my misfortunes."[84] The officers who had enumerated her property "insisted on knowing" how much she had paid the Governor's officer on June 10. When she told them, the Treasury officials demanded 200 tickals of the Governor. The Governor became enraged with Mrs. Judson and threatened retaliation on her husband. Always anxious to make a religious point, Ann later wrote that she told the Governor that it was against her religious scruples to lie. "My religion differs from yours—it forbids prevarication," she supposedly said.[85] Ann was able to offer the Governor a pair of beautiful opera glasses and the promise that, with his continued help, she would "endeavor, from time to time, to make him such presents as would compensate for his loss."[86] The Governor responded favorably to this arrangement but acted to restrict her entreaties by telling her that she could intercede for her husband only. Ann Judson pleaded for her husband's colleague and friend, Dr. Price, but to no avail. Price was then returned to the inner prison for ten days, probably to demonstrate the Governor's will. Price was able to buy his way out with cloth and handkerchiefs secretly provided by Ann Judson.

In the next seven months, Ann Judson was tireless in her ministrations to Judson and the other English-speaking Christian men who were forced to endure the unremitting horrors of the prison at Ava: inadequate food, clothing, and air; brutality; and erratic torture. A pregnant Ann made daily visits to the prison (where she was allowed to converse with her husband and, for a fee, distribute food) and to members of the government, or branches of the royal family (where she sought someone with influence to destroy the impression of Judson "being in any way engaged in the present war"). She later wrote of this period:

> Oh how many, many times have I returned from that dreary prison at 9 o'clock at night, solitary and worn out with fatigue and anxiety, and thrown myself down in the same rocking chair . . . provided for me in Boston, and endeavored to invent some new scheme for the release of the prisoners.[87]

In addition to the continual and escalating extortion by the Burmese, which was draining Ann's reserves, the political climate became increasingly volatile. With each British success, the King became more hostile to foreigners and more susceptible to the extremist military leadership of Bandoola. At some point in 1825, Mrs. Judson presented before Bandoola, in public, a petition written by her husband arguing for his release. Not surprisingly, the petition was accompanied by another "present of considerable value."

Bandoola listened but authorized his wife, the following day, to tell Mrs. Judson that her husband would be freed only after the British were expelled from Burma.[88]

Bandoola's pronouncement forced Ann Judson, for the very first time, to consider the alternatives to immediate release. She expressed her deepest fears in the 1826 letter she wrote to her brother-in-law at the close of hostilities:

> My prevailing opinion was, that my husband would suffer violent death; and that I should, of course, become a slave, and languish out a miserable though short existence, in the tyrannic hands of some unfeeling monster.[89]

Mrs. Judson was able to face the day-to-day challenge of survival because of the consolations of religion: "It taught me to look beyond this world, to that rest, that peaceful happy rest, where Jesus reigns, and oppression never enters."[90] After Bandoola's dictum, she "gave up the idea of [Adoniram's] being released from prison" and concentrated on courting the favor of those who could insure a tolerable situation for the prisoners. At the request of Mrs. Judson, Adoniram was allowed to erect a small bamboo shelter, within the prison enclave, where he was able to visit with his wife and be alone.[91]

The Governor of Ava continued to be Ann Judson's most crucial contact in monitoring government attitudes toward the English-speaking prisoners. According to her later reports, she was teaching the Governor about America, during the "greater part of every other day," throughout the last few months of her pregnancy. When Maria Judson was born on January 26, 1825, Ann was probably unattended by any English-speaking or Christian person. The birth of the child meant that she was unable to visit the Governor as regularly as before, and she lamented a considerable loss of influence in this period. When Maria was two months old, her father and all the "white prisoners" were put back in the inner prison in five pairs of fetters each.[92] Mr. Judson's bamboo hut, which had become a veritable sanctuary, was removed. In the midst of the Burmese hot season, Judson joined one hundred other men in a room with inadequate ventilation. Ann later wrote: "The white prisoners, from incessant perspiration and loss of appetite, looked more like the dead than the living."[93]

Mrs. Judson immediately sought the ear of the Governor, whom she addressed with customary deference, praising him for his protection. The Governor informed her that the prisoners' removal to the barbarous inner quarters was, in effect, his way of keeping them out of sight. He disclosed that, on three occasions, he had received orders to "assassinate all the white prisoners, privately." On the basis of his friendship for Mrs. Judson, he made the following avowal: ". . . though I execute all the others, I will never execute your husband."[94]

While the Governor's promise was reassuring, Ann Judson was unable to mitigate the horrors of the prison or the political turmoil in Burma. With the death of Bandoola, the King accepted the military leadership of the Pakan Woon, a former British prisoner, who was attempting to raise a new army as he stepped up the torture of Portuguese and Bengali residents.[95] Adoniram Judson was taken with a fever and not expected to live so long as he remained in the "noisesome place." Again, the Governor of Ava provided the means for relieving the Judsons' distress: Ann was allowed to nurse Adoniram in another bamboo hovel on the prison grounds. This she was able to do for about three days. On the third day, she was called to the Governor's home on the pretext of talking about his watch. "I found afterwards," Ann wrote, "that his only object was, to detain me until the dreadful scene, about to take place in the prison, was over."[96]

When Ann returned to the prison, all the white prisoners, including the ailing Judson, had been carried off. Anxiety drove her through the streets of Ava, asking every person she saw where the prisoners had been taken. In despair, she checked the local execution site, but found nothing to indicate that the Burmese had been there recently. Eventually, she turned to the Governor for an answer. He told her that Judson was on his way to Amarapora. He also told her, with an air of finality, "You can do nothing more for your husband, take care of yourself."[97]

Ann's undeterred perseverance led her next to Amarapora, and to the "never to be forgotten place," the Oung-pen-la prison. After depositing two or three trunks with the Governor, she left her home at Ava, and with three-month-old Maria, Mary and Abby Hasseltine, and a Bengali cook, she set off for Amarapora in the "burning sun." Two days later she found her husband:

> . . . what a scene of wretchedness was presented to my view! The prison was an old shattered building, without a roof . . . under a little low projection outside . . . sat the foreigners, chained together two and two, almost dead with suffering and fatigue. The

first words of Adoniram were, "Why have you come? I hoped you would not follow, for you cannot live here."[98]

Judson's words were a mark of his desperation. According to Ann's later reports, the forced march from Ava to Amarapora and then to Oung-pen-la almost killed her husband. Already weakened by the fever he took at Ava, he was compelled to march eight miles on hot sand and gravel, without shoes, in the searing midday sun of a Burmese May. As his feet blistered and then the skin fell off, Judson was supported by his partner in chains, a Captain Laird; the Bengali servant of Henry Gouger,[99] an imprisoned English merchant, arrived in time to wrap the missionary's feet in his headdress and carry him the rest of the way. The forced march to Oung-pen-la was so bad that Adoniram Judson apparently considered suicide;[100] twenty years later, when he returned to the United States, Judson's travails on this march were immortalized in words and pictures in *The Judson Offering*.[101]

In addition to her anxiety over her husband's suffering and despondency, Ann had no water, food, or shelter for the three children in her care. She was, however, able to approach one of Judson's Burmese jailers with a request for help. Through him, she was provided with a low-ceilinged room, half-filled with grain: "in that little filthy place," she later wrote, "I spent the next six months of wretchedness."[102]

Ann had no furniture or provisions of any kind. The morning following her arrival, the Burmese girl, Mary Hasseltine, was taken with smallpox. Ann began to divide her time between the ill child and her suffering husband "whose fever still continued . . . and whose feet were so dreadfully mangled, that . . . he was unable to move."[103] Rumor had it that the prisoners were to be burnt, en masse, at Oung-pen-la, but repairs to the prison led Ann to conclude that they instead faced a "lingering death." Eventually, despite the innoculations she was able to administer, Maria was afflicted with a bad case of the smallpox and Ann with a lesser one. Just as Adoniram's condition began improving and the children were returned to health, Ann was "struck down by one of the diseases of the country, which is almost always fatal to foreigners."[104]

With the idea that she would return to die at Oung-pen-la, Ann managed to struggle back to Ava to obtain a medicine chest she had left with the Governor. She returned to her family in a cart, taking laudanum[105] regularly, ill, tired, and wet—for it was now the rainy season. According to her postwar reports, she spent the next two months on a mat in the grain-filled room, her devoted Bengali cook insuring her survival. When Maria cried in the night for the milk her mother's fever-wracked body could not supply, the infant was taken to her father, who, now able to walk, gave presents to the jailers, and roamed the village looking for a Burmese wet nurse.[106]

As the war drew to a close, Adoniram's potential services as a translator became apparent to the Burmese. A release order, obtained by one of the Treasury officials who had enumerated the Judson's property, led to the welcome exit from Oung-pen-la.[107] Adoniram, under heavy Burmese guard, was separated from his wife and transferred to a prison at Ava. During this period, the already frail Mrs. Judson came down with "spotted fever," creating a desperate situation. With her hair shaved and her head and feet covered with blisters, her Burmese neighbors took her for dead. "I could not rise from my couch," she later wrote. She was powerless: "I could make no efforts to secure my husband; I could only plead with that great and powerful Being, who had said 'Call upon me in the day of trouble, and I will hear.' "[108]

Adoniram was involved, as the Burmese promised, in the peace settlement with the British.[109] By late February 1826, the Treaty of Yandabo had been signed and the hostilities ended.[110] A posthumous biographer attributed the following to Adoniram Judson, as he looked back on the captivity:

> One evening several persons at our house were repeating anecdotes of what different men in different ages regarded as the highest type of sensuous enjoyment; that is, enjoyment derived from outward circumstances. 'Pooh!' said Mr. Judson; 'these men were not qualified to judge. I know of a much higher pleasure than that. What do you think of floating down the Irrawaddy, on a cool, moonlight evening, with your wife by your side and your baby in your arms, free—all free! But *you* cannot understand it either; it needs a twenty-one months' qualification, and I can never regret my twenty-one months of misery, when I recall that one delicious thrill. I think I have had a better appreciation of what heaven may be ever since.[111]

Ann Judson, ostensibly recovered from her near-fatal illness, joyfully shared in the decision to relocate the family and the postwar mission in Amherst, British Burma. Adoniram Judson regarded a British victory as a victory for Christ:

> Here have I been ten years preaching the Gospel to timid listeners who wish to embrace the truth but dare not . . . and now, when

all human means seem at an end, God opens the way by leading a
Christian nation to subdue the country.[112]

In their new home in British Burma, with Maria and the Hasseltine
girls, Ann began running another school for heathen women. When
he was asked by John Crawford, the British Resident, to assist in
negotiating a secondary treaty, including provisions for religious
toleration, Adoniram Judson left Amherst temporarily for Rangoon. He never saw his wife again. In October 1826, after a two-
week illness, Ann Hasseltine Judson died at Amherst. Her physician
judged that she was the victim, not of the climate at Amherst, but
of the "weakness of her constitution, occasioned by the severe pri-
vations and long protracted sufferings which she endured at
Ava."[113] Her life, her character, and her apostolate were marked by
the hopia tree at the head of her grave.[114]

In February 1827, Adoniram Judson wrote his mother-in-law in
Bradford about the death of Ann. His remarks, laden with the sad-
ness of the occasion, reveal the traditional reading of Ann Judson's
life and of her sacrifice. "Oh, with what meekness, patience, mag-
nanimity and Christian fortitude she bore those sufferings!" wrote
the bereaved husband.[115] Certainly there was no quarrel with Judson's analysis of his wife's character: hers was the kind of Christian
self-denial that evangelicals applauded. In fact, Ann Judson's hopia
tree, often repeated as a religious motif, came to symbolize both her
life and her sacrifice.[116] The question to be asked is why generations
of religious women immortalized Ann, and why she entered the
realm of American Christian hagiography?

The basis of Ann Judson's sainthood lay not only in the sacrifice
of her life for the American Christianizing mission but in the manner in which her life broadened the notion of woman's salvific role.
In addition to providing food supplements, replenishing scanty
clothing, nursing the sick and, ultimately, dying, Ann Judson exhibited a full measure of Christian ingenuity and self-assertion. She
had, after all, kept Adoniram alive, saved the other Christian prisoners, and preserved the translation work. She did this, *not* by honoring the conventions of female delicacy, but by demonstrating her
concerns and capabilities as a Christian woman.

According to Judson's fellow survivors, Ann Judson was herself
"the author of those eloquent and forcible appeals to the government [of Burma], which prepared them by degrees for submission
to terms of peace."[117] When she believed they were being mis-

treated, she argued the prisoners' case before Burmese government officers and the royal family. Ann Judson also showed herself to be something of a pragmatist, willing to work the Burmese system of extortion in order to attain her own, Christian ends. Her British admirers, who found her "amiable and humane," agreed that she was also "eloquent and forcible."[118] Wayland, who called Ann Judson "one of the most remarkable women of her age," verified the fact that she had direct contacts with Burmese officialdom and described her as "fertile in resources,"[119] an encomium rarely applied to persons considered purely decorative or passive.

In addition to demonstrating the power of the apostolate of women, the story of "Ann of Ava" foreshadowed the way in which future generations of Christian women might choose to "honor Christ by the fruits of their pens."[120] Since there was no biblical justification for female authorship, the evangelicals were using the Bible in a less-than-literal way, adjusting their reading to the economic, social, and political exigencies of their day. A final measure of Ann Judson's self-assertion was the fact that she, not Adoniram, articulated the emotional realities of the Judsons' life in Burma. If her epistolary story was, in fact, one of many feminine duties she performed, she still told the story well. It was, after all, Ann, not Adoniram, who acted as the dramatist of the Burmese mission and of the imprisonment at Ava and Oung-pen-la. Gammell was simply another observer who commented on how well Ann told the story:

> her own pen . . . traced, in lines that will never be forgotten by those who read them, the affecting story of the dismal days and nights of her husband's captivity. We followed her alike with admiration and deepest sympathy.[121]

In the very act of telling it, Ann made the Judson story preeminently her own.

The story of Ann Judson's travails became a symbol of the resilience and competence of religiously inspired women. The Baptist historian, William Gammell, wrote that Ann Judson's grave "will be rendered forever sacred to Christians in every land by the memory of one in whom genius and heroism and piety were combined with the highest graces both of person and character."[122] Edward Porter claimed that one could "search the annals of Greek or Roman, medieval or modern heroism, and . . . find no name worthier" than Ann Judson's.[123] A collection of didactic biography,

aimed at adolescent girls, used Ann Judson's life as a model of female activity: "Those women, whose indolence induces them to
draw back from everything that requires the slightest exertion, under the plea of inability to perform it, may blush to read what Mrs.
Judson did and suffered."[124] According to William Hague's report,
the Bishop of Calcutta regarded Ann Judson as a symbol of "an order of [American] woman, to whom . . . the pen of history will do
justice as having been the glory of the nineteenth century."[125]

Undoubtedly, Ann Judson's autonomy was both temporary and
circumscribed, lasting only so long as her husband was in Burmese
fetters. Her public appeals and her personal conniving, all of which
continued during her second pregnancy, were acceptable because
she acted on behalf of the Cross, and because she stood alone, without male Christian protectors. In *Sketches of American Character*
(1833), Sarah Josepha Hale articulated the conditions that made for
acceptable female self-assertion or "exertions of decisiveness." Hale
posited that "decision of character . . . [was] rare in women," and
attributed that lack to either a more "delicate organization" or "the
dependent situation in which nature and education" have placed
woman. "Such decision," she wrote, "only becomes necessary to
woman in adversity. Let no one imagine its exertion contributes to
the happiness of the female. It may be her *duty*, it should never be
her desire."[126]

To legitimize woman's self-assertion, even in the limited name
of adversity and duty, was to invest women with new prerogatives,
namely, the creation of their own personalized versions of the religious "mission for life." In this sense, evangelicalism provided an
important impetus for the widespread introduction of women into
a host of religious and quasi-religious activities: Sunday school and
Bible societies; temperance; moral and prison reform; foreign and
domestic missions; charitable societies for orphans and widows;
antislavery; Sabbatarianism; and public education. Certainly the
evangelical clergy, in their unanimous acclaim for Ann Judson,
sanctioned the idea that the cause of Christianity oftentimes justified some measure of female aggressiveness.

At the same time, evangelicalism was an impediment to the development of any widespread acceptance of political feminism. The
feminist concerns of American religious women were channeled
abroad, into the foreign mission movement, where social practices
were more clearly abhorrent and where the possiblity of change
brought no threat to their own family and community relation-

ships. For every description of degraded womanhood abroad, there was a parallel invocation of Christianity's role as an elevator of woman. "To Christianity is woman indebted for a glorious revolution in her destiny," wrote Mrs. E. R. Steele in *The Missionary Memorial* (1846). "The Christian female, no longer the slave and plaything of olden time, has been exalted by [Christian] men to the rank of his friend and counsellor."[127] "Christianity alone teaches the true rank of women," stated James Knowles.[128] Lydia Maria Child and Lydia Huntley Sigourney agreed that Christianity had done much for women.[129] "If the Christian religion was a gospel to the poor," wrote Arabella Stuart Willson, "it was no less emphatically so to woman, whom it redeemed from social inferiority and degradation."[130] Richard Furman, President of the Baptist General Convention, told an 1817 meeting: "Every enlightened female must know that where Christianity exists not, the character of woman is shamefully degraded."[131] Simply in their association with Christian men who followed the path of Jesus, American Christian women were supposed to have little to complain about, and certainly nothing to fear.

What the evangelicals saw in non-Christian cultures was woman as victim, without the assistance of supportive men, without the benefits of either a moral or useful education, without the pedestal provided by Christian morality. It is both ironic and typical that Ann Judson, who never posited a direct relationship between women's education and the betterment of the sex within the United States, made that connection in the case of her Burmese sisters. Neither did she entertain the idea that educated Burmese women might turn to the great books of Buddhism. Instead, she persisted in her faith in the unilateral corrective: Christian conversion provided the most expedient and sure way for women everywhere to improve their lot.

So it was that in the foreign mission movement evangelical women were able to practice an identifiable, albeit truncated, form of religious feminism that was oriented toward the betterment of their sex, through the creation of a Christian women's *internationale*.[132] In the process of describing the condition of heathen women, evangelical women became involved simultaneously in defining their own status and function. This process of self-description was more congratulatory than critical, reflecting how much easier it is to scrutinize a neighbor than oneself. Undoubtedly, the evangelical effort to differentiate heathen from Christian women, which was a basic motivational technique in foreign mission work, contributed to the creation of the "Cult of True Womanhood," a collective, hyperbolic statement of the perfection of Christian women in America. For evangelical women, then, Gospel Christianity itself constituted the feminist revolution.

Chapter 5

Trippings in Author-Land

The popularity of Ann Judson's story pointed the way for the evangelical woman's involvement in literature, and in authorship, in the period before 1850. Within a decade of its publication, James Knowles' *Life of Mrs. Ann Hasseltine Judson, late missionary to Burma* (1829) went through ten editions. This memoir, which was said to be "universally known,"[1] relied heavily on Ann's own letters, replete with descriptions of her life, her work, and her spiritual progress. A reviewer for the liberal *Christian Examiner* praised the compiler for "permitting the subject to speak" but added that the story was becoming somewhat hackneyed: "We believe the most prominent events of her life . . . have been repeatedly published."[2]

The wide dissemination of Ann's story was an indication of the evangelicals' developing enthusiasm for female literary endeavors embodying Christian experience and principle. Although the rhetoric of Ann's story was rooted in eighteenth-century traditions of spiritual autobiography and epistolary travelogues, the literary productions of her successors, Sarah Hall and Emily Chubbuck, would

107

take different forms. Born in 1803 and fourteen years younger than Ann Hasseltine, Sarah Hall expressed her personal piety in "poetic effusions," published under religious auspices and frequently related to her reading about the Judson mission. Emily Chubbuck, born in 1817, twenty-six years after Ann Hasseltine, was a fiction writer who drew the material for her moral tales from the village life of upstate New York, while cultivating a professional relationship with the popular periodical press. By 1850, the year of the publication of Susan Warner's domestic novel, *Wide Wide World*, the "fruits" of a Christian woman's pen could have a variety of shapes and colorations.

The comparative biographies demonstrate the evangelicals' ability to adapt contemporary cultural forms to their own purposes. A dramatic representation of that quality, and of the point where religious and popular culture converged, was the 1846 marriage of the venerated missionary, Dr. Judson, to the popular fiction writer, Fanny Forester (Emily Chubbuck). That Chubbuck did what she did, and that Judson could find it both acceptable and potentially valuable, points to the basically utilitarian character of the American evangelical. It was always Judson's contention that the productions of Chubbuck's imaginative pen would be turned to a higher purpose; that the media, in this case popular fiction, could be Christianized. In this sense, Fanny Forester was potentially Adoniram Judson's most important convert.

At the time, Judson's willingness to allow Christianity to be "served up" in a popular cultural style found only limited acceptance. Both the missionary and his famous wife took a certain amount of abuse from their respective religious and literary communities. The orthodox found Fanny Forester beneath the dignity of the respected biblical translator, while the world of popular letters spurned the romantic decision that would take Fanny Forester away to do the work of zealots and to meet certain death.[3]

After her marriage, Emily Chubbuck Judson dropped both her pseudonym and the practice of fiction writing. She did, however, produce a number of religious works, like the *Memoir of Sarah B. Judson* (1848), which deliberately capitalized on her experiences with fiction. This biography, which reached its thirtieth thousand by 1855, was "regarded by some as marked too much by the sparkling manner of her magazine sketches, and wanting in the gravity which befits a record of Christian toil and self denial."[4] Because

Chubbuck enlivened an otherwise routine missionary biography, she was castigated by those who were still resistant to the new ways of marketing Christianity. What they heard, in fact, was her authentic voice, originally and most forcefully expressed in her sentimental fiction and poetry. When she translated herself into the language of pietistic literature, she lost her forcefulness and her audience. Interestingly enough, in the *Memoir of Sarah B. Judson*, she reached the evangelical audience best, employing all the devices of the sentimental novelist. Religious readers obviously enjoyed the techniques which pleased the more secular; when Chubbuck chose the more sedate forms of pious literature her popularity declined.

After Adoniram's death at sea in April 1850, his widow returned to the United States, where her remaining years were spent caring for the Judson children, publicizing the missionary cause, and waging what ultimately came to be a legal battle with a commercial publisher who was attempting to preempt the authorized version of Judson's life.

Emily Chubbuck's biography was written and her letters collected by Asahel Clark Kendrick, a Professor of Greek Literature at the newly founded University of Rochester, a Baptist institution. Her story was one of female aspiration and success, set within a Christian context, and informed by the new reality of professional female authorship.[5] In the course of the lives of the "three Mrs. Judsons," the literary productions of women had become an important evangelical tool and a major component of the national culture industry.

On April 10, 1834, at Tavoy, a remote missionary outpost which had attracted two hundred Karen converts, Adoniram Judson married his fellow missionary, Sarah Hall Boardman, the widow of George Boardman. Judson, who was by now forty-six, had been a widower for eight years. His new wife, who was only thirty-one, had lost her husband three years before.[6]

The Boardman-Judson union brought together two different generations of missionary enthusiasts. As a young woman, Sarah Hall had heard the Judsons' "Macedonian cry" and responded in the fashion of her day, with participation in female foreign mission societies and with poetry expressing her pious concern for the missionaries and for the salvation of the heathen. In 1823, Sarah Hall actually saw the famous Mrs. Judson at a Salem meeting; by 1825, she herself was on her way to Burma as the wife of a young Baptist missionary.

In the Spring of 1827, approximately six months after the death of Ann Hasseltine Judson, the Boardmans joined the widowed Adoniram, his daughter Maria, and Jonathan and Deborah Wade at Amherst, British Burma. Within two weeks of the Boardmans' arrival, on April 24, 1827, another tragedy struck Judson and, consequently, the whole of the small Baptist mission family: "Little . . . Maria breathed her last, aged two years and three months," wrote the saddened father to his mother-in-law. "Her emancipated spirit fled, I trust, to the arms of her fond Mother."[7]

Sarah Hall Boardman was part of the small community of mourners surrounding the missionary patriarch. In characteristic fashion, she chose to express her feelings about this loss in a poetic work, dedicated to Maria and conjuring up the entire history of the Burmese mission:

> Though short thy life, full many a day of pain,
> And night of restlessness, has been thy lot.
> Born in a heathen land,—far, far remov'd
> From all thy parents lov'd, in former years—
> When thou first saw'st the light, these were not there,
> To kneel beside thy mother, and implore
> Blessings upon thy little head, and sing
> The song of gratitude, and joy, and praise.
> Strangers were there; strangers to truth and peace;
> Strangers to feeling; strangers to her God.
> Thy father came not then to kiss his babe,
> And glad the heart of her who gave thee birth.
> Alas! a loathsome, dark, and dreary cell
> Was his abode,—anxiety his guest.
>   Thy mother's tale, replete with varied scenes,
> Exceeds my powers to tell; but other harps,
> And other voices, sweeter far than mine,
> Shall sing her matchless worth, her deeds of love,
> Her zeal, her toils, her sufferings, and her death.
>   But all is over now. She sweetly sleeps,
> In yonder new-made grave; and thou sweet babe,
> Shall soon be softly pillowed on her breast.[8]

Because of her own ailing health, Sarah Boardman soon left Amherst for Maulmain where medical assistance was more readily available. Before she and her husband departed for their mission to Tavoy, in March 1828, the grieving Judson visited their Maulmain home and supervised their proselytization work. Within months, Judson and the Wades moved the official mission station to that city, where they erected two houses of worship and operated a school. Judson's letters of this period indicated that he was in close, day-to-day contact with both of the young missionary couples, now his only family in the East. An 1829 letter to his mother-in-law included a poem he wrote entitled "The Solitary's Lament": "Where lie they whom I loved so dear / I call—they answer not."[9]

When George Boardman died in 1831 on a gospel-preaching tour in the Burmese jungle, Adoniram Judson provided his widow with practical advice and with spiritual support born of his own experience. "My Dear Sister," he wrote, "You are now drinking the bitter cup whose dregs I am somewhat acquainted with. And though, for some time, you have been aware of its approach, I venture to say that it is far bitterer than you expected." Judson told Sarah Boardman to expect months of "heart-rending anguish," to allow the tears to flow. Yet he assured her that there was "sweetness at the bottom" of the bitter cup: "You will find heaven coming near to you, and familiarity with your husband's voice will be a connecting link, drawing you almost within the sphere of celestial music."[10]

Judson encouraged the twenty-eight-year-old widow to remain where she was, in effect, to continue her own apostolate. Rather than have her return home or join another mission station, Judson observed: "I think, from what I know of your mind, that you will not desert the post, but remain to carry on the work which he [George] gloriously began. The Karens of Tavoy regard you as their spiritual mother. . . ." Given the fact that she had already lost two young children, in 1828 and 1830, Judson saw no need for her to part with her precious son George at this difficult time, although he pledged, for the future, his influence in "procuring for him [at home] all those advantages of education" that his mother desired. The childless missionary also promised that, should Sarah die, he would "receive and treat" George as his "own son . . . to watch over him as long as [he] live[d]." Finally, as the senior member of the Baptist mission in Burma, Judson had to explain to Sarah the official policy on her financial support: "By our regulations; a widow is entitled to seventy rupees a month, and a child ten. . . ."[11]

With the support of her "sympathizing brother," Adoniram Judson, Sarah Boardman remained at Tavoy where she proved herself an effective missionary. Judson was so impressed by the work of women missionaries that he wrote a friend in Waterville, Maine, in 1836: ". . . in regard to single females, who intend to acquire the language and instruct their own sex and the rising generation, if they are as good as those who have already come, I can only say, the more the better."[12] A lone Baptist woman by the name of Cummings operated out of the Chummerah Station in Burma with the assistance of native male converts. In 1837, Judson specifically stated that he could use two or three such persons as Miss Cummings, who was by then dead, or Miss Macomber, a missionary to the Pwo Karens.[13]

Sarah Boardman's later biographers would always describe her as a woman of extraordinary courage, one who had, in fact, survived a terrifying midnight invasion of her boudoir by a band of knife-wielding Burmese freebooters.[14] Predictably, Sarah Boardman's decision to remain in Burma was popularly interpreted as an expression of female duty rather than as an indication of her autonomy. Arabella Stuart Willson wrote that Mrs. Boardman's "natural disposition, which was singularly modest and retiring," would have led her home to the United States, but for her desire to see a nation of Christian Karens.[15]

The "modest and retiring" woman of Willson's description assumed her husband's full mantle in the years ahead. Because it had been her husband's responsibility to make tours among the remote Karen villages, preaching the Gospel, Sarah Boardman continued the practice. After her death, her biographers described the woman missionary as she threaded her way through "the wild passes of the mountains, the obscure paths of the jungle, fording the smaller streams and carried over the larger in a chair borne on bamboo poles by her followers."[16] In one memoir of her life, it was reported that Mrs. Boardman went so far from any civilized habitation that she was mistaken by an Englishman living in the wilds as an "angel visitant from a better sphere."[17]

In addition to her jungle tours, her translation work, her personal instruction of Karen women, and the care of her son and home, Sarah Hall Boardman became the primary administrator of a system of Karen schools. In January 1832, she reported upwards of 170 students under her supervision, eighty of whom attended five day schools. "The superintendence of the food and clothing of both the boarding schools," Sarah wrote, "together with the care of five day-schools under native teachers, devolves wholly on me."[18]

In the same 1832 report, the former New England school teacher observed that the "day-schools are growing every week more and more interesting." "We cannot . . . expect," she wrote, "to see among them [day-school students] so much progress, especially in Christianity, as our boarders make; but they are constantly gaining religious knowledge, and will grow up with comparatively correct ideas."[19] Sarah reported that the day schools were "entirely supported" by the Honorable British East India Company. Judson confirmed this relationship in 1833: "Mrs. Boardman got a letter of thanks from 'his lordship'; and the government . . . is authorized to expend five hundred rupees per month on schools. . . ."[20]

What Sarah Boardman was administering was part of a larger system of Bengali government schools. When the government acted, sometime in 1833, to banish religious instruction from these schools, Boardman wrote to the civil commissioner expressing her opposition to the new policy. She reasoned that even though it was "desirable" for future generations of Tavoyans to learn science and languages, "it [was] infinitely more important that they receive into their hearts our holy religion."[21] Mrs. Boardman also argued that Burmese parents understood the risks of parochial education: "parents and guardians must know, that there is more or less danger of their children deserting the faith of their ancestors, if placed under the care of a Foreign Missionary."[22] Unable to accept the notion of an educational system dedicated to "mere human science," she informed the commissioner that she would forfeit government patronage rather than drop religious instruction from her schools. The commissioner's reply indicated that Mrs. Boardman would continue to receive her monthly allowance so long as she accepted all students who presented themselves, "without any stipulation as to their becoming members of the Christian faith."[23]

While Sarah Boardman labored at Tavoy for Karen converts, Judson remained at Maulmain, working on his Burmese Old Testament translation. On January 31, 1834, twenty-two years after he left his native land, the missionary reported the completion of his task. He allegedly said at this time: "Thanks be to God, I can now say, I have attained."[24] Sarah Boardman, who was also fluent in Burmese, was probably among the first to know of his success. A letter from her to Adoniram, dated February 17, 1834, remarked on the accomplishment, mentioned the necessity of thanksgiving to God, and praised him for the "tone," "perspicuity," and "vivid manner of expression" that he demonstrated in the New Testament

translation.[25] Because she found Judson's New Testament so affecting, Sarah remarked that she would be willing to learn Burmese
simply for the sake of being able to read Judson's Bible.[26]

Fewer than two months later, Judson left Maulmain for Tavoy
where he found Mrs. Boardman's schools to be run "excellently
well," and two hundred Karen converts. Within four days of his arrival, Sarah Boardman and he were married, embarking immediately with her son, George, for a new home at Maulmain. It is unlikely that Mrs. Boardman's visible accomplishments at Tavoy
caused Judson to act impetuously. Rather, the trip to Tavoy appeared to be part of a prearranged plan whereby the two would
marry when the translation work was completed and Sarah's mour-
ning period over. As they left Tavoy, Judson wrote in his journal:

> Once more, farewell to thee, Boardman, and thy long cherished
> grave. May thy memory be ever fresh and fragrant, as the memory
> of the other beloved, whose beautiful, death-marred form reposes
> at the foot of the hopia tree. . . . And at last may we all four be re-
> united before the throne of glory, and form a peculiarly happy
> family, our mutual loves all purified and consummated in the
> bright world of love.[27]

For eleven years Adoniram and Sarah Boardman Judson were
united by their shared religious conviction and the concerns of rearing a growing family. After a painful decision to return the young
George Boardman to America so that he could be educated for the
ministry, Sarah bore a succession of children: Abby Ann (1835),
Adoniram Brown (1837), Elnathan (1838), Henry (1839),[28] Henry
Hall (1842), Charles (1843),[29] and Edward (1844). The fifty-two-
year-old Judson wrote his mother and sister during Sarah's fourth
pregnancy: "I am not so much driven in [my] studies as formerly. . . .
I have a family of young children growing up around me so that my
mind has become more domesticated. . . ."[30] His letters indicated
that he was much involved in his children's learning and behavior,
as well as their spiritual lives, his particular concern.[31] A series of
affectionate letters to George Boardman in America reveal that he
monitored the young man's Christian development from afar and
that he had specific goals in view: "May you be a growing Christian
and become a faithful minister of the gospel . . . who knows but
that you will yet be my colleague and successor in the pastorship of
the Maulmain Church?"[32] In March 1845, Judson wrote to his unconverted ten-year-old daughter, Abby Ann: "I pray every day that

somewhere during your travels with dear mama, you may receive a blessing from God, so that you will return a true Christian, and set such an example before your brothers as will induce them to try to follow your steps."[33]

The Judsons' life together at Maulmain lacked the adventure of either Adoniram's or Sarah's earlier exploits. As if he were being asked to supply the American audience with more colorful material, Judson told the Corresponding Secretary of the Baptist Mission Board: ". . . I wish it was in my power to make more copious and more interesting communications for the Magazine; but what can be expected from a man who spends his days at a study table . . .?"[34] Judson worked on his biblical revisions well into 1840; Sarah had schools to superintend, Bible classes and prayer meetings to organize, and a new maternal association for educating Burmese mothers to supervise. In addition, she was doing translation work in Burmese and Talain, while learning Peguan, the language of a people who had put themselves under the protection of the British government (thereby making them attractive conversion prospects).[35]

A year after his marriage to Sarah, Judson wrote the first of many letters that conveyed his feelings for his competent and supportive wife. "I am very happy with her," he told his elderly mother, "she is possessed of a very affectionate, amiable, pious spirit; is well acquainted with the Burmese language, and is a great help to me in all respects."[36] Judson's official correspondence with senior Baptists at home reported on conversations he had with his wife, and, on at least one occasion, he made a policy recommendation based on their dialogues. In a letter dated May 6, 1835, Judson observed that a missionary at an isolated or remote station was "forced to put forth all his efforts" and was, therefore, "worth half a dozen cooped up in one place." "I have seen this subject more clearly, from month to month, ever since my marriage," Judson wrote:

> Mrs. Judson says, that at Tavoy she was obliged to be ever on the alert, and sometimes had to run away . . . to get leisure to write a few letters. But here [at Maulmain] there are so many in the way of one another, that she can hardly find enough to do.[37]

In the same letter, Judson also reported on how he was using native assistants to "penetrate every lane and corner of this place [Maulmain] and the neighboring villages."[38] In her supervision of the

native teachers at Tavoy, Sarah Judson again had an experience
pertinent to her husband's mission. The working relationship of
Adoniram and Sarah Judson would be an important model for
evangelical marriage and a dramatic example of how a man and a
woman could ideally be "Partners in the Age of Christian Enterprise."[39]

Adoniram's letters to Sarah Judson are also filled with expressions of his love for her and their children. In February 1839, he
told her: "You know I love you more than all the world beside."[40]
When they were separated because Adoniram's chronic lung condition necessitated a sea voyage, Sarah tucked away a personal memento in his bag. "I have found your beautiful braid of hair," he
wrote her, "and I hunted for some further note or token, but in
vain." In case there was any doubt on where she stood in relation to
the memory of Ann Hasseltine, Adoniram assured her: "I feel that
no wife ever deserved her husband's gratitude and love more than
you."[41] Later in the same voyage, he thanked her for her "precious
letter of *five sheets*": "How much I enjoyed it, and how much I
loved you, during the perusal, I cannot stop to detail. No one can
tell the value of such a letter but an absent husband and father,
whose heart is wrapped up in his family."[42] Judson was consistent
in articulating the emotional pleasure he drew from marriage:

> If such exquisite delights as we have enjoyed . . . with one another,
> are allowed to sinful creatures on earth, what must the joys of
> heaven be?[43]

In the Spring of 1845, when Sarah Judson became desperately
ill from the aftereffects of the birth of her tenth child, Adoniram
decided to embark with her for England and for the United
States.[44] It was the second time that the missionary had to explain
the return of an ailing wife. He wrote the Baptist board that "nothing but a voyage beyond the tropics can possibly protract [Sarah's]
life."[45]

Judson's anxiety about the condition of the woman he loved,
and his simultaneous uneasiness about leaving, even temporarily,
"the mission for life," was reflected in a single statement: "I have
long fought against the necessity of accompanying her; but she is
now so desperately weak, and almost helpless, that all say it would
be nothing but savage inhumanity to send her off alone."[46] Therefore he chose to accompany Mrs. Judson on her voyage but brought
along two Christian Burmese assistants in order not to interrupt his

newest translation project, a Burmese-English dictionary. Abby
Ann, Adoniram, and Elnathan would also accompany their parents, to be left in America for their respective educations.

Judson was quick to point out that domestic affection was not
the sole reason for preserving the life of Sarah Judson. "There is
scarcely an individual foreigner now alive," he claimed, "who
speaks and writes the Burmese tongue so acceptably as she does,
and [for that reason] I feel that an effort ought to be made to save
her life."[47] By justifying Sarah's continued existence in this particular way, Judson proved himself to be the consummate evangelical.

Judson expected, when in the United States, to see Sarah recover and to find "his quiet corner," to work with his assistants,
"undisturbed and unknown."[48] He wrote the Board that he did not
want to do any public preaching when he came to America, that his
English was quite stale and his voice nearly inaudible. He asked
that he "be allowed to hoard up the remnant of [his] breath and
lungs for the country where they are needed most"—Burma.[49] In
July of 1845, Mrs. Judson's condition became so improved that Judson, still in the East, decided to forego the American trip; he would
return to Maulmain and Sarah would continue on to their native
land. Her last poem, written on the Isle of France in July 1845, and
entitled, "We Part on this Green Islet, Love," encouraged her husband to be steady at his task, despite the pain of their separation:

> Then gird thine armor on, love,
>   Nor faint thou by the way,
> Till Buddah shall fall, and Burma's sons
>   Shall own Messiah's sway.[50]

All their hopes and plans were dashed in August, when Mrs.
Judson experienced a serious relapse. She lingered a few days and
died, on September 1, 1845, while their ship, the *Sophia Walker*,
was in port at St. Helena. Judson later wrote an affecting account
of Mrs. Judson's death and burial in "the rock of the ocean," already famous as the resting place of Napoleon.[51] Within twenty-
four hours of the tragic event, the grieving husband and his children were on their way home. During the passage from St. Helena,
Judson wrote to a friend: ". . . this morning, the rock of the ocean,
where reposes all that is mortal of my dear, dear wife, is out of
sight. And, O how desolate my cabin appears, and how dreary the
way before me."[52]

Judson remarked in a personal letter, "I hope I feel thankful to
God that he has granted me, during my pilgrimage, the society of
two of the most excellent women and best wives that ever man was
blessed with."[53] To add to her many credits, it was reported that at
the end Sarah faced death tranquilly: "No shade of doubt, or fear of
anxiety, ever passed over her mind. She had a prevailing preference
to depart and be with Christ."[54] Her obituary in the *Baptist Missionary Magazine* made a special point to address the natural comparisons that were being made between the first and second Mrs.
Judsons:

> [Mrs. Judson's] bereaved husband is the more desirous of bearing
> . . . testimony to her various attainments, her labors and her
> worth . . . from the fact that she was often brought into compari-
> son with one whose life and character were uncommonly interest-
> ing and brilliant. The Memoir of his first beloved wife has been
> long before the public. It is, therefore, most gratifying to his feel-
> ings to be able to say in truth, that the subject of this notice was, in
> every point of natural and moral excellence, the worthy successor
> of Ann H. Judson.[55]

Almost at once Judson lamented that "there is no portrait of the second, as of the first Mrs. Judson." The bereaved widower regretted
that "her soft blue eye, her mild aspect, her lovely face and elegant
form, have never been delineated on canvas."[56] In order that her
memory be preserved, Adoniram began to think about the publication of a memoir of the life of Sarah Judson. It was in this context,
as a prospective biographer of his second wife, that the famous missionary met the popular authoress, Fanny Forester.[57]

Fanny Forester was the pseudonymous creation of Emily Chubbuck, a twenty-eight-year-old Mistress of Belles-lettres at the Utica
Female Seminary.[58] As Fanny Forester, Chubbuck caught the popular attention; for an eighteen-month period (1844-1846), her stories were published regularly in the *New York Mirror*, the *Knickerbocker, Columbian Magazine*, and *Graham's*. In the wake of her
popularity in the periodical press, she published three books: *Trippings in Author-Land* (1846), *Lilias Fane* (1846), and *Alderbrook*
(1847).[59] Her work was promoted in a particularly enthusiastic
manner by the *New York Evening Mirror*, whose editor, Nathaniel
Parker Willis, had been the first to give her national recognition:
"Among our claims to the consideration of the public, we rank as

not the least our having had the honor to be the first to introduce [Fanny Forester] to author-land."[60]

The history of Chubbuck's rise to national prominence as a literary figure had all the trappings of a female success story. Born in Eaton, Madison County, New York, in August 1817, Emily began working at the nearby woolen mill at Pratt's Hollow at the age of ten.[61] Her earnings, as a splicer of rolls, were essential to the support of her family which included, at that time, her parents and six other children.[62] Her father, Charles Chubbuck, was something of a ne'er-do-well, unable to make it as a farmer and unable to stay out of debt.[63] Emily attended school irregularly and moved about a great deal as her parents looked for better opportunities in and around Morrisville and Hamilton, New York. Apparently, the Chubbucks kept themselves fed and housed, albeit marginally, by taking in boarders, setting the children out to work, and getting small contracts to do such things as carry the mail.[64] In 1839, Ben Chubbuck, one of Emily's brothers, was convicted of horse theft and sent to Auburn State Prison, an event that did little to increase the family's respectability.[65]

Despite their poverty and their embarrassment, the Chubbucks were a pious family, typical of the evangelical constituency of the Burned-Over District. Kendrick later wrote that the parents of Emily Chubbuck Judson were "both . . . in character above any whisper of reproach."[66] An 1849 letter from Emily to her brother Walker, a printer in Wisconsin, indicated that their mother, in particular, was a staunch Baptist: "I wish you could tell me . . . how you came to be a Presbyterian. I suppose the Baptists are very weak in the west, but I should hardly think my mother's son would leave them for that."[67] Emily's parents and her two elder sisters, Lavinia and Harriet, were converted in the revivals of religion that swept upstate New York in the 1820s.[68] As a family, they took the religious papers and were attentive to the news from the Baptists' Burmese mission.[69] Lavinia Chubbuck, who died in her early twenties and was eulogized in the *New York Baptist Register*, apparently caught the missionary spirit from the young Hamilton men who came to call on her in her sickroom.[70] Emily read both the magazine coverage of the Judson story and Knowles' biography of Ann Hasseltine.[71] In later years, when it was important for Emily Chubbuck to establish her early religious credentials, it was reported that, in her early twenties, she wrote the Rev. Nathaniel C. Kendrick about becoming a foreign missionary.[72] Emily's conversion came at age seventeen, after a protracted period of shopping for a denomination. "Indeed I believe my solemn little face was almost ludicrously familiar to worshippers of every denomination," Chubbuck later wrote.[73] She became a Baptist, and, with her family, worshiped in the Baptist churches at Eaton, Morrisville, and Hamilton.

In the main, Emily Chubbuck's early secular education was left to happenstance. After the age of twelve, she was able to attend district schools sporadically, but she never spent more than a few months at the academy in Morrisville, returning always to "twisting threads" for the money it provided. Her reading was a mixture of the pious and the profane. In later life she admitted that the female operatives in the woolen factory at Pratt's Hollow supplied her with novels, "first exacting a promise that [she] would not tell [her] mother and sister."[74] When her brother Walker purchased a share in the town library, she was allowed to borrow a book a week. By her own report, her first selection was Thomas Paine's *Age of Reason*, on which she took copious notes. Her father, she reported, "looked pale and his hands trembled" when he discovered her selection.[75] She also read Gibbon, Hume, Voltaire, Byron, Shakespeare, Goethe, and Fielding, despite the fact that these did not have "the full approval of the heads of the family."[76] The books on the mantle shelf, recommended for family use, were, in addition to the Bible and the family psalm book, "Baxter's Saints' Rest, the lives of several honored martyrs and saints, two volumes of sermons, and Bunyan's Pilgrim's Progress and Grace Abounding."[77] Chubbuck later recalled that even in her pious home, "so great was the reverence for books beneath [our] poor roof, that I do not think our parents could have found it in their hearts to destroy even a bad one."[78] "We had been taught," she wrote, "from our cradles to consider knowledge, next after religion, the most desirable thing."[79]

Despite her family's reverence for education, fifteen-year-old Emily was encouraged by her mother to become a milliner. "To devote my life to making bonnets," Chubbuck wrote, "was not in accordance with my plans, and I rebelled most decidedly."[80] Instead she expressed a desire to be a teacher, a kind of woman's work that required a modicum of intellectual training. After crying all night, she left to confer with a former instructor at the local academy, whose help she sought in her new career decision. Under the guise of a visit to family friends, she secured a job for seventy-five cents a week plus board as a district school teacher for the summer term of 1832.[81] Though she "could earn as much as a milliner, and far more twisting thread," both Emily and her family were pleased with the status she was accorded. For the next five years, she taught schools in Morrisville, Smithfield, Nelsons Corners, Brookfield, Syracuse, and Hamilton, while studying intermittently at the academy at Morrisville.[82] In 1837, she became a teacher at the academy where she was formerly a student; in 1838, her family moved to Hamilton where she was tutored in Greek by a student at the Hamilton Seminary.

Emily Chubbuck's letters from this period reveal that, by her early twenties at least, she was tired of district school teaching, that her ambition had, in fact, escalated. On more than one occasion she wrote to her brother, Walker, asking, "Is there an academy in your town? If so secure me a place in it."[83] Either in preparation for a move upwards or westward, Emily began educating herself, while in Morrisville, for the responsibilities of an academy teacher. In the fall of 1837, she told her brother that by spring she would "be prepared to teach beside Geography, E. Grammar and Arithmetic: History, Natural philosophy, Chemistry, Botany, Rhetoric, Logic, Moral and Intellectual Philosophy, astronomy, French, drawing and painting."[84] In the fall of 1839, she left Morrisville with the intention of not teaching during the winter term, and "contemplated fine fun in the visiting line."[85] Financial necessity, however, forced her to engage another district school at Pratt's Hollow, where she earned three dollars per week plus her board. Near the end of the term, Emily told her brother: "I am tired to death of school teaching."[86]

As her dissatisfaction with school teaching grew, Emily became increasingly concerned about her social status and about the possibilities of marriage. In March 1840, shortly before her removal to Utica, twenty-three-year-old Emily wrote her brother Walker that she was "thinking some of getting married":

> The Damon in question is a young physician of Wayne County by the name of Redfield, a fine face and figure, genteel, pleasing manners, a good address, some talent, and heart of a turtle dove. Nothing great, nothing small—about on a level with the rest of mankind. But I don't care a fig for him . . . what shall I do. I don't love him and I don't hate him and I don't believe I ever should do either.[87]

As a woman who had been forced to earn money since her mid-teens, Emily saw the issue clearly: "Shall I . . . tie myself to a person towards whom I feel perfect indifference for the sake of a home and a protector?"[88] Redfield's suit was doomed with Emily's final comment, a telltale sign of her growing social aspiration: "If you have any young congressmen or governors . . . that are in want of a 'better half' just send them here. I will give up the Dr. anytime for a better."[89]

Chubbuck's taste for authorship and for social status were whetted by her experience in Syracuse in 1838. Despite the fact that at home her father was "dogged by creditors" and her brother Ben was intemperate, Emily was able to create her own successful position in a new location. She wrote unabashedly to Walker Chubbuck: "I have obtained a footing in the highest circles of society. . . ." "To tell the truth I was somewhat astonished myself to find my society so much courted by those who were so much my superiors," she explained, "but I have lately discovered the mighty secret."[90] The explanation for Emily's social desirability lay in her new identity; she had become a published author:

> I have written of late for several publications over the signature of
> E.E.C. People were quite anxious to find out who it was and the
> Editor of the "whig" at last bribed a little boy who carried my
> communications to the office and he betray's me. People at once
> believed because the letters were my initials and so I got to be an
> "authoress" before I was aware of it.[91]

Two years later, when she was invited to the Utica Female Seminary for study and training as a teacher, Emily Chubbuck began to write in earnest. The Utica institution represented a significant educational and social advance over the academy at Morrisville. Emily Chubbuck, who had been referred by a Morrisville friend, was taken under the protective wings of the Seminary's principal directors, the sisters Urania and Cynthia Sheldon.[92] Emily was admitted as a student at the school under a special financial arrangement: funds for her tuition, which amounted to sixty dollars a term, would be loaned on the promise of her future earnings as a teacher, either at the Utica Seminary or at some other location. In order to further defray the costs of her education, the enterprising Sheldon sisters encouraged Emily Chubbuck to write for the press during intervals from school.

In February 1840, Emily wrote from Utica to her brother in Wisconsin explaining the financial realities of female authorship. "They will pay me 2$ a column for articles for the Baptist Register and a dollar a page for the Mother's Journal but the style of both these papers," Emily observed, "is quite out of my view and I don't expect to do much at it."[93] After dismissing the overtly pious periodicals, she noted that she was "preparing a little volume of stories for children," but that this too "is quite far from the mark." Describing herself as "dissatisfied with everything" she did, Emily Chubbuck was, like many a writer, looking for the genre that suited her best.[94] In December 1840, she wrote a friend, Maria Bates, to elicit her reactions to yet another publication possibility.

> I have always shrunk from doing anything in a public capacity. . . . But O, necessity! necessity! Did you ever think of such a thing as selling brains for money? And then, such brains as mine! Do you think I could prepare for the press a small volume of poems that would produce the desired—I must speak it—cash?[95]

By May 1841, Emily Chubbuck was in debt for $120, the cost of two terms at the Utica Female Seminary.[96] She was also making plans to bring her younger sister, Catharine, to Utica to study "piano teaching." This, added to the continued need of her parents, created serious pressures for her to increase her income. In a letter to Catharine in the summer of 1841, Emily signed herself "Amy Scribbleton," and reported on placing three pieces of her work: a poem entitled, "Where Are the Dead?" in the July *Knickerbocker*; an article in the *Mother's Journal* for the same month; and a poem entitled, "Old Man," in a forthcoming *Godey's Lady's Book*.[97] *Charles Linn; or How to Observe the Golden Rule*, the children's book which she began a year earlier, was being published by Dayton and Saxton in New York City.[98]

Despite these successes, Emily had to ask her brother Wallace for money, offering to pay him back, with interest, within two years. "I have written considerable since I came here," she explained to Wallace, "but I begin to think this business more profitable to the *possessor* of money than to the *seeker* of it. Its promises are very flattering and I have hoped and hoped but never realized a single penny."[99] Emily complained to her sister, Catharine, of the same thing: "my empty wallet is lying useless in [the] trunk."[100] In fact, until October 1841, when she received $51 for the sale of 1,500 copies of *Charles Linn*, Emily Chubbuck had made virtually nothing as an author.[101] "The truth is," she told Maria Bates, "writing has become such a matter-of-fact, dollar-and-cent business with me, that I have as complete a horror of the pen as a sweep of his chimney on a holiday. Oh, there is nothing like coining one's brains into gold—no, bread—to make the heart grow sick."[102]

Necessity rather than inspiration made Chubbuck persevere. Her determination to pursue authorship in addition to teaching was evident in these remarks, written to her brother Wallace:

> I am not very healthy but I *can* work and I *will*. I shall have neither Hough [an earlier suitor], nor Dr. Redfield for I don't like them and can live alone. Besides, I calculate to take care of Pa and Ma for I believe I am the only one left to do it.[103]

In September 1841, probably as a result of her publications, Chubbuck was appointed head of the Composition Department at the Utica Female Seminary, a position which brought her the seemingly munificent sum of $150 per year plus her board. Within weeks, she purchased a home for her parents on Broad Street in the Village of Hamilton;[104] at the same time, her sister Kate commenced study, at the cost of $120 per year, in the institution where Emily taught. As Emily's salary had increased, so had her indebtedness.

During the next three years, Chubbuck was published in a number of places, but without making any real economic headway. During the period 1842-1843, she authored four books, all didactic stories for juveniles: *The Great Secret; Or How to Be Happy* (1842); *Effie Maurice: Or, What Is My God* (1842); *Allen Lucas; The Self Made Man* (1843); and *John Frink* (1843).[105] Two of these didactic tales were considered pious enough to be published by the American Baptist Sunday School Union.[106] She was able to supplement her income still further by placing an occasional piece of poetry in the *Columbian* and the *Knickerbocker*, for which she received four dollars per page.[107] Still, she lamented her financial condition: "My affairs in the business line are not very prosperous—the hard times having put a great check on book-publishing."[108] Perhaps it was her frustration that led her to found an outlet for her own work; in 1842 she began, at the Utica Female Seminary, a "ladies monthly magazine," for which she was both the editor and principal writer.[109] During this period she wrote a lengthy poem, in Spencerian stanza, entitled, "Astronoga, Or the Maid of the Rock," which drew heavily on her familiarity with Byron's *Childe Harold*.[110]

In her capacity for literary creation in a variety of forms, Chubbuck was typical of that generation of young women who were prone to "versify," to cultivate an epistolary style, and to concoct, alternatively, tales of piety, imagination, and romance. This interest in all forms of literary endeavor was summed up by an adolescent woman in the 1840's: "Lizzy, it is a fact that I am allmost [sic] as fond of using my pen as my toung [sic] which you know there is no lack of want."[111] Women, as writers and as readers, were an integral part of the popular cultural milieu of antebellum America.[112] The poet, Grenville Mellon, poked fun at the literate American woman: "Ye critics, look! She writes—and talks—and moves—a living book!"[113] As an author, Nathaniel Hawthorne was forced to compete with them. In the 1850s he decried their popularity, petulantly calling them "a damned mob of scribbling women."[114]

An audience of women readers and an expanding number of women writers were important factors in the success of literary entrepreneur Nathaniel Parker Willis.[115] As a poet, Willis had a propensity for Byronic imitation;[116] as an editor, he was closely attuned to contemporary cultural tastes and to the significance of his female audience. "It is the women who give or withold a literary reputation," he was reported to have said.[117] When Emily Chubbuck made her first trip to New York City in the spring of 1844, she did not call at the offices of Willis' *New York Mirror*. She did, however, take a number of her "pieces" to John Inman, editor of the *Columbian*, whom she later described as a "pleasant, whole souled man."[118] When she returned to Utica, she wrote Nathaniel Parker Willis the most important letter of her life, signing herself for the first time, Fanny Forester.[119]

The letter that caught Willis' attention and catapulted Fanny Forester to national prominence was an ingenuous statement of Emily Chubbuck's literary aspiration. Using the experiences of a country girl in the metropolis as a narrative device, Chubbuck described the seductions of New York fashion and inveigled support from the famous editor:

> You know that the shops in Broadway are very tempting this Spring. Such beautiful things! Well, you know . . . what a delightful thing it would be to appear in one of those charming, head-adorning, complexion-softening, hard-feature subduing, Neopolitans; with a little gossamer veil dropped daintily on the shoulder of one of those exquisite balzarines, to be seen any day at Stewart's and elsewhere. Well, you know . . . that shopkeepers have the imperti-

nence to demand a triviling exchange for these things even of a
lady; and also that some people have a remarkably small purse,
and a remarkably small portion of the yellow "root" in that. And
now, to bring the matter home, I am one of that class. I have the
most beautiful little purse in the world, but it is only kept for
show; I even find myself under the necessity of counterfeiting—
that is, filling the void with tissue-paper in lieu of bank notes, preparatory for a shopping expedition![120]

Fanny Forester explained that after conversations with her "Cousin
Bel,"[121] she had decided to tell Willis the truth: she wanted money
in order to purchase the accoutrements of New York style, not because she was an orphan, a cripple, or the victim of "some specula-
tive bubble." Fanny Forester teased Willis: "Have I read the New
[York] Mirror so much . . . and not learned who has an eye for
everything pretty?"[122]

The mysterious authoress then asked Willis outright for his literary patronage, noting that she had "a nice little feather tipped
pen," Dr. Johnson's dictionary, and a host of "little messengers rac-
ing 'like mad' through the galleries of [her] head; spinning long
yarns, and weaving fabrics rich and soft as the balzarine which
[she] so much covet[ed]."[123] "Thus prepared," she asked Willis,
"think you not I should be able to put something in the shops of the
literary caterers? something that, for once in my life, would give me
a real errand into Broadway? Maybe you of the New Mirror *pay* for
acceptable articles—maybe not. Comprenez-vous?"[124]

The publication of Fanny Forester's audacious letter promoted
speculation about her identity. Willis' published response raised the
possibility that the "anonymous lady who wished to conjure a new
bonnet and dress out of her inkstand" might be a wily old spinster,
a "practiced magazinist," or, even, a man.[125] In Utica, Emily was
amused by the amount of attention she had attracted. In September
1844, after a summer of Forester-Willis exchanges in the *New Mirror*, she wrote to her brother Wallace:

> I will send you the last New Mirror to let you know what fun I am
> having with N.P. Willis. . . . I commenced writing for [him] as
> Fanny Forester last June about the tenth no. of the Mirror I think.
> . . . Since then there has been scarcely a Mirror without something
> about me in it. Get the back numbers and then tell me if you don't
> think I am having fun.[126]

Although Willis was paying her nothing to help ease her $300 indebtedness, Chubbuck considered the relationship worthwhile. "Thro' his influence I expect to get into Graham and Godey's and then I hope to make something," she told Walker Chubbuck.[127] She wrote her sister, Kate, that she expected her correspondence with Willis to put her "in a way of making money like smoke."[128] When her identity was revealed to him, Willis took a keen interest in encouraging the young woman to further literary production and suggested that she try a novel.[129] "You are more readable than any other female writer in this country," he wrote her in September 1844, ". . . I shall go on glorifying you in our daily paper, until the magazine people give you fifty dollars an article." In November 1844 after receiving a Forester sketch entitled, "Dora," Willis wrote the author: "I have just read the proof of your exquisitely beautiful outline story, my dear Miss Chubbuck, and my heart is in my throat with its pathos, and with my interest in your genius."[130] Willis was, undoubtedly, the guiding force in Chubbuck's "literary noviatiate."[131] His letters provided her with unqualified support and an ample dose of his literary criticism. "Nobody could ever read a line of yours and see any thing but merit over-modest," he told her, "and there is no writing well without coloring from one's own heart. . . . There are two worlds, my dear . . . one imaginative and the other real life— and people of genius have separate existence in both."[132]

Within little more than one year, stories from the pen of the composition teacher in Utica were published in *Graham's, Godey's Lady's Book*, the *Columbian*, and the *Knickerbocker*. In the winter of 1845, Emily wrote to her sister, Kate: "The Columbian people pretend to think all the world of me; Graham is as good as the bank, and Willis fifty times better. . . ."[133] Literary accolades for "the sweet authoress" were everywhere. The reviewer for *Graham's* called her "fascinating."[134] Sarah Josepha Hale of *Godey's* enthusiastically endorsed the first collection of her work, *Trippings in Author-Land*: "For vivacity, feeling and naivete, Fanny is unrivaled among living writers."[135] The publisher's preface to the story of *Lilias Fane* described Fanny Forester as "a lady who has written herself into the heart of the public. . . ."[136] On the basis of her celebrity in an eighteen-month period, between June 1844 and December 1845, Fanny Forester was ranked among American literati and included in the following contemporaneous collections: Thomas Bu-

chanan Read, *The Female Poets of America* (1849); Rufus Wilmot
Griswold, *The Prose Writers of America* (1847); Caroline May, *The
American Female Poets* (1848); and Horace Binney Wallace, *Literary Criticisms and Other Papers* (1856).[137] From Edinburgh,
Hogg's Weekly Instructor observed the phenomenon of Fanny Forester and commented on its larger meaning: "The chief features of
this gifted and amiable woman's life are striking ones, and are certainly more common in Republican America than with us."[138]

In Utica, the "sensation days" of Fanny Forester apparently
brought Emily Chubbuck some small annoyances. Because she continued to teach at the female seminary, Chubbuck had the problem
of preserving her anonymity. She wrote her old friend, Maria
Bates: "Now I do not like to be an object of curiosity like the Siamese Twins or Tom Thumb."[139] A poem entitled, "To a Fair 'Tripping Forrester,' " published in the *Utica Daily Gazette*, embarrassed the young school teacher-turned-fiction writer because of its
implication:

> We have witnessed the "Trippings,"
>   And inhaled the rich sippings
> Of your own sweetly sketched "Author-Land";
>   But there are still *some things*,
>   Which a view of it brings
> That we cannot quite understand.
>
>   In truth, fair Miss Fanny,
>   You're so *au fait* and canny
> In *all the deep mysteries of love*,
>   Than when bent upon wooing,
>   You sit "billing and cooing"
> Like unto some sweet turtle-dove.
>
>   You so well *theorise*
>   It would not much surprise
> Your friends, who have witnessed your art,
>   If in threading the way
>   In which CUPID doth stray
> You had heedlessly *lost your own heart*.
>
>   Pray who is the swain
>   Who in following your train,
> Has had the good-fortune to find it?
>   For whatever his phiz
>   Our advice to him is
> With HYMEN'S fast cord quick to bind it.[140]

The fact that people were talking about her in this way, and speculating on the source of her material, prompted a letter to Willis. He replied with the following advice:

> The pain that you are suffering from the *exposure of fame* is a chrysalis of thought. You will be brighter for it, though the accustomed shroud of seclusion comes off painfully. The opinions of the "Uticanians" as to anything but your amiableness and respectability, is not worth one straw. . . . You have yet to learn that genius burns darkest near the wick, never, *never* appreciated by those who eat, drink and walk with it. You are a hundred times more admired in New York than you ever could be in Utica, and it is the charm of City life that the "solitude of a crowd" throws even your nearest neighbor to the proper perspective distance. Keep making an effort to shed neighborhood. . . .[141]

In the late winter of 1845, ostensibly because of her health, Chubbuck left Utica for warmer climes, accompanied by Cynthia Sheldon and planning to remain away approximately six weeks. In Philadelphia, she stayed with the family of the Rev. A.D. Gillette, a Hamilton graduate and pastor of the Eleventh Baptist Church. [142] With her literary reputation preceding her, Philadelphia marked the beginning of Chubbuck's personal introduction to the larger literary and social world beyond Hamilton and Utica. During her stay there she was called upon by a number of "literary lions," including George Rex Graham, [143] Rufus W. Griswold, [144] and Joseph C. Neal. [145] On her journey home, she spent a fortnight visiting with the counselor whom she had never met, Nathaniel Parker Willis; this was to be the only time that Willis and Forester would meet. When she returned to Utica in July 1845, Emily was filled with enthusiastic reports on her trip and began making plans for another, a voyage to Italy, in the company of the United States Consul to Genoa. She wrote her brother Wallace about the success she was having:

> If I go [to Europe] Mr. Graham (of Graham's Magazine) will send me and give me a salary for my letters—letters from abroad by Fanny Forester. I got to be quite a belle while I was gone—gallivanted about with Graham and R.W. Griswold in Philadelphia, went to the opera with N. P. Willis, cut up all manner of shines. Willis, as you probably know, set sail for London about five weeks ago, a week after I left. He is a noble fellow and the very best friend I have got. . . .[146]

With great excitement, Emily told her brother that Willis sent her a "magnificent New Year's present—a painting from my story of Dora, done by Hagy."[147] In case her brother was unaware of its worth, she told him: "It was valued in New York at two hundred dollars."[148]

Aside from the discomforts of being the object of local gossip, Emily Chubbuck was relishing her life as Fanny Forester. In the summer of her success, she took the time to reflect on her own history. To her old friend, Urania Sheldon Nott, wife of the President of Union College, she wrote:

> My life, from my cradle, has been full of changes. Without one of my own kindred to assist me, I have struggled with almost every kind of difficulty up to the present moment. Even *you* can not dream of half that I have borne. Heaven knows, enough to make me humble. Within the last year—one short year—I have gained for myself a position which others have been all their lives in attaining, and I have a right to be proud of it. You may tell me it is a small thing to be a magazine writer. So it is. But it is not a small thing for a woman, thrown upon her own resources, and standing entirely alone, to be able to command respect from everybody, rising by her own individual efforts above the accidents of fortune. Doest all this sound like boasting? I only want to prove to you that I understand my ground, and take too comprehensive a view of it to have my heart set a fluttering by every swing of Mr. Nobody's censer. I know precisely what my reputation is worth to me, for I have measured it carefully; and I know, too, what all their silly compliments are worth.[149]

In October 1845, because of delicate health, Chubbuck left Utica for Philadelphia and a return visit to the home of Rev. and Mrs. A. D. Gillette. There, she renewed the acquaintance of the literati of that city and became a personal friend of Horace Binney Wallace, who later wrote that Fanny Forester was in "the front rank of writers of dramatic fiction on either side of the water. . . ."[150] In December, her host, A. D. Gillette, returned home from a series of missionary meetings in Boston, accompanied by America's premier missionary, the fifty-seven-year-old widower, Adoniram Judson.

According to Asahel Clark Kendrick, Judson read *Trippings in Author-Land* before ever meeting Miss Chubbuck.[151] Detained on a train from New York to Philadelphia without any reading material,

Gillette provided him with the popular collection of Forester stories. Judson read them, either in part or in their entirety, and then gave his opinion. The venerated missionary first judged Fanny Forester's writing to have "great beauty and power," and then asked if she were a Christian. Undoubtedly Gillette replied with the particulars, that Fanny Forester was, in fact, Emily Chubbuck, a Utica Female Seminary teacher, his houseguest, and, most importantly, a Baptist. According to Kendrick, Judson then "expressed his desire to see and converse with her, as it was a pity that talents so brilliant should not be more worthily employed."[152] After meeting Emily the following day and hearing the story of her indigent parents and her laborious years of teaching and unremunerative authorship, Judson secured her services for the preparation of a memoir of his recently deceased wife.

Neither party ever revealed the manner in which this working relationship grew into their engagement and eventual marriage. Asahel Clark Kendrick described it with a decorous euphemism: "The consequences of the coming together of two persons respectively so fascinating, were what has often occurred since the days of Adam and Eve."[153] In a letter to his son in Wisconsin, Emily's excited father, Charles Chubbuck, informed Walker of the surprising relationship:

> . . . the most important news is about Emily, you know she has become one of the most popular female writers in America, well would you believe it? She is going to be married to the Rev. Adoniram Judson D.D. Missionary to Burmah, who is on a visit to this country after an absence of thirty three years . . . the agreement was finally concluded between them in January. . . . They will probably be married about the last of June, and sail for Burmah soon after. . . . Doctor J. is 57 years old, is one of the best and most noted of men, and I believe he and Emily think all the world of each other.[154]

A letter to Horace Binney Wallace prior to the public announcement of the engagement revealed what Emily Chubbuck saw ahead in her new role as a missionary wife.[155] First, she made some perfunctory statements about her desire to have the opportunity to do "real, permanent good." In Burma, she said, she expected that "every word and act will have a very important bearing," a responsibility sure to result in her own religious and moral improvement.

Most importantly, however, she envisioned Judson and herself having a significant effect on the national cultural life:

> *There* is a great nation on whose future character every pen-stroke will have a bearing. Doctor Judson has given them the entire Scriptures, written several small books in the Burmese, and has nearly completed a dictionary of the language. He will be the founder of a national literature, give its tone (a pure and holy influence he exerts) to the character of a mighty people; and I must own that I feel rather inclined to thrust in my own little finger.[156]

The union of the widely known fiction writer and the missionary-lexicographer seemed inexplicable to many in the religious community who formed their conception of marital compatibility on the basis of Scripture. In fact, they looked to Genesis and to the example of Isaac and Rebecca, who suffered great anxiety lest their son Jacob marry among the daughters of Canaan.[157] "It is the absolute necessity of real believers [to] marry only such as they have some good reason to believe are converted persons," stated the editors of the *Evangelical Intelligencer*.[158] Even though the future Mrs. Judson was a church-going Baptist who had undergone conversion in her adolescence, her public career as a writer of imaginative literature did little to support her case among the community of believers. The year before, her book, *Trippings in Author-Land*, had received its lone negative review, from the *Gospel Messenger*, which called it "namby pamby trash" having "neither wit, taste, erudition, nor instruction" to redeem it.[159]

Conceivably, Adoniram Judson saw in Fanny Forester an opportunity for a cultural conversion that closely paralleled the personal religious conversions of his missionary career. Just as Fanny Forester was attracted to Judson as a Great Man, a hero of religious society, Judson saw the sentimental fiction writer as a young woman whose talents could be converted to the cause of worldwide evangelicalism. Aside from whatever personal chemistry existed between them, each of them saw in the other a personification of a culturally desirable attribute, in a form available for appropriation through marriage.

Since it was considered both evil and dangerous "for a serious person to form a matrimonial connexion with one who gives no satisfactory evidence of being a partaker of divine grace," Adoniram Judson's proposal to Chubbuck represented a serious breach of evangelical etiquette. Letters from students at the Hamilton Seminary also indicate that Judson's decision to remarry, only months after the death of his wife Sarah, alienated him from many who revered the memory of his former wives. E. C. Lord, one of the Hamilton audience who heard Judson speak on missionary themes in the fall of 1845, had this to say about the betrothal:

> I shall forbear making any comments myself on the Dr's course in reference to this whole affair. But I greatly fear that Dr. J [would] stand before the students in a very different aspect from what he did when he stood before us, some months since, exhorting us to "look to Jesus." I do not know as any one blames the Dr. for loving; & perhaps there are not many that blame him for loving "Fanny Forester"; but that he should love under such circumstances, and that he should take such a course—at this many shake their heads.[160]

Another Hamilton student, I. N. Loomis, irreverently wrote his sister that Judson had been in town for over a week, "playing Knight-errantry . . . to perfection." "I think him well adapted to the romantic disposition of Fanny Forester," Loomis wrote, "he may play his part well. He is old and knows how."[161]

Criticism of Chubbuck's decision to forsake a literary career to become a missionary wife came from as far away as London, where a writer for the *Saturday Review* called the emerging Judson story "an exercise in the theory and practice of erotics." The same vituperative reviewer claimed that Emily Chubbuck's character could best be expressed by Pope's last couplet about Narcissa: "A very heathen in her carnal part / Yet still a sad, good Christian at her heart."[162] In America, the *Boston Evening Transcript* considered her a prime example of the religious "infatuation" of those who imagined themselves "called" to labor and die in unhealthy climes.[163]

On a deeper level, Chubbuck's entire career was a departure from the traditional world of American letters and the class-oriented code of female behavior. First, Chubbuck was a mere "magazinist" who, according to the Unitarian *Christian Examiner*, catered to "the multitudes who devour periodical literature as the locusts eat all green things."[164] Second, her career was launched by the kind of self-conscious promotional act that was considered abhorrent to "true womanhood." And, finally, the evangelicals' eagerness to justify Fanny Forester's career as an act of Christian duty (providing sustenance for the Chubbuck family) violated the idea that all women were "ladies" and members of a leisure class.[165] The requirements of gentility were, after all, incompatible with the kind of hungry literary ambition demonstrated by Emily Chubbuck.

In October 1846, the Rev. A. D. Gillette, a man who knew well both the missionary and the young authoress, was forced to take pen in hand in order to defend the future Mrs. Judson against "slander, ignorance, [and] maliciousness." In the pages of the *Christian Watchman*, a Baptist "religious and family newspaper," Gillette stated that Emily Chubbuck was not a "novel writer, a danseuse, a ball and theatre frequenter and even an actress." He attested to the fact that from September 1845 until April 1846, the young woman in question had spent "but three evenings out." He gave the exact date and place of her Baptism and remarked that many women "are *talking* more, but *doing* infinitely less good than Fanny Forester."[166]

Gillette then turned to a consideration of Chubbuck's work which he called "moral and graceful." Reminding his readers that she had written eight "religious books," four of which were published by the American Baptist Publication Society, Gillette offered his interpretation of the substance of Fanny Forester's fiction:

> [She] writes about her home, the things she and others who resided in the vicinity of her purely loved, and beautifully described *Alderbrook*, saw, and knew, and felt. Whether there be such a place in every particular, in Madison County, New York is a question of small moment to us. We know there is such a place in the heart of every home-bred, country-reared mind, and that not all the fascinations of city crowds, or congregated cares and responsibilities of professional life, can or shall erase its innocent image from our hearts.[167]

In addition to portraying Forester's fiction as an invocation of the rural-small town ideal, Gillette justified her authorship in Christian terms. Emily Chubbuck became the popular periodical writer Fanny Forester in order to support her aging and indigent parents. Filial obligation, rather than personal aspiration, motivated her writing and underlay her success. On this basis, Gillette endorsed Emily Chubbuck as worthy to become "one of the consecrated three."[168]

The correspondence between Judson and Chubbuck in the period of their engagement reveals Emily's uneasiness and lack of confi-

dence in the wake of popular criticism. In addition to her understandable anxiety about leaving home for the wilds of heathen
Burma, Chubbuck was constantly distressed by the criticism she
and Judson received. Repeatedly, she apologized for the embarrassment their association caused him: "It is impossible that I shall ever
be any thing but a weight upon your hands and heart. . . . You
were a demi-god, and I have brought you down."[169] Judson's replies
became litanized; in a variety of different and affectionate ways, he
told her that her past history held no particular embarrassment for
him, that she "had done right . . . though the publication of a few
letters might not have been wise":

> . . . you know I always thought it was exceedingly desirable that
> you should henceforth pledge yourself and vows to holier pur-
> poses. And that was the aim of my first plain and rather ungallant
> exhortation. . . . I shall always think that your own sense and love
> of right essentially aided me in my adventurous attempt on your
> heart. But by whatever means it was effected, it is the joy of my
> life that I have secured a little lodgment in that dear, dear
> heart.[170]

The man Emily called her "precious guide and teacher" did not
allow himself to be moved by the brouhaha in which they were involved. "As to what the newspapers and public say," Judson wrote
her, "can you not receive it with that cool, quiet composure which
best becomes you, nor let anyone but me know that it disturbs you?
In fact, be not disturbed. There is nothing that ought to disturb one
of your pure and high purpose."[171] The bride-elect was particularly
upset by an unauthorized sketch or likeness of herself which
adorned a "surreptitious edition" of *Lilias Fane.* Judson assured her
that his "heart's love" could not "be ruffled" by seeing [her] cari-
cature . . . by the side of Fanny Elsler, and the Fair Bandit, and
other demireps, in the low book-stalls through the country." Judson restated his commitment to her and asked: "Did you think
that my courage would quail, and that I should wish to take it all
back. . .?"[172]

Emily was contrite for what she called her "lack [of] the proper
degree of meekness" in trying to "defend [herself] from what seems
to [be] undeserved blame."[173] But she repeatedly saw herself as a
victim: "I carefully kept my name from the public eye, assumed a
nom de plume for the sake of privacy, and now every one that can
pen a clumsy paragraph, must needs drag it before the public and
make his senseless comment."[174]

Chubbuck's letters were also filled with expressions of her own religious ambivalence. "I find much among Christians which is called religion, and which is just its antipode," she wrote Judson. "There is so much in the world (particularly the refined, poetical part of the world, which perhaps, has too much of my sympathy) like the purest religion, that it attracts me in spite of myself."[175] Her efforts at renewing her spiritual faith were unabashedly anchored in her love for Adoniram:

> Pray for me dearest . . . I do love his cause more than anything else, and am happy in the thought of being permitted to do some good; but I need your constant, unremitting prayers. I do not know how far I am influenced in this important step by love to you, and how far by love to God; the two seems to be pointing so entirely in the same way, and He has made it so sweet to do right. I am sure I can not love you too much; pray for me that I may love the blessed Saviour more.[176]

Judson did little to discourage the young woman's reliance on him as her spiritual father. "Take me to your heart, and fashion me entirely," she wrote him from Hamilton. He called her "the earthly sun that illuminates my present."[177]

Physical affection appeared to be one component of Judson's love for Emily Chubbuck. He told her in the weeks before their marriage: "My thoughts and affections revolve around you and cling to your form and face and lips."[178] On another occasion he wrote, "I have some desire to see your sweet face . . . and fold you in my arms."[179] Her comments on their physical relationship were more restrained but included remarks about Mr. Judson's youthful looks. "His hair," she told her family," is black, his teeth perfect, and his face young looking." She also told her brother Walker, confidentially, about "some splendid offers" she had had "in the matrimonial line," hoping to convince him that she knew "what [she] was about" when she accepted the "good, high souled old doctor."[180]

While Emily was at home preparing for her marriage and her new life as a missionary, Judson traveled to Worcester and to Bradford to make arrangements for the care of his children.[181] The two boys, Adoniram Brown and Elnathan, were placed with pious friends in Worcester; Abby Ann was "left crying" with the Hasseltine family in Bradford.[182] George Boardman, now a young man, was scheduled to enter Brown University, his stepfather's alma mater. While in New York, Judson took time to arrange for the publication of Emily's two-volume collection, *Alderbrook*.[183] According to the rules of the Baptist Foreign Mission Board, any profits that were earned from writing done after she became Mrs. Judson, reverted to the mission treasury.[184] Judson wrote her reassuringly that "my pecuniary arrangements are such that we shall have an ample sufficiency for all our purposes, and enough to furnish your parents with what you may think necessary. . . ."[185]

On June 2, 1846, Emily Chubbuck and Adoniram Judson were married at Hamilton by the Rev. Nathaniel C. Kendrick, the acting President of the Hamilton Literary and Theological Institution and corresponding secretary of the New York Baptist Educational Society.[186] The wedding was strictly private, attended only by the Chubbuck family and two of Emily's friends, Cynthia Sheldon and Anna Maria Anable. The following week the Judsons left for New York, Boston, Plymouth, and Bradford, where they visited with family and friends.[187] On the eleventh of July, "amidst the tearful adieus of hundreds," the Judsons embarked for Burma aboard the *Fanueil Hall*.[188] A box of books, presented to Mrs. Judson by N. P. Willis, W. H. Prescott, Henry Wadsworth Longfellow, and George Bancroft, marked the conclusion of her literary career.[189] A pious letter of farewell to the Baptist churches at Hamilton, Utica, and Morrisville heralded Mrs. Judson's new life as a missionary of the Gospel.[190]

Emily Chubbuck Judson was published again in America, although never again as Fanny Forester, nor as a writer of fiction. When *Alderbrook* was reviewed by *Graham's* in March 1847, their critic observed that:

> The interest of the book is enhanced by the present position of the gifted authoress. As Mrs. Judson, she will devote her fine talents and beautiful enthusiasm of character to a new object. The present book, therefore, has almost the look of a posthumous work.[191]

In fact, after 1846, everything that Emily Judson wrote was informed by her new and strongly felt identity with the evangelical religious community. In 1854, the *Massachusetts Baptist Missionary Magazine* observed that "no one who compares her earlier life with her later writings can fail to see how the great enterprise to which her life was at length given at once heightened their tone and lent increased weight and force to her pen."[192]

As the wife of Adoniram Judson, it was Emily's intention to apply her literary style to religious and missionary themes. Although she did try her hand at a strictly didactic work—a series of Scriptural questions on the historical parts of the New Testament—she and Judson agreed that her peculiar literary talents and reputation might better be used to "win for her a class of readers not hitherto interested in missionary literature."[193] On board the *Fanueil Hall*, Emily Judson wrote her first work as a missionary publicist, "Outward Bound," for the *Columbian Magazine*.

After offering exalted paeans to her native land, Mrs. Judson described the sea voyage in great and colorful detail, speculating on treasure ships hidden beneath the sea and recording a variety of marine life. Her language was uniformly rich in natural and classical imagery. Only on reaching Burma did she write about the purpose of her sea voyage:

> To kindle the fire which shall illuminate such a people, though it be at first but the faint, fitful glimmer of a rush-light, how glorious! To plant the seed of one pure principle in natures so degraded, to place one bud of hope in the core of such misery, and watch its beautiful and beautifying expansion, to hold in hand the lever which after hundreds of years shall elevate a mighty nation . . . has a glory in it which no truly wise man would barter for the sceptre of Alexander. Good can be done every where, and nothing is truer than that "missionaries are needed at home"; yet if I have but one morsel of bread, let me give it to the famishing; if I have but a single flower, let me take it to the cell of the dying prisoner, on whose cheek the free air never plays, and who knows nothing of the pleasant sights and smells in which others are revelling.[194]

On the trip out, Emily also wrote a poetic tribute to Sarah Boardman,[195] which was followed by the proposed biographical memoir. In the *Memoir of Sarah B. Judson* (1848), which she wrote over the course of a six-month period from a sickbed in Rangoon, Emily Judson demonstrated her usefulness as a self-conscious promoter of religion in the guise of fiction. By 1855, the volume was into its thirtieth thousand. The reviewer for *Graham's* called it "deeply engaging, an affecting volume, uniting a kind of romantic character, derived from the scenes and perils it describes, with the deeper interest of a record of the evangelization of the heathen."[196] Unlike Knowles' pietistic memoir of Ann Hasseltine, which was compiled some twenty years earlier, Sarah Boardman's biography had a consciously conceived dramatic structure, which presented her life in self-contained episodes or chapters bearing suggestive titles such as "Withering and Watching," "Death in the Jungle," and "Little Sarah." Letters from Sarah and Adoniram were generally published only in part, and placed within the text as though they were dialogue between the characters. The author also used literary techniques like foreshadowing to heighten the dramatic interest.[197] The story's final denouement, the death of Sarah Judson at St. Helena, was an excruciating recitation of the heroine's superlative Christian humility and acceptance in the face of death. Adoniram was certainly pleased with Emily's production. In May 1848, he sent copies of the *Memoir* to Sarah's sons, Adoniram Brown and Elnathan. "You will be delighted to read it, so beautifully and so truthfully it is written," he told them.[198] He praised his "young romance writer," now the mother of a child, Emily Frances, not only for the *Memoir*, but for the translation and teaching she had begun.[199] He joked to his old friends, the Robarts of Philadelphia, "I hope she will yet come to some good."[200]

In July 1849, Emily wrote to a friend about the technique she had used in the popular memoir:

> though . . . I sometimes embellish my *style*, I have never been guilty of embellishing facts. . . . In the work alluded to (than which a more truthful narrative was never made), I had my reasons, and I believe good and sound ones, for departing from the beaten track of compilers.[201]

What the Judsons condoned was the packaging of explicitly Christian materials in popular cultural styles. Simultaneously, they buttressed their argument for the evangelical uses of fiction, arguing that Jesus himself had employed the parable as an educational tool. Emily wrote to a friend in July 1849: "The innocence or the usefulness of fiction, in at least one of its forms, does not lie open to discussion; for the question has been decided by the Saviour himself. But how far this mode of teaching should be used, at what point it becomes reprehensible, and when it degenerates into a vice, has puzzled too many wise hearts to allow my venturing an opinion."[202] Despite her declared reticence, Emily did offer an observation: "I will venture to assert that where one person is injured by insipid moral tales, a hundred persons are benefitted."[203]

Emily Judson's remarks anticipated literary developments to come. In the 1850s, book-length moral tales, from the pens of young women authors, constituted the nation's bestsellers.[204] "Domestic novelists," such as Augusta Jane Evans, Maria Susanna

Cummins, Mary Jane Holmes, Mrs. E. D. E. N. Southworth, and Susan Warner entered the literary world at an auspicious moment. Not only was the publishing business in halcyon times, but the tradition of female authorship had already been established. Between 1825 and 1850, the number of American periodicals and the total production of books increased by 500 percent.[205] Additionally, native-born writers like Cooper and Catharine M. Sedgwick demonstrated, in the 1820s and 1830s, the legitimacy of American fiction.

In the evangelical community, the traditional opposition to imaginative literature began to dissipate, after 1830, in the face of a burgeoning secular culture. In fact, the orthodox clergy began to supplement their incomes by editing literary annuals and giftbooks, which allowed for a modicum of fiction in a guaranteed moral and religious context.[206] In 1836, an ancillary division of the evangelical movement, the American Temperance Union, formally endorsed "prose fiction and the products of fancy" as weapons in the crusade against "Prince Alcohol."[207] A decade after this utilitarian decision, the marriage of the venerated exemplar of the Gospel movement, Adoniram Judson, to the fiction writer, Fanny Forester, at least in part suggested evangelicalism's developing interest in appropriating the very techniques of secular acculturation.[208]

The fact that the "domestic novelists" of the fifties followed on the heels of this development explains, in part, their tremendous popularity. Susan Warner's Wide Wide World (1850), which one reviewer thought might do more good "than any book outside of the Bible," went through thirteen editions in two years, selling one-half million copies.[209] Maria Susanna Cummins' The Lamplighter (1854) sold 40,000 copies in just eight weeks.[210] By the time of both these publications, the audience for moralistic fiction had expanded to include women from the Gospel movement. For the pious but aspiring evangelical, the domestic novels, with their female heroines, middle-class values, and stories of Christian fortitude and faith, were a comfortable form.[211] In fact, they followed a simple "Home and Jesus formula,"[212] proposing that the resolution of all familial difficulties lay in the realm of religion. While they were never explicitly sectarian, these novels displayed a definite evangelical orientation. Religious conversion was a central motif of most "domestic novels."[213]

In October 1851, as Susan Warner's Wide Wide World held the popular attention, Emily Chubbuck Judson returned to America. In April of the year before, she and Adoniram were forced to undergo a separation since his desperate health necessitated a sea voyage. At his bedside before he left, Mrs. Judson wrote a poem entitled "Watching," which foreshadowed the events to come: "Night deepens and I sit / in cheerless doubt, alone."[214] The most interesting thing about Emily Judson's poem is what her biographer, Nathaniel C. Kendrick, had to say about it. He wrote: "The scene is thoroughly oriental; and the vivid truths of the portrait is surpassed by nothing in the luxurious imagery of 'Lalla Rookh,' or the more simple and natural picture-drawing of Byron."[215] Kendrick was weighing the aesthetic qualities of Mrs. Judson's poetry against that of Moore and Byron. In so doing, he was expressing a popular evangelical conviction: that there was nothing in the seductions of secular writing that could not be found, in a superior form, in literature that came from the pens of the pious.

In "Watching," Mrs. Judson had expressed her fears for the worst. For some months after Adoniram's departure in December 1849, she heard nothing of his condition or of the progress of his ship. In April 1850, still unaware if her husband was alive or dead, she gave birth to a stillborn child, whom she commemorated with the poem, "Angel Charlie":

He came—a beauteous vision—
    Then vanished from my sight,
His wing one moment cleaving
    The blackness of my night;
My glad ear caught its rustle,
    Then sweeping by, he stole
The dew-drop that his coming
    Had cherished in my soul.[216]

This combination of circumstances left Emily desolate, and explains the spirit of another poem written to her mother in the same period: "Sweet mother, I am here alone / in sorrow and in pain / The sunshine from my heart has flown / it feels the driving rain. . . ."[217] On August 28, 1850, Emily Judson learned that her husband was dead, that he died aboard ship within two weeks of their parting.[218]

On account of her own failing health and the needs of her three fatherless children, Judson's widow returned home to a warm welcome. Kendrick suggested the change that had occurred in her relationship to the religious community:

. . . the welcome she now received was undoubtedly more deep and heartfelt than the tumultuous God-speed which had accom-

panied her departure. Then, misgivings existed in many minds
that would not utter them, lest the brilliant romance-writer might
fail in the practical qualities and self denying duties of the missionary. She had gone through the ordeal and come out, like gold
from the furnace, approved and refined.[219]

Emily's evangelical credentials were established by her four-year
tenure in Burma, by her reverential memoir of Sarah Boardman,
and by the fact of her widowhood.

In America, she was to act in a manner befitting the widow of
Dr. Judson. Her first priority was to bring under one roof all of
Adoniram's children.[220] Before leaving Burma, she also made arrangements, according to her husband's final instructions, for the
completion of Judson's Burmese-English/English-Burmese dictionary.[221]Two months after her arrival, she began to systematically
collect and arrange the letters and papers of her late husband. Dr.
Francis Wayland, President of Brown University, and, probably,
antebellum America's most eminent Baptist scholar, had been engaged to prepare the Judson biography, without compensation,
leaving its entire profits to the widow and children.[222] Despite her
physical debilities, Mrs. Judson went to work reading, selecting,
copying, digesting, commenting, and annotating the materials on
her husband's life. It was her intention to create a personal biography that would not "place the subject at a cloudy distance [or]
divest him of . . . attributes of humanity. . . ."[223] At the same time
she saw his life in a historical context: ". . . his life has been such a
complete exposition of the age in which it began and ended, that a
rapid but comprehensive glance at these times will be an essential
requisite to a full development of the subject."[224]

Mrs. Judson's energies in her remaining years were devoted to
the perpetuation of her husband's memory, to the advocacy of the
missionary cause, and to meeting the material needs of no fewer
than ten persons who were dependent upon her for support.[225] It
was a combination of these three considerations that led her again
to the commercial presses. In 1852, a volume entitled *An Olio of
Domestic Verse*, consisting of her published and unpublished
poetry, was issued by Lewis Colby of New York. The collection,
which included poems associated with Judson's historic mission, received only mixed response.[226] In 1853, her pious tribute of sisterly
affection for Lavinia and Harriet Chubbuck was published as *My
Two Sisters: A Sketch from Memory*.[227] In the same year, Tickenor,

Reed, and Field of Boston brought out *The Kathayan Slave and other Papers Connected with Missionary Life*, a collection of essays by Emily Judson, extracted from the Baptist magazine, the *Macedonian*.[228] Except for *The Olio*, which went through two editions, Mrs. Judson's post-1850 authorship was largely unrewarding.[229] Neither her former identity as a literary light nor her current status as the widow of Adoniram Judson did much to bolster her sales.

If the financial rewards for Emily Judson's own work were small, the market for biographies of her husband was expansive. When she arrived in Boston in 1851, she was immediately met by a proposition from a New York commercial publisher, who had already prepared a memoir of Adoniram Judson. The publisher, identified by Kendrick only as a non-Baptist, offered to pay Judson's widow fifty dollars for each 1,000 copies sold.[230] Because she did not wish to sanction such "wild-cat" projects, Mrs. Judson declined the offer and began to work on the authoritative, Baptist biography in which she had a vested financial interest. The last year of her life was spent trying to stop another interloper, E. H. Fletcher, a New York publisher with Baptist connections, from issuing an inexpensive, single-volume memoir of Adoniram Judson. At the time of her death in June 1854, Emily Judson saw herself as a legitimate foil to the "Christian pretensions" of this commercial publisher.[231]

In retrospect, Mrs. Judson's obstructionist efforts were both ineffectual and unnecessary. Even though Fletcher's book was released, Wayland's official biography sold 26,000 copies in its first year.[232] It was soon followed by other commemorative works, speaking to different audiences, which continued well into the twentieth century.[233] What Emily Judson ultimately failed to understand was the inspirational effect of the Judsons' story on both authors and audiences and its ability to encourage religious activism. Her efforts to secure for Francis Wayland and herself a monopoly on the Judson audience was, for all intents and purposes, an alien act for an evangelical interested in the widest possible dissemination of the Christian message.

In this respect, Emily Judson still had the perspective of a secular author, the capacity in which she had achieved her greatest success. In fact, her failure to develop a religious reading audience anywhere equal in size to her previous secular readership, may well be attributable to the elimination from her post-1850 writings of what had until then attracted her readers. As a secular writer, she had full play for such elements as humor, sarcasm, romance, and dialogue. In her role as the wife and widow of Adoniram Judson, she bowed to the constraints imposed by the religious community which then failed to buy her work in any significant numbers. Ironically, what she had produced in the "sensation days" of 1844 to 1846 was the wave of the future in American popular culture. Ultimately, in both her life and her work, she became more pious than the woman who had attracted Adoniram Judson.

Chapter 6

Telic Adjustments and Terrestrial Magnetism

As Judson's widow, Emily Chubbuck tried valiantly to reunite the family under one roof in the Baptist stronghold at Hamilton. Upon her death in 1854, the Judson children were left to the care of friends and denominational associates. Despite the many kindnesses bestowed upon them by people who revered their parents, the children were separated from each other, thrust into unfamiliar situations, and watched with intense interest.

In considering the lives of the Judsons' progeny, one is struck by a powerful fact—that none of their children chose careers as foreign missionaries despite the popular identification of their name with that movement. As adults, their public careers demonstrated a worldly orientation that differentiated them from their antebellum progenitors. This decision to pursue secular careers and domestic religious activity was a response both to the changing structure of opportunity in the Gilded Age and, quite likely, to the dislocations and harsh realities they experienced as the children of the first American foreign missionary generation. Although the children's retreat from the piety of their parents was ultimately symptomatic

145

of larger societal changes—changes to be described in the course of this and a subsequent chapter—the retreat surely had a personal dimension as well. Undoubtedly, the intense religious conviction of the Judsons, and the style of living necessitated by that conviction, had consequences for their offspring.

All of the children bore the emotional weight of premature separation from their parents. In the wake of his father's death, George Dana Boardman (1828–1903) was separated from his mother, Sarah, and put on board the ship *Cashmere* to be returned to the United States. Adoniram Judson, his new stepfather, carried him to the boat that would take him to the homeland he had never seen.[1] The boy never saw his mother again. She died in 1845, when he was seventeen, leaving as a memento for her eldest son a pin cushion fashioned from the scraps of her own clothing.[2]

Nine-year-old Abby Ann Judson (1835–1902), born after George left Burma for his American education, nursed her mother through the last months of her life, a period of rapid decline precipitated by the birth of a tenth child. That child, Edward Judson (1844–1913), virtually never knew his mother. While he was still an infant, his father and the older siblings–Abby Ann, Adoniram Brown (1837–1916), and Elnathan (1838–1894)—left Burma for a trip that eventually took them to the United States, leaving Edward and his brother Henry Hall (1842–1918) behind. In America, the three eldest children experienced a painful separation from their father, who, accompanied by his new wife, Emily Chubbuck, returned to Burma without them. The boys were left in the home of the Reverend and Mrs. Edward Bright of Roxbury, Massachusetts. Abby Ann, who was originally placed in the home of the Hasseltines, was soon moved to Philadelphia and put under the care of Emily Judson's friend, Cynthia Sheldon.[3]

In December 1846, when Edward was two years old and Henry Hall was four, the father they hardly knew finally returned to Maulmain, accompanied by a woman designated as their "new Mamma." A year later, there was a baby sister, Emily Frances, born of the union of Adoniram Judson and Emily Chubbuck. When Adoniram died in 1850, the Judson boys were left to their stepmother's care; Edward, the youngest, had known his father for only four years. In the United States, fifteen-year-old Abby Ann heard the news that she would never see her father again.

In 1854, the children lost the last of their parents when Emily Chubbuck Judson died at age thirty-seven after a long illness.[4] To the older children, the loss was least disruptive. George Boardman, whose bonds with Judson's widow were formed of sentiment rather than blood, was already a twenty-six-year-old Baptist clergyman about to marry a young woman from Albany, New York, named Ella Covell.[5] Abby Ann, the eldest of the children born by George's mother in her marriage to Adoniram, was nineteen and preparing for future work as a teacher at the time of her stepmother's death. Adoniram Brown and Elnathan, ages seventeen and sixteen, were living with a Reverend Aldrich at Middleborough, Massachusetts, and preparing for entrance to college.[6]

Baptist friends in and around Hamilton took over the support and nurture of the younger children. Ten-year-old Edward was placed on a permanent basis in the home of the Reverend Ebenezer Dodge, president of Madison University, formerly Hamilton Literary and Theological Institute. Henry Hall, age twelve, was provided for by another local family under the general supervision of the Reverends Edward Bright and James Granger, executors of the estate.[7] In nearby Utica, seven-year-old Emily Frances, her mother's only natural child, was put under the guardianship of Anna Maria Anabel, Chubbuck's longtime friend from her Utica days who inspired the character of "Cousin Bel" in the early Forester stories.

Emily Frances Judson came to maturity within a community that recognized, if not revered, her parents' names. As a girl, she apparently remained in and around Utica, spending time in nearby Hamilton, the hometown of her departed mother. In 1870, at the age of twenty-three, she married Thomas A.T. Hanna, the twenty-eight-year-old pastor of the Central Baptist Church in Williamsburgh, Long Island. A childhood emigré from Ireland, Hanna was a classmate of Emily's half-brother, Edward, who also graduated from Madison University in 1864.[8]

Emily Judson had impeccable credentials for the wife of a Baptist clergyman. Together the young Hannas moved to the Mount Zion Baptist Church in Philadelphia and then traveled abroad from 1874 to 1875 before settling in Plantsville, Connecticut. In that central Connecticut town, both Hannas were increasingly involved with work for the denomination, not solely for the local church. "T.A.T." Hanna became moderator of the New Haven Association, Secretary of the Baptist State Convention, and, in 1881, "missionary of the year" for general fields. Emily Judson Hanna carried on domestic missionary work among a German congregation in nearby

Meridian. Hanna resigned the Plantsville pastorate in 1881 to become Superintendent of Missions for Connecticut, preaching in French, German, and Scandinavian churches. In 1887, the family moved to the pastorate of the Falls of Schuykill Baptist Church in the prestigious Philadelphia Association.[9]

Although the quality of Emily Frances' personal life is unknown, the pattern seems familiar: born the daughter of a venerated Baptist missionary, she married within the denomination, assisted her clergyman husband in his "calls" from one field to another, and bore eight children while tending to the dual obligations of a domestic missionary field and a Victorian home.[10] Her life, which lacked both the struggle and success of her mother's, was shaped by traditional pieties and metered out in the cadence of simpler times.

Many late nineteenth-century religionists, including Emily Hanna's own siblings, did not share this apparent serenity. Industrialization, urbanization, and Darwinian science were altering the American moral as well as material landscape. According to Martin Marty in *The Righteous Empire*, the Civil War shattered the evangelical dream of a homogenous, theocratic, Protestant empire.[11] While some may regard the Gilded Age as a time of "vital regenerative faith," Paul Carter has posited that there was in fact a "Spiritual Crisis," that church-going people had a "rather bad time" as the nineteenth century drew to a close.[12]

Spiritual crisis remains, of course, an essentially private matter, hidden from historical view unless it becomes manifest in patterns of public action and in written documents. In the case of the Judson children, a complete story is limited by a lack of substantive information. It is known that Adoniram Brown Judson became an outstanding orthopedic specialist, publishing over twenty works relating to hip disease and related phenomena,[13] that Henry Hall Judson remained permanently disabled as a result of Civil War service,[14] and that Elnathan Judson was pronounced insane and hospitalized for over thirty years in Worcester, Massachusetts.[15]

Even among children who share a common heritage, considerations of gender, personality, and material circumstances create different patterns. So, too, the erosion of orthodoxy can proceed at varying rates, breaking off bits and pieces of the foundation, and resulting, ultimately, in new configurations. Consequently, the problem of which people experienced spiritual crisis in the Gilded Age, and why they did so, has many answers.

The question then is: can the adult experiences of the children associated with a pivotal foreign mission illuminate the course of evangelical religion and culture in Victorian America? Because the biographies of three of the other children are particularly telling, they comprise the substance of the remaining chapters. What the lives of George Boardman and Abby Ann Judson illustrate is the extent to which those raised on orthodox piety underwent reorientation of their religious convictions. For Gilded Age evangelicals whose education and status had moved them to the brink of modernity, there was no greater intellectual seduction than modern science. Both George Boardman and Abby Ann Judson acted out that infatuation in the course of their lives. In Abby Ann's case, her choice of a "new dispensation" was related to a personal quest for a world view that seemed both modern and emotionally supportive while allowing full authority to women. A final chapter presents the story of Edward Judson and his efforts to memorialize the first Baptist mission to Burma by building a church, in his father's name, at Washington Square, New York City. Although none of the children ever assumed the archetypal proportions of their parents, these three biographies are of considerable interest for what they convey of a new generation and the changing nature of the evangelical mission.

Charles Darwin's *The Origins of the Species* was widely reviewed in America as early as 1860.[16] At first, discussion of the Darwinian thesis and its implications occurred quietly within the professional scientific and religious communities. With the coming of the Civil War, the public discussion of evolutionary theory was delayed as men acted out more immediate questions of survival on the battlefields at Gettysburg and Antietam.

In the two decades after Appomattox, American public attention turned not only to the problems raised by Darwinism but to the general areas of scientific inquiry and applied science. Men like Edward Livingston Youmans made careers as popular lecturers on scientific subjects. In 1872, Youmans founded the *Popular Science Monthly*, an eclectic journal which soon sold 11,000 copies a month because it provided people with access to all kinds of theoretical and applied scientific news and discussion. While the *Popular Science Monthly* was the most notable journalistic success of "the scientific revival,"[17] other magazines and newspapers attempted to feed the American appetite for scientific development. The *North American Review*, *Appleton's*, *Atlantic Monthly*, *Nation*, New York *World*, and New York *Tribune* each ran articles on Darwin and on his most effective popularizer, Herbert Spencer, and carried both supportive and critical analyses by Asa Gray, John Fiske, and Louis Agassiz.[18] Because of popularization and the fact that both *The Origin of Species* and *The Descent of Man* (1871) could be read and generally understood by most educated men and women, the debate over Darwin was not confined to scientific circles. While few nonscientists followed the intricacies of the debate over scientific proof of evolution, most people had, by 1900, an intuitive understanding of the basic question and had encountered Darwin, even in diluted form. Surely, popular skepticism must have intruded on the dinnertime discussions of even church-going Victorian families.

Many of the questions raised by evolutionary theory obviously struck at the heart of orthodoxy. According to Vernon Parrington, "the discovery of a vast impersonal cosmos," such as the one proposed by Darwin, "annihilated the petty egocentric world of good and evil postulated by the theologians."[19] Darwinian answers to the question of how the human species originated cast a long shadow on the evangelical Protestant tradition of biblical inerrancy or literalism. Orthodox religionists were faced with a host of difficult questions rooted in their literal, ancestral faith: if mankind was, in fact, derived from another species, what did that imply for the Book of Genesis, for the story of Adam and Eve? How could the processes of Darwinian evolution, namely, natural selection and survival of the fittest, be reconciled with the Calvinist concept of original sin? Where in the Darwinian scheme of things was there room for God the Creator? And did the currency of Darwin among the American scientific community mean that religious men and women had to forego science? Was the time coming when all "intangible realities" must be turned into measurable laws?

The fact of the matter is that while Darwinism was never embraced by the orthodox, science itself commanded so much attention and prestige that it could not be ignored. Ministers from all the Protestant denominations cultivated avocational interest in the subject and wrote regularly for *Popular Science Monthly*.[20] Unwilling to have religion portrayed as "backward," many who saw themselves as modern preachers concurred with Henry Ward Beecher: "The providence of God is rolling forward a spirit of investigation that Christian ministers must meet and join. There is no class of people upon earth who can less afford to let the development of truth run ahead of them than they."[21] Anxious to establish their own claim to the future, many religious leaders sought to emphasize their basic harmony, rather than discord, with men of science.

Among the evangelical clergy who took up the cause of reconciling science with religion was George Dana Boardman, the eldest son of Sarah Boardman Judson. In 1855, after his graduation from Brown University, Boardman married Ella Covell and began service to a congregation at Barnwell Court House, South Carolina. Although Boardman had been in the South before, his tenure in South Carolina was short-lived. After South Carolinian Preston Brooks clubbed abolitionist Senator Charles Sumner in May 1856 and was hailed as a hero at home, Boardman resigned the pastorate "because he could not conscientiously live among slave holders."[22] He went almost immediately to Rochester, New York, a Baptist stronghold and a center of abolitionist activity. There he assumed the spiritual leadership of the Second Baptist Church, a congregation of nearly 500, and became a close personal friend of Martin B. Anderson, the Baptist president of The University of Rochester. Boardman remained at that post for eight years before being invited in 1864 to the pulpit of the First Baptist Church of Philadelphia, a prestigious congregation dating from the seventeenth century and housed in an impressive Romanesque building on the corners of Broad and Arch. The incentives for coming to Philadelphia were obvious. Besides a somewhat warmer climate, Philadelphia offered $3,000 per year and a generous ten-week vacation; additionally, the church no longer required its clergyman to do pastoral visitations.[23]

The pattern of Boardman's thirty-year career at the First Baptist Church can be explained, in part, by the nature of his position. Free from the time demands of the traditional clerical pattern of personal visitation, he was able to turn instead to writing, public lecturing, and publishing. Between 1878 and 1903, Boardman published twelve books and an enormous number of articles, lectures, and sermons.[24] In Philadelphia, Boardman earned a reputation for his civic-mindedness due to his Wednesday evening biblical exegesis, his Tuesday noon lectures, and his Sunday afternoon presentations to University of Pennsylvania students. In many ways, his lifestyle approximated that of a college professor and made him something of a celebrity in Philadelphia's intellectual galaxy.[25]

With his economic comfort insured and the status of a resident intellectual, Boardman's career was a definite departure from traditional Baptist practice, given its bias against intellectualism and

its preference for material simplicity. Although he joined the city's
evangelical clergy in extending an invitation to revivalist Dwight
Moody in 1875, Boardman's own career was largely uninvolved
with evangelistic conversion techniques or with the mathematics of
bringing on the millennium.[26] In fact, Boardman's ministry in Philadelphia was never expansively evangelical, and most of his time
was spent within circles of people from his own social milieu.

This is not to say that Boardman forsook orthodoxy completely
or that he significantly altered his faith. What he attempted to do
was to push his religious inheritance into the modern world. Yet,
beneath his sophisticated urban patina, Boardman appears to have
spent much of his life wrestling with the intellectual implications of
biblical inerrancy. His writings indicate that he continued to see
biblical exposition as the primary role of the pastor. "To me," he
told his congregation, "the Bible is the one great classic of literature, and I hold its study to be of preeminent importance. The
dominating ideal of my ministry among you [is that] I desire to unfold the word of God as written in the Bible."[27] In retirement,
Boardman would write:

> I am one of those old fashioned students who believe that . . . the
> Bible is still true, and that it has yet many a fresh and authori-
> tative lesson to teach even the swiftly advancing twentieth cen-
> tury.[28]

Thus, Boardman's distance from an earlier generation of Baptist
pietists and from his contemporaries, the popular revivalists, was
marked out in the issues that he chose to address and in his attempt
at a rationalistic interpretation of the heritage of Christian values.
In so doing, he put aside his parents' essentially rural language of
Protestant piety and devotion and keyed his rhetoric to the modern
middle-class of an urban and scientific age.[29]

Because of the phenomenal population growth of American cities, as well as industrialism's ever-widening social and economic re-
percussions, many of the Protestant clergy were forced to examine
the role of their churches in relation to American society. George
Boardman was convinced that the teachings of Jesus and the message of Christian salvation could be applied to the social, political,
and economic problems of his day. This view of religion, as a corrective for the diseases of secular society, was actually a traditional
part of the evangelical litany.

Boardman's orthodox commitment to internal, individual regeneration apparently gave way to a developing social conscience. In 1881, he had written:

How little Jesus Christ makes of surroundings, herein taking issue with the world's philosophers and reformers. They say: "Alter your conditions, and you will alter your character." He [Jesus] says, "Alter your character and you will alter your conditions." After all, the Christian—the man who lives in Jesus Christ—is the only really independent man. Like his Master, he lives above the weather.[30]

By the early 1890s, Boardman was sufficiently moved to join with a fellow Baptist, Walter Rauschenbush, and two other young New York City pastors, Leighton Williams and Nathaniel Schmidt, to create the Brotherhood of the Kingdom, an organization designed to keep the Christian ministry in touch with the common people and to interject the social aims of Jesus into the life of the nation.[31] To accomplish the latter, Boardman charged the churches to "secularize Christianity in order to Christianize secularity."[32]

All of the Brotherhood's interests in the difficult social questions of the day were supposed to be viewed in the light of the religious ideal of the Kingdom of God. Boardman never assailed the social order with the intensity of some of his colleagues in the group, probably because of a lingering ambivalence over the relative primacy of character versus conditions. Neither did he develop the kind of far-reaching economic critique associated with his colleague, Walter Rauschenbush. Thus, Boardman's association with the Brotherhood confirms the connection between antebellum evangelicalism and the Social Gospel but does not place Boardman at the heart of that movement.[33]

Rooted as he was in the foreign missionary tradition, Boardman might also have connected his religious mission to the expansionist foreign policy of the 1890s. Instead, as national attention turned to the Caribbean and the Pacific, Boardman took up the cause of international peace. His pacifism found expression in a number of outlets, including memberships in the Christian Arbitration and Peace Society, Pennsylvania Peace Society, Universal Peace Union, Boston Peace Society, British National Peace Society, La Societé de la Paix, International Bureau de la Paix, Belgian Peace Society, and the International Arbitration and Peace Association.[34]

In 1890, as a representative of the first of these groups, he spoke for the cause of disarmament before a Washington, D.C., audience that included the Secretary of State and members of the Cabinet and Congress.[35] In 1893, he presented his disarmament pleas at the Peace Congress arranged for the Columbian Exposition.[36] He sent his popular pamphlet, "The Disarmament of Nations," to government officials, Booker T. Washington, the Czar of Russia, Queen Victoria, and the Archbishop of Canterbury.[37] President William McKinley apparently read, but ignored, Boardman's treatise before issuing the declaration of war in 1898.[38] In 1901, Boardman wrote the new President, Theodore Roosevelt, that war was an "antiquated policy" in international relations. Boardman spent the years prior to his death in 1903 coupling his peace advocacy with a call for Christian unity. In these last years, he blended his devotion to irenics with a dose of millennialism:

> I believe that the spirit of Jesus Christ will be the dominant force in the coming century; that his Mountain Sermon will become more and more the supreme constitution for Mankind; . . . that Christendom will disarm, that the whole world will become one neighborhood, that human units will grow into human unity, men into man; that the Golden Rule will become more and more the law of society; . . . in brief, that the twentieth century will be in very truth a century of Christocracy.[39]

Boardman had told all who would hear: war violates the spirit of Jesus and the New Testament. "The whole New Testament," he affirmed, "is distinctly and emphatically against all war. . . . I do not think you can cite from it a solitary statement that even hints that Jesus Christ or his apostles ever approved of war."[40]

Boardman's pacifism, however, was only partially based on biblical injunction. In addition to his distinctly evangelical arguments based upon a "right" reading of the text, Boardman rooted his pacifism in a rudimentary social science that regarded society as a social organism. According to his widow, Boardman had a compelling interest in all things scientific and considered himself a "Christian sociologist." Using a biological analogy, he likened the relationship between nations to the body and its specialized component parts, positing that war was the equivalent of disease, self-maiming, or suicide.[41]

Boardman's writings indicate that he paid close attention to modern scientific theory, particularly Darwinian evolution. In fact, his willingness to adopt scientific and quasi-scientific language suggests that, in many respects, he perceived himself as a "harmo-nizer," as one of those special people who could make peace be-tween science and religion.[42] While most of the harmonizers came from within the liberal denominations, Boardman did not. Conse-quently, his efforts to reconcile Darwin with the scriptural account of creation were fraught with special tensions.

Biblical inerrancy was a formidable tradition which Boardman did his best to keep intact, all the while cultivating his own pseudo-scientific, but basically religious, explanations of the natural world. In "The Scriptural Anthropology," an essay published in the *Baptist Quarterly* for April 1867, he distinguished between three compo-nent parts of human nature: *soma* (the body), *psyche* (the soul), and *pneuma* (the spirit).[43] Predictably, it was the latter, identified as the religious faculty, which he considered most important. In an address before the Philadelphia Academy of Natural Sciences, called "Archetypal Forms and Telic Configurations," Boardman demonstrated a fundamental knowledge of the structure of crystals but concluded that the very complexity of crystals pointed to God's power as Creator and Arranger.[44] In 1882, in *Nature a Pledge of Grace: A Sermon Suggested by the Transit of Venus, December 6, 1882*, he posited that the stability of natural laws confirmed the sta-bility of moral law and, therefore, the existence of an omnipotent God.[45]

Although he always upheld the validity of Scripture, Boardman himself was not an absolute literalist. In 1875, more than a decade after Darwin was introduced in America, Boardman wrote the fol-lowing:

> I do not believe that the Creation Record is to be taken literally.
> . . . The words describing creation [are] figurative, or parabolic.
> And parable is the highest form of truth.[46]

The most important thing, claimed Boardman, was the spiritual meaning of the text. This interpretation of the Bible, as a record of spiritual rather than historical truths, left him considerable room to maneuver. He consistently emphasized the didactic qualities of bib-lical study and the manner in which the Bible, unlike Darwin, pre-sented a beneficent vision of the destiny of man:

> Darwin busies himself with what man has been; Paul with what
> he can be. Darwin dwells upon the past and present; Paul looks
> toward the future. Darwin's evolution ends in himself; Paul's evo-
> lution ends in Christ.[47]

In *The Kingdom* (1899), Boardman laid out his position on the great question:

> We hear a great deal said in our day about "Evolution." Whether this doctrine, as applied, at least by some of the scientists who hold it, to the formation (not creation) of the universe is true or not, is, I feel bound to say, an open question. I see but little in the Bible, to oppose it; I see much in the Bible to uphold it.[48]

Essentially, Boardman was a theistic evolutionist, one who accepted the process of gradual development of the species but refused to reconsider the first cause. In his view, life simply could not be the result of some fortuitous natural event; the evolutionary process, which he granted, had unfolded "along the ideal of a Divine thought out plan."[49] As for natural selection and Darwinian nomenclature: Boardman believed that God envisioned general archetypal forms that were shaped by new conditions and environments. God was the ultimate Arranger of the universe and a professor of taxonomy, to boot. "What Mr. Darwin calls Natural Selection," Boardman wrote, "I would call God's Telic Adjustment, configuring the Archetypal Form to a special need."[50] Darwinism, then, pressed to its logical conclusions, led inevitably to God.

Despite his intention to harmonize, George Boardman was never able to bring science and religion into accord in his own work. All of his writing on the subject is based on the assumption that the natural and the spiritual are two distinct ontological categories, that science (the natural) and religion (the spiritual) are like two parallel lines. Boardman wrote repeatedly that there were really two Bibles: one scriptural, the other based in the natural world.[51] In 1903, in *Ethics of the Body*, he asserted that science and religion "are complemental, science being the natural side of religion, religion being the spiritual side of science."[52]

Even though Boardman posited that the natural and spiritual worlds were complemental and equally legitimate, he inevitably placed science in a subservient role. For him, the parallel lines really could intersect, but only at the point where science served the larger spiritual mission. Religion, he wrote, had nothing to fear from science because "when science does discover a new fact, it will also discover that the Bible has from the outset morally implicated it."[53] If, as Boardman stated, all the discoveries that resulted from modern scientific investigation were foreshadowed in the Bible, then science was simply the name given to another new technique in the seminally important field of biblical criticism.[54] Boardman proved himself to be a consummately orthodox evangelical on this issue: no matter where contemporary intellectual currents took him, he ultimately returned to the Bible. "Science has no higher calling then to decipher the Scriptural cipher," he explained.[55]

In minimizing the importance of scientific facts, Boardman revealed the true nature of his position: he admired scientific language but did not admit the significance of the scientific process. According to his own description, discoveries of important new information, either about the geological formation of the earth or the biological origins of humankind, led him to Scripture, which he then used as a concordance to help him interpret the natural world. If Boardman was as unscientific as this process suggests, why did he adopt so much pseudo-scientific language and why is his writing fraught with so many allusions to the biological and physical sciences?

What Boardman exhibited in his attraction to modern science was a constitutional evangelical predisposition. In their commitment to the continued expansion of Gospel Christianity, evangelicals were inextricably tied to the rhythms of popular culture. Christianity, they believed, was best dispensed in the forms that people liked and found comfortable. Just as his stepfather, Adoniram Judson, argued that Emily Chubbuck's fiction could be drawn in such a way that it embodied moral truths, Boardman was willing and eager to develop a superficially scientific vocabulary for religious ends.

If sentimental fiction was the growing infatuation of the 1840s, science was a central intellectual seduction of the Gilded Age. George Boardman, who considered himself a modernist, was not immune. In his selective acceptance of scientific discoveries, he demonstrated the way in which evangelical religion could absorb secular trends without altering its own essential message. In the case of nineteenth-century science, the accommodation was made possible by the naive way in which Boardman chose to read Darwin and others—not as spokesmen for a basic intellectual process with a modern world view, but as technicians with new tools for explaining old verities.

In a very real sense, George Boardman discarded the intense Christian piety that was the hallmark of his parents' day. In its place, he substituted a brand of Christian cosmopolitanism that allowed him to mix easily in a complex, pluralistic society and still serve evangelical ends.[56] With even a nominally scientific outlook as part of his public persona, Reverend Boardman appeared to be in step with the music of his times.

In faraway Minneapolis, Boardman's half-sister heard the same music but played it with a different coda. In 1890, after fifty years of practicing Gospel Christianity, Abby Ann Judson proclaimed herself a Spiritualist, a believer in direct communication with disembodied spirits. This sudden departure from the orthodox tradition was certainly controversial, a fact which the Spiritualist weekly, *Banner of Light*, did not fail to point out:

> It was with feelings of profound surprise that the Church listened to a report that the daughter of Dr. Judson had renounced her former belief, or rather non-belief, became a Spiritualist, and was zealously engaged in advancing a knowledge of the truths of modern Spiritualism; that she had organized a Spiritualist society in a western city and was its inspired teacher . . . it remains to be seen in what manner the Christian world will regard one of their own who, having seen a great light, turns her face toward it, even though in doing so she is forced to turn from ways that for nearly half a century she has followed.[57]

For the Spiritualists, Abby Ann Judson was an important, identifiable convert. In the decades ahead, she proved herself an able lecturer for the cause and demonstrated a willingness to use her celebrity status to its best advantage. In a typical lecture series, such as the one given before the First Spiritual Society of Lowell, Massachusetts, in 1895, she included a talk on "reminiscences of life in Burmah, and the way in which [she] was led out of the gloomy depths of dogmatic Calvinism on to the bright uplands of Spiritualism."[58]

Like many who were attracted to Spiritualism in post-Civil War America, the explanation of her new faith was couched in terms of free, scientific inquiry.[59] Because the techniques of scientific argument were familiar to her, Judson asserted that Spiritualism rested on observable facts—things that people could see, or touch, or hear. In the spirit of scientific inquiry, "I would investigate the subject to see how much fraud, how much delusion, and how much imagination was in play," reported Abby Ann. Her aim, she claimed, was empirical knowledge. "I entered upon this investigation with a candid mind and a desire for real truth, wherever it might lead," she explained, assuming the stance of an independent, scholarly investigator.[60] When asked if there was life beyond the

grave, Judson replied, "This question, like every one in this generation must be answered on a scientific basis," and, then, she recommended Spiritualism.[61]

Judson's belief, which was based on the notion of progression in
the physical and spiritual worlds, indicates the ways in which Spiritualism incorporated elements of evolutionary theory and still allowed room for the presence of God the Creator. Judson told an
1896 audience in Greenwich, Connecticut: "All living germs
whether implanted in the most simple organism, as the early
moner,[62] or the most complex, as that of man himself, have the law
of progress stamped on their being."[63] The year before, in an address before the Massachusetts Convention of Spiritualists entitled
"Why I am Opposed to Vivesection," this errant child of orthodoxy
presented her world view:

> Nature is an affect, of which God is the cause. God is life, and this
> life always works from lower to higher. The lowest organic forms
> share in this divine life: From crystal to moner, from moner to
> amoeba, from simple to complex, and more and more complex,
> the sensations ever becoming more acute, until the various grades
> of mammals appeared on our planet, reaching their acme in man.
> . . . The life in a man or woman is no more truly a part of infinite
> life, or God, than is the life of the lowest creature on earth. With
> the advancement in the forms of life has gradually evolved the su-
> premacy of mind over mere physical force.[64]

For Judson and her Spiritualist compatriots, the law of progress
had its most important application in the realm of mind or spirit.
The typical late nineteenth-century Spiritualist believed that all individual souls had a continued existence after death, a term that
they generally exorcised from their vocabularies. Because individual spirits survived the demise of their "physical husks," the moment when biological life ceased was termed the "transition." After
the transition, individual spirits were never reincarnated but continued their progress toward perfection, ultimately becoming part
of the infinite soul of the universe.

In the effort to explain their philosophy, Spiritualists oftentimes
invoked the name of Emerson. In an 1895 essay for the "Woman's
Souvenir Number" of the *Banner of Light*, Judson reported the following anecdote:

> . . . Ralph Waldo Emerson was an ideal Spiritualist. Someone
> once said to him, "They say the world is coming to an end." "Very
> well," said Mr. Emerson, "I can do without it."[65]

Judson found Emerson's stance admirable because it demonstrated a basic alienation from the world and the flesh. What separated the Emersonian concept of the Over-Soul from Judson's construct of "infinite soul" was that the latter, according to Spiritualist belief, was empirically based.

Good Spiritualists worked throughout their lives on earth to develop an independence of the material world. In this process, they were sensitized to communication with disembodied spirits and often acted as conduits, or mediums, through which spirits might contact those who remained "below" or "behind" in earthly bodies. Abby Ann Judson, like so many who shared her enthusiasm for the "new dispensation," followed a seemingly scientific system for building receptivity to spirits, broadly known as "soul culture." A significant portion of her public lecturing revolved around this theme, as did some of her books.

In *Development of Mediumship By Terrestrial Magnetism* (1891), Judson espoused techniques for cultivating increased receptivity to disembodied spirits. Terrestrial magnetism referred to magnetic, or electric, currents that allegedly flowed between the temporal and spirit worlds. Because Judson believed one side of the body was positive and the other negative, she diagramed exercises that would improve receptivity to spirit communication. In addition, she included recommendations on diet, clothing, exercise, and sexual practice. She made medical claims that the conditions requisite for the proper functioning of spirit communication could also cure insomnia, overweight, and even organic disorders. The ultimate proof of the scientific nature of Spiritualism came from data collected at the séance where believers found empirical proof of disembodied spirits in the forms of alphabetical rappings, table tipping and knockings, spirit music, signs from the planchette, and materialization.

Judson was critical of contemporary Christian orthodoxy precisely because it failed to admit empirical inquiry. "The religion doled out to American babes in the last century," she wrote, "is a sort that a reasonable man, who thinks without shackles, does not receive."[66] Particularly adamant on the subject of Christian miracles, Judson repeatedly asserted that there was no supernatural, that the things "fancied" to be so by "the old theologians, as a direct revelation from God Almighty in the Hebrew Scriptures, [i.e.] the resurrection of the fleshly body of Jesus and the so-called miracles of him and his apostles, never transcended nature at all."[67]

For Abby Ann Judson, it was not that these events could not or

had not occurred. In fact, she believed that they had but that traditional Christianity resorted to reactionary interpretations. "The
'miracles' were all in accordance with natural forces, misunder-
stood in that ignorant age," she wrote in the *Banner of Light*.[68] Judson undoubtedly saw herself as a modernist, as part of what she
called "the new orthodoxy, the vanguard of which is led by Spiritualists, advocating progression of every kind. . . ."[69] She wrote also to
her former associates in the Christian church explaining the essential difference in their faith: "Friends, progression is a better thing
than redemption or salvation; development is better than fall; and
continued and advancing life is better than resurrection."[70]

In 1894, Abby Ann Judson published *From Night to Morn; or
An Appeal to the Baptist Church*, documenting her complaints
against Christian orthodoxy and signifying her ultimate rejection of
the evangelical credo. In her critique of organized Protestantism,
she dismissed the concepts of the Trinity, human depravity, predestination, vicarious atonement, a final judgment, conversion, and a
divinely inspired Bible.[71] In *The Bridge Between Two Worlds*
(1894), she faulted the apostle Paul for the "Jewish materialistic notion" of Christ's physical resurrection which she considered an
"absurdity."[72] Despite the legacy of her parents' careers, she admitted that she found it increasingly difficult "to believe that all who
were not evangelically converted should be in a hell of torment forever."[73]

Judson took contemporary Christianity to task for its worldly
nature, despising its sectarian quality and calling it a "set of
creeds."[74] As a Spiritualist, she considered all religions equally irrelevant to the larger process of identifying oneself with the infinite
soul of the universe:

> All creeds have been useful to certain souls at certain periods of
> human development, but no creed of a less advanced age will ex-
> press the consciousness of the human race as it goes on to the
> ultimatum of development.[75]

Of all the archaic religions, Christianity had deteriorated more
than the others, causing it to be "less spiritual" than either Moham-
medanism or Confucianism.[76]

Judson maintained that Jesus was "the most perfect medium between mortal man and the spirit world."[77] Unfortunately, Jesus's
church had "won its way to temporal rule by intolerance, torture
and blood; and has opposed every human reform that the progress
of the race has brought to the front, being in this decade the ad-

vocate of monopoly and of the money power."[78] Although Christianity was founded by "one [who was] truly spiritual," it had become mired in the politics of the world.

Judson's disillusionment with Christian orthodoxy went unrevealed until later in life. Between the time of Emily Judson's death in 1854 and her own removal to Minneapolis in 1879, Abby Ann was associated with schools in Worcester, Bradford, and Plymouth, Massachusetts; in Warren, Rhode Island, and in College Hill, Ohio. She was also a governess for some time with families in New York City, Albany, and Fall River. From 1869 to 1875, she taught in the high school at Plymouth, Massachusetts, her father's hometown.[79] In 1879, at the age of forty-four, she moved to Minneapolis where she founded and became principal of the Judson Female Institute, an interdenominational Christian school for girls in which the Bible was read daily and "its truths made the basis of moral teaching."[80] She later confessed that when she became principal of the seminary she felt compelled to "keep her Spiritualism quiet."[81] Given her name, her position, and her associates, she was, understandably, reluctant to identify herself with the Spiritualist movement, despite the fact that it had achieved some degree of popularity in the 1870s.[82]

Although she claimed that she had never heard of "materialization," "circles," "séances," "controls," "going under influence," or "conditions" before the fall of 1887, Judson liked to recount the secret history of her move to Spiritualism. She told American Baptists that after surviving a forbidden interdenominational communion service while a student in Hanover, New Hampshire, she began to question the validity of any sect that codified a set of beliefs. In June 1854, when she was seventeen, Abby Ann Judson saw her first spirit incarnation, "a white form."[83] The following day her stepmother died at Hamilton.

Judson tended to link her own experiences to those of her mother and stepmother. She reported that Emily Judson was always "troubled" with religious doubts, that in the awful months in 1850 when Adoniram's fate was unknown, Emily longed to have his spirit visit her and "tell her if he was dead."[84] Abby Ann also found religious ambivalence in the life of her sainted mother, Sarah:

My father and Ann [Hasseltine] never doubted after their conversion; but my precious mother, so loving, devoted and intuitive, was troubled at times by painful doubts. I well know this from the conversations I heard as a child. There was in her a constant strife between her determination to cling to what is orthodoxy and her intuitive perceptions of infinite justice and love.[85]

To hear her tell it, Judson spent the major portion of her adult years, as she believed her mother had, trying to reconcile her inherited orthodoxy with a developing belief in the existence of individual spirits outside the body. Throughout the 1880s, she maintained her connections with the Baptist community in Minneapolis, proceeding with her "church work, Bible class, work with the Temple Builders, . . . and commenting on the scripture that [was] read daily in her seminary."[86] She found that her minister, Dr. William T. Chase, shared her belief that it was Christ's spiritual rather than physical body that clothed him after the Resurrection. So long as Chase remained in the pulpit of the First Baptist Church of Minneapolis, Abby Ann Judson continued her traditional association, praising her pastor for his "disposition to probe to the bottom of every subject he undertook" and masking her own orientation to the spirit world.[87]

An incident involving the death of a Reverend Wilder, sometime in 1887, provided Abby Ann Judson with what she considered proof of the existence of disembodied spirits. Some weeks before Wilder's death, his son's fiancee died. The family chose not to tell the ailing pastor who was fond of the young woman, named Dell. As Wilder lay dying, he began to talk to persons whom others in the room could not see. After speaking to many who were known to be among the dead, Wilder burst out: "Why, Dell, are you there?"[88] Confident that Wilder had no prior knowledge of the young woman's demise, Judson certified the existence of Dell's spirit in Wilder's home.

In December 1887, as she sat with two women friends in the recitation room of the Judson Institute, Abby Ann Judson received her first visit from the spirit of her father. Afterwards, she testified that neither of the two women knew anything about Baptist missions or her early life in Burma. However, the spirit communicating with her knew Burmese names and places and was able to quote the last words of her mother, which were unknown to anyone outside the Judson family.[89] Within the year, she began to "discern other spirits," including an infant sister who allegedly died in 1839, and the wives of other missionaries to Burma. In August 1888, when the centenary of her father's birth was celebrated at Malden, Massachusetts, Abby Ann Judson sent the following message to mark the occasion:

> Adoniram Judson has been alive one hundred years. Nearly two-thirds of this time he dwelt here in the flesh. The remaining years of this century of existence he has dwelt in the land of souls. But he is not idle there. He is not dead.[90]

Although the Malden audience probably regarded the letter as her solemn tribute to Adoniram's continued influence, Abby Ann knew differently. She said of her centenary contribution: "It was Spiritualism from the beginning to end, except that the *word* was not used."[91]

Inevitably, she came into conflict with the new pastor of the First Baptist Church, Dr. Wayland Hoyt. In April 1890, she ceased attending Bible classes and in May "disposed" of her school.[92] Because of Dr. Hoyt's "unfavorable allusions to Spiritualism" and her discomfort in the church, Abby Ann Judson finally left the denomination of her birth. In the very same year that her secret history became a public issue, her pastor, Dr. Hoyt, contributed $50 towards the Adoniram Judson Memorial Baptist Church Edifice Fund administered by her brother Edward in New York City. "There was no place for me in the [Baptist] church," she later wrote:

> . . . the pastor and those whom he influenced were against me. They were against me, not because of my character or my works. They were against me because I had found evidence that my father and other dead friends were sometimes with me to influence and help me, and could, on rare occasions, even communicate with me.[93]

During the summer of 1890, after her position became known, Judson left Minneapolis and attended a Spiritualist camp meeting at a site called Mt. Pleasant, on the bluffs overlooking the river near Clinton, Iowa.[94] Upon her return to the city, she formed a Spiritualist association and began giving public lectures. Within the next year she left Minneapolis and "went alone, from town to town and from state to state to spread far and wide the light of the New Dispensation."[95]

From 1890 to 1896, Judson traveled extensively from Illinois and Missouri to Philadelphia, Boston, and points in between, relying upon a network of Spiritualist associations to generate engagements for her.[96] During her itinerancy period, she sent letters to the

Banner of Light describing her experiences. From St. Louis, she wrote about her stay in Decatur, Illinois:

I found there a struggling persistent little society, meeting in the parlour of one of its members each Sunday, and dependent usually on local inspirational and mediumistic talent. My heart goes out to these many towns, all through our great country, either crying for the light, or else sunk in the apathy of creedal bondage and conventionality. Do we need more faithful workers who will go like those sent through Palestine by the great medium of Nazareth, without scrip and only a staff in hand?[97]

Given her differences with Christian doctrine, Judson's style was still distinctly evangelical. In Attleborough, Massachusetts, she was heralded as the "missionary of liberalism."[98] "Church-going people," drawn to hear her because she was the daughter of missionaries, were not uncomfortable with her blend of evangelical emotion and pseudo-scientific fare. For example, in Melrose Highlands, Massachusetts, in 1895, Judson's theme was "Shall We Know Each Other There?" She gave the following answer, drawn from her repertoire of Spiritualist explanations:

By psychical development in accord with natural forces, we may while still envisioned in the flesh, cognize the spirit-world, or the condition of a far more rapid vibration; and thus clairvoyance, clairaudience, and clairsentience are not abnormal. They are normal, and indicate that the inner consciousness can cognize an outside world by the use of its psychical body, as well as by the sense of the fleshly body. These things being so, we need not ask whether we shall know our friends after we leave the physical body. . . . It would be against nature and natural law if we did not.[99]

Despite her heavy reliance on Spiritualist terminology, Judson claimed that her audience was visibly moved. In fact, she described their reactions in terms reminiscent of the revival and the manner in which converted Christians turned their thoughts to reunions in a celestial heaven:

The glorious fact of personal recognition beyond the grave was put upon a scientific basis, and tears on many faces attested to the tenderness awakened in our hearts by the anticipation of meeting and clasping our loved ones by and by—not as uncanny ghosts, not as denuded souls, but as truly and naturally as when we dwelt together in the earth-life.[100]

Similarly, Judson had a successful engagement in Waverly, New York, where she reveled in the way "church-going people" responded to her message, dropping their "old fetters" and walking "with sandals loose" upon the "sunny heights" of her new faith.[101]

In March 1895, Judson reported a schedule of her forthcoming Sunday appearances in the *Banner*. "My engagements during the remainder of the season are as follows," she wrote:

> March 24 and 31, Haverhill; April 7 and 14, Meridian, Connecticut; April 21, Manchester, N.H.; April 28, Malden, Massachusetts; May 12 and 19, Lawrence, Massachusetts; June 2 and 9, Stafford, Connecticut. During the above I will, if my physical strength permits, speak once a week between Sunday services in any town near the one where I am engaged.[102]

In the effort to secure longer engagements, Judson explained to the readership that these "constant kaleidoscopic changes" sapped her strength and "frittered away" her influence.

Judson's audience actually extended beyond the parlors and halls where people came to see and hear her. Between 1891 and 1899, she published five books: *Why She Became A Spiritualist* (1891); *From Night to Morn; or An Appeal to the Baptist Church* (1894); *The Bridge Between Two Worlds* (1894); *Development of Mediumship by Terrestrial Magnetism* (1891); and *A Happy Year: or Fifty Two Letters to the Banner of Light* (1899). All noted on their title pages that the author was the daughter of Adoniram Judson. Each also included, in abbreviated or complete form, transcripts of "inspired utterances" that Judson received, through a medium, from the disembodied spirit of her father.

Abby Ann Judson began communication with her father's spirit while she was still in Minneapolis. Seated before a window on a sunny Thanksgiving morning in 1888, she saw her father's etherialized form. "I found myself in my father's arms," she later wrote, "and we held tender converse together." On the same occasion her Grandmother Judson, whom she "never saw in earth life," materialized before her. Overcome by what was happening, she immediately felt a "great force" that "bowed [her] head into [her] lap." "I did not like it and moaned," she reported, and soon the spirits faded wholly away.[103]

Judson's descriptions of the time and location of spirit communications with her parents were factually inconsistent but always evoked the memory of their premature separation and their life in

Burma. Typical of these recitations is this account from *The Bridge Between Two Worlds*:

> . . . one day being weary from sweeping a large school room, I went into my parlour and sat down to rest in a large easy-chair. I was thinking of nothing in particular, was expecting nothing, was therefore perfectly passive, and found myself sitting in my father's arms! The forty years since he had passed to spirit life were annihilated, I was a child again and was held to his breast again by his loving fatherly arms. This was not fancy nor phantasy—*I felt his arms*. I spoke to him and he to me.[104]

Judson qualified this account of her contact with her father in this way: "He did not materialize on this occasion. It was my spirit body that he held in his spiritual arms, and we talked together just as we shall by and by when I shall be so happy as to have left forever the inswathing tabernacle of clay." Because she considered materialization unnecessary where there was true faith in the spirit world, Judson explained: "My father never materializes for me. I should be very sorry to have him do so, for it is not necessary."[105]

Unwilling to make materialization the absolute proof of the presence of Adoniram's spiritual existence, Abby Ann turned to mediums to bring her another kind of verifiable evidence in the form of testimony from the spirit world. In *Why She Became A Spiritualist*, Abby Ann reported communicating with both parents by means of an independent "slate writer."[106] According to this report, her father was in sympathy with her Spiritualist convictions and concerned about her brother Edward, the New York clergyman, because he had not adopted the new faith. Judson supposedly sent the following message: "How best to unfold the soul is the question. I am anxious that Edward should enjoy the truth."[107]

Four years later, in a communication received from Mrs. R.S. Lillie, a medium, Adoniram Judson's spirit praised his daughter for her public efforts on behalf of the spirit world and referred again to her erring brothers:

> The light is spreading, and most people are breaking some fetters, and your brothers will yet see the light. [George] who has been kindest to you, and who has least to fear of men will receive this light, and walk in it, acknowledging it before men. His added testimony will have effect with the others, and before they pass on, they will know that you have been in the right.[108]

In *Night to Morn,* her personal statement to the Baptists of America, Abby Ann again claimed that she alone had the support and encouragement of the spirits of Adoniram and Sarah Judson:

> . . . though my brothers may never recognize the existence of the spirit world until they pass into the clearer light of the world beyond, our parents rejoice over me with a yet greater joy, because to me it has been vouchsafed to receive direct evidence of spirit existence, and of life, in spite of death and the grave, and to know that they are often with me with their sympathy and love.[109]

Neither the brothers nor the evangelical community could have anticipated Abby Ann's startling new use of the family name and tradition. While she discredited the faith of her brothers in her books, Judson's columns in the weekly *Banner of Light* often contained information about family relationships—information that was designed to dispel rumors that she had been rejected by them. During the autumn of 1894, she made her first trip to the East to visit family since her adoption of the Spiritualist faith four years before. She stayed with her mother's surviving brothers, George and Charles Hall, and her Aunt Nancy at Skaneateles Lake before journeying to New York City for a twenty-four-hour visit with her younger brothers, Edward, the clergyman, and Adoniram Brown, the surgeon. In the *Banner* she praised them for their honorable work and presented a picture of a cordial, respectful reunion:

> They are both doing noble work for humanity in their chosen lines, and very kind were they to their sister, though she has departed from the lines of thought which they still hold dear—they would be poor Christians, and I would be a poor Spiritualist if we loved each other less fondly than of yore because we do not see all things in heaven and earth in the same light. If they were bigoted or harsh, or if I were the same, it would be more difficult. Anyway, let us all love each other for what we really *are*, and not for the sort of glimpse that we may get of eternal truth.[110]

On another occasion she wrote that she was frequently asked in conversation, "How do your ministerial brothers in New York and Philadelphia receive you?" Her reply was that Edward Judson and George Boardman were "right brotherly," although they were "not yet ready to receive her truth." Yet, "blood is thicker than water," Abby Ann affirmed, "and it is sweet to know that the links that will continue to bind members of the same family together in the spirit-world have begun to brighten here."[111]

Of course, what Judson did not discuss publicly was her brothers' reactions to her claims of communication with their sainted parents. In the absence of a transcript or supporting correspondence, it is impossible to tell what really happened in the brief twenty-four hours the three children were together. Was her brothers' reported kindness simply the careful handling that is meted out to those who are considered unbalanced? Did kindness mean that her brothers avoided the delicate issue of how she communicated with their sainted father? Or did kindness imply that they spoke openly to one another, evaluating Abby Ann's claims in a civil, detached manner—as though she were not one of their own and as though the family's tradition carried no special meaning?

The personal dynamics of the 1894 Judson reunion are probably obscured forever. On the other hand, it makes sense to point out that the structure of Abby Ann's belief did not allow for alienation of affection on religious grounds. No matter how much her brothers may have berated her for turning her back on the Baptist faith or for invoking their parents' names and reputations in a disreputable cause, she could not cease to love them. She regarded her brothers' creed, after all, as an expression of an "ignorant age" for which they should be forgiven. Her Spiritualist belief held the comforting promise of reunion with all her family after death, as well as advice and support from her parents' spirits in the time remaining for her here on earth.

The fact that she wrote and spoke so lovingly of the comfort provided by the disembodied spirits of her parents must have attracted others who were bereaved or had experienced some significant loss.[112] One can only speculate as to how many people were attracted to Spiritualism by the prospect of conversing with the spirits of deceased luminaries like Adoniram Judson. The possibilities, of course, were limitless and must have included the "medium of Nazareth," Jesus himself. In fact, Abby Ann claimed to have had a conversation, channeled through her father, with Jonathan Edwards. The disembodied spirit of the eighteenth-century divine allegedly gave her a number of cryptic but encouraging messages, including, "Dear Friend, my mission to earth was to enlighten the world. You have taught in your way. You are called to a higher school."[113]

Abby Ann's propensity for using her father's name in support of the Spiritualist cause was demonstrated in the twenty-first chapter of *The Bridge Between Two Worlds*, where she attached verbatim copies of communications received from the spirit of Adoniram Judson. Her invocation of her father's reputation, and her attribution to him of a Spiritualist point of view, constituted a religious endorsement. Through these communications, Adoniram's spirit spoke directly to the question of his daughter's legitimacy, as his spiritual heir, stating unequivocally that hers was a new and "great truth." "The great mass of mankind who knew me once," Judson reportedly said, "must know me again through you."[114] His admission of the power of the "new dispensation" was expressed in a single statement, indicating a commitment to continual spiritual development: "I fell at my post battling for the right, as I then conceived it."[115]

In a manner that was characteristic of the nineteenth-century evangelical, Adoniram Judson's spirit lauded his daughter's published works for the influence they had: "Your book has accomplished a great deal more than you know of, while it is my pleasure to see and sense much more than you can."[116] Like the man who gave the Bible to the Burmese, Abby Ann Judson saw the progress of her new faith linked to her capacity as a publicist, an essentially evangelical technique.

The verbatim words of the disembodied spirit of Adoniram Judson were regarded by his daughter as empirical evidence that the spirit world was alive and functioning. Wherever she traveled and whenever she wrote, Abby Ann Judson described the solace and joy that she found in communing with her departed parents, regardless of whether or not they materialized completely. Evidences from the séance and the medium, which were so important to Judson's own identity as a Spiritualist, inevitably became the movement's primary drawing card and, also, the source of its major criticism.

In an 1895 issue of the *Banner of Light*, Judson asked the question that plagued Spiritualists everywhere: "Is Spiritualism synonymous with mediumship?" Judson's response was pointed:

Many use the two terms [Spiritualism and mediumship] interchangeably. Some become Spiritualists because they have been told that they could become mediums; if their powers do not develop as they expected, they give up being Spiritualists. Many Spiritualists of long standing claim that Spiritualism is the same as mediumship. While we all know that knowledge of the continuity of life first comes to most of us through a medium, . . . Spiritualism as an agent for the development of the inner soul, and of the race in general, involves far more than that first knowledge.[117]

Judson believed that good Spiritualists were made by their serious preparation for life on "the other side," not by mere accumulation of proofs of spirit existence. She was impatient with those who rested their Spiritualist belief on the capacity of mediums to produce such evidence of a spirit's presence as raps, tips, independent slate writing, music, or materialization. While nonbelievers clamored for demonstrations of these mediumistic powers, Judson urged true Spiritualists to prepare instead for their own continued existence "by living aright, in thought and word and deed."[118] Having "sold" the faith as an answer to scientific skepticism, the popular interest in seeing and hearing spirits pushed many in the movement to the point where they disavowed mediums entirely, particularly those for whom mediumship was a paying occupation.

Abby Ann Judson, who relied on mediums for much of her own important communication with her parents, wrote repeatedly of the need to establish the benign character of mediums. "It is often said," she remarked, "that we should not demand moral character in our mediums, that all the spirits want is an organism through which they can communicate. We think this doctrine is a pernicious one, and a main cause of the disrepute of what is called Modern Spiritualism."[119]

In *The Bridge Between Two Worlds*, Judson wrote extensively about the problems of unenlightened mediumship and the need to move, ultimately, beyond material proof of the spirit world. She disavowed all uses of mediumistic talent that either limited individual decision making or involved making financial decisions. "It is pitiable," she wrote, "to see a medium encouraging these tendencies in a spirit in order to aid her [the medium] to make money for grasping men by her 'gifts' as a 'business medium.' Such a use of mediumistic power is a prostitution of the gift."[120]

Judson's derogatory use of the term prostitution was probably no accident and signified where she stood. Spiritualist women in Victorian America were likely to be characterized in terms of sexual impropriety for a number of reasons. As R. Laurence Moore has so aptly pointed out in his scholarly study of nineteenth-century Spiritualism, *In Search of White Crows: Spiritualism and Parapsychology in American Culture*, the profession of mediumship was disproportionately female, or at least was perceived as such. For many, mediumship represented the ultimate corruption of femininity in that women as mediums used their allegedly feminine virtues of passivity and sensitivity to provide questionable services for money. Additionally, female mediums gave public performances, in defiance of the Pauline proscription against such activity, and were tied, through a number of notorious cases, to divorce and infidelity.[121]

The flamboyant career of Victoria Claffin Woodhull, the Feminist candidate for the presidency in 1872, shaped many a Victorian's thinking on what Spiritualism was all about. Having declared her personal advocacy of free love from the rostrum at Steinway Hall, New York City, in 1871, "The Woodhull's" notoriety grew when she charged the distinguished minister, Henry Ward Beecher, with adultery involving the wife of a friend and parishioner. Woodhull, who was an outspoken critic of conventional Victorian sexual mores, met her second husband, Colonel James Harvey Blood, through a "clairvoyant consultation" in St. Louis. They became lovers, divorced their respective mates, and took up Spiritualism together. Victoria's service as president of the American Association of Spiritualists in the 1870s helped link women's rights, free love, and Spiritualism in the public mind.[122]

Spiritualism's reform orientation was similarly revealed in the careers of three popular mediums, Laura Cuppy, Eliza Pitsinger, and Cora Hatch—all of whom considered feminism a logical outgrowth of their faith in progression.[123] Judson, who obviously sought to dispel any association between Spiritualist mediumship and sexual impropriety, wrote in March 1898: "It gives a true lover of Spiritualism a great pain to hear this constant cry of fraud by its opponents and when to the disgraceful fraud is added the still more opprobrious term of filth, it requires some nerve to say unflinchingly in the face of those who revile the name, 'Yes, I am a Spiritualist.'"[124]

"It was not just the half-baked, the uneducated and the credulous who appeared at séances or spirit circles," writes R. Laurence Moore. In fact, the number of Americans who experimented with spirit manifestations is intriguing and included such well-known nineteenth-century figures as Alexander Jackson Downing, William Lloyd Garrison, George Ripley, Benjamin Wade, Horace Greeley, Rufus W. Griswold, Lydia Maria Child, William Cullen Bryant,

Robert Owen, William Dean Howells, Benjamin O. Flower, Nathaniel Parker Willis, James Fenimore Cooper, George Bancroft, Hamlin Garland, and Harriet Beecher Stowe.[125] At the turn of the century, a wealthy Geneva, New York, nurseryman, William Smith, was dissuaded from founding an expressly Spiritualist college for women on the shores of Seneca Lake. Smith, who was simultaneously interested in all things scientific, built his own observatory and hired William R. Brooks, the noted comet discoverer, to move to Geneva as his personal resident astronomer.[126] In Britain, science and Spiritualism were fused in the life and career of Alfred Russell Wallace, Darwin's collaborator and a proponent of political and social equality for women.[127]

The relationship between Spiritualism and nineteenth-century Feminism remains tenuous because it requires greater clarification and definition. It is germane to point out, however, that the two causes were fused in the life of the daughter of another distinguished evangelical family, Isabella Beecher Hooker (1822–1907). For the youngest daughter of Lyman Beecher, participation in the Abolition, Dress Reform, and Women's Rights movements was preparatory to her adoption, in the 1870s, of a radical suffrage view, and then Spiritualism, both of which were embodied in her personal and public support of Victoria Woodhull. According to Marie Caskey, a recent biographer of the Beecher family, Isabella, in the years after 1877, became increasingly preoccupied with spirit manifestations. Following the death of her daughter, Mary, in 1876, she not only spoke with Mary's disembodied spirit but saw her materialize on a mountaintop.[128]

In a number of rather obvious ways, Spiritualism provided women like Abby Ann Judson with positions of religious authority that were not available to them in the evangelical denominations. In the 1870s, Cora L.V. Richmond, as well as the flamboyant Woodhull, served as pastors of the National Spiritualist Association headquartered in Chicago.[129] A cursory view of the structure of Spiritualist associations in the decade of the 1890s reveals that women were as likely as men to be presidents of the local associations.[130] Just as Donald Meyer suggested for "mind-cure" in the *Positive Thinkers*, Spiritualism can be read as a grasping for female power within a religious context.[131] Spiritualist doctrine itself, with its emphasis on direct communication with the spirit world, effectively circumvented male-dominated church hierarchies. Finally, Spiritualist

women were able to pursue careers as mediums and as public lecturers and writers. Elizabeth Stuart Phelps (Ward) (1844–1911)
wrote *The Gates Ajar*, a Spiritualist novel that sold 80,000 copies in
the   United States in the three decades after its publication in
1868.[132] Phelps, who was married but wrote under her own name,
was the granddaughter of Moses Stuart, a president of Andover
Theological Seminary, the Congregationalist institution where
Adoniram Judson prepared for the ministry. Her father, Austin
Phelps, was Professor of Sacred Rhetoric and Homiletics at Andover
at the time the best-selling novel was issued. Thus, Elizabeth Stuart
Phelps provides another example of how the daughters of orthodoxy
had moved into the realm of popular culture, tasting the fruits of
science and modernity.

Abby Ann Judson's biography is particularly instructive when it
is set against the Gilded Age pattern of Spiritualist-Feminist connections and the earlier evangelical background, "The Apostolate
of Women." Although she never indicated any interest or support
for late nineteenth-century *political* Feminism, Abby Ann Judson's
career indicates a certain impatience with the role bequeathed to
her by her mother's generation. Her ideological clash with her minister in Minneapolis and her public differences with her brothers
over who was the true heir to their father's spiritual legacy reveal a
woman unrestrained by either Pauline proscription or by cultural
assumptions about female deference. In fact, the tensions with her
brothers and her minister suggest that Abby Ann had emotional difficulty accepting the notion that positions of religious leadership
were closed to her because of her gender. When she had the opportunity, as she did in 1894, to speak in a Spiritualist capacity
from the pulpit of the Baptist Church at Waverly, New York, she
enthusiastically accepted what had been a male mantle:

> Never did I feel a greater influx of spiritual power than when ad-
> dressing that throng of people, mostly church-members and
> preaching a sermon from the Baptist pulpit on the text I. Corin-
> thians XV:44, "There is a natural body, and there is a spiritual
> body."[133]

Whatever feminist impulses underlay the American woman's
involvement in antebellum foreign missionary work, "the apostolate" was simply not an expansive enough role for a late nineteenth-

century woman of Abby Ann Judson's particular education and experience. While brothers Edward and George proceeded naturally
to positions of power within the evangelical church, Abby Ann's
religious activities, prior to 1890, did not differentiate her from
other religious women, nor did they convey the importance that her
own sense of lineage demanded. The antebellum evangelical call to
female activism had, by the 1890s, produced a structure of "ladies"
auxiliaries and organizations which, while providing women
important opportunities for Christian sociability and activity outside the home, also kept them confined to the laity. Even as a
mature woman and principal of the Judson Female Institute, Abby
Ann was subject to the direction of a "Board of Reference," composed of eight men, six of whom represented the Protestant religious world of Minneapolis.[134] At fifty-five, when she contemplated
the years of teaching behind and ahead, her enthusiasm may have
waned. Living alone, without any apparent familial support, it is
not surprising that she found solace in a movement that provided
her with emotional comforts as well as equal opportunity for participation and recognition. The life of a lecturer on the Spiritualist cir-
cuit conceivably held the promise of interesting travel, regularized
sociability, public recognition, and, possibly, some economic rewards.

Judson also found Spiritualism attractive because of the promise
it held for ultimate moral perfection through the demonstration of
the healing powers of the spirit world. Having rejected all Calvinist
precepts, she saw progressive religion—in the form of the Spiritualist faith—as a curative for all the physical and moral diseases of
mankind. Her previously mentioned advice on vegetarianism,
regular exercise, sensible clothing, personal cleanliness, and the
control of sexual passion were all part of her "scientific" conception
that a purified body could serve the progressing soul. Through physical purification and the process of "harmonizing" one's own soul,
the mortal was united with the whole earth sphere.

In fact, the procedural stages through which an individual had
to pass in order to throw off "all inharmonious personal magnetism," approximated the later stages of the evangelical decision of
character, or conversion. Gone, however, was the Calvinist emphasis on initial religious anxiety and self-doubt. Instead, Judson
the Spiritualist offered to all who would follow it the following five-
point program, neatly charted for convenience and easy mastery,

and providing specific physical activities based on her understanding of electrical, magnetic theory:

SYNOPSIS OF THE PROCESS[135]

Inner	Outer
1. Throw off all cares, unkindness and anger.	1. Facing the north, throw off magnetism by turning three and a half times to the left, while all the time drawing the magnetism toward the body and the hands and arms.
2. Be receptive.	2. Making yourself a horse-shoe magnet, receive magnetism from the south, and then turn to the right, to the north.
3. Aspire.	3. Turn around once to the right, with hands and eyes raised, repeating the Invocation.
4. Take possession of yourself.	4. Take possession of your magnetic sphere by turning three and a half times to the right, all the time drawing the magnetism towards the body with the hands and arms.
5. Become ready for action.	5. Facing the south, lock up your magnetism by the reciprocal motions of the hands.

In December 1895, Abby Ann Judson told readers of the *Banner* that she now made headquarters in Worcester, Massachusetts, where her "invalid" brother Elnathan was hospitalized.[136] Judson explained to her readership that her lecturing, hereafter, would be restricted to within a hundred miles of Worcester since her brother was becoming "more feeble and also more dependent" on her.[137] According to records at the Union Theological Seminary, where her brother prepared for the ministry between 1859 and 1862, Elnathan Judson was pronounced insane and institutionalized in the

McLean Hospital at Sommerville, Massachusetts, in 1864, before being transferred to Worcester a decade later.[138] According to Abby Ann's report, Elnathan suffered sunstroke while rowing in a Fourth of July regatta at Providence in 1860; sunstroke was followed by "brain fever." Unable to forsake him, she sent gifts on birthdays and Christmas, and, supposedly, visited him "from time to time" although it "gave her great pain."[139] By 1895, Elnathan Judson had been institutionalized for nearly thirty years. Her brother's case would provide the Spiritualist lecturer and writer with her most important demonstration of the new religion that was also a science.

In the later part of January 1896, Elnathan Judson suffered a "stroke of paralysis, affecting his whole left side." By the end of February, his sister had "removed him from the Insane Hospital, after an incarceration of thirty-two years," and took him to live in her "hired rooms" in Worcester.[140] Incapacitated herself by a fall which allegedly led to the formation of cataracts on both her eyes, she said that she undertook "the sole and entire charge of [her] insane and paralyzed brother." According to her first report, she fed her brother "every morsel" until, on February 8, 1897, he "rose . . . from a bed of harrowing pain to that brighter region."[141] Judson noted, however, in this report, that her brother was extremely cooperative, thanking her for all that she did, up until the last.

In January 1898, Judson's weekly letter used the case of her "lately arisen" brother to illustrate the therapeutic relationship that she perceived between Spiritualism and insanity. In this report, Judson presented a different picture of her brother and indicated her displeasure with the kind of treatment that Elnathan received from alleged "experts on insanity" during his long incarceration. (The quotations were hers.) Additionally, she now revealed that Elnathan had been a less-than-docile patient, that she had needed assistance to subdue him:

> When his left side became paralyzed I was allowed to take him home. Then came the tug of war, for the dark spirits that had held him for so long came the very first evening, and dreadful oaths and frightful obscene words came from lips that never before spoke wrongly in my presence. Dismayed to my heart's core, I engaged the aid of a male nurse, who stayed nine weeks and then left for other easier work. He was succeeded by one who came well recommended for hospital work, whom I discharged in six weeks for pounding my brother in the night. After discharging him I made

no engagements to lecture and from June 17, 1896 until his transition . . . I took entire charge for him, day and night.[142]

Judson's ensuing description of the eight months in which she alone cared for her troubled brother reveal the manner in which she believed Spiritualism could be used to cure the insane and prepare them for transition. "Alone in the house with him," she wrote, "as his screams forbade other[s] . . . I fought the battle with those dark, revengeful or despairing spirits; and at last through spirit aid, and spirit aid alone, I conquered."[143] The disembodied spirits of both her parents were in the rooms at Worcester, helping her to identify "the lines of thought" that "opened the doors" to Elnathan's perversities. By teaching her brother "how to think and how to use will against them [the low spirits]," she was able to eliminate his "spells of obsession" and his "violence."

When Elnathan was finally subdued and submissive because of his new "receptivity to pure spirits," sister and brother took up residence in the home of a family of Seventh Day Adventists whom Judson described as patient and sympathetic although "antipodal" to her own religious views. Of Elnathan's final days in his "physical husk," his Spiritualist sister wrote: "My will, reinforced by his own, made the last four months of his earth-life so calm and sweet. . . ."[144]

In the "tug of war" that occupied the final months of Elnathan Judson, his sister devoted her complete attention to the task of preparing him for his death. In this process, which she called harmonization, Abby Ann Judson revealed her basic evangelical belief in the annihilation of individual will through a transforming religious experience. After all was said and done, Elnathan Judson's period of preparation for "transition" had the core elements of an evangelical deathbed conversion: the final subordination of his own perverse will and the acceptance of a higher spirit. Reared in a tradition where deathbed conversions had become a literary formula, and having nursed her own mother through the last months of an exemplary Christian life, Judson abandoned the liberal Spiritualist view that human nature evolved toward perfection and applied the kind of intense pressure associated with evangelical parenting. We can only surmise if the day-to-day operations were strictly Spiritualist since Abby Ann did not detail whether she moved her troubled brother back and forth between magnetic poles. However, the process she did describe—of purging Elnathan of "dark" and "revengeful" spirits—indicated a persistent remnant of her family's evangelical Protestant temperament.[145]

Like her half-brother George Boardman, Abby Ann Judson had developed a religious vocabulary infused with information and terminology extracted from the scientific literature of her day. For both of them, science was more a metaphor for modernity than an actual process of empirical research and investigation, despite Judson's claims to scientific skepticism. What is surprising in both cases is the extent to which residual forms of evangelicalism persisted, despite Boardman's apparent adoption of a modern theology and Judson's new liberal faith.

This is not to say that Adoniram Judson's children were bypassed by the religious crisis of the Gilded Age. Boardman wrestled with the implications of Darwin before adopting a comfortable stance as a theistic evolutionist and Christian cosmopolitan, oriented toward the future rather than the world of his venerated stepfather. Although she was loath to admit it, Abby Ann was caused considerable personal discomfort by her public espousal of a religious ideology that dismissed Calvinist precepts and counted among its adherents spokespersons for both the spirit world and unorthodox lifestyles. Religious crisis, then, came in different forms—some intellectual, some personal.

There are, however, some important postscripts. Among these children of orthodoxy there was a decline in traditional piety as they increasingly interjected religion into the social world, breaking down the old polarities between the spiritual and the secular. In addition, both Boardman and Judson were forced to recognize that the "facts" of any given religion might, in time, become untrue. Boardman handled that dilemma by his insistence on a spiritual rather than a literal interpretation of text. Abby Ann resorted to the enumeration of a new set of scientific-sounding facts or evidences drawn from a projected world beyond the grave.

Yet, for both Boardman and Judson, the evangelical heritage was certainly the intellectual backdrop against which they set all categories of new information. The persistence of this tradition, in the face of the actual diffusion of the family after 1854, confirms the assertion that pious evangelical parents successfully fixed the basic character and consciousness of their children in their earliest years.[146] Ultimately, it was the strength of this tradition of family piety that explains the nature of their spiritual crises and why neither George Boardman nor Abby Ann Judson could ever come to perceive religion as irrelevant.

Chapter 7

Benevolent Extortion

In 1875, the youngest son of the Burmese missionaries, Edward Judson, left a wealthy Baptist congregation in North Orange, New Jersey, to minister to a pastorate that was composed almost entirely of immigrant poor. Judson told the people when he was leaving North Orange that he felt "called" to the work of "building up a church in the lower part of New York [City]." He accepted the invitation of the struggling Berean Baptist Church and spelled out the following conditions for acceptance of their offer: that all seats in the church be "without exception free" and that the expenses of public worship be met by purely voluntary contributions.[1] Acting as a domestic missionary, Edward Judson chose to live and work in a densely populated area of lower Manhattan, close to the tenements and lodging houses that sheltered the immigrant masses. The thirty-year-old pastor's transfer from North Orange to lower Manhattan was later called a "sacrificial act worthy of his parentage."[2]

Edward Judson apparently grasped the evangelistic potential of the American city. Most of the nineteen million immigrants who came to the United States between 1820 and 1900 settled in urban

180

centers, thus forever altering these environments. Where once English was heard in the streets, the alien sounds of Italian, German, and Yiddish now mixed with the dialect of the Irish poor. In the decade of the 1880s, close to one-half million Italians, Jews, and other Southern and Eastern Europeans poured into the crowded districts of New York City's Lower East Side, augmenting the already substantial number of immigrants from western Europe.[3] For a person accustomed to thinking about the evangelization of foreign, non-English-speaking groups, these immigrant communities appeared to be a likely field for religious endeavor.

From his home at 35 West Washington Square, where he lived with his young wife, the former Antoinette Barstow, Judson spoke and wrote a great deal about the relationship between Christian and immigrant.[4] He noted, correctly, how new patterns of residential segregation and social stratification were changing the face of the American city. "The tendency is," he wrote, "for the intelligent, well-to-do, and church going people to withdraw from this part of the city."[5] Judson lamented the way in which the church also followed a policy of "abandonment," forsaking "just these sections of the city where they are needed most."[6] In 1833, there had been fifteen Baptist churches in New York City south of Fourteenth Street; by 1898 that number had diminished to only five.[7] As evangelical people fled northward, in and beyond Manhattan, downtown churches fell into "disrepair." This "policy of retreat," he wrote, "is fatal to Christianity, as in dropsy the water rises little by little until it submerges the vitals."[8]

Judson wanted the evangelical churches to remain downtown, to muster their best resources for the evangelization of the immigrant. Judson undoubtedly believed that a Protestantism so oriented was the best response to the social disorder of lower New York, its "pauperism, prostitution, intemperance, and crime."[9] In fact, he argued that Protestant neglect of the immigrant masses posed a serious threat to the American way of life:

> . . . these people in the lower wards of our city have a revenge. They are a constant menace to our distinctive institutions. We cannot escape them. They cling to our flanks and follow us as we proceed northward on our narrow island. We catch their diseases. They have a saloon on every corner. They outvote us at our elections. A miasma stealing up from the widening social swamps infects our whole municipal life.[10]

Later, Judson equivocated, "I have come to regard foreigners not as a menace but an opportunity."[11] Yet his attempts to stimulate interest in the evangelization of these immigrants inevitably raised the spectre of social disorder. "We must conquer these people," he advised, "or they will conquer us."[12]

Judson's writing evidenced a certain distaste for both the color and vitality of immigrant life in New York as well as the continuity of Old World traditions. He described the immigrant as "prolific" and likened the streets of his district, which were filled with children, to a "rabbit-warren."[13] The intellectual milieu of Eastern and Southern Europeans was, according to his assessment, "thin mental soil."[14] While some of the immigrants were congenial and even responsive to Gospel Christianity, Judson was still distressed by their general adherence to Old World traditions, to "materialistic and sacramentarian notions."[15] In addition to his bias against Catholicism, Judson wrote about "alien races"—Latin, Celt, Slav, and Semite and their "stiff presuppositions against the church."[16] In fact, the immigration process itself never evoked any sympathetic feelings from this important advocate of immigrant evangelization. "Italians," he once wrote, "have a glamor and picturesqueness in Italy, which disappears upon their arrival in America. Like their own olives, they seem to lose their flavor through transportation over sea water."[17]

Under Edward Judson's leadership, special efforts were made to evangelize the Italian Catholic population. Adoniram Judson had spent virtually his entire life making the gospel accessible to the Burmese; Edward, in turn, believed that "the gospel preached to [the Italians] in their own tongue will remove materialistic and sacramentarian prejudices, so that they will not prevent their children from flocking into our churches."[18] Beginning in the 1890s, Judson's church held services in Italian at least twice a week. Rev. Victor L. Calabrese, a minister, and a female missionary, Rosa Cignarole, were listed in the church's weekly schedule of activities. In 1906, Judson wrote to Dr. Hinton S. Lloyd urging the creation of an Italian Department at Colgate, his alma mater. "Nothing could be more timely," Judson wrote, "as all our denominational societies are in danger of muddling the immense and exigent Italian problem through the lack of an educated Italian ministry. A divinity school of this kind will shape the character of Italian Baptist churches in this country."[19] In 1907, when Colgate inaugurated the Italian Department, located on Hewes Street in Brooklyn, Edward Judson presided at the opening ceremonies. Like many in his denomination, Judson equated evangelization with Americanization, believing that conversion to Gospel Christianity held the promise of a materially, as well as spiritually, better life for all Catholic immigrants.[20]

With this conception in mind, Judson's work in lower New York took on distinctly missionary overtones. In fact, he criticized the "spectacle of Christendom sending missionaries to the heathen beyond the seas" but ignoring "the heathenism in the very vitals" of America.[21] Judson believed that it was his task in Manhattan, as it had been his parents' in Burma, to demonstrate the attractiveness of the Christian way of life and to educate heathen immigrants in Christian values. Deploring the current tendency "to concentrate religious efforts upon the more favored classes," Judson argued that the masses of New York should receive the best in Christian "preaching, architecture and music":

> If I had my way, I would put the most beautiful churches among the homes of the poor, so that it would be only a step from the squalor of the tenement house into a new and contrasted world. The rich have beautiful objects in their homes. They should be content with plainness in church. But when we bring together the poor and the sad, let their eyes, grown dim with tears and weariness, find repose and inspiration in the exquisite arch, and the opalescent window, through which shimmer the suggestive figures of saints and martyrs. Let their ears hear only the sweetest and most ennobling music. Let everything in church be educational and uplifting.[22]

Judson's ideal church was also cosmopolitan and democratic, eschewing identification with a single nationality or class. He wanted the most vigorous and attractive congregations downtown, on the home turf of the immigrant poor. "The strongest medicaments of the gospel," he advised, "should be injected into the most diseased tissue of the body municipal."[23] At the same time that he revealed a constitutional inability to regard non-Protestant culture with any real respect, Judson disliked the mannered, docile Christianity practiced by the more affluent in their private enclaves in and around New York City.

Edward Judson posited that in American society, which was characterized by deep "social crevasses," the local church was the best agency of social amelioration. Rich and poor, literate and illiterate, native born and foreign, management and labor, were, he thought, best able to cooperate in the context of the local church. "In the churches," Judson wrote, "resides a potency adequate to the cure of every social sore."[24] Although he collaborated with private and municipal welfare groups, Judson's hope was "in the ministry of the local church, not in the service of Christian people through other organizations":

> Rescue missions, gospel halls, and the like are only feeble and hectic substitutes for vigorous church organizations. The church should have its mission in a social swamp, and begin by being itself a mission.[25]

Judson's aversion to secular charity and philanthropic services appeared to be an indication of his traditionalism. Like his father, he saw each individual church as the loving heart of "The Righteous Empire."

On a number of occasions, Judson publicly expressed his reservations about the multiplication of Christian services associated with the Social Gospel movement. In an address in Chicago, he took the Y.M.C.A. to task for erecting a set of buildings at "an enormous expense," while churches lay idle.[26] Another time he said:

> Let no other society displace in our consciousness the local church. The Y.M.C.A., for instance, cannot take its place. It is simply auxiliary. It may serve, like the wings of a net, by soft persuasion, to draw people within the embrace of the church.[27]

It was Judson's argument that "had the church done its duty, amid the changing and complicated conditions of modern life, the Y.M.C.A. would hardly have cause for existence."[28]

Judson's effort to stake out the Church's claim to the field of social service was the fundamental and, ultimately, most frustrating issue of his clerical life. His response to the social problems created by immigration, urbanization, and industrialization was the Institutional Church, a concept he elaborated in a number of written works and then brought to fruition in 1890, with the dedication of the Judson Memorial Church in Washington Square. That church, which was the focus of much of Edward Judson's professional career, joined three other Institutional Churches—St. George's (Episcopal), St. Bartholomew's (Episcopal), and the Madison Square Presbyterian Church—in doing the work of organized Christian benevolence in the city of New York.[29]

At an Institutional Church, "outreach" efforts were part of a twenty-four-hour-a-day program. Judson reportedly told his congregation: "If a business firm should erect an expensive building, and use it only during six or seven hours a week, could it expect to succeed?"[30] Facilities at the prototypical church had to be large enough to accommodate hundreds of persons for lectures and even "entertainments" like a "Gospel Meeting with Stereopticon Views of Pilgrim's Progress." There were also the following types of departments of work and worship in an Institutional Church: Sunday School, Church Choir, Junior Choir, Young People's Society of Christian Endeavor, Union Choral Class, Nursery, Kindergarten, Primary School, Teachers' Class, Industrial School for Girls, Gymnasium Class, Memorial Home for Children, Tract Depository, Dressmaking Establishment, Icewater Fountain, Flower Mission, Fresh-Air Work, and Memorial Young Men's Class.[31] In the two decades after the dedication of the Judson Memorial Church more activities and services were developed; the Judson Health Center, a dispensary employing a staff of doctors and nurses, and the Judson Memorial Basketball Team typified the wide range of activities associated with an Institutional Church.

Activities for immigrant children were obviously an important part of the church program, reflecting the characteristic evangelical interest in the process of Christian nurture. "They [the children] want to learn our language," Judson wrote, "and they are allured by the life and joy and music in our churches and Sunday schools."[32] Describing the American Sunday School as "magnetic," Judson concluded from his experience in lower New York that the same immigrants who were afraid of Protestant churches were not reluctant to send their children to the Sunday School, where they received instruction in the English language. "There is such a joyous life within the Sunday Schools," Judson maintained, "that it wins the foreigners and they will come to it."[33]

Children up to the age of three were received in the church's day nursery; from three to seven they were included in the kindergarten. Those between seven and nine were instructed in a primary school also housed within the church building. On Mondays, there were gymnastics for girls; on Tuesdays and Thursdays, children's prayer meetings; on Wednesdays, gymnastics for boys; and on Saturdays, a sewing and singing school. "Let the church take over the whole educational charge of the child from infancy up to the age of nine or ten, when it can enter public school," Judson recommended. Following in the tradition of Horace Bushnell, Judson maintained that the first "plastic years" of a child's life required the

"constant touch of a consecrated Christian teacher."[34] By exposing
the immigrant child to Gospel Christianity, evangelicals could assure the future: "The key to the solution of the hard problem of city
evangelization lies in the puny hand of the little child."[35]

Judson's conception of the Christian mandate was developed in
a 1907 article which likened the Institutional Church to an octopus:

> The social forms through which the church expresses its sympathy
> and compassion are like the soft tentacles which some creature of
> the sea stretches out on every side in order to explore the dim ele-
> ment in which it swims, and to draw within itself the proper good.
> The church needs just such organs of prehension with which to lay
> hold upon the community about it. The institutional church is a
> kind of tentacular Christianity.[36]

The support of such a comprehensive urban ministry ultimately required either an expanding church congregation or a wealthy benefactor. Given the harsh economic realities of immigrant life in
lower New York, as well as the immigrants' understandable resistance to Protestant evangelization, Judson was never able to count
on his local congregation for the costs of operating an expansive and
seductive church program. As a result, he turned to affluent Baptists within the city of New York, asking them to underwrite his
work at the struggling Berean Church. In early 1882, probably as a
result of his name and his association with the denomination's City
Mission Society, Edward Judson was visited at the Berean Church
by a fellow Baptist, John D. Rockefeller. This meeting, which provided the Berean Church pastor with his first real entrée to an enormous industrial fortune, was an important turning point in his ministerial career.

The relationship that developed between Rockefeller and Judson continued for over three decades, ultimately serving the needs
of both men. For Rockefeller, Judson was only one of many Protestant clergy whose company he kept; ministers sought access to
Rockefeller because he was known to give widely to a variety of
Protestant denominations and to individual churches.[37] However,
the personal association with Edward Judson was unique in that it
tied the Rockefellers to a distinguished religious family whose credentials probably served them well in the face of mounting contemporary criticism of their part in the new industrial order. For Edward Judson and his vision of extensive urban evangelization,
large-scale philanthropy was an absolute necessity. While Judson
sought gifts from the pious rich wherever he could find them,[38] the

enormity of John D. Rockefeller's resources made him a particularly tantalizing personality for the evangelical preacher. Rumored to
be the nation's wealthiest man, Rockefeller was also avowedly traditional and moralistic in his private life and, very importantly,
willing to identify himself with the Baptist denomination. Throughout the relationship, Judson played to the private Rockefeller, acting as a family friend and religious counselor, and avoided consideration of Mr. Rockefeller's rapacious presence in the oil industry.

Yet the clergyman's letters to the controversial industrialist occasionally belied his ignorance of Rockefeller's public business roles.
In 1887, after Rockefeller was called as a prosecution witness in a
Buffalo, New York, case (which charged a Standard Oil affiliate
with sabotage against a small, competitive refinery), Judson wrote
to him expressing his support:

> I felt sorry that you should be put to so much trouble about the
> Buffalo suit. I know that there could be but one result. But [it]
> does seem a pity, that one in your position should be thus an-
> noyed. It seems to be one of the painful incidents of greatness that
> it should be expressed to adventurers and black-mailers who have
> nothing to lose and who itch for notoriety.[39]

The fact that Judson was quick to rise to the defense of the industrialist surely cemented what could only be, from the perspective of
the pastor, a beneficial relationship. A few years later, when the
Standard Oil Trust was under fire, Judson wrote Rockefeller, praising him for his "bearing . . . coolness . . . dignity . . . and courtly
behavior" in an unpleasant situation. "Part of the press," Judson
observed, "actuated by a demagogic spirit, may give voice to malignant envy; but I hear only one opinion from grave and sensible
men."[40]

Despite the claim for unanimity, a January 1889 letter from
Judson indicated that there was already division within the Baptist
ranks over the question of financing religious work with monies
"tainted" by Rockefeller's business practices. Judson reported to
Rockefeller that at a "meeting of the Baptist ministers of Philadelphia and its suburbs," probably in 1887, "some very shallow and ill-
advised . . . vehement insinuations were made against the Standard
Oil." Judson conveyed this information in making the case for a
young Long Island clergyman, who at that meeting delivered "a
brave, ringing speech" in which he defended Rockefeller's largess
against his fellow clergy's accusations. "I took note of his 'clear grit'
and loyalty on that occasion," wrote the dutiful Judson. "It oc-

curred to me that perhaps you might like to know the circumstances and might desire to give him a little gift."[41]

Judson's written commentary on the "public" Rockefeller never dealt with the content of the accusations. In fact, Edward Judson was probably incapable of evaluating the "public" Rockefeller so long as Rockefeller monies were linked, in his mind's eye, to the work of urban evangelization. As a result, the private conversations of the two men must have been limited in scope—if not stilted—by their mutual need to retain certain traditional distinctions between the religious and the profane.

This is not to say that Judson totally avoided any connection with Mr. Rockefeller's secular employments. On a number of other occasions, he recommended to the industrialist young men who were seeking work. In September 1887, he wrote Rockefeller about a Mr. Henry Moore, whom he described as a "good man" for a position as an agent of Standard Oil.[42] There is no evidence to suggest, however, that Rockefeller took the pastor's advice or that the two men agreed on what made for a competent oil industry agent. Rockefeller generally subscribed to Judson's definitions of "good men" but only in terms of clerics, organists, teachers, and missionaries, whose work he underwrote on numerous occasions.

Judson's friendship with Rockefeller and his unrelenting quest for Rockefeller's support of his religious work were symptomatic of a world view that ultimately reconciled godliness and economic gain and, at the same time, allowed traditional Christian social values to be separated from the exigencies of the marketplace.[43] In many respects, the relationship between the two men demonstrated the demise of traditional evangelical theory that was organic in nature; in its place, Judson and Rockefeller, like religion and industry, forged a relationship built on their separate, but oftentimes symbiotic, needs. Although he liked to think of himself in terms of the purity of his spiritual mission, Edward Judson became almost totally enmeshed in the work of financing religion, an area in which he looked to Rockefeller for advice as well as money. And however much the Rockefeller name was associated with questionable business practices, Judson continued his attempt to tie that family's resources to his earthly, religious goal: the creation in the heart of lower New York of an elegant Institutional Church edifice, replete with meeting and work spaces, where he could carry on the full-time business of evangelization among the immigrants.

In order to build the Memorial Church that Judson envisaged, major philanthropy was required. Mere mites were not enough to employ the nation's leading ecclesiastical artists: Stanford White, the architecture; St. Gaudens, the sculpture; and La Farge, the stained glass windows.[44] The fact that Edward Judson conceived of attracting the "neglected masses" of New York City through the creation of a church building offering the best in Christian aesthetics was also an important departure from the minimalist philosophy of his parents' generation. In the 1830s, Adoniram and Ann Judson had both articulated their religious distance from the Bumese by expressing their distaste for sacred decorations in pagodas, decoration itself suggesting both heathenism and Romanism. By the 1880s evangelicals were able to reconcile their religious sentiments with contemporary tastes in architectural style and decorative detail, demonstrating once again the confluence of religious and secular culture.

To support materially the vision of inspiring church edifices, the evangelical clergy had to make common cause with the rich, often titans of the new industrial order. In December 1898, Edward Judson addressed the paper manufacturers of the city of New York on the subject "The Development of Civic Righteousness." Not surprisingly, Judson found righteousness in the benevolent use of wealth as in the example of John D. Rockefeller.[45] An article by Judson in the *Baptist Home Mission Monthly* had the same message and was entitled rather crassly, "Worship God by Giving Money."[46] This kind of exhortation heralded a new day for all Christian organizations that sought the largess of the wealthy and explains why the idea of an eternal judgment biased against the rich was dropped from the evangelical credo. Although Judson organized an extensive fund-raising campaign involving Baptists all over the world, the Memorial Church's inception was linked to large philanthropic gifts. Judson, who saw no contradiction between the Bible and the clergy's interest in money, repeatedly told audiences that "Jesus was a man of affairs."[47] It was no wonder, then, that he integrated the religious imperative in all his complicated business dealings with the industrialist.

John D. Rockefeller gave considerable support to the Memorial Church project. However, his fortune eventually became so large, and the petitioners so numerous, that he began, in the 1890s, to systematize his charitable giving. Rockefeller's manifold religious contributions were increasingly channeled through centralized denominational bureaucracies rather than allocated to individual churches. In so doing, he put the Judson Memorial Church on equal footing with other applicants. Whatever personal feelings he had for the son of Adoniram Judson, they were cast aside in the interest of a more efficient philanthropic system, an executive assignment taken on by the inexhaustible Fred T. Gates, a former Baptist pastor who began his business career as an adviser and estate manager for George A. Pillsbury.[48]

Fred Gates, like John D. Rockefeller, spent his early life in the pious, agricultural communities that bordered New York's Burned-Over District. In fact, Gates' father was the preacher at Centre Lisle, a tiny mill hamlet on the Otselic River, only ten miles distant from Richford Springs, the settlement where Rockefeller was born. Gates' autobiographical record of those times revealed his distaste, as an adult, for the intense religiosity associated with the revivalism that swept the area. The mature Gates gave his greatest praise to those adults who, in his youth, "had too much tact" or "too much delicacy of feeling" to "annoy" or press him on the matter of "personal religion."

This is not to say that Gates was irreligious. In fact, he was converted at about age sixteen, but without feeling, he said, "the deep sense of guilt, [which] the revivalists sought to create." After a move westward, when his father joined the service of the American Baptist Home Missionary Society, Gates taught in district schools to support his university attendance, a common nineteenth-century career pattern. Eventually, he studied at The University of Rochester, graduating in 1877, and at the Rochester Theological Seminary before assuming the pastorate of the Fifth Avenue Baptist Church of Minneapolis in 1880. In Minnesota, Gates became involved with the effort to raise funds to support a Baptist academy in the state, modeled on Phillips Exeter. George A. Pillsbury, who had the money to make the academy a reality, followed Gates' advice and committed the necessary funds. In the next few years, Gates became secretary of the newly formed American Baptist Education Society and, in that capacity, was dedicated to the idea of seeing the Baptists build a "powerful college, to become later a university," at Chicago.[49]

Under the careful eye of Gates, Rockefeller's resources became increasingly inaccessible to Edward Judson. This occurred for a variety of reasons, not the least of which were new priorities for the denominational leadership, including the creation of a great Baptist university at Chicago, and the passage of the ideal of the individual church as the central machinery of moral transformation. Additionally, after years of listening to Rockefeller's advice on the need to make his church self-supporting, Judson was roadblocked by the accomplishment of that very goal. Judson's persistent claims on Rockefeller's fortune were repelled by Gates on the grounds that religious institutions, unlike secular ones, need not rest on secure financial foundations. In his assertion that churches should not have endowments, Gates, ironically, became the spokesperson for the traditional evangelical injunction against worldliness.

Ultimately, Edward Judson failed as a practitioner of finance capitalism. Yet his professional life, which was a dogged attempt to link an industrial fortune to religious imperatives, prefigured new patterns and associations for American religionists, regardless of denomination. Judson was not, after all, the only minister to make common cause with a titan of industry. But, in so doing, he differentiated himself from his Spiritualist sister, Abby Ann, a pointed critic of the Church's collaboration with "the money power," and from his half-brother, George Boardman, an advocate of limited capital accumulation.[50] For the youngest son of Adoniram Judson, the resources of John D. Rockefeller posed a practical rather than a moral problem.

––––––––◆◆––––––––

In July 1882, Rockefeller wrote to Judson praising him for his religious work and enclosing "a draft order on Standard Oil for $500, from Mrs. Rockefeller and myself to yourself and family with our kindest regard." Rockefeller expressed regrets that the two had not seen each other since their first meeting, a few months before, at the Berean Church:

> I hoped to have seen you again but the winter and spring flew by
> and I failed to do so. I appreciate very much what you have done
> in New York City and believe its influence extends through all our
> denomination.[51]

Although the initial gift to Judson was for an expressly personal use, the fact that Rockefeller spoke in terms of "our denomination" was a harbinger of marvelous things for the Baptist clergy and their work. Given the fact that a typical minister's salary at this time was probably not in excess of $2,500, the Rockefeller gift was both a sizeable boost to the family's assets and an attractive inducement to expect more, from the same source, for urban evangelization.

Edward Judson's reply was typical of the many letters he wrote Rockefeller in his lifetime. In addition to expressing his profuse thanks and making reference to the friendship of the two families, the cleric inevitably blessed Mr. Rockefeller for his largess and for "the manifold stewardship" to which he had been called:

> Thank you for your kind letter with its generous gift. I cannot tell you how deeply I was affected by this expression on your part of thoughtful solicitude for myself and of confidence in my work. I shall not soon forget the fine faithful friends who have given me aid and succor during the trials and difficulties of my first beginning in New York. Please accept dear friend, on behalf of myself and Mrs. Judson . . . our sincerest thanks. Praying that the blessing of our Saviour, whose service is so sweet, may rest upon this as well as upon the many other noble gifts which you have laid at his altar, I remain yours with greatful affection.[52]

Judson's prototypical letter also included some explicit statement directing Rockefeller to the continued use of his economic resources for religious purposes. "I know that it is your aim," wrote Judson in 1886, "to use your wealth in the way that will be most pleasing to the One, whose we are and Whom we serve, and that we will be guided by the wisdom that is from above."[53]

On other occasions, Judson thanked Rockefeller for supplementing his salary and noted that the extra income provided the family with a measure of security and a sense of well-being they would not ordinarily have. "I confess that I have been barely able to get along," Judson wrote to Rockefeller while he was at the Berean Church, "and what you have given me imparts a feeling of ease and freedom at an exceedingly critical period in my life."[54] Rockefeller's pattern of gifts to the family, which included making mortgage payments on their house at 106 West Seventy-ninth Street, as well as Christmas and special anniversary presents of $100 each, continued for over three decades, no matter what transpired in the realm of Rockefeller's philanthropic giving or in his business activities.

Upon receipt of an unsolicited $250 personal gift in 1886, Judson wrote: "It is a very great satisfaction to me while striving to do mission work in New York to be able thus to lay aside something for the future of my wife and children."[55] In fact, the Judsons tied their children's futures to their benefactor's gifts, indicating their material as well as spiritual concern for their offspring. From the late 1880s throughout the 1890s, Edward and Antoinette Judson's annual Christmas letter of thanks mentioned that a "portion [of the

gift] has been put away for the girls . . . in a savings bank."[56] By
1908, the girls—Elizabeth and Margaret—had become stockhold-
ers in Mr. Rockefeller's business enterprise, owning one share each
of Standard Oil.[57]

What Judson extended to Rockefeller, in exchange for the latter's material support, was an invitation to religious colleagueship
and the opportunity to join him in the work of urban evangelization. On one occasion Judson told Rockefeller:

> As I come in contact with leading Christians in other denomina-
> tions, I find that this question of the salvation of the cities occupies
> a large place in their minds. They are all advancing aggressively in
> this direction and I am convinced that you and I may be building
> better than we know, and we in the forefront of a movement the
> significance of which will be even more apparent a decade hence.
> In what you have done and may be led to do along these lines . . .
> it will be seen that you have a deep apprehension of the true
> religious [back]wardness of our troubled times, and that, as a
> broadminded and progressive Baptist, you are a good many steps
> in advance of the main body, which must ultimately reach your
> standpoint.[58]

Judson posited, in fact, that the Supreme Being had selected Mr.
Rockefeller for this particular assignment. In February 1885, when
Rockefeller sent him another $250 check for a payment on his
house, Judson replied in a manner that tended to obscure the dis-
tinction between support for his program and support for his person:

> Many thanks for this token of your regard. I prize it, most highly
> as such, and shall never cease to feel grateful to you as well as to
> my Heavenly Father for raising me up such a friend and helper. I
> do not see how I could ever get along without you during these
> first years in New York. Your guiding and supporting hand has
> been so kindly, wisely, and steadily applied! Perhaps it will be
> permitted to us Baptists to form an epic in City Evangelization as
> truly as our Fathers did in the Foreign Missions.[59]

When Judson invoked their "fathers'" generation and foreign
missions, he was pointing to his own distinguished parenthood and
to Rockefeller's maternal heritage. It was Eliza Davison Rockefeller
who was the staunch Baptist; Rockefeller's father, in fact, had been
something of a ne'er-do-well. As a Cayuga County, New York,

farmer, part-time businessman, and occasional patent medicine salesman, his career also included an 1849 indictment for the rape of a domestic servant and, in 1850, a judgment against him for debt, brought by his own father-in-law.[60] When Judson called on the Rockefellers at their various homes and vacation retreats, he came as a celebrity and plied them with family stories, contributing to their sense of intimacy with the famous Burmese mission. In March 1883, John D. Rockefeller wrote Judson, thanking him for "the new edition" of Adoniram's life, which Edward had just completed.[61] Edward Judson also presented Lucy Spellman, Rockefeller's resident sister-in-law, with a "little tragedy from Burman life, composed by Fanny Forester."[62]

In May 1883, in anticipation of another hot New York summer, Rockefeller made plans to leave with his family for Saratoga and invited the agreeable Reverend Judson to come along. He also asked the clergyman to describe the Berean Church's summer activities for the urban poor: ". . . write [me] care of the Adelphi Hotel, Saratoga, how you are getting on and what prospects [there are] for funds to carry forward the work. I may contribute a further mite."[63] The most notable of the Berean Church's services to the immigrant poor was the Fresh Air and Cool Water Fund which Rockefeller supported consistently, beginning in 1882 with ad hoc contributions of fifty and one hundred dollars. Fresh air work was, according to Judson, an important component of an urban ministry. The aged, the sick, working girls, and children were provided by the church with two weeks in the country. In the early years, the city visitors were placed in a home at Hamilton; by 1892, Judson had secured from George E. Crowell, editor of the *Household Magazine*, the use of a large Queen Anne style home or "cottage" at Brattleboro, Vermont.[64] Judson assured Mr. Rockefeller and other supporters that places at Brattleboro would not go simply to the most aggressive. "In the case of many charitable enterprises it is the clamorous and obtrusive that get the main benefit," Judson wrote, "while too often the weak and shy and more needy are altogether passed by." In the case of his church, Judson emphasized to Rockefeller that the "intimate acquaintance which we have formed through our teachers and missionaries with hundreds of poor families . . . enables us to select the most needy and deserving."[65]

In addition to the two-week vacations at Hamilton, the Berean Church operated an ice-water fountain at the corners of Bedford and Downing Streets, which provided the densely populated neighborhood with cool, safe water during the summer months. By 1892, the Cool Water Fountain had become a downtown institution; in the new Memorial Church building it took the following form:

> We have a box in the basement of the Church large enough to hold a ton of ice. The ice rests upon a coil of pipe connected with the Croton [reservoir] system. During the six warmer months the fountain supplies the passer-by with cool water ranging in temperature from 39° to 45° Fahr.—cool enough to be pleasant to the taste, and yet not so cold as to be injurious to the health.[66]

In addition to providing a cool beverage for laborers and for the sick, the cool water fountain was presented by Judson as a natural deterrent to immigrant drinking: "Workmen may be seen sending their pails to our fountain to be replenished at noon, instead of to the beer saloon across the street, and thus, on the principle of deplacement, the nuisance of intemperance is somewhat abated in our neighborhood."[67]

In the effort to respond to the crucial physical and economic needs of the immigrant community, Judson led the Berean Church into a wide array of services. The church sponsored an orphanage in Somerville, New Jersey, and, as early as 1885, ran a kindergarten charging five cents per week for its childcare services.[68] In December 1886, Judson wrote Rockefeller about the aim of the latter project, which was supervised by Lilian Isham whom Judson identified as a graduate of Madame Kraus'[s] school, "the best Kindergarten training school in the country." He said of the kindergarten: "The idea we have is to gather in these little ones before they begin going to public school and win their hearts and train them in Scriptures. This work is necessary and fundamental, if we propose to change materially the character of our community."[69]

In addition to its commitment to Christian nurture, the Berean Church also operated an employment bureau, a flower mission, an adjunct chapel on Broome Street near Thompson, and a wood and coal yard, all designed to assist "the worthy poor."[70] For a number of years the Berean's Department of Practical Benevolence ran its own "milk depot," bottling and delivering "warranted pure milk" at seven cents a quart.[71] When profits accrued from the sale of milk, they were utilized for the establishment of a free reading room but not for the church's operational support. Wherever he could, Judson looked for ways to expand the manifold activities of the Berean Church, a prototype of the Institutional Church that came almost a decade later.

John D. Rockefeller was obviously impressed by Edward Judson's ability to get things done. Judson, in turn, reported to him regularly during the summers of 1883 and 1884 about the work of the Berean Fresh Air and Cool Water Fund. In June 1883, after Judson visited with the Rockefellers at the Adelphi Hotel in Saratoga, he wrote to Rockefeller: "I have the tenderest recollections of the little visit I had with you and your family at Saratoga."[72] Rockefeller responded: "You could not have enjoyed more than each member of my family did your visit with us in Saratoga, and we hope to see more of you next winter."[73]

In the earliest years of their relationship, visiting between the two men was easy and fairly frequent. When Judson needed funds to hire a gospel singer or to initiate outdoor "tent work," he was able to discuss these matters on Saturday evenings at Mr. Rockefeller's home, generally with the family in attendance. Judson almost always declined Rockefeller's Thursday and Friday night invitations, reminding him that he was "engaged to preach for [his] people every night except Saturday."[74] Occasionally, the Rockefellers made a special effort to worship at the Berean Church, rather than in their own congregation, the Fifth Avenue Baptist Church. "Do you preach on Thanksgiving Day," Rockefeller wrote to Judson in November 1884, "if so, at what hour, and where?"[75]

In the Saratoga interlude, Rockefeller had committed himself to $200 a month for a year in support of the Berean Church program and its minister. Judson wrote the following letter of confirmation in September 1883:

> When I met you in Saratoga, you were kind enough to intimate your willingness to help me during the coming year beginning October 1. I think you even specified that, if I was in need, I might look to you for one or two hundred dollars a month. I write to learn if you still think favorably of investing in the missionary and philanthropic work that I am trying to do in lower New York. I have so far no assurances whatever of help from any other quarter and accordingly would be extremely gratified if I could look to you for two hundred dollars a month for one year.[76]

In addition, Judson observed that he "did not think [he] should need [this support] for a longer period" than one year. In fact,

Rockefeller's personal and institutional support of Edward Judson would continue until 1910. In April 1884, Rockefeller was giving $275 per month, $50 of which he had "kindly designated for [Judson's] own personal use." By 1886, $100 of the $275 monthly dole was going towards Judson's salary.[77] In this early period, Rockefeller appeared to be receptive to almost all of Judson's ad hoc appeals for support, writing him, "If you do not secure the amount required do not hesitate to advise me. If I have to give [I] will do so cheerfully, and if I find I cannot I will say [to] you nay, and hope to be better prepared for the next call."[78]

Rockefeller's willingness to give his mite to religious work, a practice he began as a youngster, did not pass Judson by. Prior to 1890, Judson's letters were filled with spontaneous requests for $50 and $100 gifts above and beyond the regularly monthly allocation. The requests were always for religious work: upkeep of the church, employment of an organist or gospel singer, charity relief for the poor, or assistance for a needy ministerial colleague.[79] "You kindly told me to come to you under such circumstances," Judson wrote, "and although you have done so much for me that I feel almost ashamed to ask you for any more, yet I venture to assure you that a check for $50 or a $100, just at this time would be most welcome, and would enable me to sleep a little better o'nights."[80]

The only documented instance of Judson's refusal of a Rockefeller gift came in January 1884 when the millionaire offered to supply the Berean Church at 117 West Fifteenth Street, with $150 to renovate the baptistry. Judson, who probably already had larger things in view, wrote Rockefeller that he was "quite chary of spending money on [the] building, because it is capable of absorbing so much money without yielding very much to show for it."[81] The declination, based on sound business principles, won Rockefeller's favor and another invitation.

On April 8, 1884, Judson left with Rockefeller and a party of twelve aboard the Pullman car Bremen for a trip to California. Judson's wife, Antoinette, remained behind as indicated by her April 30th acknowledgment from New York of Rockefeller's monthly dole.[82] Three days after leaving Jersey City, the Bremen took on provisions at Atlanta, including an unusually large ration of apples, oranges, and raisins. From there they were on to New Orleans, where the grocery bills again indicated the Victorian fondness for fruit. Between New Orleans and Houston, less than a day's travel by train, the Rockefeller party apparently consumed six dozen apples, twenty-four boxes of strawberries, and four dozen oranges and lemons. On the twenty-second of April, the Bremen reached Los Angeles. The party made a brief side trip to San Pedro before heading northward to San Francisco, where they divided their time between the Palace and the Baldwin Hotels. In San Francisco, the Rockefellers visited Chinatown, took the ferry across Oakland Bay, and planned side trips to Rock Creek, Wyoming, and Ogden, Utah. Their carriage bills for this period indicate that they continued to attend church while on vacation and that they paid charitable visits on May 14 and 15 to the Point Park Alms House.[83]

For the minister who accompanied them, the California excursion was heady fare. First, the trip provided Judson with the opportunity to travel in great style and see the country, something which his $2,400 salary ordinarily would not allow.[84] Second, the circumstances of life aboard the train put him in easy proximity to all the family members, including the children for whom he apparently displayed great affection and in whom he took great interest. After the California trip, notes and drawings by the Rockefeller children adorned the writing table in his new home on West Seventy-ninth Street, "reminding [him] of their sweet faces and voices."[85] Finally, the six-week excursion gave Judson the opportunity to broach the subject of making wider religious use of Mr. Rockefeller's resources. Although he was already giving $5,000 a year to the Baptist City Missionary Society, Judson probably deduced that Rockefeller really could, and might, do more. In one of his perennial letters of request, Judson apologized: "I am afraid you will think I am like the tramp I told you about once who came to a country house and said to the women who opened the door, 'Will you please give me a drink of water, I am so hungry, I don't know where I shall stay tonight.' "[86]

Within the next two years, Judson asked Rockefeller to commit special funds, above and beyond the continuing $275 per month, to all of the following: payment of the Berean Church's $800 operating deficit (1884-85), support of his plan to rent Cooper Union for Sunday afternoon services, and removal of the "$6,000 encumbrance" or church debt.[87] In order to allay Rockefeller's fears that the Berean Church was becoming too dependent upon him, a single benefactor, Judson always presented his need for money in terms of the "stimulative" effect it would have on others: "If you saw fit to make a conditional subscription I am sure it would prove very stimulating, and might be almost equivalent to paying the whole amount."[88] When Rockefeller refused to pay off the entire Berean debt, Judson wrote him: "I was tempted into asking [so much] by the extreme difficulty of raising money for a church debt. It is such a prosaic and dead issue that it fails to awaken much interest."[89] Judson was able, however, to secure the necessary support with Rockefeller subscribing $1,000. By January 1887, the Berean Church was an unencumbered property and the way had been prepared for launching a larger Institutional Church project, to be named in honor of Adoniram Judson.

The campaign to build the Judson Memorial Church was directed at an international Baptist community. At the start, it was Judson's conception that every Baptist could contribute ten cents to the Adoniram Judson Memorial Baptist Church Edifice Fund. Individual Baptists who purchased a ten-cent share in the prospective church building received a brief biography of Adoniram Judson, with his portrait, produced by the London Tract Society. Judson intended to sell the shares to "every Baptist man, woman and child in the world."[90] The mailings required to do this kind of fund raising were actually underwritten by a $1,000 gift from Rockefeller which, with his approval, Judson redirected from another purpose.[91] In November 1887, Judson reported having raised $2,500 through the ten-cent appeal, a figure obviously inadequate to the scope of his proposed project. Within the next two years, Judson traveled widely, raising as much as $2,000 a week for the cost of constructing the Memorial Church. What Judson was forced to confront was the extent to which the Baptist public was already overburdened with local, more immediate requests for financial support.[92] In addition, many of the larger gifts that he received, such as a $2,500 pledge from the heirs of J. B. Hoyt, were encumbered, in that the funds were earmarked for memorial windows or other kinds of monuments within the church.[93]

As a result, Judson returned repeatedly to John D. Rockefeller for the seed money to secure the project. This is not to say that Rockefeller supplied the bulk of the money: an 1892 statement indicates that Rockefeller gave a total of $40,000 but that $256,331 was raised from other sources including contributions, sale of annuities, and the sale of the Berean Church property.[94] However, from 1887 until 1891, when the Memorial Church opened its doors, Edward Judson pushed unrelentingly for more and more Rockefeller money. Judson's letters to the industrialist were filled with business propositions, many of which attempted to escalate Rockefeller's involvement in the project.

In November 1887, Judson laid out a preliminary formula for Rockefeller participation in the new church:

> May I look to you say for one dollar for every dollar I will raise over and above the expenses of securing the contributions and over and above the value of our present church edifice[?] So that when I begin to build you will offset the cash I have in hand with an equivalent sum. Or, if that should seem to you more than your share, will you be so kind as to indicate what fractional proportion of the sum raised you will assume[?][95]

Judson explained that he chose to put the question in the form of a letter rather than disrupt Mr. Rockefeller's domestic solicitude: "When a man . . . like yourself comes home after business hours and is enjoying the society of his family by the fireside, I think he must sometimes find it trying to have the burden even of mission work in lower New York laid upon him in such a way as to tax his sympathy and consideration."[96] Rather than "talking shop" when they were together, Judson adopted the form of the persuasive letter.

Because he received no reply to his initial request for a percentage, Judson followed with another letter in February 1888, indicating that he and Rockefeller had, in fact, "talked shop" in the very recent past:

> You have been so kind as to express your willingness to subscribe towards the Memorial Church Edifice; and in harmony with our conversation the other evening I beg leave to submit the following questions. Let us assume that we have $50,000. We said $45,000 the other evening, but $50,000 is a rounder number and I doubt not that the 10 cent movement with the value of our present [Berean Church] property will in the end swell our sum up to that figure. Now what proportion will you give of the $50,000 required to bring the amount up to $100,000? What proportion will you give of the $75,000 required to bring the amount up to $125,000? What proportion will you give of the $100,000 required to bring the amount up to $150,000? And lastly, if we should need $200,000 in order to realize most completely our ideal, for what fraction of $150,000 may I depend on you?[97]

Rockefeller's concise reply came within five business days. If a site could be found that was not competitive with existing Baptist churches, Rockefeller agreed to the following formula: if $50,000 had to be raised beyond the Berean Church assets and money on hand, he would contribute $15,000; if the total cost was $150,000, he would give $27,500; if $200,000 was the final figure, he would donate $40,000. All of Judson's fund raising would have to be accomplished within six months. Additionally, Rockefeller wanted the mortgage for the church to be turned over to the Baptist Association of Southern New York in order to insure that the property retained its ecclesiastical function.[98] Rockefeller was willing to begin the campaign with a check for $10,000.

Judson, of course, accepted Rockefeller's conditions but with one proviso. He suggested, in a reply written a day after Rockefeller set out the terms, that the American Baptist Missionary Union would be a more appropriate denominational affiliation for the church because it was "country-wide [in] character" and because it was organized in 1814 "for the express purpose of supporting [his] father in Burmah." Other than that, his letter of thanks verged on the ecstatic:

> When a friend comes to us in our great straits and gives such a lift to enterprises into which are woven our life's hopes and our very heartstrings, as you have done to me within the last two days, it is hard indeed to express one's gratitude. Words seem cheap and unable. But I do want to say *thank you* on paper, and, I may say, tears of gratitude fill my eyes as I write on these lines, and think of what a firm, true, kind friend you have been to me since the day we first met down in the old church. I know it is the *Lord's doing* for I never dared to seek your aid, and I know that I could never have brought these things about myself. I can truthfully say *I thank my God upon every remembrance of you.*[99]

For Judson, the recollection of trips with the Rockefellers to California in 1884 and to Yellowstone in 1886 now took on a larger, providential meaning. If his earlier effort to involve Rockefeller as a trustee of the Berean Church had failed, it had only been a temporary test of the staying power of both men.[100] Edward's brother, the surgeon, Adoniram Brown, received the good news and wrote the great benefactor within twenty-four hours: "Thank you for your most generous offer in connection with the project of building a church in memory of my father. I will not dwell on the good which I trust will, in many ways, follow your action."[101]

Judson followed Rockefeller's proposal with six months of intense fund raising in New York, Brooklyn, Albany, Boston, and

Philadelphia. Also, a future site for the church was selected, on Washington Square, where he felt a congregation might be drawn from among the middle and upper classes as well as the immigrant poor. The cost of the 105-by-100-foot property was $111,000, and the building bids, based on a design by McKim, Mead, and White, came to $128,500. The church design, based on Italian Renaissance forms, was intended as a lure to the Italians in the area. The architectural plans for the Institutional Church also included a revenue-producing residential complex alternately called by Judson "the Young Men's building" and, later, "the apartment house."[102]

The total cost of building the Judson Memorial Church, then, came to nearly $250,000—fifty thousand more than the uppermost figure that Mr. Rockefeller was committed to support. Judson admitted in his letter of December 8, 1888, that he had raised only $120,000, including the $10,000 that Rockefeller had contributed to initiate the fund drive. The financial package that would insure the creation of the church had not been put together in time.[103]

Undaunted by this difficulty, Judson sent Rockefeller a number of alternative propositions that were accompanied by a series of illustrations that brutalized the architects' conception of the church. The illustrations, which removed towers and parts of the configuration, demonstrated how the McKim, Mead, and White design could be adapted for gradual implementation, at different cost levels. One of Judson's propositions included clearing the lot, by the following May, and building just the church basement and the apartment house with a temporary roof over both. Judson argued that this scheme (which cost $194,500) was financially and psychologically sound. "I find upon consultation with experienced and sagacious businessmen," he told Rockefeller, that the apartment "will yield at the lowest computation a net annual rental [income] of between $6,000 and $7,000." In addition, he argued that an "unfinished building will itself be an eloquent appeal for further contributions." Judson urged Rockefeller to make other propositions that could help him raise the money that he was short, either for an incomplete building or a completed building costing $250,000. He reported that he had 3,000 personal letters and flyers ready to be signed and mailed to ministers, Sunday school superintendents, and influential Baptist laymen throughout the country.[104]

Judson wrote two letters to Rockefeller in March 1889 indicating that, while he awaited a new Rockefeller offer, he had not stopped raising money. From Boston, he reported that he thought he "could keep up an average of a thousand or two a week for a long time . . . but [was] painfully aware" of the work he had left behind at his home base. On March 12, he queried Rockefeller: ". . . in the first instance [the church building only] we must raise $61,402 and in the second instance [the completed church and apartment] $149,832. In either alternative what aid may I expect from you?"[105]

Rockefeller responded with a check for $5,000 which was to be used immediately towards the purchase of the church land.[106] His support of the Memorial Church project now amounted to $15,000. He also expressed his concern to Judson that a May 1, 1889 ground-breaking date was rushing things too much. Unwilling to alienate his most important benefactor, Judson replied that "in a matter of distinctly business character" he "did not hesitate to defer" to Rock-efeller's "judgement and experience."[107] Prone to profuse expressions of deference in matters of money, Judson wrote in another instance when they failed to agree:

> . . . your long experience in such enterprises, your consummate business judgement, your strong steady support of my work in the past, and my hope of help and sympathy and advice from you in the future, . . . all these make my acquiescence in your . . . decision a cheerful necessity.[108]

During the remaining months of 1889, Judson worked frenetically to raise the required funds. A fourteen-week tour in the spring netted $21,188. "I find a kind response everywhere," he wrote, "both to my father's memory and to the work of evangelization."[109] By January 1890, the land for the Judson Memorial Church had been paid for; still wanting was the $140,000 needed to erect the church building and its important apartment complex. Judson wrote Rockefeller repeatedly that the revenue-producing apartments would, in effect, create an endowed church, a church where he could do the work of urban evangelization without counting on outside sources—namely Rockefeller—for a monthly operational supplement.

Judson continued to ply Rockefeller with various schemes for financing the church and for manipulating those resources already in hand. For example, in July 1890, Judson considered how best to use a $40,000 pledge by Hiram Deats, $25,000 of which was specified for support of a home for children, in Deats' name, and the remaining $15,000 for the Memorial Church project. Since Rockefeller was paying in increments based on what Judson had raised, the

minister suggested that the total amount of the Deats' contribution
be temporarily considered as a pledge to the Memorial Church
fund.[110]

Even during the process of construction, the financial negotia-
tions continued. By his own admission, the minister used the industrialist's contributions as a lever to secure more funds; at the same
time, Judson used the other funds to prod Rockefeller to give more.
By February 1891, Rockefeller had already given $38,000, just
$2,000 short of his ultimate initial commitment, despite the fact
that Judson's fund raising never progressed at the rate that the original proposition required. Since the church construction continually ran in excess of the contractors' predictions, Judson was forced
to consider other fund-raising techniques: taking a larger or second
mortgage on the apartment house and perhaps combining with
another New York Baptist church, preferably one with unencumbered property.[111]

By April 1891, the main church building was completed without debt, but the auditorium required $15,000 for interior finishing
and furniture. The revenue-producing building, the apartment
house, carried a $100,000 debt and required nearly $25,000 of additional expenditures. Reluctant to admit that Memorial Church subscriptions were shrinking significantly, Judson asked Rockefeller for
the $2,000 that was still outstanding on his original pledge with the
admission that he really had not met the conditions.[112] At the same
time, he also attempted to secure Rockefeller's continued commitment to providing $225 per month in support of the church's pro-
gram and promised that these requests would taper off in the near
future, when the apartment house scheme began to bear fruit. "If
you will help me just one more year," promised Judson, "then I can
safely transfer to the [apartment] house the many interests which
you have been so long carrying. . . . I have so exhausted everyone
with my missionary appeals that I have become an old story."[113]

In the same letter to Rockefeller, the cleric described himself as
a "tired swimmer who ha[d] almost reached shore. With my right
hand I have been holding fast to your firm outstretched arms, until
my left hand almost touches the bank."[114] Saturated and overburd-
ened by his involvement in religious financing, Judson explained to
Rockefeller that he did not want his life to be this way. "It is far
more to my taste to build a *spiritual* house than one of brick and
stone," he wrote.[115]

Yet, his single-minded dedication to creating an expansive and
self-supporting Institutional Church created a situation whereby

Judson was constantly in pursuit of what he called "ecclesiastical appliances," rather than spiritual work. At one point, the forty-five-year-old pastor expressed his frustration to Rockefeller:

> I do not wish to be merely a *manufacturer of agricultural implements*. I want to give my best years to the actual work of *husbandry*. It is so easy to be drawn aside to the task of making *tools*, and so to forget that all these appliances are merely helps in the work of building up the Kingdom of God in the hearts of men and so to change for the better the character of a debased community. You will not wonder at my reluctance to being simply a *toolmaker*. God has given me so many tokens of His favor in *spiritual* work that I do not want my life entirely secularized.[116]

Judson used the same rhetoric again, over a decade later: ". . . in our modern . . . complicated civilization, one sometimes needs to invent and manufacture implements before he can either sow or reap effectively."[117]

What the technological reference indicated was Edward Judson's staunch commitment to providing the best in material equipment for evangelization through finance capitalism. As tired as he was of fund raising, he tied himself in the decades ahead to another material goal: the total elimination of the Memorial Church's indebtedness. The fact that he tried to do this from 1893 to 1894, in the midst of an industrial depression, illustrated the religious imperative that infused his financial planning. "People will naturally think these times are too hard for raising money," Judson wrote Rockefeller, "but I think they are just the time to test what Christians can do when they have a good cause."[118] Hoping to eliminate the debt, which he then estimated at $50,000, Judson asked Rockefeller for a "definite subscription," which he would augment, within six months, using funds raised through annuities, legacies, and outright gifts. Offering Rockefeller the opportunity to give "the finishing stroke" to a project that he had, in fact, begun, Judson told him that "such a victory scored during these times of peculiar stringency would have great moral value."[119]

Typically, Rockefeller's reply was brusque and to the point. In a letter dated November 15, 1893, composed of simply three sentences, Rockefeller rejected Judson's request and mapped out the new directions his philanthropy would take:

> I duly received yours with reference to the proposed effort to cancel the balance of the indebtedness upon the "Judson Memorial Church" property. I must ask you to excuse me. I have just made

another large committal for Chicago, and must observe my limitations.[120]

Within the next two weeks, Rockefeller did send Judson two
checks, but each for only $100, to be applied to the church's pro-
gram for relief of the poor within his district.

Rockefeller's claim to "limitations" reflected his enormous financial commitment to the process of building and staffing the University of Chicago, a project that involved many Baptist denominational leaders and was secured as a Rockefeller priority by Fred T.
Gates.[121] In 1891, at age thirty-seven, Gates left his Morgan Park,
Illinois, home and his position as a fund raiser for the new university to come to New York to assist Mr. Rockefeller in his benevolent
work "by taking the interviews and inquiries and reporting results
for [Rockefeller's] action."[122] It was Gates' job to make some order
out of the chaotic frenzy of appeals that surrounded the nation's
wealthiest man, a process that he described in this way:

> Mr. Rockefeller was constantly hunted, stalked, and hounded al-
> most like a wild animal. In calling me from the West for his par-
> tial relief he had not exaggerated his trials and annoyances. But he
> had determined an escape. He meant what he said. And so nearly
> all comers, near or remote, friend or guest, high or low, were
> blandly sent by his ushers to my office. . . . I did my best to soothe
> ruffled feelings, to listen fully to every plea, and to weigh fairly
> the merits of every cause. I found not a few of Mr. Rockefeller's
> habitual charities to be worthless and practically fraudulent. But
> on the other hand I gradually developed and introduced into all
> his charities the principles of scientific giving, and he found him-
> self in no time laying aside retail giving almost wholly, and enter-
> ing safely and pleasureably into the field of wholesale philan-
> thropy.[123]

The transition from "retail" to "wholesale" philanthropy after
1891 meant that Rockefeller monies would no longer be distributed
to individual churches but channeled through denominational organizations which, according to Gates, "were conducted by responsible men, under suitable rules carefully thought out, [and] the
result of experience." By centralizing distribution in the official denominational agencies, such as the New York City Mission Society,
the Baptist Foreign Mission Society, and the American Baptist Education Society, Gates believed he was actually increasing the
amount of available funds and, simultaneously, basing their award

on "disinterested inquiry and comparative merit." Within the Rockefeller organization itself, applications were reviewed by committee. "Scientific giving" was Gates' contribution to Mr. Rockefeller's growing arsenal of defensive mechanisms and, also, Edward Judson's nemesis. "It was a long time," Gates admitted, "before I was able to rescue him [Rockefeller] from these begging churches."[124]

Despite Gates' opposition to individual gifts, the Rockefellers continued to support the Memorial Church program and its pastor throughout the 1890s and well into the next decade, at the rate of $3,000 per year. However, neither Rockefeller, Senior or Junior, made any effort to assist Reverend Judson in his efforts to remove the church's indebtedness. By April 1906, that indebtedness had grown to $90,000, an increase that Judson attributed to the burden of paying the annuitants, individuals, all over sixty, who had contributed to the Memorial Church and drew six percent interest on their contribution for the remainder of their lives.[125] The necessity of paying the annuitants their due appeared to put Judson under enormous pressure. Consequently, his brother Adoniram Brown wrote to Mr. Rockefeller in the hope that a frank assessment of his brother's condition would stimulate some more Rockefeller money. The industrialist's reply indicated that he would not succumb easily to the statement of personal distress:

> I have yours of the 27th . . . in reference to your dear brother with whom I have been associated in his beautiful work in New York for many years. We prize him very highly, and it would be a source of great regret to a multitude of people to have him break down under his heavy burdens. . . . [But] as you know, I have already put into the property and current expenses, during the last twenty years more or less, a large sum of money, and I regret that I do not see my way clear to carry out your suggestion with reference to the cancellation of the debt.[126]

Despite what appeared to be a definitive refusal, Rockefeller agreed on June 5, 1906, to commit $40,000 toward the elimination of the Memorial Church debt on the condition that Judson would raise $50,000, for the same purpose, within six months.[127] By September 1906, Edward Judson had met the stipulations of the Rockefeller pledge.[128] At last, it would seem that the Judson Memorial Church was finally on solid ground and that the work of urban evangelization could go forward without continual buttressing from the Rockefellers.

However, no sooner was the debt paid off than Edward Judson sought to escalate Rockefeller's annual support of the church program, disclaiming that he was "a party to any form of benevolent extortion."[129] The family, as previously mentioned, had been giving to the Memorial Church at the rate of $3,000 per year. With the gift of the $40,000 to eliminate the debt, Judson agreed to a reduction of the annual gift figure to $1,400. Rockefeller's advisory committee on philanthropic giving, headed by Fred T. Gates, reasoned that the $1,400 figure was fair, given that the Memorial Church no longer had to pay the $1,600 interest, figured at four percent, on the $40,000 portion of the total debt that Rockefeller had eliminated. Thus, Judson's October 1906 request for $1,800 in support for the year violated the terms of the pledge and put Gates and him at loggerheads. In actuality, they were arguing over little more than $400, yet the financial sophistication of the argument marshaled by Judson indicated that the minister had imbibed both the rhetoric and techniques of the captains of industry.

Judson used the "problem of the annuitants" as a justification for his claim to the additional $400 per year. In the process of raising the required funds to meet Rockefeller's stipulations, Judson, in fact, raised $25,000 more than was necessary, largely by resort to annuities on which he had to pay six percent interest. This put the church in a situation of paying six percent interest on money that was expended to pay off a debt requiring only four percent interest per year. Judson argued that the two percent difference set the church finances back, creating a $460 deficit, which Mr. Rockefeller should help to offset.[130]

Judson's shrewd analysis did not sway Fred T. Gates. Gates pointed out that the problem was being caused by the fact that Judson had raised an "overplus" of $25,000 which he was trying to use as an endowment for the church. He wrote to Judson on October 31, 1906:

> . . . why should you be so worried about this little deficit of $460? . . . You take this burden only because you assume that you must preserve your surplus intact—but why preserve your surplus intact? You have $57,000 of annuities, $32,000 of which is necessary to your debt, and $25,000 is pure overplus. Every dollar of it was contributed, not for endowment or for current expenses, but for debt, and this should be its first use. Your resources are so generous that you are amply prepared to pay the 6% on the whole $57,000 indefinitely, with the exception of $460. Is not your sur-

plus of $25,000 sufficient to take care of this little $460? You are perfectly safe in taking it annually from the $25,000 until such time as enough of your annuitants pass away to release you from paying this amount.[131]

On the issue of annuitants, Gates and Judson never saw eye-to-eye. Gates maintained that Judson had a real asset in his annuitants. "Annuitants die and there is a handsome net profit in the annuities," he told Judson. "You welcome them precisely because they do *not* eat up the principal."[132] In other words, Gates realized that Judson would not pay these elderly people six percent forever, that eventually the money paid out to them would become revenue for the church's operations. Judson, on the other hand, persistently portrayed the annuitants as an albatross around his neck. Judson ridiculed Gates for his statement of November 2, 1906, that "it is highly probable that within a year or two years at most this whole deficit will be cut off by death." The sixty-year-old Judson regarded Gates' attitude on this question as callous and implied that he would not participate in wishing for the annuitants' early demise. In fact, he claimed that those who had contributed to the church in this way lived exceptionally long lives. He told Gates that "the relief from care experienced by a Judson annuitant is so promotive of longevity, that even one's nearest relatives and expectant heirs could hardly hope for so speedy a departure as you require." The minister also repeated to Gates a jingle which a friend of his attributed to Byron:

Tis said that persons living on annuities
Are longer lived than others—God knows why.
Unless to plague the grantors—yet so true it is.
That some I really think do never die.[133]

Gates not only saw the revenue-producing potential of the annuities; he also advised Judson to use the "overplus" and went on record against the very concept of church endowments. According to Gates, he and Mr. Rockefeller shared a common vision "that the permanent endowment of evangelistic agencies [was] not desirable." Gates stated that there was no precedent in Rockefeller's pattern of gifts for supporting a church with an endowment. "For myself," he told Reverend Judson, "I think that history justifies the statement that a church debt tends more to the prosperity of Zion than a church endowment."[134] To Rockefeller, Gates wrote a more pointed statement of his case: "[Dr. Judson] is, in a nutshell, asking you for endowment and nothing else; and it illustrates also the flimsy pretext on which even our best men, if the personal channel is once created, will come back to you after having received the most generous treatment, and compel us, painfully to all concerned, to resist and deny them."[135] Judson's counterarguments—that aggressive missionary work among the immigrants justified an endowment and that "other communions like the Presbyterians and Episcopalians" supported their institutional churches by the revenues of endowment—were to no avail.[136]

The Rockefellers continued to authorize their $1,400-a-year contribution on the assumption that Reverend Judson maintained a balanced budget each year. It was, therefore, with great surprise and disappointment that John D. Rockefeller learned in November 1910, that the Memorial Church was back in debt, to the extent of $20,000.[137] Gates had learned of this situation somewhat earlier when he asked Judson to provide information on whether or not his yearly estimates for receipts and expenditures were, in fact, accurate. This resulted in a lengthy correspondence which disclosed the "floating indebtedness." Gates blamed the situation on Judson's failure to report his receipts and expenditures accurately. Although he claimed to balance his budget each year, Judson was actually spending $5,000 to $6,000 more per year than he was taking in.[138] Even with this admission, the cleric unabashedly asked Mr. Rockefeller to consider increasing his 1910-1911 contribution from $1,400 to $2,400.[139]

Gates made the following recommendation to Rockefeller: "I am now inclined to think that the best service you can render to the Memorial Church and to the Baptist denomination, is to decline to make the usual annual contribution or any contribution." Gates also advised that the church be turned over to the Baptist City Mission Society, one of the denominational agencies that was already a part of the Rockefeller system of centralized philanthropic giving.[140] Disappointed by Judson's inability to steer a clear financial course, the Rockefellers agreed to Gates' recommendation and authorized the committee to inform Judson that he would no longer receive operational or any other kind of financial support from them.

The disclosure of the true nature of the church's finances opened up the larger question of the value and effectiveness of the Reverend Judson's work. While no one in the Rockefeller organization ever questioned Judson's personal veracity, their internal correspondence suggests that, under Gates' leadership, the Memorial

Church program and its minister underwent careful scrutiny. An illustration of this increasingly critical view came from the pen of John D. Rockefeller, Jr., who had known and respected the pastor all his life. "Dr. Judson is a true and good man," he told Fred T. Gates, but he followed with a less than deferential question: "If [Judson's] work has and has had the merit to warrant us in our contributions to it, how is it that all of New York and his large acquaintances outside fail to respond to [his] needs[?]"[141]

Gates had been developing his own response to that question for a number of years. His relationship with the pastor of the Memorial Church never had the warmth or intimacy of the Judson-Rockefeller relation, which was distinguished by familial gatherings, interest in the development of their respective children, mutual recognition of special wedding anniversaries, and the like. Gates maintained an absentee relationship with Judson's church, supporting it to the extent of $50 per year, and worshiped in his home church in Montclair, New Jersey. In 1897, when Judson wrote to him asking for an increase in his contribution, Gates declined in a manner that foreshadowed the position he would take as the architect of "scientific giving": "I am in such close personal touch with our various societies, such as Home Missions, Foreign Missions, Education, etc. that I prefer to make my contributions directly to their treasuries unless there are special reasons why I should do so through the Memorial Church."[142]

Because Judson was never able to come up with a "special reason" that satisfied Gates, the contribution remained at the $50 level until as late as 1906. It seems that Judson considered this long-standing token gift an affront and wrote Gates, in March 1906, inquiring as to what he was doing with his money for the cause of religion and, apparently, asking questions about his doctrinal beliefs. Gates recounted all his denominational giving and stated that he gave the customary ten percent.[143] In May of the same year, Gates returned to Judson copies of sermons that the cleric had sent him, along with his critique of Judson's views. After describing his own "little creed" as "helpful and reasonably satisfying," Gates told Judson that much in the sermons was "assumed without discussion to be true." Indeed, he took issue with Judson's apparent statement of the need for Christians to uphold an orthodox creed:

> I greatly doubt whether these fundamental assumptions necessary to orthodoxy, have much moral value. I am convinced that the things for which you contend in these sermons, while comforting,

are not at all essential to one who, without avowing belief or dis-
belief in any of them, is yet quite certain that the Spirit of Jesus . . .
is the salvation of the individual and of society, and who is seeking
to possess that Spirit in its fullness, to practice it in its daily life and
to propagate it as best he can in the world.[144]

The doctrinal jousting between Gates and Judson was an indication of the former's unwillingness to treat the latter with any special delicacy, despite his distinguished position within the denomination.[145] In a series of memos that preceded the Rockefellers' 1910
withdrawal from the Memorial Church, Gates spelled out, in no
uncertain terms, his reservations about the voracious Reverend Judson and his work in lower New York. At the start, Gates objected to
Judson's constant manipulation of his personal friendship with
Rockefeller, his "illgrace" in admitting that he created an endowment, and his constant recitation of "great personal sacrifices,"
when, in fact, "the denomination has given him the money to meet
all his requirements."[146] In noting Judson's "granitelike determination" to build an endowed church, Gates sarcastically suggested
that Judson had "missed his calling . . . [and] should have been a fi-
nancier, a politician or a diplomat," rather than a minister to the
spirit:

> I want to pause here to call attention to the marvelous money-get-
> ting qualities of this man. Starting in thirty years ago with noth-
> ing, in the heart of New York, he has created a Church property
> worth more than half a million dollars; he has got it, not from the
> City of New York chiefly, but from other cities all of which have
> their own affairs to attend to, besides the unceasing denomina-
> tional calls from every direction, in my opinion very much more
> worthy and imperative than his. Imagine, if it is possible to pic-
> ture in the imagination, the extraordinary tact, persistence, diplo-
> matic skill and personal charm required to extract more than half
> a million dollars from such sources! What might not such a man as
> this have done had he been at the head of one of our great denomi-
> national societies. . . . What might not he have done in business as
> the head of a great corporation, or in politics had he been am-
> bitious for high place![147]

Despite Judson's enormous fund-raising talents, Gates saw no
payoff in the actual religious work of the Memorial Church. "The
service which the church has rendered for many years and is rendering to the community in which it lives," Gates told Rockefeller,
"is by no means proportionate to the enormous amount of money

that has been put into the plant and to the $20,000 which it annually costs."[148] Just in case the message was not clear, Gates made the following report to the Rockefellers:

> His [Judson's] church numbered, three years ago, 613; two years ago, 622; last year, 637. The Baptisms numbered, three years ago, 8; two years ago, 13; last year, 14. His Sunday School numbered, three years ago, 350; two years ago, 250; last year, 325. When one considers that these meagre results represent thirty years of work, with many helpers . . . and that he has at no time been able to give any considerable visible and tangible moral and spiritual achievements that can be expressed statistically, the marvel of his success in getting money for this enterprise borders closely on the miraculous.[149]

Simply put, "the results [were] not commensurate with the costs in a lifetime," wrote the efficient Fred T. Gates.

In fact, Judson, by this point, had little evidence to the contrary. Although he attributed the Memorial Church's difficulties to an improper location, he could hardly blame his lack of quantitative success on a site that he himself chose and then "sold" to Mr. Rockefeller. The question of why his Institutional Church failed to make significant inroads among the immigrants, despite its program of education and social service, was consistently tied, in his mind, to the need for larger and better implements of evangelization and not to the difficulties of cultural assimilation and religious conversion. Judson's letter to his longtime friend, Rockefeller, Senior, indicated that he did not differ, essentially, with the committee's negative evaluation of his present situation:

> I only wonder that during these declining days of my work, when I have had such meagre results to show, as compared with my first years in New York, that you have held out so long and patiently in helping me; and my heart is full of gratitude to you for your gift of continuance, when such kindness on your part must have seemed to many a kind of *waste*, and about the only thing that kept me from well-deserved disaster. My undertaking, however, has been so long sick, without actually dying, that I am almost inclined to think that it may get well after all, and that the good Father will somehow see to it that the work to which I have given the best thirty years of my life will not prove at last a kind of *Judson's Folly*.[150]

Nearly three years later, on June 17, 1913, the Judson Memorial Church property was transferred to the New York City Baptist

Mission Society, thereby placing the church's administration in the hands of the executive committee of that society.[151] The transfer was the culmination of a process set in motion by Fred T. Gates who, undoubtedly, disliked Judson for his capacity to slip through the rational screening procedures he was creating to administer the Rockefeller philanthropies.

Even within the world of religion, standardization began to take precedence over personal relationships and, supposedly, meritocracy would reign.[152] The transfer of the church property, then, was a function of scientific giving and signaled the decline of the power of the individual church polity and minister. Yet, in the context of each church, persons of wealth took on increasing importance, revealing how the essential relationship between the pastor, as almoner, and the individual Christian had changed. In the Gilded Age, aggressive religious work required millions rather than mites, a new reality that was symbolized in the story of Edward Judson and John D. Rockefeller. In countless communities across the country the pattern was repeated: wherever accumulations of wealth became obvious, the evangelical clergy sought access to it. The fact that Edward Judson ultimately failed does not change the case. One has only to contrast the angular simplicity of antebellum church architecture with what came after 1880 to see the discontinuity, to discover the character of evangelicalism at the turn of the century. After 1880, and certainly by 1900, a large number of heretofore struggling evangelical congregations were affluent enough to support a mannered and grandiose church architecture as well as the employment of celebrity clerics. At the same time, the popular values of Victorian America led families like the Rockefellers into the cultivation of clerics as personal friends and advisors.

The elder Mr. Rockefeller continued to send the Judson family personal gifts and to make spontaneous small gestures of support. In the summer of 1911, when Edward Judson visited the Rockefeller family at their Forest Hills estate, he was authorized to purchase, at the industrialist's expense, a victrola for the Memorial Church.[153] In December 1913, when the Baptists celebrated the Judson Centenary, marking the one-hundredth anniversary of Adoniram Judson's mission to Burma, the Rockefellers participated in the denominational festivities. In addition to a $300 contribution for the Judson Centenary dinner, John D. Rockefeller, Jr., sat at the head table for that event.[154] In the same year, both father and son also contributed to a testimonial fund for Edward Judson.[155] When the Rockefellers celebrated their Golden Wedding Anniversary in 1914, Judson did not neglect to send a special message of congratulations. Neither did the ailing pastor miss the opportunity to invite John D. Rockefeller, Jr., to serve as toastmaster at his conference dinner in February 1914. Hoping that he could attend, and "bring that great father of [his] along," Judson promised father and son a "rousing welcome."[156]

The relationship between Edward Judson and John D. Rockefeller persisted for over three decades. When the cleric died, in October 1914, his daughters, Margaret and Elizabeth, received the following telegram from Rockefeller's son, John, Jr.: "My heart is deeply saddened by the news which reaches me this morning. Your father was my dearly beloved and honored life long friend."[157] Two years before his death, in a letter of thanks for his perennial $100 Christmas check, Judson had told Rockefeller: "I count your friendship as one of the most inexpressibly precious things in my life, not only for the direct aid which you have given me . . . but especially that you have let me feel something of the friendly warmth of your home since I first met you down in the old Berean Church. . . ."[158]

If the evangelical pastor was induced, by his own ideology and the circumstances of life in modern America, to seek the company of rich rather than humble men, he often paid the price in terms of a personal crisis of spirit. Edward Judson's career certainly exemplified the evangelical malaise. Caught between his ideological presuppositions about the content and value of a Christian life and the social problems of an urbanized, industrialized, and heterodox America, he forsook piety for the intricacies of finance capitalism, the only earthly guarantor of a continually expansive religious program. By his own definition he had failed in the essential task. "The important thing, after all," he wrote, "is not the building up of the Church, but the Christianizing of the community."[159]

In tying himself to the rationalistic use of capital and to problems of interest and endowments, Edward Judson changed his vocabulary and abdicated the role of moral leader that his father had marked out. For Adoniram Judson, Jesus and the Apostles were the primary models for behavior, his generation admiring those men and women who could spiritually feed the multitudes. Because he both admired and coveted Rockefeller's capacity to materially feed the multitude, Edward Judson put himself in a position whereby his life and religious work depended, to a large extent, on the approval of that man. It was no accident, then, that Judson exalted their "personal relation" even in the face of the committee's rejection of his life's work, or that Rockefeller continued to befriend the pastor despite an essentially bureaucratic decision to terminate their former financial relationship. Whatever anger or disappointment Judson and Rockefeller may have felt with each other's failures, they cloaked their emotions in the garments of cordiality that inevitably characterized this reciprocal but self-serving relationship. In the process of building a material memorial to Adoniram Judson, the industrialist and the pastor played out the dynamics of "benevolent extortion," heralding the dawn of a new era for American evangelical religion.

In the century between the inception of Adoniram Judson's Burmese mission and the death of his youngest son, the Judson family walked many of the main routes that American evangelicals traveled. For all its emphasis on a literal biblical tradition, evangelicalism was not a static concept, proving itself remarkably resilient in the face of wide-scale social and economic change.

Throughout the nineteenth century, evangelicals both resisted and accommodated themselves to contemporary cultural forms and ideologies. In this respect, the Judson family personified the evangelicals' consistent adaptability and helped to shape it. Beginning in the last decades of the eighteenth century, the evangelical clergy increasingly directed their efforts to the conversion of American youth. By the 1840s, the print-oriented evangelical community adopted popular fiction as well as the tract, acting as a spur to the national publishing industry and to the flowering of a sentimental culture. In the 1890s, evangelicals were able to incorporate and infuse contemporary science and industrial capitalism with their own religious imperatives. This pattern of religious expropriation of secular trends appears to be one of initial resistance, followed by absorption whenever the deluge seems inevitable. So it is, that, in our own time, the cultural manifestations of evangelical religion are remarkably coextensive with our popular culture.

Afterword

Because the past and present work together to illuminate our understanding, I have chosen to conclude the story of the Judson family with a brief postscript touching on the characteristic spirit and form of evangelical religion in our own time. In the 1970s, evangelical Protestant expansion has become so notable that it is not unfitting to describe the period as a "Fourth Great Awakening."[1] Moreover, in addition to the traditional constituency for Protestant evangelicalism, there are now evangelical Episcopalians and an estimated one million evangelical Catholics, all of whom share a basic faith in the authority of the Bible and personal experience with Jesus Christ.[2]

In many ways, evangelical Protestantism demonstrates remarkable continuity. Despite the unprecedented social and economic changes that have reshaped American life in the past century, contemporary evangelicals continue their staunch and self-defining adherence to the necessity of an individual conversion experience, the acceptance of Christ as the personal savior, and the importance of intimate acquaintance with the word of God, as set forth in Scriptures. Today, as in the nineteenth century, the evangelicals are passionate in articulating their sense of the divine in every aspect of life. In this respect, Adoniram Judson and his family would not be uncomfortable with the thrust of the modern movement.

Almost everywhere one looks in contemporary American society one can find "born again" Christians: in politics, in entertainment and sports, in business, and even in the universities among an estimated 300 different sections of the Campus Crusade for Christ.[3] A 1976 Gallup Poll revealed that one American in three, or thirty-four percent have been born again. This fact translates into the following startling figure: among Protestants, nearly half—or forty-eight percent—identify themselves as born again Christians.[4] All of the following individuals have acknowledged publicly their personal conversion experience: James Earl Carter, Eldridge Cleaver, Charles Colson, Walter Hoving (Tiffany's), Michael Ford (son of Gerald and Betty Ford), Julian Carroll (Governor of Kentucky), Jesse Helm (U.S. Senator from North Carolina), Archie Griffin (Heisman Trophy winner), Graham Kerr (The Galloping Gourmet), Dale Evans, Kent Benson (basketball player), Pat Boone, Stan Smith (tennis player), Lindsay Wagner and Dean Jones (actors), B. J. Thomas (musician), Donna Fargo (musician), and Mark Hatfield (United States Senator from Oregon).

Regarded by the more secular as an eccentric relic, religious conversion—the touchstone for all evangelicals—has become an integral part of American life in the "Me Decade." In fact, personal religious experience with God is as much a part of life in our narcissistic culture as many of the more flamboyant, hedonistic behavioral expressions against which the evangelicals preach.[5] For, when all is said and done, the marketing of the conversion process in America has extracted from the product all but a residual Calvinist flavoring. Individuals are now enjoined to submit to a kindly God not because they are degraded sinners but rather to realize their full potential. The titles of a number of recent religious best sellers reveal how much today's born again Christians have in common with the constituency of the secular human potential movement: *Feeling Free, Give Yourself a Chance, The Joy Robbers*.[6] In today's evangelical Christianity, the love of, by, and for Jesus is purported to have a therapeutic effect. To be born again as a Christian is to be allowed and encouraged to practice religion as an act of self-love and not simply as an act of traditional Christian self-denial.

This change is important, but its direction is actually quite predictable on the basis of the nineteenth-century record. In the history of the Judson family, we have observed how the practitioners of evangelical religion, beginning in the early stages of industrial development, were willing and able to adopt secular packaging in the interest of selling their product and extending their religious message. It should come as no surprise, therefore, that contemporary evangelicals are not cut off by their religious faith from either popular cultural expression or from the possibilities of worldly, material success. The evangelical community continues to build its constituency through a network of what Edward Judson called "tentacular" forms, geared to the needs and tastes of contemporary Americans, particularly Christian publishing and bookstores; a Christian rock music and entertainment industry; and worldwide radio, television, and satellite communications programming.

The capacity to harness technology to the service of religion has been a persistent fact of American cultural life since the early nineteenth century. Colportage wagons and chapel cars journeying to the West, as well as the deployment of printing presses to foreign fields, were the nineteenth-century expression of this leitmotif. Today, the Christian Broadcasting Network brings the nightly PTL (Praise the Lord) Club to seventy percent of the television households in America and operates (since 1978) an earth satellite transmission and receiving station capable of relaying the same religious telecast in up to thirty-two different languages.[7] Missionaries, such as the Akron, Ohio-based Humbard family, regard television as a "Christian miracle" which has extended their names and influence around the world. Like many other contemporary religious entrepreneurs, the Rex Humbard World Wide Ministry, Inc., offers such diversified Christian services as travel tours and estate planning; its publications and Sunday morning television programs are both professionally produced and filmed in order to display the choral skills of three generations of the family in a Christianized, variety show format. Billy Graham and Oral Roberts, two of the best known of the nation's estimated 2,000 broadcast preachers, are each reported to have drawn as many as 60 million viewers with a single TV performance.

The evidence suggests that a significant number of contemporary Americans substitute evangelical religious programming, on radio and TV, for the once traditional weekly and semiweekly worship service in the local church. The reasons for this are complex and they reflect a number of important changes in American society having to do with geographic mobility, standards of living, communications theory, and religious faith in general. One line of argument is that families without long-standing community roots may feel more comfortable worshiping in the privacy of their own living room than in a church among strangers. Another explanation may be that television has so conditioned American responses that people prefer to receive their weekly religious supplement from a distant, larger-than-life figure rather than from an ordinary minister known to grasp for words or suffer from human foibles. What is interesting about this phenomenon of "arm chair evangelicalism" is that it has not even remotely freed its constituency from the burden of financing religion. The typical broadcast preacher in the 1970s still devotes a sizeable portion of his airtime to the traditional moral exhortation that is the evangelical fund-raising style. Because the cost of television ministries is so high, the broadcast preacher must generate enormous funds in order to buy airtime and expand the work. Despite the fact that these television ministries must inevitably compete for gifts with local evangelical churches and ministers, just as nineteenth-century itinerant revivalists challenged the settled clergy's capacity to "bring in the sheep," both fields continue to grow. According to the editor of *Religious Broadcasting* magazine, there is "one new religious radio station going on the air each week and one new Christian TV station starting each month." The National Religious Broadcasters Association claims that it reaches 130 million Americans every week.[8]

The rapid increase in religious broadcasting over the past decade is paralleled in the realm of publishing, where religion is also good business; Christian book sales in the United States exceed $600 million annually.[9] Within a four-week period in the autumn of 1978, the Zondervan Corporation of Grand Rapids, Michigan, sold 1.2 million copies of a new evangelical translation of the Bible.[10] Billy Graham's most recent work, *Holy Spirit*, sold 300,000 copies for Word Books in Waco, Texas, within 90 days, boosting the evangelist's all-time sales to over 20 million books.[11] A recent national report on religious publishing revealed that retail sales in Christian bookstores increased on an average of seventeen percent annually over the past five years, while retail sales in the secular bookmarket rose by only nine percent.[12] It is no wonder that *Publishers Weekly*, the journal of the secular book trade, now devotes two special issues a year to the religious book market and that trade publishers like Doubleday, Scott Foresman, and Harper and Row have developed their recent lists with an eye to the growing audience for a contemporary Christian literature. These media successes suggest that, in the decade of the seventies, the nation's 45 million evangelicals probably comprise one of the single most expansive sectors of the American economy.

The aggressive entrepreneurial posture of the evangelicals has permeated the national political life as well. On one level, the direction of mainstream evangelical politics is primarily defensive, embodying the social and economic values of an increasingly middle-class constituency that sees itself as self-made, hard-working, and too easily preyed upon by big government, labor, minorities, and inflation. Certain segments of the contemporary evangelical community, however, have moved beyond these middle-class attitudes to a patently aggressive position on a number of related social issues, all of which have to do with the status and role of women in American society. In this sense, the selling of anti-Feminism has become a major preoccupation among many on the so-called "evangelical right."[13]

Evangelical anti-Feminism emanates from a number of different sources which are passionately involved with the defense of the patriarchal family and with the simultaneous assertion of women's social uniqueness.[14] The personification of the anti-Feminist evangelical is Marabel Morgan, an ex-beauty queen from Ohio State University and former staff member of the Campus Crusade for Christ, whose two books, *The Total Woman* (1973) and *Total Joy* (1976), have sold more than three million copies. Morgan, who posits that women find happiness only when they make their husbands the center of their lives, details the techniques of sexual enticement and subordination to men in her "Total Woman" courses which are taught in 60 cities throughout the United States.[15]

More typical is the kind of contemporary advice literature generated by the Thomas Road Baptist Church of Lynchburg, Virginia, under the direction of its pastor, the successful broadcast preacher, Dr. Jerry Falwell. In *Faith Aflame*, the free magazine that serves as an organ of the Falwell ministry, evangelical readers are warned against the disintegration of the American family, a phenomenon that is linked to the assertion of female authority and autonomy within the family. According to Dr. Ed Hindson, Director of Counseling for Thomas Road Baptist Church Ministries:

"Someone once said: 'Anything with two heads belongs in the zoo!'
That includes your family. Two-headed families are as confusing as
they are clumsy. . . . When no final authority exists in the family,
confusion and arguing always result."[16] Hindson goes on to detail
the proper form of patriarchal family governance. And he uses biblical explication to color the story, the point of which is to demonstrate the injury feminist women do to men and to their own delicate emotional structure:

> The Bible clearly states that the wife is to submit to her husband's
> leadership and help him fulfill God's will for his life (cf. Eph.
> 5:22-24; Col. 3:18). There can be no doubt as to the meaning of
> these passages. She is to submit to him, just as she would submit to
> Christ as her Lord. This places the responsibility of leadership
> upon the husband, where it belongs. In a sense, submission is the
> wife learning to duck, so God can hit the husband. He will never
> realize his responsibility to the family as long as she takes it. If the
> wife wants her husband to be more of a leader, she must let go of
> the reins. Most men do not enjoy fighting their wife for control of
> the family, so they sit back and do nothing. In time, the wife has a
> nervous breakdown trying to run something God did not call her
> to run.[17]

At the same time that she is directed to submit to her husband's
jurisdiction in familial matters, the evangelical woman of the 1970s
unabashedly pursues a public role, as a political activist on behalf
of the anti-ERA, antiabortion, or antigay rights campaigns. Anita
Bryant, voted "Most Admired Woman" in a 1978 *Good Housekeep-
ing* poll, is a born again Christian who mobilized thousands in her
crusade to prohibit homosexuals from teaching in Dade County,
Florida. As in the nineteenth century, the majority of evangelical
women probably still choose to identify themselves with spiritual,
rather than political, movements. However, many of the evangelical churches have put aside their traditional distaste for women in
politics and have attempted, much in the spirit of nineteenth-century reform, to harness female energies to the work of expressing
the voice of what Jerry Falwell calls "the moral majority."

In the decades ahead, it would not be surprising to see evangelical women attempt to forge the kind of cultural dominance they
had in mid-nineteenth-century America. After all, many born again
Christian women see themselves as combatants in the struggle for
control of American culture and society. A May 1979 mailing from
Maude Aimee Humbard was cast in these terms. Written in long-
hand on cream and blue stationery, as if it were a personal letter

among women friends, the wife of the Akron evangelist spoke about the blessings of grandchildren, a beautiful family, and her husband of thirty-eight years. She also expressed the "heartache" she felt for her grandchildren's future, a future threatened by "sick values and filth." As a Christian mother and grandmother, Maude Aimee Humbard sees the issue clearly: "I know Satan is roaring through this country, spreading his garbage everywhere."[18]

In order to insure both moral and financial support for this point of view, the Humbard letter included a "Christian Survey and Support Poll," designed to increase the sense of participation in this socioreligious campaign to control secular culture. Recipients of the letter were asked to make a donation only after registering their approval or disapproval of the following statements:

> I'm offended by immorality, crime and violence in America.
> I believe the decay of the American family unit is increasing.
> I believe America must turn back to God to save our land.
> YES, Maude Aimee, I agree with you, and I will do my part to bring the cleansing power of Jesus to all the families in America.

To date, Maude Aimee's efforts to sample and shape popular feelings about American society have not had a specific political outlet or connection. Maude Aimee, however, is not the only popular evangelical to undertake the assault on contemporary American social values. Jerry Falwell, the Lynchburg evangelist, recently launched a similar effort, the "1979 Clean Up America Campaign," on the steps of the nation's capital.[19] Political organizations of born again Christian women, freed from the traditional evangelical proscription against female political activity, have already begun to coalesce around a number of important public policy issues: prayers and sex education in the schools, textbooks, community sanctions against pornography and obscenity, the Christian School movement, protective legislation for the family, and content control of television programming. As even the secular begin to cry for a return to "basics" in American education, the evangelical cultural critique may become extremely seductive. Should the "Christian revival" continue, "the moral majority" will surely intersect with national and local politics in ever-increasing ways. In modern dress, the evangelicalism of Adoniram Judson and his family persists and, consequently, it remains a significant motif in our cultural life even as we approach the twenty-first century.

Notes

Introduction

1. Robert Middleditch, *Burmah's Great Missionary. Records of the Life of Adoniram Judson* (New York, 1854), p. 26. This is Judson's terminology, not that of the author of the memoir.
2. Martin Marty, *Righteous Empire* (New York, 1970).
3. For a good overview of the debate over the concept of culture, see A. L. Kroeber and Clyde Kluckhorn, *Culture: A Critical Review of Concepts and Definitions*, Papers of the Peabody Museum of American Archaeology and Ethnology, XLVII (1952).
4. Hannah Chaplin Conant, *The Earnest Man, or The Character and Labors of Adoniram Judson* (Boston, 1856), p. 452.
5. Timothy Dwight, *A Sermon Delivered in Boston, September 16, 1813* (Boston, 1813), pp. 5–7.
6. Mary Ryan, *Womanhood in America: From Colonial Times to the Present* (New York, 1975), pp. 142–43.
7. "The Evangelicals: The Empire of Faith," *Time* 110:26 (December 26, 1977), pp. 52–58.

8. Avery Hamilton Reid, *Baptists in Alabama: Their Organization and Witness* (Montgomery, Alabama, 1967); Louise Manley, *History of Judson College* (Atlanta, 1913).

CHAPTER 1

1. Conant, p. 470.
2. For Congregationalist histories of the ABCFM, see Rufus Anderson, *Memorial volume of the first fifty years of the American Board of Commissioners for Foreign Missions* (Boston, 1862), idem, *History of the Missions of the American Board of Commissioners For Foreign Missions* (Boston, 1874); and William E. Strong, *The Story of the American Board. An Account of the First One Hundred Years of the American Board of Commissioners for Foreign Missions* (Boston, 1910). More contemporary studies are: John A. Andrew III, *Rebuilding the Christian Commonwealth: New England Congregationalists and Foreign Missions, 1800–1830* (Lexington, Ky., 1976); Charles L. Chaney, *The Birth of Missions in America* (Pasadena, Calif., 1976); Clifton Jackson Phillips, *Protestant America and the Pagan World: The First Half Century of the American Board of Commissioners for Foreign Missions, 1810–1860* (Cambridge, 1969). The first ten annual reports of the ABCFM were printed in Boston by Crocker and Brewster in 1834; these cover the important early years of the Board (1810–1820).
3. The story of Adoniram Judson's change of religious sentiment is reported uniformly by Baptist writers. Typical is the following from Jesse Clement, *Memoir of Adoniram Judson: being a sketch of his life and missionary labors* (Auburn, 1851), pp. 49–51: "During the voyage it occurred to Mr. Judson, that he should there [in India] meet the English Baptist missionaries, and perhaps, have occasion to discuss the question of baptism; accordingly, while engaged in translating the Scriptures, he examined this point very critically, and before the voyage was ended he had nearly decided that immersion was the primitive and only legitimate mode." See Middleditch, pp. 52–55; William Gammell, *History of American Baptist Missions* (Boston, 1849), pp. 6–8; and Francis Wayland, *A Memoir of the Life and Labors of Rev. Adoniram Judson, D.D.* (Boston, 1853), pp. 102–10.

   Adoniram Judson wrote letters to the following New England clergymen to explain his change of commitment: Thomas Baldwin, pastor of the Second Baptist Church in Boston and editor of the *Massachusetts Baptist Magazine*; Lucius Bolles, pastor of the First Baptist Church in Salem; Daniel Sharp, pastor of Charles Street (Baptist) Church in Boston; and Samuel Worcester, pastor of the Tabernacle

Church (Congregational) at Salem and a founder of the ABCFM. Judson's letters appeared, in part, in most of the posthumous biographies and in the pages of the *Massachusetts Baptist Missionary Magazine (MBMM)*.

4. *MBMM* III (March 1813), pp. 266–70.

5. *MBMM* III (May 1813), pp. 294–96.

6. Gammell, p. 16. William Gammell was a Professor of Rhetoric and English Literature at Brown University (1835–1850) and an editor of the *Christian Review*. See William Cathcart, *The Baptist Encyclopedia* (Philadelphia, 1881), I, p. 43.

7. This is Oliver Elsbree's estimate of Baptist membership in 1812. Most Baptists were in Virginia, Kentucky, and New York. In fact, according to Elsbree's statistics, there were "more Baptists in Virginia in 1812 than in all of New England." See Oliver Elsbree, *The Rise of the Missionary Spirit in America, 1790–1815* (Williamsport, Pa., 1928), p. 36. For a standard history of the denomination, see A. H. Newman, *A History of the Baptist Church in the United States* (New York, 1894).

8. Walter Wyeth, *Ann Hasseltine Judson: A Memorial* (Cincinnati, 1888), p. 76. For a description of Rice's important role as an agent and publicist for the Baptist foreign mission cause, see L. T. Gibson, "Luther Rice's Contribution to Baptist History," unpublished Ph.D. dissertation, Temple University, 1944; and E. B. Pollard, *Luther Rice: Pioneer in Missions and Education* (Philadelphia, 1928). There is also an antebellum biography: James Barnett Taylor, *Memoirs of Luther Rice* (Baltimore, 1840). See also Charles Wesley Brooks in *A Century of Missions in the Empire State* (Philadelphia, 1900).

9. Elsbree, pp. 116–17.

10. Wyeth, p. 76.

11. Letter published in *MBMM* III (September 1813), p. 321.

12. For a listing of all of the American editions, see Edward Starr, *A Baptist Bibliography, being a register of printed material by and about Baptists* (Philadelphia, 1947–1976), XII, pp. 194–95.

13. Reported in Phillips, pp. 35–37.

14. Judson answered these charges in a letter to Rev. Thomas Baldwin, published in the *MBMM* IV (September 1816), pp. 346–48.

15. Enoch Pond, *Nott's Testimony in Favor of Judson. Examined in a Letter Addressed to Rev. Samuel Nott. Late Missionary to India* (Boston, 1819). For an additional Congregationalist critic of Judson, see Moses Stuart, *A Sermon Preached in the Tabernacle Church, Salem* (Andover, 1818).

16. Samuel Nott, *A Letter Addressed to Rev. Enoch Pond on the Insinuations and Charges Contained in His Reply to Mr. Judson's Sermon on Baptism* (Boston, 1819).

17. Gordon Hall, *Anecdotes of the Bombay Mission for the Conversion of the Hindoos* (London, 1836), p. 29. This tension between sectarianism and denominational cooperation is basic to an understanding of Protestant evangelical religious culture in the period 1790–1850. While sectarian controversy was officially discouraged because it was divisive, and a "roadblock" on the way to the millennium, it had value as a means of "energizing" and "awakening" Christians. As in the Judson case, sectarian controversies, which resulted in the extension of the evangelical enterprise through the formation of more organizations, were usually explained as the working out of God's will. The broad outlines of relationships between the evangelical sects are described by Sidney Mead in "Denominationalism: The Shape of Protestantism in America" in *The Lively Experiment* (New York, 1963), pp. 103–33; and Marty, pp. 67–77.

18. For studies of male geographical mobility, see Stephan Thernstrom and Peter R. Knights, *Men in Motion: Some Data and Speculations about Urban Population Mobility in Nineteenth-Century America* (Los Angeles, 1970); Stephan Thernstrom, *The Other Bostonians: Poverty and Progress in the American Metropolis, 1880–1970* (Cambridge, 1973); and Joseph F Kett, *Rites of Passage: Adolescence in America 1790 to the Present* (New York, 1977). Information on female mobility is almost nonexistent. See Thomas Dublin, "Women Workers and The Study of Social Mobility," *Journal of Interdisciplinary History IX* (1978–79), pp. 647–65.

19. Whitney Cross, *The Burned-Over District: The Social and Intellectual History of Enthusiastic Religion in Western New York, 1800–1850* (Ithaca, 1950), p. 8. Cross does observe that it may have been easier to switch sects in "youthful" regions than in New England. (There is evidence, however, that denominational mobility was not restricted solely to upstate New York.) Cross's work describes the surface manifestations of the Second Awakening. Other relevant studies are: Sydney E. Ahlstrom, *A Religious History of the American People* (New Haven, 1972); Richard Birdsall, "The Second Great Awakening and the New England Social Order," *Church History XX-XIX* (1970); Richard Carwadine, "The Second Great Awakening in the Urban Centers: An Examination of Methodism and the New Measures," *Journal of American History LIX* (1972); Nancy F. Cott, "Young Women in the Second Great Awakening in New England," *Feminist Studies III* (1975); Charles R. Keller, *The Second Great Awakening in Connecticut* (New Haven, 1942); Donald Matthews, "The Second Great Awakening as an Organizing Process," *American Quarterly XXI* (1969); William McLoughlin, *The American Evangelicals, 1800–1900* (New York, 1968), idem, *The Meaning of Henry Ward Beecher: An Essay on the Shifting Values of Mid-Victorian*

America, 1840–1870 (New York, 1970); William Warren Sweet, *Revivalism in America* (New York, 1944), idem, *Religion in the Development of American Culture, 1765–1840* (New York, 1952).

20. Cathcart, I, p. 93.

21. Ibid., p. 603.

22. Quoted in Gerda Lerner, *The Grimke Sisters from South Carolina* (New York, 1967), p. 68.

23. Ernst Cassara, "Augusta Jane Chapin," in Edward T. James, ed., *Notable American Women* (NAW) I (Cambridge, 1971), p. 321.

24. *NAW*, I, p. 122. See Kathryn Kish Sklar, *Catharine Beecher: A Study in American Domesticity* (New Haven, 1973).

25. Lyman A. Eddy, "Private Diary and Journal of Passing Events," August 1829–November 1831, Warren Hunting Smith Library, Hobart and William Smith Colleges.

26. For a local history study of the way in which Presbyterians and Episcopalians maintained their hegemony in one Western New York town, see G. David Brumberg, "Geneva, N.Y.: A Community Study, 1780–1860," unpublished Ph.D. dissertation, Miami University, Oxford, Ohio, 1977.

27. *The Columbian Star*, March 6, 1824, quoted in Daniel Gurden Stevens, *The First Hundred Years of the American Baptist Publication Society* (Philadelphia, 1925), pp. 5–6.

28. Gammell, p. 177.

29. Harriett Raymond Lloyd, ed., *Life and Letters of John Howard Raymond* (New York, 1881), p. 149.

30. Middleditch, pp. 359–60.

31. William Hague, *The Life and Character of Adoniram Judson. A Commemorative Discourse before the American Baptist Missionary Union, Boston, May 15, 1851* (Boston, 1851), pp. 22–23. Hague (1808–1878) was author of *Home Life: Twelve Lectures* and served as pastor of Baptist churches in Utica, Boston, Providence, Newark, Albany, and New York City. He also served on the editorial board of the *Christian Watchman*, a Baptist weekly begun in Boston in 1819. Cathcart, I, p. 485.

32. Cathcart, I, pp. 648–49. See Florence Hopkins Kendrick Cooper, *An American Scholar: A Tribute to Asahel Clark Kendrick, D.D. 1809–1895* (New York, 1913).

33. Letter from Hezekiah Harvey to Lucy Loomis, November 1845, Hezekiah Harvey Papers, Colgate University Archives.

34. Ibid.

35. Ibid.

36. Trumansburg Baptist Church Records, May 12, 1832, Department of Manuscripts and University Archives, Olin Library, Cornell University.

37. There are indications that a number of male children were named for Adoniram Judson; Middleditch, pp. 354–55, says that "not a few had rejoiced to enroll it [Judson's name] in the registers of their families." At least three young men who became Baptist ministers were named for him: Adoniram Judson Frost (b. 1837, Parishville, N.Y.) who graduated from the Hamilton Seminary in 1867; Adoniram Judson Gordon (b. 1832, New Hampton, N.H.) who graduated from Brown University in 1860; Adoniram Judson Joslyn (b. 1819, Nunda, N.Y.) who organized the Union Park Baptist Church in Chicago and was editor of the Elgin, Illinois, *Gazette*. Their biographies are in Cathcart, I, pp. 419–20, 459–60, 625. A more bizarre case involved the murder of one Adoniram Judson Burroughs, brother of the president of the Baptist Theological School in Chicago. The July 1865 trial was brought to my attention by Mary Beth Norton and Karen Kaufmann Richards of Cornell University.

    Middleditch also observed that "seminaries and young men's Christian societies" bore Judson's name.
38. *New York Baptist Register* XX (January 16, 1846), p. 2, and XX (January 23, 1846), p. 3. Sectarian purpose was almost consistently disavowed by religious publicists of the period.
39. Middleditch, pp. 354–55.
40. Conant, p. 472.
41. Gammell, pp. 178–79.
42. The most elaborate literary remnant of Judson's visit is a giftbook, John Dowling, ed., *The Judson Offering, intended As A Token of Christian Sympathy with the Living, and A Memento of Christian Affection for the Dead* (New York, 1846), which was in its fifth thousand by 1847. Dowling, pastor of the Berean Church in New York City and author of *The History of Romanism* (New York, 1845) retold the story of the Judsons' trials in Burma and included selected poetry and prose which dealt with either the Judsons or missionary themes. The commemorative volume had at least a dozen engravings of scenes from the Judsons' life in Burma. For other Judson volumes issued in 1846, see: *The Missionary Offering: A Memorial of Christ's Messengers in Heathen Lands, dedicated to Dr. Judson* (Auburn, 1846) and *Statistical Sketch of Dr. Judson's Missionary Life* (New York, 1846); and Abram Dunn Gillette, "Adoniram Judson," *Christian Souvenir I* (December 1846), pp. 295–300.
43. Wayland, I, p. 127.
44. Copy of a letter from Samuel Colgate to Mary Colgate, January 30, 1846, in Colgate University Archives. William Learned Marcy was not actually a senator at this time, but was, in fact, Secretary of War in Polk's cabinet. Cathcart, II, p. 748.
45. *Utica Daily Gazette* IV (October 22, 1845), p. 2.

46. Middleditch, p. iii.
47. James D. Knowles, *Memoirs of Ann H. Judson* (Boston, 1835), p. 9.
48. Benjamin B. Wisner, *Memoirs of the late Mrs. Susan Huntington, of Boston, Mass.* (Boston, 1826), p. viii.
49. Asahel Clark Kendrick reports this in *The Life and Letters of Mrs. Emily C. Judson* (New York, 1861), p. 394. The memoir in question was either withheld at Mrs. Judson's request, or, if we construe "New York publisher" to mean New York State, it could be Jesse Clement, *Memoir of Adoniram Judson: being a sketch of his life and missionary labors* (Auburn, 1851). Clement was a layman. The Auburn edition reached at least 7,000; later in the decade it was printed in Buffalo and in New York City.
50. Letter reprinted in Kendrick, p. 394.
51. See above, n. 3. Middleditch was born and educated in England and was sent as a Baptist missionary to Jamaica, West Indies, in 1844. He came to the United States in 1846 and was ordained in New Jersey in 1848. He was the pastor at Red Bank, New Jersey, from 1850 to 1867. Cathcart, II, pp. 790–91.
52. See Kendrick, pp. 398–403 for the exchange of letters between Emily Chubbuck Judson and E. H. Fletcher. In 1854, a case was brought by Fletcher against C.B. Norton (of the *Literary Gazette*) for publishing uncomplimentary remarks made about him by Francis Wayland. Because the letters between Emily Chubbuck Judson and E. H. Fletcher were offered as evidence at the trial, they were published in a number of newspapers. Norton was acquitted.
53. R. W. Cushman, *Grace and Apostleship: Illustrated in the Life of Judson. A discourse delivered, before the Maryland Union Association, May 5, 1851* (Philadelphia, 1854). For biographical information on Cushman and other Baptist biographers, see Cathcart, I, II.
54. Ibid., p. 3.
55. Edgar Harkness Gray, *The Christian Hero of the Nineteenth Century: a discourse on the life of A. Judson* (Shelburne Falls, Mass., 1851). In 1865, Gray was one of four clergymen who officiated at Lincoln's funeral; the others represented the Presbyterian, Episcopal, and Congregationalist denominations.
56. Abram Dunn Gillette, *A Sketch of the Labors, Sufferings, and Death of the Reverend Adoniram Judson, D.D.* (Philadelphia, 1851). Gillette was responsible for introducing the young author, Fanny Forester (Emily Chubbuck), to Adoniram Judson. See Chapter 5 for that story.
57. Rufus Babcock, *A Discourse Commemorative of the Life and Labors of the Rev. Adoniram Judson, D.D.* (New York, 1851). Babcock served as president of the American Baptist Publication Society and was editor of the *Baptist Memorial* from 1841 to 1845.

58. For biographical information on Hague, see n. 31 above.

59. See n.4 to the Introduction. Conant's book was designed for a juvenile audience. As editor of *The Mother's Journal*, Hannah Conant knew Emily Chubbuck Judson and began work on this volume, at her request, after Judson's widow became too ill to complete it.

60. Daniel C. Eddy, *A Sketch of Adoniram Judson, D.D. The Burman Apostle* (Lowell, 1851). See n. 65 below.

61. Starr, XII, p. 189.

62. Samuel Lorenzo Knapp, *Female Biography: Containing Notices of Distinguished Women, in different nations and ages* (New York, 1834), p. 279.

63. Cecil B. Hartley, *The Three Mrs. Judsons, the Celebrated Female Missionaries* (Philadelphia, 1863), p. 3.

64. See Chapter 4.

65. Daniel C. Eddy, *Heroines of the Missionary Enterprise, or Sketches of Prominent Female Missionaries* (Boston, 1850); idem, *Daughters of the Cross; or Woman's Mission* (New York, 1855); idem, *The Three Mrs. Judsons, and other daughters of the Cross* (Boston, 1859). See Cathcart, I, p. 112 for information and bibliography on Eddy.

66. *Godey's Lady's Book* XXXII (August 1848). The engraving was accompanied by an article by Rufus Wilmot Griswold, "The Heroism of the Knights Errant and of the Female Missionaries of America," pp. 61–68. In addition to the two Mrs. Judsons, the article and engravings highlighted Harriet Newell, Harriet Bradford Stewart, and Elizabeth Baker Dwight. Newell, a Congregationalist, had gone off with her husband at the same time as the Judsons, under ABCFM sponsorship. She died at the age of nineteen, before reaching the missionary field. See *The Life and Writings of Harriet Newell* (Philadelphia, 1831).

67. *Geneva Gazette* IV (July 22, 1848), p. 2.

68. Arabella Stuart Willson, *The Lives of Mrs. Ann H. Judson and Sarah B. Judson, with a biographical sketch of Mrs. Emily C. Judson* (Auburn, 1851). Arabella Stuart Willson resided in Canandaigua, Ontario County, N.Y., in 1851. There is no evidence that she was a Baptist. She also wrote *Disaster, Struggle, and Triumph, The Adventures of 1000 "boys in blue." Dedicated to the 126th Regiment of New York* (Albany, 1870).

69. Starr, XII, pp. 206–7.

70. Willson, p. iv.

71. James D. Knowles, *Life of Mrs. Ann H. Judson, late missionary to Burma. With an Account of the American Baptist Mission to that Empire* (Philadelphia, 1830). Knowles (1798–1838) studied with William Staughton in Philadelphia before becoming pastor of the Second Baptist Church in Boston (1825). He was appointed to a professorship at

the Newton Theological Institution where he began his connection with the *Christian Review*, a religious quarterly. He was the author of a memoir of Roger Williams. Cathcart, I, p. 655. It is difficult to determine the publication figures. This information has been culled from Starr, XII, pp. 203–5 and *The National Union Catalogue, Pre-1956 Imprints* (Mansell).

72. Harvey Newcomb, *A Practical Directory for Young Christian Females, Being a Series of Letters from a Brother to a Younger Sister. Written for the Massachusetts Sabbath School Society and Approved by the Committee of Publication* (Boston, 1833), p. 268. Newcomb does not refer to the Knowles volume by the author's name. He suggests "memoirs" as a generic category and simply lists the subjects' names. Knowles' was the obvious and only volume of this type at that time.

73. Lydia Maria Child, *Good Wives* (Boston, 1833), p. 246.

74. Elizabeth Camp's comments were called to my attention by Fay Dudden of The University of Rochester. Camp Family Papers (#555), Department of Manuscripts and University Archives, Olin Library, Cornell University.

75. *Geneva Courier* XV (January 4, 1842), p. 4; Starr, XII, p. 204.

76. Emily Chubbuck Judson, *Memoir of Sarah B. Judson, member of the American Mission to Burma* (New York, 1848). Publishing information from Starr and Mansell.

77. Asahel Clark Kendrick, *The Life and Letters of Mrs. Emily C. Judson* (New York, 1861). Asahel Clark Kendrick was the nephew of Nathaniel Kendrick, president of the Hamilton Literary and Theological Institution. Publication figures are from Starr and Mansell.

78. A popular treatment of Sarah Josepha Hale is Ruth Finley's *The Lady of Godey's* (Philadelphia, 1931). On Sigourney, see her own autobiography, *Letters of Life* (New York, 1866); Gordon S. Haight, *Mrs. Sigourney: The Sweet Singer of Hartford* (New Haven, 1930); Ann D. Wood, "Mrs. Sigourney and the Sensibility of Inner Space," *New England Quarterly* (NEQ) XLV (1972).

79. Sarah Josepha Hale, *Woman's Record; or, Sketches of All Distinguished Women* (New York, 1855), p. 369.

80. Lydia Huntley Sigourney, "On Reading the Memoir of Mrs. Judson," reprinted in Knowles, pp. 348–49, and *Judson Offering*, p. 146.

81. Lydia Huntley Sigourney, "Burial of Mrs. Judson at St. Helena," reprinted in *Judson Offering*, p. 241.

82. H.B.H., "Mrs. Judson's Funeral," in *Judson Offering*, pp. 236–39. H.B.H. is probably Horatio Balch Hackett (1808–1875), who was reared as a Congregationalist and educated at Phillips Academy, Amherst, and Andover Theological Seminary before becoming a Baptist and a professor at Brown University. Cathcart, I, pp. 483–84.

83. Pamela S. Vining, *Christian Herald*, date unknown, poetry clipped and pasted to a personal copy of Clement's biography of Judson.

84. Maria Mansfield Papers, Department of Manuscripts and University Archives, Olin Library, Cornell University.

85. Margaret Fuller manuscripts, November 1839, quoted in Judith Kennedy Johnson, ed., *The Journals of Charles King Newcomb* (Providence, 1946), p. 14.

86. On the relationship between Romanticism and Transcendentalism, see Octavius Brooks Frothingham, *Transcendentalism in New England* (Gloucester, Mass., 1959) and Kenneth Walter Cameron, *The Transcendentalists and Minerva: Cultural Backgrounds of the American Renaissance* (Hartford, 1958). An interesting piece of evidence for the relationship between the two movements is Kenneth Walter Cameron, ed., *Transcendental Reading Patterns: Literary Charging Lists for the Alcotts, James Freeman Clarke, Frederick Henry Hedge, Theodore Parker, George Ripley, Samuel Ripley of Waltham, Jones Very, and Charles Stearn Wheeler—New Areas for Fresh Exploration* (Hartford, 1970). On Romanticism and evangelicalism see Ralph Gabriel, "Evangelical Religion and Popular Romanticism in Early 19th Century America," *Church History* XIX (1950), pp. 34–47.

87. S. Washburn (lyrics) and L. Heath (music), "The Burial of Mrs. Judson at St.Helena, September 1, 1845" (Boston, 1846). I am indebted to Mildred O'Connell and to Mary Gallagher Durfee for locating this piece of Judsoniana. Mary Gallagher Durfee also supplied me with information about Charlotte Newcomb, who was her great aunt.

88. Ibid.

89. Marty, p. 167.

90. P. Douglass Gorrie, *The Churches and Sects of the United States* (New York, 1850), p. 132, estimates that there were only 30,000 Unitarians at mid-century. Other Protestant groups that might be construed as hostile to evangelical religious practice and/or activities were the Protestant Episcopal Church (70,000), the Universalists (100,000), the Anti-Mission Baptists (20,000), and the Old School Presbyterians (192,000). Baptist, Methodist, and Presbyterian/Congregational evangelicals numbered over 30 million, according to Gorrie.

91. Kett, p. 83, describes the connection between evangelicalism and educational institutions for youth.

CHAPTER 2

1. See Thomas Baldwin, *A Brief Account of the Late Revivals of Religion* (Boston, 1799), p. 4; *The American Baptist Magazine and*

Missionary Intelligencer (January, 1817), p. 24; *A Narrative of the Late Revivals of Religion in the Bounds of the Geneva Presbytery* (Geneva, N.Y., 1832), p. 7; *Memoirs of the late Miss Lucy Richards of Paris, Oneida County, N.Y.* (New York, 1842), p. 12; *Evangelical Intelligencer* (October, 1808), p. 488; Bennet Tyler, *New England Revivals, As They Existed at the Close of the Eighteenth and the Beginning of the Nineteenth Century* (Boston, 1846); Edwin D. Starbuck, *The Psychology of Religion: An Empirical Study of the Growth of Religious Consciousness* (New York, 1906); G. Stanley Hall, *Adolescence: Its Psychology and Its Relations to Physiology, Anthropology, Sociology, Sex, Crime, Religion and Education*, I and II (New York, 1905).

On sexual composition in revivals, see Maurice Armstrong, "Religious Enthusiasm and Separation in Colonial New England," *Harvard Theology Review* (1945), pp. 111–40; Cedric Cowing, "Sex and Preaching in the Great Awakening," *American Quarterly* XX (1968), pp. 624–44; Herbert Moller, "Sex Composition and Correlated Culture Patterns in Colonial America," *William and Mary Quarterly* II (1945), pp. 113–53.

On the developmental needs of adolescents and their expression in evangelical religious conversion, see Kett, pp. 62–85; Cott, pp. 20–21; Eric Erikson, *Identity: Youth and Crisis* (New York, 1968).

Erikson's well-known description of the growth process is certainly suggestive for a study of the involvement of youth in evangelicalism. Evangelicals were not only concerned about youth but extended to them opportunities for involvement and status. In turn, youth found in evangelicalism the kind of "mission for life" that is associated with their developmental needs.

2. Knowles, p. 11.
3. Clement, p. 2.
4. Wayland, I, pp. 14–15.
5. Willson, p. 13.
6. Wayland, I, p. 23.
7. Clement, p. 25; Knowles, pp. 49–50; Willson, p. 22.
8. Leonard Woods, *History of the Andover Theological Seminary* (Boston, 1888), p. 36.
9. The neglect of the mothers in the biographies of the Judsons is peculiar given the evangelical emphasis on the mother's role in Christian nurture. This is not to say that the mothers are absent or unconcerned about their children's spiritual state; they simply are not portrayed in any real detail. See Ann Douglas, *The Feminization of American Culture* (New York, 1977), pp. 74–76, 99–100; Ann L. Kuhn, *The Mother's Role in Childhood Education: New England Concepts, 1830–1860* (New Haven, 1947).

10. Adoniram Judson, Sr., *A Sermon Preached in the New Meeting House, Plymouth, December 22, 1802 in Memory of the Landing of Our Ancestors* (Boston, 1803), p. 11. Judson, Sr., was born at Woodbury, Connecticut, in 1752. He was descended from William Judson, who emigrated from Yorkshire, settling at Concord. Judson, Sr., married Abigail Brown of Tiverton, R.I., in 1786. Before going to Plymouth, he held pastorates in Wenham, Malden, and Braintree.

   According to Lemuel Hall Barnes, *Pioneers of Light: The First Century of the American Baptist Publication Society, 1824–1924* (Philadelphia, n.d.), p. 9, Adoniram Judson, Sr., was a Congregationalist home missionary in Vermont. Adoniram Judson, Jr., never mentioned his father's activity in this regard. However, a letter from Arthur W. Smith to Edward Judson, in December, 1913, states that Edward's grandfather was, indeed, a Congregationalist missionary to Vermont for twelve weeks prior to assuming his pulpit in Plymouth. Edward Judson Collection, American Baptist Historical Society.

11. Judson, Sr., p. 12.
12. Ibid., p. 21.
13. Ibid.
14. Ibid., p. 14.
15. Cotton Mather, *Magnalia Christi Americana* (Hartford, 1855), p. 564.
16. Jonathan Edwards, *An Account of the Life of the Late Reverend Mr. David Brainerd* (Boston, 1749).
17. Willson, p. 17; *An American Lady, Sketches of the Lives of Distinguished Females Written for Girls with a View to their mental and moral Improvement* (New York, 1833), p. 192; Knowles, p. 36. Sarah Hall also read Brainerd's biography. Knowles, p. 34.
18. Woods, p. 169. Woods knew Adoniram Judson personally and delivered the sermon at his ordination. See *A Sermon Delivered at the Tabernacle Church in Salem, February 6, 1812 on the Occasion of the ordination of Rev. Messrs. Samuel Newell, Adoniram Judson, Samuel Nott, Gordon Hall and Luther Rice* (Stockbridge, 1812). In addition to his professorship at Andover, he was a member of the Prudential Committee of the ABCFM for twenty-five years.
19. See F. A. Cox, *History of the English Baptist Missionary Society from A.D. 1792 to A.D. 1842* (Boston, 1844), for a description of the origins of this endeavor.
20. Carey, the first British Baptist missionary, wrote *An Enquiry into the Obligation of Christians to Use Means for the Conversion of the Heathen* (Leicester, 1792). Joshua Marshman and William Ward joined him in the field in 1799. All three were of humble back-

ground. Carey was a shoemaker prior to his missionary involvement; Joshua Marshman had been a weaver. William Ward, son of a carpenter, had been apprenticed to a printer. See George Smith, *The Life of William Carey, D.D., Shoemaker and Missionary, Professor of Sanskrit, Bengali, and Maratni in the College of Fort William, Calcutta* (London, 1885).

21. *Panoplist* (March, 1806), pp. 462–64; *Connecticut Evangelical Magazine* (April, 1806; January, 1807), pp. 342–43, 270–71; Elsbree, pp. 105–6.

22. See Elsbree, pp. 51–55, 77–80; Chaney, Chapter I; Helen Emery Fall, "Women in Missions Support in the Nineteenth Century," *Baptist History and Heritage* XII (January, 1977), pp. 26–36; and James A. Patterson, "Motives in the Development of Foreign Missions among American Baptists, 1810–1826," *Foundations: A Baptist Journal of History and Theology* XIX (October-December, 1976), pp. 298–319. Most of the writing done on foreign missions has been the product of "professional religionists." See n. 24 below for an exception.

23. Elsbree, p. 63.

24. Andrew, pp. 70–81.

25. Edwin Dwight, *Memoir of Henry Obookiah, a Native of Owhyhee, and a Member of the Foreign Mission School* (New Haven, 1818), pp. 6–11.

26. Dwight, p. 17.

27. On Mills and the Brethren, see Gardiner Spring, *Memoirs of the Rev. Samuel J. Mills* (New York, 1820); Richard Donald Pierce, "A History of the Society of Inquiry in the Andover Theological Seminary, 1811–1920 and a Brief History of the Brethren, 1808–1873," unpublished thesis, Andover-Newton Theological Seminary, n.d.; *Memoir of American Missionaries formerly connected with the Society of Inquiry Respecting Missions in the Andover Theological Seminary* (Boston, 1833). Other relevant material is in Elsbree, pp. 100–101; Phillips, pp. 23–26; and John Haskell Hewitt, *Williams College and Foreign Missions* (Boston, 1914), pp. 73–76.

28. Dwight, p. 22.

29. Henry K. Rowe, *History of Andover Theological Seminary* (Newton, 1933), p. 14; Daniel Day Williams, *The Andover Liberals: A Study in American Theology* (New York, 1941), pp. 2–7.

30. Gordon Hall, *Anecdotes of the Bombay Mission for the Conversion of the Hindoos: Exhibiting an Account of the Travels and Missionary Labors of Messrs. Hall, Newell, Judson, Mills, Richards, Rice and Nott* (London, 1836), p. 3.

31. Dwight, p. 23.

32. Ibid.

33. Those who departed in 1812 to do the work of evangelization were Gordon Hall, Luther Rice, Newell, Nott, and Judson. Mills never became a foreign missionary. In the spring of 1812, the ABCFM appointed him to take a tour in the western and southern states. Mills became the premier domestic missionary of his day and founded the American Bible Society.

34. Phillips, pp. 90–91.

35. Lyman Beecher, *A Sermon Delivered at the Funeral of Henry Obookiah* (New Haven, 1818), pp. 33–34.

36. See Rufus Anderson, *Memoir of Catherine Brown, a Christian Indian of the Cherokee Nation* (Boston, 1824); Elias Cornelius, *The Little Osage Captive* (Boston, 1822); Francis Mason, *The Karen Apostle: or, Memoir of Ko Thau-Dya, the First Karen Convert* (Boston, 1843); Harlan Page, *A Memoir of Thomas Hamitah Patoo, a Native of the Marquesas Islands, Who Died July 19, 1823, while a Member of the Foreign Mission School, in Cornwall, Conn.* (Andover, 1825); William Richards, *Memoir of Keopuolani, Late Queen of the Sandwich Islands* (Boston, 1825); *Sketches of Pious Nestorians Who Have Died at Oroomiah, Persia* (Boston, 1857); Deborah B.L. Wade, *The Burman Slave Girl: Also, Narrative of the First Burman Inquirer, and of the First Converted Burman . . .* (Boston, n.d.).

37. Evangelical religion was the primary organizational force behind higher education in the antebellum period. Between 1800 and 1850, in New England, New York, and Ohio, Congregationalists spawned Amherst, Middlebury, Western Reserve, Oberlin, and Marietta. Presbyterians were linked to Union, Hamilton, New York University, University of Buffalo, Elmira College, and Muskingum. Baptists founded Colby, Colgate, The University of Rochester, Alfred, Vassar, and Denison. The Methodists organized Wesleyan, Baldwin-Wallace, and Ohio Wesleyan. Episcopalians founded Trinity, Hobart, and Kenyon. Universalist-sponsored institutions (e.g., Tufts and St. Lawrence) came after 1850, with the exception of Norwich (Northfield, Vermont). Fordham University was the lone Catholic institution in New England and New York prior to 1850. See Donald G. Tewksbury, *The Founding of American Colleges and Universities before the Civil War, with Particular Reference to the Religious Influences Bearing upon the College Movement* (New York, 1932), Appendix, pp. 211–20. In the national context, Presbyterians founded 49 colleges before the Civil War; Methodists, 34; Baptists, 25; Congregationalists, 21; Catholics, 14; Episcopalians, 11; Lutherans, 6; Disciples of Christ, 5; German Reformed, 4; Universalists, 4; Friends, 2; Unitarians, 2; Dutch Reformed, 1; United Brethren, 1.

　　See also Thomas Woody, *A History of Women's Education in the United States I* (New York, 1929), pp. 319–414; Harry C. Reiner, "A

Study of the Decline of the Academy in New York State and the Disposition of the Property," unpublished Ph.D. dissertation, Cornell, 1932, p. 19. On the relationship between religion and education, see Bernard Bailyn, *Education in the Forming of American Society* (New York, 1960), p. 40; Laurence Stone, "Literacy and Education in England, 1640–1900," *Past and Present* (February, 1969), pp. 69–139; Richard Altick, *The English Common Reader: A Social History of the Mass Reading Public, 1800–1900* (Chicago, 1957), pp. 99–128.

38. *Narrative of the Presbytery of Geneva*, p. 5.
39. I. M. Laurence, Geneva, N.Y., to Ruth A. Whitaker, Benton, Yates County, N.Y. January 31, 1831, Geneva Female Seminary Collection, Archives, Geneva (N.Y.) Historical Society.
40. C. Woolsey, Geneva, N.Y., to Ruth A. Whitaker, Benton, Yates County, N.Y., January 31, 1831, Geneva Female Seminary Collection, Archives, Geneva (N.Y.) Historical Society.
41. *Narrative of the Presbytery of Geneva*, p. 6, and James Harvey Hotchkins, *History of Western New York* (New York, 1848), p. 144.
42. From the *Milwaukee Sentinel* (November 14, 1877) quoted in Walter F. Peterson, "Mary Mortimer: A Study in Nineteenth Century Conversion," Presbyterian Church in the U.S.A., Department of History Journal XLI (1963), p. 83.
43. Knowles, pp. 16–17.
44. Ibid.
45. Ibid., p. 25; Willson, p. 18.
46. Knowles, p. 18.
47. Ibid.
48. Journal of Fanny Kingman, (n.p.), collection of the author.
49. Kett, p. 63.
50. Teaching after conversion was a common sequence of events for young women. One of the issues faced by the young convert-turned-teacher was the question of whether or not to begin school with a prayer. In the 1830s, Fanny Kingman labored over this decision; in the first decade of the century, Ann Hasseltine faced a similar question. She opened her schools in Salem, Haverhill, and Newbury with prayer and was thankful she was "enabled" to do so. "The little creatures seemed astonished at such a beginning," she wrote, "probably some of them had never heard a prayer before." Knowles, p. 53. It is unlikely that these New England youngsters had never heard a prayer. What seems more plausible is that there was some question about the etiquette of prayer in the publicly supported common schools where sectarianism was inadmissible.
51. Fanny Kingman to New Bedford Sabbath School Class, March 1843, in Journal of Fanny Kingman (n.p.).

52. Peterson, pp. 83–88. Mary Mortimer, founder of the Milwaukee Female College (1851), was an associate of Catharine Beecher. In 1852, Beecher, her sister, Harriet Beecher Stowe, and Mortimer formed the American Women's Educational Association.

53. Ibid., p. 83.

54. Knowles, p. 22.

55. Kingman Journal.

56. Knowles, p. 28.

57. John and Virginia Demos, "Adolescence in Historical Perspective," *Journal of Marriage and the Family* XXXI (November, 1969), pp. 632–39, claim that the concept of the "adolescent" and the "peer group" was an impossibility before the city. According to Demos, it was urbanization and subsequent spacial disintegration of the family that gave children the opportunity to develop peer contacts. It is my intention to suggest throughout this chapter that, in the evangelical crusade, peer group associations and situations were important at least two decades before the 1830s, when urbanization became a fact of life in the United States.

58. Phillips, pp. 29–31.

59. Quoted in Hewitt, p. 75.

60. Tewksbury, p. 67, and Kett, p. 74. See also Henry Wood, "Historical Sketches of Revivals of Religion in Dartmouth College, Hanover, New Hampshire," *American Quarterly Register* X (November, 1836), pp. 177–82; David Allmendinger, *Paupers and Scholars: The Transformation of Student Life in 19th Century New England* (New York, 1975). On college revivalism and foreign missionary societies, see Shedd, pp. 48–75; Chaney, pp. 98–100; and Phillips, pp. 29–31.

61. Letter of Leonard Woods, November 20, 1850, in D. C. Eddy, *A Sketch of Adoniram Judson. The Burman Apostle* (Lowell, 1851), pp. iv–v.

62. Fletcher, p. 15; Wayland, p. 22, wrote "young Judson did not escape the contamination." Although Brown was founded by Baptists (1764) and maintained a certain percentage of Baptists on its Board, there is no evidence that the experience at Brown had any direct bearing on Adoniram Judson's later switch to that denomination. His home town of Plymouth was, after all, about equidistant from Providence and Cambridge (Harvard). Given recent events at Harvard, the Judsons probably chose the Baptist college.

63. Shedd, p. 41.

64. Fletcher, p. 15.

65. Adoniram Judson, *The Elements of English Grammar* (Boston, 1808) and idem, *The Young Lady's Arithmetic: a complete mercantile system* (Boston, 1808).

66. Wayland, p. 23, and other biographers. Also mentioned in Appleton's *Cyclopedia of American Biography* III (New York, 1888), p. 483.
67. See Chapter V.
68. Williams, p. 8.
69. Woods, p. 136.
70. Woods, p. 136; Wayland, pp. 24–25.
71. Thomas Boston, *Human Nature in its Fourfold State of primitive integrity, entire depravity, begun recovery, and consummate happiness or misery* . . . (Boston, 1796); Claudius Buchanan, *The Star in the East; A Sermon, Preached in the Parish Church of St. James, Bristol, on Sunday, February 26, 1809* (Boston, 1809).
72. Quoted in Fletcher, pp. 21–22. Gammell, pp. 2–3, and Wayland, p. 29, also credit the Buchanan piece with having great influence on Judson. In addition to its independent circulation, which went through ten editions, Buchanan's sermon was reprinted in *The Massachusetts Baptist Missionary Magazine* in September 1809, the same month Judson recalled reading it.
73. Edward Judson, *Adoniram Judson*, p. 562.
74. *Narrative of the Presbytery of Geneva*, pp. 6–7.
75. Modernization theory provides one way of approaching the organization and "system" characteristic of antebellum evangelicalism. See Richard D. Brown, "Modernization and the Modern Personality in Early America, 1600–1865: A Sketch of a Synthesis," *Journal of Interdisciplinary History* II (1972) and *Modernization: The Transformation of American Life, 1600–1865* (New York, 1976). See also E.P. Thompson, "Time, Work, Discipline and Industrial Capitalism," *Past and Present* XXXVII (1967), pp. 56–97 and Keith Thomas, "Work and Leisure in Pre-Industrial Society," *Past and Present* 29 (1964), pp. 50–66.
76. The Graham Society was organized in 1816 by Isabella Graham, a devout Presbyterian. The purpose of the group was to promote Sabbath schools in New York. Douglas, p. 112.
77. The Corban Society was founded in Boston in 1811 in order to raise money to support worthy candidates for the ministry. See *Act of Incorporation and Constitution of the Corban Society* (Boston, 1817).
78. Benjamin B. Wisner, ed., *Memoirs of the late Mrs. Susan Huntington* (Boston, 1826), p. 128.
79. With all the dangers inherent in youthful association, the evangelical denominations continued to generate institutions and organizations that brought young people together. From the perspective of some students of nineteenth-century American culture, this collectivization of religious experience in the period 1790–1850 was a hedge against heterodoxy. For the "social control" interpre-

tation, see John R. Bodo, *The Protestant Clergy and Public Issues,
1812–1848*: Charles I. Foster, *An Errand of Mercy: The Evangelical
United Front, 1790–1837* (Chapel Hill, 1960); Clifford S. Griffin,
*Their Brothers' Keepers: Moral Stewardship in the United States,
1800–1865* (New Brunswick, 1960); Paul E. Johnson, *A Shopkeeper's
Millennium: Society and Revivals in Rochester, N.Y., 1815–1837*
(New York, 1978). For a critical assessment of this interpretation, see
Lois W. Banner, "Religious Benevolence as Social Control: A Cri-
tique of an Interpretation," *Journal of American History* LX (June,
1973), pp. 23–41.

80. See Henry Dwight, *The Centennial History of the American Bible
Society* (New York, 1916), pp. 93–94. Also, Elsbree, p. 55, notes the
existence of an interdenominational Young Men's Missionary Society
of New York (1809) and the Presbyterian Youth's Assistant Missionary Society (1809).

81. *Geneva Gazette* (March, 1831), p. 2. See Arthur C. Cole, *A
Hundred Years of Mt. Holyoke College* (New Haven, 1940), for a description of many student-initiated projects. Mt. Holyoke actually
had a Judson connection: Mary Lyon, founder of the institution, was
converted by Joseph Emerson, a New England educator and Congregationalist. Emerson was married to Rebecca Hasseltine, sister of
Ann.

82. For a detailed account and interpretation of the beginnings of the
ABCFM and the involvement of the Congregationalist leadership in
the foreign missions projects, see Andrew, pp. 70–81.

83. See *Memoirs of American Missionaries, Formerly Connected with
the Society of Inquiry Respecting Missions in the Andover Theological Seminary* (Boston, 1833), pp. 20–21; Hinton S. Lloyd, "Adoniram Judson and the Institution at Hamilton," *Watchman-Examiner*
(January 29, 1914), p. 2.

84. David Bogue, *A Sermon Preached at Tottenham Court Chapel
Before the Founders of the Missionary Society, September 24, 1795*
(Cambridge, 1811).

85. Records of ABCFM quoted in Phillips, pp. 20–21.

86. On the way to England, Judson's ship was captured by a French
privateer. All of his biographies include some brief mention of the
fact that he spent several weeks in a French prison at Bayonne.

87. On Hopkinsian Calvinism and its influence, see Chaney, pp. 74–76;
Elsbree, pp. 141–45; Phillips, pp. 6–8; Joseph Haroutunian, *Piety
Versus Moralism: The Passing of the New England Theology* (New
York, 1932), p. 87; William Warren Sweet, *Religion in the Develop-
ment of American Culture, 1790–1815* (New York, 1952), p. 147.
See Woods, pp. 45–50 and Rowe, pp. 12–22 for information on the
Hopkinsian party in the founding of Andover.

88. A typical article by Morse promoting the foreign mission cause is "Concern for the Salvation of the Heathen," *Panoplist* V (May 1810), pp. 545–46.
89. *Panoplist* VI (September 1811), p. 180. Probably Worcester was abandoning South America because of Catholic missions there.
90. S. M. Worcester, *Life and Labors of Rev. Samuell Worcester* II (Boston, 1852), p. 123.
91. From the *Monthly Anthology*, quoted in Williams, p. 7. William Bentley called the missionary plan a "mad scheme [that] cannot be too much reprobated." See *Diary of William Bentley* (Salem, 1911), V, p. 82. Andrew, p. 198, identifies another Unitarian critic of missions: Thomas Robbins of Connecticut.
92. Bogue, pp. 22–23.
93. See Chapter 4 for further discussion of the evangelical presentation and view of non-Protestant culture.
94. Bogue, p. 22.
95. Ibid., pp. 18–19. Bogue takes on all these objections, pp. 3–20.
96. *Memoirs of Mrs. H. Newell, Wife of the Reverend S. Newell, American Missionary to India* (London, n.d.), p. 7.
97. James Colman died in 1818, Edward Wheelock in 1817. The strange circumstances of Wheelock's death are recounted in *American Baptist Magazine (ABM)* II (March 1820), pp. 305–6. See *ABM* IV (January 1823) for an account of Colman's death.
98. *Christian Examiner* VI (May 1829), p. 257. The reviewer, according to *Poole's Index*, is Francis Parkman; the article, however, is unsigned.
99. Quoted in Emily Chubbuck Judson, *The Kathayan Slave and Other Papers Connected with Missionary Life* (Boston, 1853), p. 29.
100. *New York Express* (1846) is reported to have written that notices of female missionary sailings are "too often followed by accounts of early death." Quoted in *Kathayan Slave*, p. 29.
101. Ibid., pp. 35–36.
102. *Boston Evening Transcript* XVII (March 27, 1846), p. 4807
103. Phillips, pp. 307–13.
104. Two examples of the literature of childhood sacrifice are: *The Missionary Daughter: A Memoir of Lucy Goodale Thurston of the Sandwich Islands* (New York, 1842); and *The Persian Flower: A Memoir of Judith Grant Perkins, of Oroomiah, Persia* (Boston, 1853).
105. Richards, pp. 267–68.
106. Ibid., p. 268.
107. Quoted in William W. Fenn, "The Revolt Against the Standing Order," *The Religious History of New England* (Cambridge, 1917), p. 112.

CHAPTER 3

1. Adoniram Judson, *The Holy Bible, containing the Old and New Testaments: translated into Burmese*, 2nd ed. (Maulmain, Burma, 1840).

2. Adoniram Judson, *Burman and English Dictionary*, Burman-English portion edited by E. A. Stevens (Serampore, 1852).

3. See pp. 69–70 and n. 36 below.

4. For a suggestive discussion of why Protestantism emerged in the sixteenth century as a "culture of the book" (as opposed to Tridentine Catholicism, a "culture of image"), see Lawrence Stone, "Literacy and Education in England, 1640–1900," *Past and Present*, (February, 1969) pp. 77–78. See also R. M. Kingdom, "Patronage, Piety and Printing in Sixteenth Century Europe," in D. H. Pinkney and T. Rupp, eds., *A Festschrift for F. B. Artz* (Durham, 1966), p. 26.

5. Issac F. Shepard, ed., *Christian Souvenir: An Offering for Christmas and the New Year* (Boston, 1843), p. 300.

6. *New York Baptist Register* XX (June 30, 1843), p. 1.

7. Such secular publications as the *Boston Recorder* V (December 16, 1820 and December 23, 1820) would occasionally print interesting extracts from the Judson journals. Also, until the news of his switch to the Baptists, there were preliminary reports of the mission in the Congregational *Connecticut Evangelical Magazine* VI (January-May 1813).

8. Almost all of the primary source material on the Judsons was printed in the nineteenth century, indicating a popular interest in any material pertaining to their lives. Wayland refers to the unfortunate destruction of Adoniram's personal papers prior to his death in 1850. Ann Hasseltine and Sarah Hall have no extant, unpublished papers, as far as I know. Some letters by Emily Chubbuck, which were not printed in the Kendrick biography, are in the Jerome Chubbuck Collection, State Historical Society of Wisconsin. Many letters that never made the magazines while the Judsons were alive appeared in the posthumous biographies.

9. Ann Hasseltine Judson, *A Particular Relation of the American Baptist Mission to the Burman Empire. In a Series of letters addressed to Joseph Butterworth, Esq., M.P., London* (Washington City, 1823).

10. *MBMM* IV (December 1814), p. 11.

11. Knowles, p. 91.

12. Ibid., p. 71.

13. Ibid., p. 96.

14. Ibid., p. 136.

15. *Western New York Baptist Missionary Magazine (WNYBMM)* II (February 1817), pp. 26–28.
16. Knowles, pp. 137–45.
17. Knowles, pp. 136–37.
18. Ibid., p. 272.
19. Wayland, I, p. 174. Pali is a dialect of Sanscrit that was introduced into Burma with the Buddhist religion. Many Pali words were in common usage by the Burmese and many theological words were Pali in origin.
20. *WNYBMM* II (May 1817), p. 49. Scriptural translations by Protestants became an issue within the nondenominational American Bible Society in 1836. Although the group initially paid $5,000 toward printing Judson's Burmese translation, controversy developed over the translation of the word *baptism* as *immersion* in a Bengali version. Baptists left the cooperative endeavor and formed their own Bible Society: the American and Foreign Bible Society. See *New York Evangelist* VII (May 7, 1836), pp. 102, and (May 14, 1836), p. 3; Henry Otis Dwight, *The Centennial History of the American Bible Society* I (New York, 1916), p. 130; John M. Gibson, *Soldiers of the Word: The Story of the American Bible Society* (New York, 1958), pp. 87–88. An interesting statement of the Baptist point of view is W. H. Wyckoff, *The American Bible Society and the Baptists; or, The Question Discussed, Shall the Whole Word of God Be Given to the Heathen?* (New York, 1841).
21. *WNYBMM* II (May 1817), p. 49.
22. Conant, p. 440.
23. This idea can be found in Buchanan's *Star in the East*, pp. 22–23.
24. Knowles, p. 105.
25. *WNYBMM* II (August 1817), p. 93. Printers early became a basic component of foreign missions. By 1836, the *New York Evangelist* VII (May 7, 1836), p. 1, reported that the Baptists had twenty-three different missions, which employed six printers and five presses.
26. *ABM* I (September 1817), pp. 183–84.
27. Adoniram's tract was either *The Way to Heaven* or *On the True God.* Both were in manuscript in 1816. See Starr, XII, p. 193.
28. *ABM* I (January 1818), p. 265.
29. Starr, XII, p. 194.
30. *ABM* I (November 1817), p. 224.
31. Fletcher, pp. 254–55. Confirmed by Starr, XII, pp. 176–209. Baptist missionaries in Burma took the mastery of the vernacular languages very seriously. Translations of the catechisms were made by different men and women for each of Burma's distinct language groups.
32. Adoniram Judson, *A Cry from Burmah. A Letter to Rev. Mr. Grow of Connecticut, March 4, 1831*, p. 1. Judson's letters and journal extracts often stressed the need for more money and more missionaries

to do the work. See *ABM* I (May 1817), p. 98; II (November 1819), p. 214, for some examples.

33. Knowles, pp. 358–59, 368.

34. Starr's bibliography indicates the Burmese mission's role as a generator of tracts well into the twentieth century. Edward Judson's 1883 biography of his father, p. 459, included the following anecdote which reflects on Judson's career:

> [In 1846] he had come home to find that his native country was almost a strange land. The railroad system had sprung into existence during his absence. He entered the cars at Worcester one day, and had just taken his seat, when a boy came along with the daily newspapers. He said to Mr. Judson, "Do you want a paper, sir?" "Yes, thank you," the missionary replied, and taking the paper began to read. The newsboy stood waiting for his pay until a lady passenger occupying the same seat with Mr. Judson, said to him, "The boy expects to be paid for his paper." "Why," replied the missionary, with the utmost surprise, "I have been distributing papers gratuitously in Burmah so long that I had no idea the boy was expecting any pay."

35. Fletcher, p. 269.

36. Wayland, pp. 160–61.

37. Ibid.

38. Knowles, p. 149.

39. *MBMM* IV (December 1816), pp. 393–95.

40. *ABM* I (September 1817), p. 184. Similar statements by Ann Hasseltine Judson can be found in *WNYBMM* VIII (November 1818), p. 233; X (May 1819), p. 301. Cushman, p. 46, described a general "drawing back" from the mission enterprise during this period and likened Judson to George Washington "on the western bank of the Delaware."

41. *ABM* II (March 1820), p. 290.

42. Ibid., p. 291.

43. *ABM* II (July 1820), p. 379.

44. *ABM* II (November 1820), p. 435.

45. Knowles, p. 150.

46. *ABM* I (May 1817), pp. 96–97.

47. Ibid., p. 98.

48. Knowles, p. 154.

49. *ABM* III (January 1822), p. 253.

50. *ABM* III (March 1821), pp. 63–68; III (January 1822), p. 255.

51. *ABM* III (March 1821), p. 66; III (July 1821), p. 143.

52. *ABM* III (July 1821), p. 144.

53. *ABM* III (May 1822), p. 343.

54. Andrews, p. 111, says that the ABCFM offered free transportation back to the United States for wives of missionaries who were unable to cope with life in the Sandwich Islands.

55. *WNYBMM* II (August 1822), p. 339. The prevailing medical opinion was that Mrs. Judson's "liver complaint" would benefit from a cold climate.

56. Knowles, p. 226; Willson, p. 109.

57. The best account of Ann Hasseltine Judson's stay in England is in Knowles, pp. 226–28.

58. Ibid., p. 226.

59. *ABM* III (May 1822), p. 344.

60. Mrs. Chaplin was probably the mother of Hannah Chaplin Conant, a Judson biographer, and wife of Jeremiah Chaplin, president of Waterville College from 1820 to 1833. Knowles, p. 235.

61. Ann Hasseltine Judson (AHJ) to Francis Wayland, December 5, 1822, in Knowles, p. 233. Ann's New York prayer meeting may have been her first missionary fund raiser. Certainly, giving was part of the "true missionary spirit" she described. She told Wayland that at the end of the evening she was "exhausted" and that she "began to fear whether [she] should be able to continue the journey."

62. The *ABM* (January 1823) notes contributions of over $700 received by Mrs. Judson for the Female School in Burma. A Boston address for receiving further contributions was given and donations were published in subsequent *ABM* issues.

63. Knowles, p. 231.

64. AHJ to Mrs. Chaplin, December 1822, in Knowles, p. 237.

65. AHJ to Mary Hasseltine, December 1822, in Knowles, p. 238.

66. AHJ to Mrs. Chaplin, December 1822, in Knowles, p. 238.

67. AHJ to Francis Wayland, January 1823, in Knowles, p. 240.

68. AHJ to her sister, March 1823, in Knowles, p. 246.

69. AHJ to Francis Wayland, April 1823, in Knowles, p. 248.

70. *ABM* IV (July 1823), p. 140; Ann Hasseltine Judson, *A Particular Relation of the American Baptist Mission to the Burmese Empire. In a Series of Letters Addressed to Joseph Butterworth, Esq., M.P.* (Washington City, 1823).

71. *ABM* III (May 1822), p. 345. Judson suggested, in a letter to Dr. Baldwin, that in Burma "favorable access" to power was often bought with gifts.

72. *ABM* IV (July 1823), p. 141.

73. *ABM* IV (May 1824), p. 330.

74. AHJ to her sister, February 1823, in Knowles, p. 243.

75. *ABM* IV (May 1824), p. 330.

76. *ABM* IV (March 1823), p. 57.

77. AHJ Journal, October 1822, in Knowles, p. 257.

78. *ABM* IV (July 1824), p. 376.

79. Ibid.

80. Ibid.

81. AHJ to her parents, February 1824, in Knowles, p. 273.
82. For a description of the complicated causes of the First Anglo-Burmese War, see D.G.E. Hall, *Europe and Burma: A Study of European Relations with Burma to the Annexation of Thibaw'a Kingdom in 1886* (London, 1945), pp. 108–20. See also Chapter 4.
83. *ABM* V (January 1825), p. 47.
84. *ABM* V (February 1825), p. 50.
85. *ABM* V (March 1825), p. 84.
86. *ABM* V (April 1825), p. 118.
87. *ABM* V (June 1825), p. 180.
88. *ABM* (November 1825), p. 338.
89. Ibid.
90. *ABM* VI (January 1826), p. 30.
91. Ibid., p. 31.
92. *ABM* VI (January 1826), p. 30.
93. *ABM* VI (March-June 1826).
94. *ABM* VI (October 1826), p. 314.
95. Ibid., p. 315.
96. Knowles, p. 282.
97. *ABM* VII (March 1827), p. 74. The story of "Ann of Ava" is in Chapter 4.
98. Ibid., p. 96.
99. Fletcher, pp. 209–10.
100. *Judson Offering*, p. 132.
101. Cushman, p. 89. In 1881, Cathcart II, pp. 737–38, observed that "It is not easy for us to appreciate the eagerness with which in thousands of Baptist families the letters and journals of Boardman and Judson . . . have been read, and what an impulse has been given by their perusal to the great work of evangelizing the nations of the earth." Oliver Elsbree (1928), pp. 104–5, argued that "what the missionary magazines in America accomplished was not simply the stimulation of popular curiosity, but as a more significant result, the enlargement of the conception of duty on the part of American Christians." Phillips, pp. 314–21, talks briefly about "the romance of missions."
102. Daniel C. Eddy, *A Sketch of Adoniram Judson, D.D. The Burman Apostle* (Lowell, 1851), p. iv.
103. Quoted in Charles Wesley Brooks, *A Century of Missions in the Empire State* (Philadelphia, 1900), p. 154.
104. See Wesley Norton, *Religious Newspapers in the Old Northwest to 1861: A History, Bibliography and Record of Opinion* (Athens, Ohio, 1977); Henry Smith Stroupe, *The Religious Press in the South Atlantic States, 1802–1865* (Durham, 1956). Antebellum religious periodicals can also be approached denominationally. See the previously cited *Baptist Union List* and Gaylord P. Albaugh, "American

Presbyterian Periodicals and Newspapers, 1752–1830," *Journal of Presbyterian History*, 41 and 42 (September, December 1963; March, June 1964).

105. John Peck and John Lawton, *An Historical Sketch of the Baptist Missionary Convention of the State of New York* (Utica, 1837), pp. 149–53; Brooks, p. 160.

106. New York Baptist Missionary Convention Report (1836), quoted in Brooks, p. 153.

107. Stroupe, p. 106.

108. John William Tebbel, *A History of Book Publishing in the United States: The Creation of an Industry 1630–1825* I (New York, 1972), pp. 184–89.

109. *An Appeal to the Christian Public on the Evil and Impolicy of the Church Engaging in Merchandise . . .* (Philadelphia, 1849), p. 4. This work was published by King and Baird printers and may well be the product of their combined pens.

110. Ibid.

111. Ibid., p. 11.

112. William Charvat in Matthew Bruccoli, ed., *The Profession of Authorship in America, 1800–1870: The Papers of William Charvat* (Columbia, 1968), p. 310.

113. American Baptist Publication Society Report (1828), p. 155; (1835) p. 1. The publishers were Cephas Bennett and Edward Bright.

114. Philomathesian Society Records, I (1821–1823) (n.p., October 1821; March 1822; April 1823), Colgate University Archives.

115. Cox, p. 243.

116. John Quincy Adams, D.D., *An Old Boy Remembers* (Boston, 1935), p. 20.

117. Stroupe, p. 27.

118. For incomplete circulation figures, see Stroupe, pp. 24–28; Joseph C.G. Kennedy, "Catalogue of the Newspapers and Periodicals in the United States," in *Livingston's Law Register for 1852* (New York, 1852); Oliver Roorbach, *Bibliotheca America* (New York, 1852). Frank Luther Mott, *A History of American Magazines 1741–1850* I, p. 251, says that the *ABM* had a circulation of 8,000 by June 1817.

119. David Benedict, *Fifty Years Among the Baptists* (New York, 1860), p. 25. There were religious periodicals before the American evangelicals embraced the form. Mott, *Magazines* I, pp. 78–80.

120. Horace Bushnell, *New Englander and Yale Review* II (1844), pp. 605–7.

121. Roorbach, pp. 644–652.

122. Mott, *Magazines* I, p. 341.

123. Frank Luther Mott, *American Journalism: A History, 1690–1960* (New York, 1962), p. 216.

124. Wayland, II, pp. 153–54.
125. *Religious Telescope* (Circleville, Ohio) November 27, 1839, p. 1. The *Telescope* was a United Brethren paper.
126. New York Baptist *Register* XX (June 30, 1843), p. 1. Advocacy of the press as the great modern evangelizing tool probably did not sit well with traditionalists, who remained committed to the extension of the word through Gospel preaching. The New York Baptist Missionary Convention in 1836 was careful to recommend the *Register* as an efficient agency "without devaluing the living teachers." Judson's biographers had to explain the fact that after 1830 he worked almost solely on translation. Fletcher, p. 300, wrote: "This task was not one to which he would have given himself of his own choice. The preaching of the word was a far more congenial employment, and it was only in consequence of the urgent representations of his American friends that he gave himself to the labors of the study."
127. *New York Evangelist* VII (May 7, 1836), p. 2. Stroupe, pp. 12–13, reports that in the South of the 1830s Baptist magazines and newspapers exceeded in number not only those of the Methodists, but those of the Presbyterians, the leaders before 1830. It is possible to extract from Norton and Stroupe all the Baptist periodicals that potentially reported the Judson story in the period 1812 to 1850.
128. On the increase of reading, see Carl Bode, *Antebellum Culture* (Carbondale, Illinois, 1959), pp. 109 ff.; Norman F. Cantor and Michael S. Werthman, eds., *The History of Popular Culture* (New York, 1968), pp. 84–94. Ann Douglas, *The Feminization of American Culture* (New York, 1977), pp. 60–68, predicates her case for the Victorian alliance of liberal Protestant clergy and middle-class women on the presence of a mass market of women readers as "consumers of literature."
129. Emily Chubbuck Judson, *Memoir of Sarah B. Judson* (New York, 1848), p. 21, and Wyeth, *SBJ*, p. 15. According to the memoir, as a young woman Sarah Hall wanted to become a member of the Indian mission in Central New York State. She wrote a letter to a missionary society in that area regarding her qualifications to work among the Oneidas, and a poem, "Catherine's Grave," about a Cherokee Indian girl whose evangelization she prayed for. The poem is reprinted in Wyeth, pp. 174–75. Also, there is a one-stanza poem entitled, "Come Over and Help Us," in the *Memoir*, pp. 28–29.
130. *Memoir of SBJ*, pp. 26–27.
131. Aracan is a province in lower Burma on the Bay of Bengal. From the fifteenth century until 1782, it was autonomous, resulting in the differentiation of its language from the Burmese. When Aracan was annexed by the Burmese in the late eighteenth century, the Burmese and British India became immediate neighbors.

132. *MBMM* IV (March 1823), p. 80; Willson, pp. 196–97; *Memoir of SBJ*, pp. 134–35. In 1823, Sarah Hall read this elegy in the presence of Ann Hasseltine Judson at a women's missionary society meeting in Salem. Mrs. Judson, who was thirty-four, was about to return to Burma; Sarah Hall was twenty.

133. Wyeth, *SBJ*, pp. 28–29; Willson, pp. 195–96.

134. Wyeth, *ECJ*, pp. 37–38; Kendrick, pp. 28–30. Emily Chubbuck was born in 1817. Therefore, she was only six when Ann Hasseltine Judson made her visit to the United States. She reported that she read Knowles' biography of the first Mrs. Judson sometime in her teens, probably after 1830. The story she is referring to here was reported in the *Western New York Baptist Missionary Magazine* when she was only ten.

135. A. L. Vail, "The Mysterious Library that Helped Judson," *The Journal and Messenger* LXXXIII (February 19, 1914), p. 3.

136. John Cawelti, *Adventure, Mystery and Romance: Formula Stories as Popular Culture* (Chicago, 1976), pp. 23–24, uses the term to designate the kind of communications theory that posits a direct relationship between art and human behavior. Cawelti suggests that there is some truth to the idea that "we carry a collection of story plots around in our heads and that we tend to see and shape life according to these plots." In the twentieth century, "seeing and shaping life" has a linear (print) and a visual (image) dimension. Can we then ascribe the same considerations to the making of early nineteenth-century popular culture? This line of thinking is related to the work of psycholinguistic structuralists like Noam Chomsky and may have bearing on this study.

    Cawelti argues, and I think reasonably so, that all the major formulas of a particular culture require definition. While he restricts his analysis to self-consciously literary forms (genres of fiction), I have tried to delineate the conventions in the biographical formula that evangelicals developed.

137. New York Baptist *Register* XX (June 16, 1843), p. 1.

138. Stone, pp. 85–86. The best analysis of the controversy over reading in Britain is in Richard Altick, *The English Common Reader: A Social History of the Mass Reading Public, 1800–1900* (Chicago, 1957). Altick, pp. 99–128, discusses the role of evangelical religion in the development of the British common reader.

139. Paul L. Lord, ed., *The New England Primer* (New York, 1962), pp. 3–4.

140. Quoted in Stone, p. 86.

141. *Boston Magazine* I (April 1784), pp. 238–39.

142. In the lives of Nathaniel Hawthorne, Herman Melville, Henry David Thoreau, and James Fenimore Cooper, there is little evidence of personal involvement with the evangelical movement.

143. The evangelical opposition to novels is found everywhere in their writing. The *Moral and Religious Souvenir* (1828), p. 18, called the novel a "moral dyke against religion." In an otherwise inadequate interpretation of the domestic novelists of the 1850s, Helen Papashvily described novel reading as "one of the great battlegrounds of conscience in the 19th century." "Again and again," she wrote, "diaries and letters of the period record the soul struggles of readers who succumbed to fiction one day and repented their indulgence the next." See *All the Happy Endings* (New York, 1956), p. 5. G. Harrison Orian, "Censure of Fiction in American Romances and Magazines, 1789–1810," *Publications of The Modern Language Association (PMLA)* LII (March 1937), pp. 195–214, described literary comments on novel reading at the turn of the century, but does not tie it to religion.

144. Tebbel, p. 516.

145. *Moral and Religious Souvenir* (Boston, 1828), p. 2.

146. Charvat, p. 49.

147. "On Reading," *Christian Examiner* XXVII (September 1839), p. 1.

148. "Selection in Reading," *Southern Literary Messenger* II (February 1836), p. 171.

149. "The Encouragement of Good Habits of Reading in Pious Young Men Preparing for the Ministry," *American Quarterly Review* X (February 1838), p. 228.

150. The availability of cheap reading material is obviously an important consideration in the development of a popular reading audience. That inexpensive material was available is confirmed by Frank Luther Mott, *American Journalism*, p. 228; William Charvat, p. 128; A. S. Collins, *The Profession of Letters: A Study of the Relation of Author to Patron, Publisher and Public, 1700–1832* (New York, 1929), p. 29; James D. Hart, *The Popular Book: A History of America's Literary Taste* (New York, 1950), pp. 158–60.

151. Grenville Mellon, *The Age of Print: A Poem Delivered before the Phi Beta Kappa Society, 26 August 1830* (Boston, 1830), pp. 5–6.

152. Ibid., p. 7.

153. Rev. G. T. Bedell, ed., *Religious Souvenir for 1833* (Philadelphia, 1833), p. 200.

154. Anna B. Warner, *Susan Warner* (New York, 1909), p. 84.

155. Harvey Newcomb, *A Practical Directory for Young Christian Females, Being a Series of Letters from a Brother to a Younger Sister* (Boston, 1833), pp. 267–29. Newcomb's book was published by the Massachusetts Sabbath School Society.

156. *Religious Souvenir for 1833*, p. 200.

157. See Ralph Thompson, *American Literary Annuals and Giftbooks 1825–1855* (New York, 1936). Thompson's work is primarily a bibli-

ography; its analysis of giftbook content is more literary than cultural.

158. Some typical statements to this effect can be found in Rev. John A. Clarke, ed., *The Christian Keepsake and Missionary Annual* (Philadelphia, 1840), p. 269; Rev. Chauncy Colton, *The Religious Souvenir for 1837* (Philadelphia, 1837), p. 141. Clarke was an Episcopal clergyman in Philadelphia.

159. Rev. Issac F. Shepard, ed., *The Christian Souvenir: An Offering for Christmas and the New Year* (Boston, 1843), p. 150.

160. *Religious Souvenir for 1833*, p. 4.

161. Rev. S. D. Burchard, *The Laurel Wreath* (Hartford, 1846), pp. iii–iv.

162. Rev. John O. Choules, *The Christian Offering for 1832* (Boston, 1832), p. i.

163. *Christian Keepsake and Missionary Annual*, 1840, p. vii.

164. Ibid., 1839, p. v.

165. The Judson story was supplemented with pictures beginning with the publication of Knowles' biography in 1829, which contained an engraving of Ann Hasseltine Judson. The hopia tree, under which Ann Hasseltine was buried, appeared in a number of biographical publications, as well as Howard Malcom's *Travels in South-Eastern Asia, embracing Hindustan, Malaya, Siam, and China; with notices of Numerous Missionary Stations, and a full account of the Burman Empire* (Boston, 1839), p. 36. Fletcher, p. 385, had a montage engraving of the hopia tree, the rock at St. Helena, and the ocean with a setting sun, entitled "Graves of the Judsons." Some of the Judson biographies and commemorative volumes had plates that depicted scenes in Burma or events of the British-Burmese War. For example, Fletcher, p. 199, featured an engraving of a shackled Judson, surrounded by his Burmese captors, entitled, "The Blood Tracked March." *The Judson Offering* had over a dozen plates depicting various "Judson scenes," including the 1812 departure. There were at least three different popular engravings of Adoniram (by J. Andrews in Wayland; by J.C. Buttre in Middleditch; and by L.W. Orr[?] in Fletcher). Ann's likeness was also reproduced in three other biographies. There is no portrait of Sarah Hall Boardman Judson, a fact which Judson lamented when her *Memoir* was published in 1848. Two portrait engravings of Emily Chubbuck Judson were published, one in Kendrick and another in Willson. Edward Judson's biography of his father includes an engraving, done from an 1853 ambrotype taken at Hamilton, of Judson's widow, three of the children, and a Burmese girl. Johnson, Wilson and Company, Publishers, New York City, issued an engraving in 1872 of Emily Judson, done from a painting by Chappel.

166. Newcomb, p. 147.
167. How to establish a "point of contact" is still an issue in twentieth-century Protestantism. It has been treated by Karl Barth, Emil
Brunner, and Paul Tillich in a theological way; Malcolm Boyd considered it in relation to the mass media, advocating the use of "mass
media missioners." See Malcolm Boyd, *Crisis in Communication: A
Christian Examination of the Mass Media* (Garden City, 1957), for a
description of current application of this principle. Also interesting is
Martin Marty, *The Improper Opinion: Mass Media and the Christian Faith* (Philadelphia, 1961).
168. Samuel Miller, *Letters on Clerical Manners, and Habits, Addressed
to a Student in the Theological Seminary in Princeton, New Jersey*
(New York, 1827), pp. 137–38. Miller was an evangelical Presbyterian.

Chapter 4

1. See Chapter 2, n. 1.
2. See Cross, pp. 173–77 for a brief discussion of the "New Measures."
3. *Panoplist* XI (April 1815), pp. 178–81. See also ABCFM, *Manual for
Missionary Candidates; and for Missionaries before entering their
fields* (Boston, 1853) for "qualifications . . . requisite in females
whether married or unmarried. . . ."
4. See R. Pierce Beaver, *All Love's Excelling: American Protestant
Women in World Mission* (Grand Rapids, 1968); Elizabeth Anthony
Dexter, *Career Women of America 1776–1840* (Boston, 1950).
5. Willson, p. 1.
6. See Cross, p. 178, for a statement on the superior female susceptibility to religion. The mere observation of the quantitative data,
that women joined the churches in greater numbers than men, has
led many to a "biologically deterministic" interpretation of women's
involvement with organized religion.
7. For the best statement on homo-social bonding among antebellum
women see Nancy Cott, *The Bonds of Womanhood: "Women's
Sphere" in New England, 1780–1835* (New Haven, 1977).
8. On the separation of women from the commodity production process and the consequent development of the nuclear family, see Wally
Seacombe, "The Housewife and Her Labour Under Capitalism,"
New Left Review 83 (January-February, 1973), pp. 3–24; Ira Gers-
tein, "Domestic Work and Capitalism," *Radical America* VII (July-
October, 1973), pp. 101–128; Ann Oakley, *Woman's Work* (New
York, 1974); Barbara Ehrenreich and Deirdre English, "The Manufacture of Housework," *Socialist Revolution* 26:5 (October-December, 1975), pp. 5–40.

9. I have co-opted the term "The Apostolate of Women" from James D. Hill, *The Immortal Seven: Judson and His Associates* (Philadelphia, 1913), p. 33. Hill, a Baptist writer, used the centenary of the Judsons' departure to compare the Tabernacle Church at Salem (where the ordination took place) to Mt. Vernon, Gettysburg, Waterloo, Plymouth, and Bethlehem.

10. See Barbara Welter's popular monograph, "The Cult of True Womanhood, 1820–1860," *American Quarterly* XVIII (Summer 1966), pp. 151–74; Ronald W. Hogeland, "The Female Appendage: Feminine Life-Styles in America, 1820–1860," *Civil War History* XVII (June 1971), pp. 101–14; Gerda Lerner, "The Lady and the Mill Girl: Changes in the Status of Women in the Age of Jackson," *Midcontinent American Studies Journal* X (Spring 1969), pp. 5–14; Ryan, pp. 139–91.

11. Jonathan Allen, *Sermon Delivered at Haverhill, February 5, 1812 on the Occasion of Two Young Ladies Being About to Embark as the Wives of Rev. Messieurs Judson and Newell, going as Missionaries to India* (Haverhill, Mass., 1812), p. 2.

12. *Moral and Religious Souvenir* (Boston, 1828), p. 43.

13. Knowles, p. 58.

14. Allen, p. 3.

15. Sarah Josepha Hale, *Woman's Record; or, Sketches of All Distinguished Women* (New York, 1855), p. ix.

16. *New York Evangelist* VII (May 28, 1836), p. 4.

17. This story was told in the *Moral and Religious Souvenir* (1828), pp. 61–64; *The Christian Souvenir* (1843), pp. 122–26; and *Christian Keepsake and Missionary Annual* (1839), pp. 43–48.

18. See David T. Kimball, *The Obligation and Disposition of Females to Promote Christianity, An Address Delivered June 15, 1819 Before the Female Education and Charitable Societies in the First Parish of Ipswich* (Newburyport, 1819), p. 1. Kimball invokes the history of all these biblical women.

19. See Walter Harris, *A Discourse delivered to the Members of the Female Cent Society in Bedford, New Hampshire, July 18, 1814* (Concord, 1814); Ethan Smith, *Daughters of Zion Excelling. A Sermon Preached to the Ladies of the Cent Institution, in Hopkinton, New Hampshire* (Concord, 1814); Ashbel Green, *The Christian Duty of Christian Women, A Discourse delivered in the Church of Princeton, New Jersey August 23, 1825 before the Princeton Female Society for the Support of a Female School in India* (Princeton, 1825). There are countless examples of this approach.

20. Kimball, p. 10.

21. Phineas Camp Headley, *Women of the Bible: Historical and descriptive Sketches of the Women of the Bible, as maidens, wives,*

and Mothers, from Eve of the Old to the Marys of the New Testament* (Boston, 1850).

22. In *Coelebs in Search of a Wife* (1808), Hannah More wrote that Paul was "still more uncivilly explicit than Milton," meaning that the apostle outdid the poet on the issue of woman's conjugal obedience. See *The Complete Works of Hannah More* II (New York, 1835), p. 10.

   In addition to St. Paul, justification for the inferior status of women can be found in I Timothy II:11–12: "Let the woman learn in silence with all subjection. But I suffer not a woman to teach to usurp authority over the man, but to be in silence." Evangelical religionists obviously did not follow this injunction against female teaching. What this indicates is that the movement generally chose what they wanted, and what was functional, from among biblical proscriptions.

23. Elizabeth Cady Stanton, *Woman's Bible* (New York, 1896). In the introduction to Elizabeth Cady Stanton, *Eighty Years and More: Reminiscences 1815–1897* (New York, 1971), Gail Parker makes the point about Stanton's anticlericalism.

24. Ann Douglas attributes the liberal clergy's collaboration with middle-class women to the clergy's loss of economic security and social status in the disestablished New Republic. This may be so, but it is important to note that the same alliance, between clergy and women, existed in evangelicalism where the clergy suffered no loss of power or status but were, instead, "on the rise." It was their reading of the New Testament's portrait of women that provided the justification for the collaboration.

25. Samuel Lorenzo Knapp, *Female Biography; containing notices of distinguished women, in different nations and ages* (New York, 1834), p. ix.

26. Ibid.

27. An American Lady, *Sketches of the Lives of Distinguished Females Written for Girls with a View to their mental and moral improvement* (New York, 1833), p. xiv.

28. *Moral and Religious Souvenir* (1828), pp. 43–47.

29. Willson, p. ii.

30. *ABM* IV (January 1823), pp. 18–20.

31. Ibid., p. 19.

32. Ibid.

33. Ibid., p. 20. The degraded position of women abroad was a major concern of women's foreign missionary activities well into the twentieth century. A 1910 pamphlet by Mrs. Moses Smith, a Congregationalist, entitled *Woman Under the Ethnic Religions* (Woman's Board of Missions of the Interior) reiterated the themes that were

raised by Ann Hasseltine. Smith's analysis mentioned child marriage, infanticide, suttee, consecreated prostitution ("Nautch or dancing girls"), polygamy, divorce, female seclusion, purdah, and bound feet. Smith attributed "the cruel brutal degradation of women . . . not to race or environment or accident" but to a lack of Christianity. The same stories, accompanied by glossaries that defined terms such as zenana, purdah, and suttee, can be found in a number of publications from the Woman's American Baptist Foreign Mission Society: *Woman of Burma: Heathen and Christian* (c. 1910), *Bridal Pictures* (c. 1915); and *A Crusade for Compassion* (c. 1910).

34. Adoniram Judson, *A Letter Addressed to the Female Members of the Christian Church in the United States of America* (New Haven, 1832), pp. 11–12.
35. New York Baptist *Register* XX (May 5, 1843), p. 1.
36. Phillips, p. 273.
37. Marilla B. Ingalls, *Ocean Sketches of Life in Burma* (Philadelphia, 1857), pp. 83–84.
38. Willson, p. 45.
39. Knowles, p. 120.
40. Ibid., p. 70.
41. Willson, p. 237.
42. Gammell, pp. 30–31.
43. *Moral and Religious Souvenir* (1828), pp. 55–56.
44. Knowles, p. 115.
45. A zenana is a living space in which women and young girls are segregated.
46. In *The Kathayan Slave*, p. 117, Emily Chubbuck Judson did report a case of adultery by a Burmese woman, who was subsequently converted:

> I do not know much about her girlhood, but of one thing I am quite certain, that the less said about it the better; for virtue is not forced upon Burmese women, as on those of some other eastern nations, by means of locks and bars, and mutilated guards. Since her marriage, it must be owned she has been quite a model woman, for this part of the world, having been found guilty of unfaithfulness in that relation but once; and then being able to prove, in self-defense, that she was under the influence of *arrack*—the Burmese substitute for *gin*.

Emily Chubbuck Judson, honoring evangelical decorum, did not speak about virginity or chastity, but chose, instead, to speak of "virtue." Her story, which had to evoke some sexual imagery, closed with this enticement: "Do I write with such plainess as to shock the sensibilities of my readers? I do it unwillingly, and I assure them that I have dared to lift only the tiniest corner of the veil." Emily Chubbuck Judson's remarks suggest that the American Christian woman's interest in her degraded sisters was probably fed by an "underground" stream of information about sexual immodesty and impropriety in non-Christian lands.

47. *The Missionary Memorial: A Literary and Religious Souvenir* (New York, 1846), p. 120.
48. Lydia Maria Child, *The History of the Condition of Women; In Various Ages and Nations* (Boston, 1835), p. 87. A Unitarian and an abolitionist, Child's critique of heathendom is reminiscent of abolitionist explanations of the dynamics of the slave South.
49. See Louis Whitney, *Primitivism and the Idea of Progress* (Baltimore, 1934); George Boas, *French Philosophies of the Romantic Period* (Baltimore, 1925).
50. *ABM* (January 1823), p. 19.
51. Judson, *Kathayan Slave*, p. 111.
52. Ibid., p. 12.
53. Ibid., p. 114.
54. See Ralph Gabriel, "Evangelical Religion and Popular Romanticism in Early 19th Century America," *Church History* XIX (1950), pp. 34–47.
55. John A. Clarke, ed., *The Christian Keepsake and Missionary Annual* (Philadelphia, 1838), p. 9. This giftbook was under Episcopal sponsorship in 1833. However, the editor stressed that it was his hope that the volume was not "sectarian" but "Christian" in purpose.
56. Child, p. 111.
57. Issac F. Shepard, ed., *The Christian Souvenir: An Offering for Christmas and the New Year* (Boston, 1843), pp. 81–83. See Dorothy K. Stein, "Women to Burn: Sutee as a Normative Institution," *SIGNS* 4:2 Winter 1978, pp. 253–73.
58. *MBMM* III (December 1813), pp. 355–56.
59. *The Vehicle; or Madison and Cayuga Christian Magazine* II (August 1814), p. 61.
60. *New York Evangelist* VII (May 28, 1836), p. 4.
61. *ABM* XXVI (May 1846), p. 123.
62. Emily Chubbuck Judson, *Memoir of Sarah B. Judson of the American Mission to Burmah* (New York, 1855), p. 28. Also reprinted in *A Little Book of Judson Verse* (Chicago, 1908), p. 7.
63. Knowles, p. 135.
64. Ibid.
65. Ibid., p. 153.
66. Ibid., pp. 168–69, 272.
67. Ibid., p. 144.
68. Ibid., p. 163.
69. Knowles, p. 179.

70. *ABM* V (January 1825), p. 22.

71. Knowles, pp. 186, 214.

72. The first woman convert was Mah Men-la in 1820. By that time, ten men had already been converted by Adoniram. Neither Ann Judson nor her husband ever wrote about the familial difficulties Burmese women faced if they chose to become Christians.

73. From Starr's bibliography we can extract the translation works for which Ann Judson was responsible: a translation of Matthew in Siamese (1810); a Burmese catechism (1817); the stories of Jonah and Daniel in Burmese (1818); a translation of a tract into Burman (1817); a Siamese vocabulary (n.d.); and a translation of a Siamese Sacred Book, into English, containing an account of the incarnation of a Siamese deity, when he existed as an elephant. See Starr, XII, pp. 208–9.

74. Knowles, p. 325.

75. Ibid., pp. 286–87.

76. Ibid., p. 288.

77. Ibid., p. 289.

78. Ibid.

79. Ibid., pp. 289–90.

80. Ibid., p. 291.

81. This story is in *The Judson Offering* and a number of other late nineteenth- and early twentieth-century versions of the Judson saga. I cannot find any direct statement to that effect from Ann or Adoniram Judson.

82. Knowles, p. 293.

83. Ibid.

84. Ibid., p. 294.

85. Ibid.

86. Ibid., p. 294.

87. Ibid., p. 296.

88. Ibid., pp. 297–98.

89. Ibid.

90. Ibid.

91. Ibid., p. 299.

92. Ibid.

93. Ibid., p. 300.

94. Ibid.

95. Ibid., p. 301.

96. Ibid., p. 303.

97. Ibid.

98. Ibid., p. 305.

99. Gouger wrote his own account of the ordeal. See Henry Gouger, *Personal Narrative of Two Years Imprisonment in Burmah* (London, 1860).

100. Knowles, p. 306; Gouger, pp. 213–14.

101. *Judson Offering*, pp. 102–10.

102. Knowles, p. 306.

103. Ibid., p. 309.

104. Ibid., p. 310.

105. Laudanum is a tincture of opium.

106. Knowles, p. 312. Adoniram Judson wrote a poem entitled, "To My Baby from the Prison of Ava," which was published in *ABM* for July 1827 and in *The Judson Offering* (1846). It was also reprinted in some of the Judson biographies and was considered an indication of the missionary patriarch's spiritual sensitivity.

107. Ibid., p. 313.

108. Ibid., p. 316.

109. Ibid., pp. 316–35.

110. Hall, pp. 118–19.

111. Wyeth, p. 200.

112. Gouger, pp. 234–35.

113. Knowles, p. 338. See *ABM* VII (May 1825), p. 160, for Ann Judson's obituary.

114. The Judsons' second child, Maria, died at Amherst on April 24, 1827, and was buried next to her mother.

115. Knowles, p. 338.

116. The hopia tree is a persistent motif in all the Judson literature. It is reprinted in Malcom's *Travels*, in D. C. Eddy, in Clement, and in *The Judson Offering*, as well as in late nineteenth- and early twentieth-century versions of the story. A poem entitled, "The Hopia Tree," by Lydia H. Sigourney, was reprinted in Malcom, p. 37.

117. Knowles, p. 325.

118. Ibid.

119. Wayland, I, pp. 329–30.

120. Kimball, p. 7, told his audience that in 1812. The designation "Ann of Ava" was used as a title for a 1913 book by Ethel Daniels Hubbard, *Ann of Ava* (New York, 1913). Hubbard, a non-Baptist, retold Ann Judson's story, accompanied by illustrations, for the nondenominational Missionary Education Movement of the United States and Canada.

121. Gammell, pp. 73–74.

122. Gammell, p. 75. Even the Unitarian *Christian Examiner* VI (May 1829), p. 253, observed that the Judson story was universally known: "We believe the most prominent events of her life, connected as they inseparably are, with the history of foreign missions, have been repeatedly published. And probably the readers of the Missionary Herald, and of similar publications, will not find much in this volume, not already familiar to them."

123. Porter, pp. 24–25.

124. Ingalls, pp. 222–23.

125. Hague, pp. 10–11.

126. Sarah Josepha Hale, *Sketches of American Character* (Boston, 1833), p. 90.
127. *Missionary Memorial* (1846), pp. 16–17.
128. Knowles, p. 9.
129. In J. Clement, ed., *Noble Deeds of American Women: with Biographical Sketches of Some of the More Prominent* (Buffalo, 1851), p. xiv, Lydia Huntley Sigourney is quoted as saying that Christianity changed the status of women. Even Child, a religious liberal, saw Christianity as an elevator of women (pp. 210–11).
130. Willson, p. ii.
131. *WNYBMM* III (August 1817), p. 74.
132. Certainly political feminism is not the only avenue for woman's expression of concern about her status. Daniel Scott Smith has argued effectively against a dichotomy between the powerless, static role of woman-in-the-home and women who engage in public activism (woman's rights, abolition, temperance, etc.). See Smith, "Family Limitation, Sexual Control, and Domestic Feminism in Victorian America," in Mary Hartman and Lois Banner, eds., *Clio's Consciousness Raised: New Perspectives on the History of Women* (New York, 1974), pp. 119–36. Smith's thesis is "that over the course of the nineteenth century the average woman experienced a great increase in power and autonomy within the family." Smith's primary evidence is taken from marital fertility data, which indicates that Victorian women acquired "an increasing power over sex and reproduction in marriage."

CHAPTER 5

1. See Chapter 1, n. 69.
2. *The Christian Examiner* VI (May 1829), p. 253. Another measure of Ann Hasseltine's reputation was the number of anthologies that included her biography. See Chapter I, pp. 18–22.
3. See Chapter 2, pp. 53–54, for the comment of the *Boston Evening Transcript*.
4. Asahel Clark Kendrick, *The Life and Letters of Mrs. Emily C. Judson* (New York, 1861), p. 273.
5. I do not mean to suggest that women were accorded full equality in the world of letters. I use terms like "authoress" and "female authorship" precisely because women writers were considered a separate species of artist, to be judged by different standards from men's. For an interesting discussion of the situation of women authors in the Victorian period in England, see Elaine Showalter, "Women Writ-

ers and the Double Standard," in Vivian Gornick and Barbara K. Moran, *Woman in Sexist Society: Studies in Power and Powerlessness* (New York, 1971), pp. 452–79. Ann D. Wood recognizes the same double standard in " 'The Scribbling Woman' and Fanny Fern: Why Women Wrote," *American Quarterly* XXIII (Spring 1971).

6. Wayland, II, pp. 82–83.
7. Wayland, I, p. 428.
8. Knowles, pp. 343–44. Poetry was an accepted literary form for even the most pious evangelical because it was both a biblical form and an expression of religious emotion rather than intellect. At the age of thirteen, Sarah Hall composed a "versification of David's lament over Saul and Jonathan." Starr, XII, p. 221.
9. Wayland, I, p. 476.
10. Ibid., p. 526.
11. Ibid.
12. Wayland, II, p. 115.
13. Wayland, II, p. 115.
14. This incident is illustrated in *Women of Worth: A Book for Girls* (New York, n.d.), p. 110. Emily Chubbuck's memoir of Sarah B. Judson also included this story.
15. Willson, p. 290.
16. Willson, pp. 300–301. Willson characteristically described this as a duty Mrs. Boardman did not like.
17. Emily Judson, *Memoir of Sarah B. Judson of the American Mission to Burmah* (New York, 1848), pp. 167–69. It is interesting to note that the title of this volume identified the second Mrs. Judson as part of an American, rather than a Baptist, mission to Burma.
18. Willson, pp. 294–95.
19. Ibid.
20. Wayland, II, p. 73.
21. Emily Judson, *Memoir of SBJ*, p. 160.
22. Ibid., p. 161.
23. Ibid., p. 163. Thus Mrs. Boardman was presented by Emily Judson and others as a spokesperson for the idea that all education should be Christian education. This axiom of evangelical faith was well represented by Mary Lyon's famous dictum: "Study and teach nothing that cannot be made to help in the great work of converting the world to Christ." See Louis Porter Thomas, *Seminary Militant: An Account of the Missionary Movement at Mt. Holyoke Seminary and College* (South Hadley, 1937), p. 29.
24. Willson, p. 302.
25. Emily Judson, *Memoir of SBJ*, p. 165.
26. Ibid., p. 166.

27. Wayland, II, p. 83.
28. Henry died at one year and seven months.
29. Charles died in 1845.
30. Wayland, II, p. 147.
31. Wayland, II, pp. 136–37, has verses Adoniram wrote to his children.
32. See Wayland, II, pp. 110, 136, 190, for Judson's letters to his step-son.
33. Wayland, II, p. 193.
34. Ibid., p. 128.
35. The following publications are attributed to Sarah Boardman Judson: a New Testament translation into Peguan (1837); the Life of Christ translated into Talain (1838); a translation into Talain of Adoniram Judson's *The Investigator*; a translation into Burmese of George Boardman's *The Dying Father's Advice* (1837); a chapel hymn book in Burmese; questions on the life of Christ (1837); scriptural questions for Sabbath schools in Burmese (1837); and a Burmese translation of the first part of Bunyan's *Pilgrim's Progress*. See Starr, XII, pp. 219–21.
36. Wayland, II, p. 94.
37. Ibid., p. 99.
38. Ibid., p. 101.
39. This expression comes from Ashbel Green, *The Christian Duty of Christian Women. A Discourse Delivered in the Church of Princeton, New Jersey, August 23, 1825* (Princeton, 1825).
40. Wayland, II, p. 133.
41. Ibid., p. 134.
42. Ibid., p. 139.
43. Ibid., p. 140. On the same voyage, without Sarah, he read Mrs. Heman's poetry.
44. Judson had refused all prior invitations to come home. He repeatedly stated his idea that a foreign missionary should "come out for life, and not for a limited term." Ibid., pp. 38, 62. He liked to tell the story that, when Eugenio Kincaid was asked by a Burmese official how long he intended to stay, Kincaid replied: "Until all Burma worships the eternal God."
45. Ibid., p. 198.
46. Ibid.
47. Ibid., p. 198.
48. Ibid., p. 199.
49. Ibid., p. 200.
50. This poem was published in a number of places: Wayland, II, p. 211; Willson, pp. 314–15; and *A Little Book of Judson Verse from the Writings of Sarah Boardman Judson and Fanny Forester* (Chicago, 1908). It was also published in the *Mother's Journal* within a year after Mrs. Judson's death.

51. For Judson's account, see the *Baptist Missionary Magazine* XXVI (February 1846), pp. 42–43; Wayland, II, pp. 202–5. Most of Sarah Judson's biographers commented on the fact that St. Helena held the mortal remains of two such dissimilar figures. Phebe A. Hanaford's description in *Daughters of America* (Boston, 1883), p. 485, is typical: "The island has become noted as the place where Napoleon died, but it is dearer to Christian hearts the world over as the place where Sarah B. Judson's body rests. The warrior is eclipsed by the woman missionary."

52. Wayland, II, p. 203.

53. Ibid.

54. From her obituary in the *Baptist Missionary Magazine* XXVI (February 1846), p. 43.

55. Ibid., p. 42.

56. Wayland, II, p. 210.

57. Kendrick, p. 143.

58. Emily Chubbuck (EC) to Walker Chubbuck (WC), March 25, 1842, Chubbuck Family Papers, File #1837, State Historical Society of Wisconsin (SHSW), Archives Division. Emily described her teaching position to her brother in this way.

59. Fanny Forester, *Trippings in Author-Land* (New York, 1846); *Lilias Fane, and Other Tales* (Boston, 1846); *Alderbrook: A Collection of Fanny Forester's Village Sketches* (Boston, 1847).

60. *New York Evening Mirror* III (December 13, 1845), p. 160.

61. Kendrick, p. 16.

62. There were six other Chubbuck children at the time Emily went to work in April 1828 for the mill at Pratt's Hollow. They were: Lavinia (b. 1806); Benjamin (b. 1809); Harriet (b. 1811); John Walker (b. 1815); Sarah Catherine (b. 1816); and William Wallace (b. 1824).

63. EC to WC, February 18, 1838, reports that "our folks are in trouble," and dragged by creditors, Chubbuck Family Papers, SHSW.

64. EC to WC, October 18, 1837, Chubbuck Family Papers, SHSW.

65. EC to WC, April 2, 1839, Chubbuck Family Papers, SHSW. Kendrick, p. 14, notes that Ben was a "constant source of anxiety" to his family but does not mention the prison sentence. In 1844, Emily reported, in a letter to Wallace, that Ben was in jail again, this time for stealing a cow. She called him a "canker-worm" and said it was "too mortifying for anything." EC to WC, September 27, 1844, Chubbuck Family Papers, SHSW.

66. Kendrick, p. 10.

67. EC to WJ, August 15, 1849, Chubbuck Family Papers, SHSW.

68. Emily Chubbuck Judson, *My Two Sisters: A Sketch from Memory* (Boston, 1853), p. 15.

69. See Chapter 3, p. 94.
70. Lavinia Chubbuck died in 1829; Harriet Chubbuck in 1831. In *My Two Sisters*, Emily gives a detailed account of her education at the hands of her pious older sisters, suggesting that in the lives of many who were formally uneducated, elder siblings played a crucial role.
71. Kendrick, pp. 38–39.
72. Ibid. Nathaniel C. Kendrick was then pastor of the Baptist church at Eaton, New York.
73. Ibid., p. 20.
74. Ibid., p. 18.
75. Ibid.
76. Emily Judson, *My Two Sisters*, pp. 23–24; Kendrick, p. 22. At different points in her teens, Emily borrowed books from a person described as Miss L.W.F., a "rhetoric and natural philosophy teacher," and from students at the Hamilton Literary and Theological Institution.
77. Emily Judson, *My Two Sisters*, pp. 23–24.
78. Ibid.
79. Kendrick, p. 21.
80. Ibid., p. 26. In a number of stories, Chubbuck used her personal work experiences. See "Florence Evelyn" in *The Great Secret, or, How To Be Happy* (New York, 1842); "The Unuseful" and "Grace Linden" in *Trippings in Author-Land*. Many of Chubbuck's stories dealt with questions about the aspirations of young people and social values in a democratic society. Generally, she combined her egalitarian credo with formulaic devices whereby the truest, the neediest, and the most democratic got their rewards.
81. Ibid., p. 30.
82. Philip Floram, "Fanny Forester: A Critical Estimate of Her Prose and Poetry," unpublished M.A. thesis, Department of English, St. Bernardine of Siena College, Loudonville, New York, 1953, p. 4.
83. EC to WC, October 18, 1837, Chubbuck Family Papers, SHSW. Emily offered to move to Wisconsin, and even to keep house for her brother, if he planned to remain unmarried.
84. Ibid.
85. EC to WC, March 22, 1840, Chubbuck Family Papers, SHSW.
86. Ibid. Chubbuck's letters never fully clarified this statement. She did not indicate if her feelings about school teaching were the result of difficult experiences, low wages, or interest in other pursuits. However, when she became a fiction writer, she wrote a great deal about the situation of district school teachers. See *Allen Lucas; The Self-Made Man* (New York, 1843); *The Great Secret; Lilias Fane and Other Tales*. In these stories, Chubbuck dealt with questions relating to the character and motivation of teachers, the uses of discipline

versus moral suasion in the classroom, itinerating and credentialing of teachers, and age heterogeneity in the common school. In the use of her teaching experiences as a resource for her later writing, Chubbuck revealed something of her essentially evangelical educational philosophy. While she upheld childhood self-government as the ideal, she also favored a careful program of parental and teacher scrutiny of all behaviors.

87. EC to WC, March 22, 1840, Chubbuck Family Papers, SHSW.
88. Ibid.
89. Ibid.
90. EC to WC, February 18, 1838, Chubbuck Family Papers, SHSW.
91. Ibid. A letter from Emily to Walker, April 28, 1840, reveals that Emily had also published some poetry over the name "Eloise" in the Cazenovia, New York, paper sometime during 1838.
92. Urania Sheldon, who was a contemporary of Emily Chubbuck, married the Rev. Eliphalet Nott, the Presbyterian president of Union College, in August 1842. Nott (b. 1773) was sixty-nine years old at the time of his marriage and he had been widowed twice before. Surely Urania's marriage had some influence on Emily Chubbuck's own future.
93. EC to WC, February 5, 1840, Chubbuck Family Papers, SHSW.
94. In the same letter to Walker, Emily hinted at her interest in fiction: "I believe if I have any genius it is for things not useful and can never be turned to account."
95. Kendrick, p. 103.
96. EC to WC, May 17, 1841, Chubbuck Family Papers, SHSW.
97. Kendrick, p. 65.
98. Emily Chubbuck, *Charles Linn; or How to Observe the Golden Rule* (New York, 1841). According to Kendrick, p. 59, Emily's contact with Dayton and Saxton, the New York publisher, was supplied through Mr. Hawley, a Utica book dealer and later a publisher himself.
99. EC to WC, May 17, 1841, Chubbuck Family Papers, SHSW.
100. Kendrick, pp. 65–66.
101. EC to WC, March 25, 1842, Chubbuck Family Papers, SHSW.
102. Kendrick, p. 72.
103. EC to WC, May 17, 1841, Chubbuck Family Papers, SHSW.
104. EC to WC, January 16, 1841, Chubbuck Family Papers, SHSW.
105. Emily Chubbuck, *The Great Secret, or How to be Happy* (New York, 1842); *Effie Maurice: or, What is My God* (Philadelphia, 1842); *Allen Lucas; The Self-Made Man* (New York, 1843); *John Frink: the third commandment* (Philadelphia, 1843).
106. *Effie Maurice* and *John Frink*.
107. Kendrick, p. 90.

108. Ibid., p. 73.

109. Ibid., p. 77. The magazine lasted for only one year.

110. EC to WC, March 25, 1842, Chubbuck Family Papers, SHSW. In this letter, Emily told Walker that she sent "Astronoga" to a Mr. Gaylord in New York in the hopes of publication. Astronoga is the Indian name for Little Falls, twenty miles east of Utica. "Astronoga" was published in the *Knickerbocker* after its author became famous as Fanny Forester.

111. Edna to Lizzy Ives, December 6, 1866, Lizzy Ives Papers, #1266, Department of Manuscripts and University Archives, Olin Library, Cornell University.

112. John S. Hart, *The Female Prose Writers of America* (Philadelphia, 1852), pp. 89–91. Hart says, "first as readers, then as writers, women took over the novel." Hart's book had chromolithographed plates for the frontispiece; on one of the ribbons decorating the bottom of the page, the name "Judson" is inscribed.

   Historians of literature who have observed women's central role in antebellum publishing are E. Douglas Branch, *The Sentimental Years: 1836–1860* (New York, 1934); H. R. Brown, *The Sentimental Novel in America, 1789–1860* (Durham, 1940); James D. Hart, *The Popular Book: A History of America's Literary Taste* (New York, 1950); Meade Minnigrode, *The Fabulous Forties, 1840–50* (New York, 1924); Frank Luther Mott, *Golden Multitudes: The Story of Best Sellers in the United States* (New York, 1947); and Fred Lewis Pattee, *The Feminine Fifties* (New York, 1940).

113. Mellon devotes a large portion of his poem *The Age of Print* to woman who "rules the printer and the page." See *The Age of Print* (Boston, 1830), pp. 7–8.

114. Hart, p. 93.

115. A graduate of Andover and Yale, Nathaniel Parker Willis (b. 1806) became a nationally known literary bon vivant who, as a young man, tried his hand at poetry, verse paraphrases of biblical themes, editing, travel letters, and playwriting. He wrote widely for Graham's and Godey's before joining George Popee Morris in a partnership that resulted in the daily *Evening Mirror* (successor to *New Mirror*). As editor of the daily, he met Edgar Allen Poe and published his work. In 1845, his wife, the Englishwoman, Mary Stace, died in childbirth; in 1846, three months after Chubbuck's departure for Burma, Willis remarried a woman twenty years his junior.

   For Willis' life after 1846, see *Dictionary of American Biography*, pp. 307–8; H. A. Beers; *Nathaniel Parker Willis* (Boston, 1885); Cortland P. Auser, *Nathaniel Parker Willis* (New York, 1969).

116. William Ellery Leonard, in *Byron and Byronism in America* (New

York, 1964), p. 93, includes Willis as one of the American imitators of Byron.

117. Pattee, p. 93.

118. EC to WC, September 27, 1844, Chubbuck Family Papers, SHSW.

119. As far as I can ascertain, Chubbuck was the first to use this kind of alliterative pseudonym that suggested a naive and unsophisticated child of nature. Fanny Fern (Sara Payson Willis Parton) and Grace Greenwood (Sarah Jane Lippincott) were later imitators, who wrote for the *New York Ledger* and the *New Mirror*, respectively. Fanny Fern was in reality the sister of Nathaniel Parker Willis. Greenwood was one of his discoveries. See Robert P. Eckert, Jr., "Friendly, Fragrant Fanny Ferns," *Colophon* XVIII (1934); Ann D. Wood, " 'The Scribbling Woman' and Fanny Fern: Why Women Wrote," *American Quarterly* XXIII (Spring 1971).

120. Forester, *Trippings*, p. 13; originally published in the *New York Mirror* on June 8, 1844.

121. "Cousin Bel" was, in reality, Chubbuck's friend, Anna Maria Anable.

122. Forester, *Trippings*, p. 14.

123. Ibid.

124. Ibid., p. 15.

125. *New York Mirror* (June 8, 1844), p. 2.

126. EC to WC, September 27, 1844, Chubbuck Family Papers, SHSW.

127. Ibid. In this letter, Emily told her brother that she had given up on writing books.

128. Kendrick, p. 101.

129. Ibid., p. 99. Kendrick called Willis "the foster father of [Emily's] intellect."

130. Ibid., p. 106. Willis told Chubbuck that he considered "Dora" semiautobiographical. In that story, which was collected in *Trippings*, Chubbuck wrote about an orphaned girl who came to work as a seamstress in the village of Alderbrook. Dora, who, in fact, had the voice and spirit of a "song bird," was whisked away by a composer, against the wishes of her good aunt. The aunt told her explicitly that her voice was a gift from God, to be left in its natural state. After becoming famous, but finding success spiritually empty, Dora returns to Alderbrook and her aunt.

   The story is interesting because its conservative message, that worldly success brings women little happiness, did not represent the pattern of Chubbuck's life.

131. Kendrick, p. 109.

132. Ibid., p. 108. Willis gave Chubbuck all kinds of gratuitous information. However, when she mentioned the possibility of marriage, Willis wrote her this decidedly Romantic advice: "Let the majority

of women marry for convenience, but you are brimfull of romance, delicacy, and tenderness, and a marriage without love, for you, would be sealing up a volcano with a cob-web. . . . You must love— you *must* and *will* passionately and overpoweringly." Kendrick, p. 134.

133. Ibid., p. 120.
134. *Graham's Magazine* XXXII (April 1848), p. 240.
135. *Godey's Lady's Book* XXXII (January 1846), p. 47.
136. Forester, *Lilias Fane*, p. i.
137. Thomas Buchanan Reed, *The Female Poets of America* (Philadelphia, 1849); Rufus Wilmot Griswold, *The Prose Writers of America* (London, 1847); Caroline May, *The American Female Poets* (Philadelphia, 1848); Horace Binney Wallace, *Literary Criticisms and Other Papers* (Philadelphia, 1856).
138. "Fanny Forester" in *Hogg's Weekly Instructor* II (1848–49), p. 409. The liberal *Christian Examiner* XLIII (May 1847), pp. 393–402, observed that *Alderbrook* appeared to be the creation of a religious woman, "feeling with all the depth of a pious nature how beautiful are all the works and dealings of God." While the reviewer praised the fact that she did not "mingle doctrinal religion with sentiment" and described a few of the tales as "well told," he objected on principle to compilations or collections of periodical literature. The reviewer felt that the quantity of "light reading rained down upon the community through magazines and newspapers constituted a growing calamity."
139. Kendrick, p. 118.
140. *Utica Daily Gazette* IV (December 8, 1845), p. 2. One of Chubbuck's students, Jane Wright, wrote a complimentary poem about Fanny Forester that was published in a New York paper. EC to WC, September 27, 1844, Chubbuck Family Papers, SHSW.
141. Kendrick, p. 108.
142. Cathcart, I, p. 455.
143. Graham was the editor of the magazine of that name which (in March 1842) claimed 40,000 subscribers and a profit of $50,000 annually. See *DAB* IV, pp. 471–72.
144. Griswold, who was friend and literary executor to Edgar Allen Poe, counted among his proteges, Alice and Phoebe Cary, Charles Fenno Hoffman, and Bayard Taylor. Griswold's own works include: *The Songs of the Beranger in English* (1844); *The Poets and Poetry of England in the Nineteenth Century* (1844) and the first American edition of Milton. See *DAB* IV, pp. 10–12; Killis Campbell, "The Poe-Griswold Controversy," *PMLA* XXXIV (1919).
145. Neal was the editor of the *Saturday News and Literary Gazette*. See *DAB* VII, pp. 399–400.
146. EC to WC, July 2, 1845, Chubbuck Family Papers, SHSW.

147. Kendrick, p. 108. Chubbuck may have meant John C. Hagen, a genre painter popular in New York City at this time. See George Groce and David Wallace, *Dictionary of Artists in America 1564–1860* (New Haven, 1957), p. 282.
148. EC to WC, July 2, 1845, Chubbuck Family Papers, SHSW.
149. Kendrick, p. 129. In the same letter, Emily reported that Bryant had ranked her ahead of Catherine Sedgwick.
150. Ibid., p. 137. Horace Binney Wallace (b. 1817) studied both medicine and law as a young man. In 1838, he wrote a novel, *Stanley, or The Recollections of a Man of the World*, which was published anonymously. He was primarily a critic and wrote extensively in the fields of art, law, and literature. See *DAB* X, pp. 370–71.
151. Ibid., p. 142.
152. Ibid. These are Kendrick's own words. There is no account of this incident in Wayland.
153. Ibid., p. 143.
154. Charles Chubbuck to Walker Chubbuck, February 21, 1846, Chubbuck Family Papers, SHSW.
155. For an engagement gift, Judson gave Chubbuck a gold watch that had been used by Ann Hasseltine and Sarah Boardman. Kendrick, p. 147.
156. Ibid., pp. 159–60.
157. *Evangelical Intelligencer* III (February 1809), p. 82.
158. Ibid.
159. Reprinted in *Utica Daily Gazette* IV (December 25, 1845), p. 3. Chubbuck's friend, Horace Binney Wallace, protested the *Gospel Messenger* review in this way: "If I can find any proper place I will cuff this reverend booby over the mazard, in a way that his insolent coarseness deserves." Wallace, p. 191.
160. E. C. Lord to Hezekiah Harvey, n.d., Harvey Papers, Colgate University Archives.
161. I. N. Loomis to Lucy Loomis, n.d., Harvey Papers, Colgate University Archives.
162. "Life of Mrs. Emily C. Judson," *Saturday Review* (April 1861), reprinted in *Littell's Living Age* XIII–LXIX (June 1861), p. 69.
163. See Chapter II, p. 54, for the exact quotation.
164. *The Christian Examiner* XLII (May 1847), p. 393.
165. Kate Millett, in *Sexual Politics* (New York, 1971), makes this point about women and work. According to Elaine Showalter (cf., p. 459), in England, all Victorian women writers came from the middle or upper classes, and literary ambition, that is, making money from one's publications, was *verboten* until mid-century.
166. *Christian Watchman* XXVII (October 1846), p. 162.
167. Ibid.
168. Ibid. All of Chubbuck's biographers attributed her self-assertion in

the literary world to her poverty. Kendrick repeatedly made this point. He also felt the need to establish the religious identity and moral purity of the third Mrs. Judson. After so doing, he said that Adoniram Judson "may be pardoned if he took the authoress for the sake of obtaining the woman. . . ." Ibid., p. 168.

169. Ibid., p. 199.

170. Ibid., pp. 178–79. Judson reiterated many times that Emily could turn her talents to better use. She, in turn, expressed a desire to redirect the energies of her friend, N. P. Willis. She wrote to Adoniram: "I have been thinking almost constantly of Willis for a few days past. . . . I am anxious to do him good and it seems as though I might. If he would only become a truly pious man and turn his singular talents to good. . . ." In the same letter, Chubbuck wrote Judson that Charles Fenno Hoffman told her that some of their literary friends had been "powerfully" affected by her decision. Emily Chubbuck to Adoniram Judson, February 22, 1846, Colgate University Archives.

171. Kendrick, p. 179.

172. Ibid., p. 185.

173. Ibid., p. 185.

174. Ibid., p. 176.

175. Ibid., p. 177.

176. Ibid., pp. 183–84.

177. Ibid., p. 252.

178. Ibid.

179. Ibid., p. 259.

180. EC to WC, May 24, 1846, Chubbuck Family Papers, SHSW.

181. According to the report of Kate Chubbuck, Adoniram and Emily left America with a "complete outfit," which included a "library and a great many beautiful presents besides, such as lamps, rocking chair, chinaware silver forks and spoons." In addition, Emily had a "common outfit," which was provided in part by the Utica Female Missionary Society. Kate Chubbuck to Walker Chubbuck, August 4, 1846, Chubbuck Family Papers, SHSW.

182. Kendrick, pp. 195–96. At the last minute, Emily wrote Adoniram urging that they take Abby Ann back with them to Burma. She reasoned that her years as an instructor of young women would qualify her to take care of his daughter, who was now approaching the critical period of her adolescence. Abby Ann was the only Judson child who was reported to have read Fanny Forester's work. *Effie Maurice*, according to Adoniram, was one of his eleven-year-old daughter's favorite books. Ibid., p. 174.

183. Ibid., pp. 200–204.

184. Ibid., p. 178. Kate Chubbuck reported to Walker Chubbuck that Emily earned $150 for the Baptist Mission Board in the year after her

marriage. This was strictly from the sale of her works in America and did not include the *Memoir of Sarah B. Judson*, which was still in press. KC to WC, December 12, 1847, Chubbuck Family Papers, SHSW.

185. Before she left for Burma, Emily and Adoniram Judson paid for the Chubbucks' house at Hamilton, for their furniture and for clothes for Kate. Judson also purchased, in Emily's name, three acres of land near Hamilton, where Charles Chubbuck could "pasture his horse, raise a few oats, etc." EC to WC, May 24, 1845, Chubbuck Family Papers, SHSW.

186. Cathcart, I, p. 649; *Utica Daily Gazette* V (June 5, 1846), p. 2; *Democratic Reflector* (Hamilton, New York) IV (June 4, 1846), p. 3.

187. During this period, Emily wrote a farewell poem to her mother which was published in the *Geneva Gazette* (September 25, 1846).

188. The Judsons were accompanied by Lydia Lillybridge, an unmarried teacher from the Utica Female Seminary. Emily Judson's first choice for a companion was Anna Maria Anable, who was either unable or unwilling to go.

189. Kendrick, p. 210; Wyeth, pp. 100–102. Willis was supposed to come to Boston to see the Judsons off, but he did not. Ibid., p. 201.

190. Ibid., pp. 212–15.

191. *Graham's Magazine* XXX (March 1847), p. 204.

192. *MBMM* XXXIV (August 1854), pp. 364–65.

193. Kendrick, p. 273.

194. Reprinted from the *Columbian Magazine* (August 1847), in Kendrick, pp. 233–34.

195. Wyeth, pp. 170–71.

196. *Graham's Magazine* XXXII (April 1848), p. 240.

197. For example, Mrs. Judson wrote of George Boardman while he was in the jungle, preaching and alive: "He was very near his eternal home." She also used poetic selections to head each chapter.

198. Wayland, II, p. 308. Throughout 1848–1850, Judson sent the *Memoir* to friends and associates.

199. Emily Frances Judson, whom her mother immortalized in a poem entitled "My Little Bird," was born December 24, 1847. See Chapter 6.

200. Wayland, II, p. 314.

201. Kendrick, pp. 308–9.

202. Kendrick, p. 310.

203. Ibid., p. 215.

204. See Mott, *Golden Multitudes*, pp. 307–8. Between 1850 and 1859, the sales of the following "domestic novels" reached one percent of the national population: Susan Warner, *Wide Wide World*; Mrs. E.D.E.N. Southworth, *The Curse of Clifton* and *The Hidden Hand*;

Maria S. Cummins, *The Lamplighter*; Mary Jane Holmes, *Tempest and Sunshine* and *Lena Rivers*; Augusta J. Evans, *Beulah*.

205. Extracted from information supplied by Hart, p. 90, and Mott, *Golden Multitudes*, pp. 340–41.

206. See Chapter 3, pp. 101–104, for a discussion of giftbook literature.

207. H. R. Brown, p. 201. Another significant bit of evidence for the case that evangelicals were adopting popular cultural styles is Henry Ward Beecher's novel, *Norwood* (New York, 1868). The *New York Ledger* commissioned twelve ministers to write a novel each for the paper. *Norwood* was one of that series.

208. I am not suggesting that the evangelicals adopted fiction uncritically. They remained highly suspicious of imaginative literature of all kinds and uneasy about its unsupervised use. Sometime after her return to the United States, Mrs. Judson wrote her step-daughter, Abby Ann:

> I would not object to a volume of Scott for you in vacation . . . I would rather, however, you would do but little [general] reading in term time, for the reason that I suspect your general reading already to be in advance of your school education. Scott is a healthful writer . . . and Campbell's poetry is a thing for you to read and re-read. . . . But I do not like to have you read Moore [Lalla Rookh]. . . .

209. Mott, *Golden Multitudes*, pp. 123–24.

210. Ibid.

211. For still other interpretations of the domestic novelists, see Helen Papashvily, *All the Happy Endings* (New York, 1956); William R. Taylor and Christopher Lasch, "Two Kindred Spirits: Sorority and Family in New England, 1839–46," *NEQ* XXXVI (1963); Nina Baym, *Woman's Fiction: A Guide to Novels by and about Women in America, 1820–70* (Ithaca, 1978).

212. This is Frank Luther Mott's term.

213. James Hart, p. 93. In addition, the heroines of the domestic novels come largely from the "democratic" churches. Catholics, Episcopalians, and Mormons were all suspect. See Papashvily, p. 161.

214. Kendrick, pp. 330–32.

215. Ibid., p. 330. The amusing thing about the evangelicals' constant comparisons between the pious and profane writers is that they assume a knowledge of the latter.

216. Kendrick, pp. 337–39. Reprinted in *A Little Book of Judson Verse*, pp. 24–25.

217. Kendrick, p. 341.

218. Ibid., p. 342; Wayland, II, p. 351.

219. Kendrick, p. 363.

220. Ibid., p. 350.

221. Ibid., pp. 345–46. Another missionary, E. A. Stevens, would complete the work.

222. Ibid., p. 366. Mrs. Judson declined the regular widow's pension out of "motives of delicacy." The Board voted to turn over to her any further profits from the sale of the *Memoir of Sarah B. Judson*.
223. Ibid., p. 354.
224. Ibid., p. 355.
225. Chubbuck had responsibility for her parents, her sister, Kate, George Boardman, Abby Ann, Elnathan, Adoniram, Henry, Edward, and Emily Frances Judson, and a Burmese woman she brought to America.
226. Kendrick, pp. 379–81.
227. Emily Chubbuck Judson, *My Two Sisters*.
228. In addition to her defense of missionary motives, Chubbuck depicted the foreign missionary movement as a grass roots crusade, involving the young and the poor on two continents. See *The Kathayan Slave*, pp. 31–34.
229. *Alderbrook*, however, went through eleven editions by 1860. The *Memoir of Sarah B. Judson* began its thirtieth thousand in 1855.
230. Kendrick, pp. 394–404.
231. See Chapter 1, p. 16, for a discussion of the Judson-Fletcher controversy. Kendrick, p. 404, describes a case that was brought by Fletcher against C. B. Norton, the publisher of the *Literary Gazette*, for printing uncomplimentary remarks about him by Francis Wayland. Mrs. Judson's correspondence with Fletcher was part of the evidence submitted at the trial; in this way the controversy became public. For Emily Chubbuck Judson's obituaries, see *New York Herald* (June 3, 1854), p. 1; and *New York Weekly Tribune* (June 10, 1854), p. 5.
232. Starr, XII, p. 189.
233. Nineteenth-century works on Adoniram Judson are detailed in the notes to Chapter 1. In the twentieth century, the following are noteworthy: Courtney Anderson, *To the Golden Shore: The Life of Adoniram Judson* (Boston, 1956); D. Babcock, *Adoniram Judson* (Grand Rapids, 1953): Faith Coxe Bailey, *Adoniram Judson, Missionary To Burma* (Chicago, 1955); J. Batten, *Golden Foot: The Story of Judson in Burma* (London, 1956); Floyd LaVerne Carr, "Adoniram Judson," in *Life Stories of Great Missionaries for Teenage Boys* (New York, 1925); Austen Kennedy DuBois, *Fighters for Freedom. Heroes of the Baptist Challenge* (Philadelphia, 1929); Orin Philip Gifford, *Adoniram Judson: An Address Delivered on the Occasion of the Judson Centennial Celebration in Tremont Temple, Boston, Mass., June 24, 1914* (Boston, 1914); Howard Benjamin Grose, *The Judson Centennial, 1814–1914* (Philadelphia, 1914); Gordon Langley Hall, *Golden Boats from Burma* (Philadelphia, 1961); Eugene Meyer Harrison, *Heroes of Faith on Pioneer Trails* (Chicago, 1945); James Langdon Hill, *The Immortal Seven: Judson and His Associates* (Phil-

adelphia, 1913); Randolph L. Howard, *It Began in Burma* (Philadelphia, 1942); Vernon Howard, *Adoniram Judson, Hero of Burma* (New York, c. 1949); John Mervin Hull, *Judson the Pioneer* (Philadelphia, 1913); Adoniram Brown Judson, *How Judson Became a Baptist Missionary* (Philadelphia, 1913); James Gilchrist Lawson, *Famous Missionaries* (Grand Rapids, 1941); Walter McCleary, *An Hour with Adoniram Judson* (New York, 1929); Laura Helen Percy, *Adoniram Judson, Apostle of Burma* (Anderson, Ind., 1926); Anna Swain, *Twenty Months a Prisoner* (Canada, 1927); Philip Allen Swartz, *Judson's High Adventure* (Little Compton, R.I., 1962); Stacy Warburton, *Eastward! The Story of Adoniram Judson* (New York, 1937); Pat Yates, *The Book in the Pillow* (New York, 1942).

The fact that this is an incomplete listing suggests the truth of Hannah Chaplin Conant's title for her 1877 book on Judson, *Our Gold Mine, the Story of American Baptist Missions in India*. It should also be noted that Judson's life was translated into the following languages for universal dissemination: French, Spanish, German, Swedish, and Hindi.

CHAPTER 6

1. William Dean to George Dana Boardman, March 1866, in Boardman Papers, American Baptist Historical Society (ABHS); *Memoir of SBJ*, p. 195. Boardman later reported that he was accompanied on this journey by a pet goat. The goat, however, was killed by the *Cashmere's* crew. As an adult, Boardman reported that this brutality left permanent effects on his nervous system. See "Men I Meet: George Dana Boardman," *Chicago Standard* (September 7, 1893), clipping (C), ABHS.
2. Mitchell Bronk, "George Dana Boardman," unpublished address, February 25, 1948, First Baptist Church of Philadelphia, ABHS.
3. Kendrick, p. 385. Recall that Emily Chubbuck Judson wanted to have Abby Ann return to Burma with her father and new wife. Chubbuck's letters indicate that she and Abby Ann discussed this possibility but could not convince Adoniram. Kendrick, pp. 363–65.
4. Kendrick, p. 407, describes Emily Judson's final illness as "ulcerated lungs," probably either tuberculosis or pleurisy.
5. Kendrick, p. 392.
6. Ibid., p. 383. Adoniram Brown Judson graduated from Brown University in 1859, attended Harvard Medical School, and received an M.D. from Jefferson Medical College in 1864 and from the College of Physicians and Surgeons, Columbia University, in 1868. Elnathan Judson attended his father's alma mater from 1858 to 1860

but graduated from Union Theological Seminary in 1862. Information provided by Martha Mitchell, University Archivist, John Hay Library, Brown University (BU).

7. Kendrick, p. 410. Edward Judson graduated from Hamilton in 1864. His education and career are described in Chapter 7. Henry Hall Judson attended Brown University from 1860 to 1861 and then transferred to Williams College. In January 1864, during his junior year, he enlisted in the Fifteenth New York Heavy Artillery. He was permanently disabled in the engagements before Petersburg, Virginia, and was mustered out by December 12, 1864. (BU).

8. Cathcart, I, pp. 493–94.

9. Ibid.

10. The Hannas eight children were: Emily (b. 1871), Thomas (b. 1872), Adoniram (b. 1875), Arthur (b. 1877), Miriam (b. 1879), Annabel (b. 1881), Edward (b. 1885) and Alexander (b. 1888). Emily Judson Hanna died in Perkasie, Pennsylvania, in 1911.

11. Marty, pp. 133–43.

12. Kenneth Latourette, *A History of the Expansion of Christianity*, 7 vols. (New York, 1937–1945) cited in Paul A. Carter, *The Spiritual Crisis of the Gilded Age*, pp. 7, viii.

13. See n. 6 above for Adoniram Brown Judson's medical education. He was an assistant surgeon in the United States Navy in 1861 and became a surgeon in 1866, serving until 1868. From 1868 until his death in 1916, he practiced medicine in New York City where he was involved in a number of public medical positions: medical inspector of the Board of Health of New York (1869–1877), U.S. Pension examining surgeon (1877–1884, 1901–1914), and medical examiner of the New York State Civil Service Commission (1901–1909). He was the orthopedic surgeon to the out-patient department of New York Hospital from 1878 to 1908.

14. See n. 7 above.

15. Elnathan Judson's history is recounted on pp. 231–34.

16. Richard Hofstadter, *Social Darwinism in American Thought* (New York, 1944), p. 13.

17. Ibid., p. 23; Paul F. Boller, Jr., "New Men and New Ideas: Science and the American Mind," in H. Wayne Morgan, ed., *The Gilded Age: A Reappraisal* (Syracuse, 1963), p. 243.

18. Hofstadter, pp. 15–26.

19. Quoted in Carter, p. 14.

20. Ibid., p. 17.

21. *Popular Science Monthly* I (July, 1872) quoted in Carter, p. 18.

22. Joseph Ide Mortenson, "The Career of the Reverend George Dana Boardman," unpublished Th.D. dissertation, Boston University School of Theology, 1966, p. 39. This is the only complete account of

Boardman's career. I am indebted to Mortensen and Janet Kerr Morchaine, "George Dana Boardman: Propagandist for Peace," *Foundations* IX (April-June 1966), pp. 145–58, for the thrust of this biography.

23. Mortensen, pp. 40–43.

24. The most complete listing of his work is in Starr, III, pp. 209–12. The books are: *Studies in the Creative Week* (New York, 1875); *Studies in the Model Prayer* (New York, 1879); *Epiphanies of the Risen Lord* (New York, 1879); *Studies in the Mountain Instruction* (New York, 1881); *The Divine Man, from the Nativity to the Temptation* (New York, 1887); *The Ten Commandments* (Philadelphia, 1889); *The Problem of Jesus* (Philadelphia, 1902); *The Kingdom (Basilica)* (New York, 1899); *The Church (Ecclesia)* (New York, 1901); *Our Risen King's Forty Days* (Philadelphia, 1902) and *Ethics of the Body* (Philadelphia, 1903).

25. Boardman supposedly gave thirty-one Wednesday evening Bible lectures. He gave the Tuesday noon lectures for fourteen weeks in 1877. In 1880, he gave an ethics course at Association Hall in Philadelphia. He also lectured at the Home Mission Society for the Spread of the Gospel, Relief of the Worthy Poor, and Care of Destitute Children; the Chestnut Street Seminary; the Historical Society of Pennsylvania; the University of Lewisburg; Drexel Institute; and Hamilton Theological Seminary. Ibid., pp. 74–76.

26. Bernard A. Weisberger, *They Gathered at the River. The Story of the Great Revivalists and Their Impact upon Religion in America* (Chicago, 1958), p. 207.

27. Mortensen, p. 38.

28. Ibid., p. 65. In 1891, Boardman published "Titles of a Pastors' Course of Weekly Lectures on the Holy Bible, from Genesis to Revelation," which was, in actuality, a topical index to those biblical themes that he had pursued in sermons delivered at the First Baptist Church between October 5, 1864 and December 29, 1890.

29. Marty, p. 104, makes the point about the rural quality of antebellum evangelicalism.

30. George Dana Boardman (GDB), *Studies in Mountain Instruction*, p. 52.

31. The authoritative work on the Social Gospel in America remains: C. Howard Hopkins, *The Rise of the Social Gospel in American Protestantism, 1856–1915* (New Haven, 1940). Other important viewpoints on the Social Gospel can be found in Aaron I. Abell, *The Urban Impact on American Protestantism* (New York, 1943); Henry F. May, *Protestant Churches and Industrial America* (New York, 1949); Donald B. Meyer, *The Protestant Search for Political Realism, 1919–1941* (Berkeley, 1960); and Robert T. Handy, ed., *The*

Social Gospel in America, 1870–1920 (New York, 1966). On the Brotherhood, see C. H. Hopkins, "Walter Rauschenbusch and the Brotherhood of the Kingdom," *Church History* VII (June 1938), pp. 138–45.

32. GDB, "The Lay Element in the Missionary Field," *Baptist Missionary Magazine* LXII (June 1882), p. 173.

33. A good summary of the important historiographical questions that illuminate the Social Gospel movement can be found in Ronald C. White, Jr. and C. Howard Hopkins, *The Social Gospel: Religion and Reform in Changing America* (Philadelphia, 1976), pp. xi–xix. Timothy Smith, *Revivalism and Social Reform in Mid-Nineteenth Century America* (Nashville, 1957) makes the classic case for the relationship between antebellum evangelicalism and the Social Gospel movement.

34. Mortensen, p. 153. Boardman vacillated somewhat on the question of "just wars." Although he was opposed to the Spanish-American War, he did find some "relatively right" wars—the wars of the Old Testament, the American Revolution, and the Civil War—all of which he attributed to the primitive character of past ages. All present and future wars he considered "absolutely wrong." His pacifism, then, was built on a notion of progress. Morchaine, p. 147.

35. Mortensen, p. 150; Morchaine, p. 150.

36. Mortensen, p. 155.

37. Ibid.

38. Kerr Boyce Tupper, *George Dana Boardman: A Memorial Discourse* (Philadelphia, 1904), pp. 27–29.

39. Mortensen, p. 143.

40. Mrs. George Dana Boardman, *Life and Light: Thoughts from the Writings of George Dana Boardman* (Philadelphia, 1905), pp. 123–24.

41. Ibid.

42. "Harmonizer" is Paul Carter's term.

43. GDB, "The Scriptural Anthropology," *Baptist Quarterly* I (April 1867), pp. 177–85.

44. Mortensen, pp. 91–92.

45. GDB, *Nature a Pledge of Grace* (n.p., n.d.), p. 1.

46. GDB, *Studies in the Creative Week*, pp. 14–15.

47. Quoted in Mortensen, p. 76.

48. GDB, *The Kingdom*, pp. 62–63.

49. GDB, *Studies in the Creative Week*, p. 124.

50. Quoted in Mortensen, p. 76.

51. Mortensen, p. 57.

52. GDB, *Ethics of the Body*, p. 12.

53. GDB, *Studies in the Creative Week*, p. 91.

54. For an assessment of the biblical criticism of the Gilded Age, see Ira V. Brown, "The Higher Criticism Comes to America, 1880–1900," *Journal of Presbyterian Historical Society* 38 (December 1960); Arthur Meier Schlesinger, "A Critical Period in American Religion, 1875–1900," *Proceedings of the Massachusetts Historical Society* LXIV (June 1932).

55. GDB, *Studies in the Creative Week*, p. 91.

56. Martin Marty identifies the same trend, calling it "decorous worldliness."

57. *Banner of Light (BL)* (June 20, 1891), p. 3.

58. *BL* (February 21, 1895), p. 7.

59. The best modern historical study of late nineteenth-century Spiritualism is R. Laurence Moore, *In Search of White Crows: Spiritualism, Parapsychology and American Culture* (New York, 1977). Moore presents the Spiritualist claim to science. "In all cases," he writes, "the strategy of Spiritualism was to sell itself by language and by deed as a scientific endeavor," pp. 14–28. See also Russel M. and Clare R. Goldfarb, *Spiritualism and 19th Century Letters* (London 1978) which is extremely informative on Spiritualism in British and American literary life. The Goldfarbs (p. 11), also confirm the point: "Orthodoxy was defensive, but Spiritualism was aggressive and modern. Spiritualists saw no contradiction between science and religion, and they welcomed scientific investigation of mediums and seances." See also Frank Podmore, *Modern Spiritualism* (London, 1902).

60. Abby Ann Judson (AAJ), *From Night to Morn; or An Appeal to the Baptist Church* (Norwich, Conn., 1894), p. 23.

61. *BL* (October 28, 1894), p. 2.

62. Moner refers to the classification *monera*, or organisms of the simplest form without condensed nuclei, i.e., bacteria and blue-green algae.

63. *BL* (January 11, 1896), p. 2.

64. *BL* (February 7, 1895), p. 7.

65. *BL* (October 12, 1895), p. 5.

66. AAJ, *Why She Became A Spiritualist: Twelve Lectures delivered before the Minneapolis Association of Spiritualists* (Minneapolis, 1891), p. 243.

67. *BL* (October 12, 1895), p. 5.

68. Ibid.

69. *BL* (October 28, 1894), p. 2.

70. AAJ, *Why*, p. 243.

71. Ibid., pp. 94–95, 106–07, 109, 110–11, 244.

72. AAJ, *The Bridge Between Two Worlds* (Minneapolis, 1894), p. 19.

73. AAJ, *Night to Morn*, p. 18.

74. AAJ, *Bridge*, p. 8.

75. Ibid., p. 12.

76. Ibid., p. 10.

77. AAJ, *Why*, p. 74.

78. AAJ, *Bridge*, p. 9.

79. AAJ, *Why*, p. 7.

80. *Catalogue of the Judson Female Institute*, Minneapolis, Minnesota, 1880–1881, p. 12. Minnesota Historical Society Library.

81. AAJ, *Night to Morn*, p. 26.

82. Moore, p. 64.

83. AAJ, *Night to Morn*, pp. 16–17.

84. Ibid.

85. Ibid.

86. Ibid., p. 21. The Temple Builders were a young people's foreign missionary society.

87. Ibid., p. 20.

88. Ibid., p. 21.

89. Ibid., p. 24.

90. Ibid., p. 25.

91. Ibid.

92. Ibid., pp. 26–27.

93. Ibid. "Some of the Subscribers of the Adoniram Judson Memorial Baptist Church Edifice Fund," 1890, Pamphlet, Rockefeller Archive Center, Pocantico Hills.

94. AAJ, *Why*, pp. 8–9; *History of Clinton County, Iowa* (Clinton, Iowa, 1978), p. 228; Merrill E. Jarchow, "Social Life of An Iowa Farm Family, 1873–1912," in *Iowa Journal of History and Politics* L:2 (April 1952), pp. 150–52.

95. AAJ, *Bridge*, p. 59.

96. An itinerary of Abby Ann Judson's Spiritualist lecturing, based on notices in the *Banner of Light*, includes all of the following, although not in chronological order: Philadelphia (First Spiritual Society); New York City (Adelphi Hall); Boston (Ladies Industrial Society, First Ladies Aid, Berkeley Hall, First Spiritualist Temple); Cincinnati (Spiritual Union); Louisville (Independent Spiritual Church); Providence; Dayton; Lynn, New Bedford, Attleborough, Springfield, Malden, Melrose Highland, N. Scituate, Haverhill, Northampton, and South Deerfield, Massachusetts; Waverly and Skaneateles, New York; Greenwich and Willimantic, Connecticut; and Sayre, Pennsylvania.

97. *BL* (January 14, 1893), p. 3.

98. *BL* (January 19, 1895), p. 4.

99. *BL* (November 17, 1894), p. 2.

100. *BL* (January 19, 1895), p. 4.

101. *BL* (October 20, 1894), p. 5.

102. *BL* (March 30, 1895), p. 5.

103. *BL* (October 21, 1894), p. 5.

104. AAJ, *Bridge*, p. 147.

105. Ibid.

106. A popular spiritualistic performance in which writing appears on a slate. The medium and the sitter occupy opposite ends of a table in a typical séance. Both hold an ordinary slate and pencil pressed against the underside of the table and wait for a message from the spirit world to be inscribed on it. Harvey E. Wedeck, *Dictionary of Spiritualism* (New York, 1971), p. 318.

107. AAJ, *Why*, p. 260.

108. AAJ, *Bridge*, p. 166.

109. AAJ, *Night to Morn*, pp. 7–8.

110. *BL* (October 20, 1894), p. 5.

111. *BL* (March 30, 1895), p. 5.

112. Moore, p. 5, also makes the point that séances attracted a great many of the elderly and the bereaved. Goldfarb, p. 61, reports that Harriet Beecher Stowe described Spiritualism, in a letter to George Eliot, as "a sort of Rachel-cry of bereavement towards the invisible existence of the loved ones. . . ."

113. AAJ, *Why*, p. 261.

114. AAJ, *Bridge*, p. 207.

115. Ibid., p. 210.

116. Ibid., p. 214.

117. *BL* (October 19, 1895), p. 5.

118. Ibid.

119. Ibid., p. 6.

120. AAJ, *Bridge*, p. 53.

121. Moore, pp. 102–129.

122. See *NAW*, III, pp. 652–55 for Woodhull's biography and for bibliographical references. There has, as yet, been no satisfactory biography of Woodhull.

123. Goldfarb, p. 45.

124. *BL* (March 19, 1898), p. 2.

125. Moore, pp. 3–4; Goldfarb, p. 139; Carter, pp. 103–104.

126. Warren Hunting Smith, *Hobart and William Smith: The History of Two Colleges* (Geneva, 1972), pp. 188–89.

127. For Alfred Russel Wallace on Spiritualism, see *The World of Life: A Manifestation of Creative Power, Directive Mind, and Ultimate Purpose* (London, 1910); on women and moral progress, see *Social*

Environment and Moral Progress (London, 1913), pp. 163–65. Warren Wagar, SUNY-Binghamton, called my attention to Wallace's Spiritualist faith.

128. Marie Caskey, *Chariot of Fire: Religion and the Beecher Family* (New Haven, 1978), pp. 101–19.

129. See Harrison D. Barrett, ed., *Life Work of Mrs. Cora L. V. Richmond* (Chicago, 1895). There is a genre of memoirs and biographies of Spiritualist lecturers and mediums. Cora Richmond began her career as a medium as a young girl in Cuba, N.Y.

130. Judson detailed the officers of many of the associations she visited. At least fifty percent of the officers were women, including the presidents of the associations.

131. Donald Meyer, *Positive Thinkers: A Study of the American Quest for Health, Wealth, and Personal Power from Mary Baker Eddy to Norman Vincent Peale* (New York, 1965), pp. 40, 46–59. Meyer does not deal explicitly with Spiritualism but with the relationship between women's needs and "mind cure."

132. Elizabeth Stuart Phelps, *The Gates Ajar*, Helen Sootin Smith, ed., (Cambridge, 1964), p. vi. See also Mary Angela Bennett, "Elizabeth Stuart Phelps," unpublished Ph.D. dissertation, University of Pennsylvania, 1938.

133. *BL* (October 20, 1894), p. 5. Goldfarb, pp. 19 f., details those portions of the Bible with Spiritualist themes that were appropriated by people in the movement.

134. *Catalogue of the Judson Female Institute*, 1880–1881, p. 3.

135. AAJ, *Bridge*, p. 205.

136. *BL* (December 12, 1895), p. 7.

137. *BL* (December 21, 1895), p. 7.

138. Information provided by Martha Mitchell, University Archivist, John Hay Library, Brown University.

139. *BL* (January 22, 1898), p. 6. Brown University Collections support the sunstroke story.

140. *BL* (September 25, 1897), p. 3.

141. Ibid.

142. *BL* (January 22, 1898), pp. 6–7.

143. Ibid.

144. Ibid. Abby Ann Judson died December 8, 1902, in Arlington, New Jersey, from burns resulting from the accidental overturning of a lamp while reading in bed. *Minneapolis Journal*, December 12, 1902, p. 4.

145. See Philip Greven, *The Protestant Temperament: Patterns of Child-Rearing, Religious Experience and the Self in Early America* (New York, 1977), pp. 21–150 for a description of evangelical child

rearing and family life, focusing primarily on the eighteenth century. Greven's important study identifies the "persistence of particular patterns of thought and action" designated as evangelical and investigates their origins in the family setting.

146. Greven, pp. 50–55.

CHAPTER 7

1. Edward Judson (EJ) to Berean Baptist Church, July 25, 1881, *Minutes of the Berean Baptist Church*, II. This letter, in the collection of the Judson Memorial Church, was brought to my attention by Arlene Carmen, the church administrator. Judson also stipulated that the pastor's salary be established at $1,200 per year and that he be allowed to bring his own staff.

2. Charles Hatch Sears, *Edward Judson. Interpreter of God* (Philadelphia, 1917), pp. 48–49. Sears was a former student of Edward Judson who served as general secretary of the New York City Baptist Mission Society.

3. See John Higham, *Strangers in the Land: Patterns of American Nativism, 1860–1925* (New York, 1963), p. 65. Many Protestants were not interested in evangelizing the immigrant. Higham describes the bigotry and fear of immigrant radicalism that led many into the nativist camp.

4. Antoinette Barstow (d. 1914) was the daughter of a Congregationalist minister in Maple Rapids, Michigan. In 1893, Charles Barstow, her father, came into an inheritance of $4,700 which Edward Judson had John D. Rockefeller administer for him. EJ to John D. Rockefeller, Sr. (JDR), August 3, 1893, the Rockefeller Archives Center (RAC), Pocantico Hills (PH), the John D. Rockefeller Collection. Some papers pertaining to Rockefeller Senior are also in Record Group II, Messrs. Rockefeller, the Rockefeller Family Archives (RFA), in New York City. Between 1894 and 1904, there is a gap in all the Rockefeller records.

5. Sears, p. 90; see Sam Bass Warner, *Street Car Suburbs: The Process of Growth in Boston* (Cambridge, 1962) for a historical description of this process in the case of one American city.

6. EJ, "The Church in Its Social Aspect," *Annals of the American Academy of Political and Social Science* XXX (July-December 1907), p. 4.

7. Salvatore Mondello, "Baptist Churches and Italian Americans," *Foundations* XVI: 3 (July-September 1973), p. 223; *Twenty-eighth Anniversary of the Southern New York Baptist Association, October 1898* (New York, 1898), pp. 55–59, ABHS.

8. EJ, *Annals*, p. 5.

9. Ibid., p. 3.

10. Ibid., p. 4.

11. EJ in the "Introduction" to Charles Hatch Sears, *The Redemption of the City* (Philadelphia, 1911), p. x.

12. EJ, *The Christian and the People* (Boston, 1886), p. 17.

13. Ibid., p. 3; Sears, p. 90.

14. EJ, *Annals*, p. 3.

15. Sears, p. 90.

16. EJ, *Annals*, p. 3.

17. Ibid., p. 4.

18. EJ, *Redemption of the City*, p. x.

19. Sears, p. 41. According to Mondello, p. 229, in 1895, the Baptists had one Italian Baptist missionary, probably Calabrese at the Memorial Church. In 1911, there were fifty Italian Baptist missionaries. By 1912 there were fifty-nine Italian Baptist Churches in the country, primarily in the major cities and in mining regions, representing a constituency of approximately 1,500 people. In 1899, the Italian Baptist Association met for the first time in Mt. Vernon, N.Y.; by 1903, they were publishing their own bilingual newspaper known alternately as *Il Messagiero*, *Il Christiano*, *L'Aurora*, and *New Aurora*.

20. Mondello, pp. 236–38, argues that Italian Baptists did in fact surpass their Catholic counterparts in terms of social mobility. See also Alfred Francis White, "A History of the Italian Baptists within the Territory of the Northern Baptist Convention," unpublished M.A. thesis, Crozer Theological Seminary, 1940, and Theodore Abel, *Protestant Home Missions to Catholic Immigrants* (New York, 1933), for further description of this kind of evangelical work.

21. EJ, *Annals*, p. 4.

22. Ibid., p. 5.

23. EJ, *Church and the People*, p. 4; *Annals*, pp. 5–6.

24. EJ, *Redemption of the City*, p. ix.

25. Sears, p. 93.

26. EJ, *Church and the People*, p. 6. For a history of the Y.M.C.A., see C.H. Hopkins, *History of the Y.M.C.A. in North America* (New York, 1951).

27. EJ, *The Institutional Church. A Primer in Pastoral Theology* (New York, 1889), p. 22.

28. Ibid.

29. See Jane Allen Shikoh, "The Higher Life of the American City in the 1890's," unpublished Ph.D. dissertation, New York University, 1972. According to Shikoh, J.P. Morgan underwrote St. George's "Memorial House" for work among the urban poor, and at St. Bar-

tholomew's, the Vanderbilts contributed the money for a facility to service the poor.

30. Reported in Sarah K. Bolton, *Famous Types of Womanhood* (New York, 1892), pp. 273–74.
31. Sears, p. 108; Program Announcement, Judson Memorial Church, n.d., New York Public Library.
32. EJ, *Church and the People*, p. 3.
33. Ibid., p. 5.
34. Ibid.
35. Ibid., p. 1.
36. EJ, *Annals*, p. 2.
37. Rockefeller did not give exclusively to Baptist causes. Records of these disbursements, throughout the 1880s and into the 1890s, can be found at the RAC, PH.
38. John H. Deane gave $5,000 a year for the first three years of the Memorial Church drive. The Rockefeller Archives Center (PH) has an 1889 list of subscribers, organized by state, and including only those who contributed $100 or more.
39. Edward Judson (EJ) to John Davison Rockefeller (JDR), May 12, 1887, RAC; Allan Nevins, *Study in Power. John D. Rockefeller. Industrialist and Philanthropist.* 2 vols. (New York, 1953), pp. 77–78.
40. EJ to JDR, March 6, 1888, RAC.
41. EJ to JDR, January 21, 1889, RAC.
42. EJ to JDR, September 14, 1887, RAC.
43. See R. H. Tawney, *Religion and the Rise of Capitalism*, for the classic statement of the development of religious thought in relation to secular business.
44. One senses that competition among the denominations motivated some of the "cathedral building" efforts of the day. LaFarge had already been involved with H. H. Richardson in the creation of the Episcopalians' Trinity Church, Copley Square, Boston.
45. Sears, p. 60.
46. *Baptist Home Mission Monthly* XIX (January 1897), pp. 33–34.
47. Judson validated the social mission of the churches with evidence from the New Testament. He believed Jesus was "intensely social." See EJ, *The Institutional Church*, pp. 19–20 for a typical statement to this effect.
48. On the subject of philanthropy and "scientific giving," see Robert Bremner, *American Philanthropy* (Chicago, 1970); Raymond Callahan, *Education and the Cult of Efficiency* (Chicago, 1962); Merle Curti and Roderick Nash, *Philanthropy in the Shaping of American Higher Education* (New Brunswick, 1965). John Davison Rockefeller said of Gates:

    Mr. Gates has been the guiding genius in all our giving. He came to us first to undertake certain business matters requiring talent of a high order and he showed phenomenal business ability. He combined with this the rare quality—born, no doubt, because he had the right kind of heart—of being able to direct the distribution of money with great vision. We all owe much to Mr. Gates, and his helpfulness should be generally recognized. He combines business skill and philanthropic aptitude to a higher degree than any other man I have ever known.

49. Fred T. Gates, *Chapters in My Life* (New York, 1977), pp. 36, 44, 96.
50. On Abby Ann Judson, see Chapter 6, p. 212, n. 78. According to Mortensen, p. 173, George Boardman reasoned that the rich were only in temporary custody of God's wealth. In "The Just Scales," *New Princeton Review* (1866), p. 206, Boardman went on record as favoring the limitation of capital.
51. JDR to EJ, July 1, 1882, RAC.
52. EJ to JDR, July [n.d.] 1882; Judson first used the term "manifold stewardship" in a November 1887 letter to Rockefeller, RAC.
53. EJ to JDR, December 10, 1886, RAC.
54. EJ to JDR, January 25, 1883, RAC.
55. EJ to JDR, March 24, 1886, RAC.
56. EJ to JDR, December 27, 1889, RAC.
57. JDR to Elizabeth Judson, August 17, 1908, RFA. As an adult, Margaret Judson served as Dean of Women at Denison University before becoming an Associate Professor of English at Vassar College.
58. EJ to JDR, February 16, 1892, RAC.
59. EJ to JDR, February 19, 1885, RAC.
60. Nevins, p. 4.
61. Edward Judson, *The Life of Adoniram Judson* (New York, 1883). Edward ostensibly wrote this book because the Wayland Memoir was out of print.
62. EJ to JDR, December 7, 1893, RAC.
63. JDR to EJ, May 21, 1883, RAC.
64. Judson Memorial Church Circular, June 29, 1892, p. 1, RAC; EJ to JDR, October 5, 1883, RAC, indicated that the home at Hamilton was called the Berean Kinmonth Home.
65. Ibid.
66. Judson Memorial Church Circular, 1892.
67. Ibid. Congregants of the Berean Church organized in the 1880s to form the Berean Baptist Church Temperance Gospel League. EJ to JDR, October 15, 1883, RAC.
68. Sears, pp. 98–99.
69. EJ to JDR, December 10, 1886, RAC.
70. EJ to JDR, June 16, 1883, RAC.
71. Leaflet, addressed "To Milk Consumers," Berean Baptist Church, c. 1882–1888, ABHS.
72. EJ to JDR, June 16, 1883, RAC.

73. JDR to EJ, June 25, 1883, RAC.

74. EJ to JDR, January 17, 1883, RAC.

75. JDR to EJ, November 24, 1884, RAC.

76. EJ to JDR, September 6, 1883, RAC.

77. EJ to JDR, April 30, 1884; December 10, 1886; RAC.

78. JDR to EJ, June 25, 1883.

79. EJ to JDR, March 3, 1884; June 25, 1883; September 16, 1884; November 19, 1884; September 30, 1885; RAC.

80. EJ to JDR, March 3, 1884, RAC.

81. EJ to JDR, January 31, 1884, RAC.

82. Antoinette Barstow Judson to JDR, April 30, 1884, RAC.

83. This description of the 1884 trip west has been culled from a folder of receipts saved by John D. Rockefeller, RAC.

84. Of the $2,400, $1,800 was the regular Berean Church salary; $600 was Mr. Rockefeller's supplement, given as part of his annual contribution.

85. EJ to JDR, September 30, 1885; October 8, 1885; RAC.

86. EJ to JDR, September 16, 1884; RAC.

87. EJ to JDR, September 16, 1884; December 28, 1885; March 24, 1886; June 1, 1886; RAC.

88. EJ to JDR, December 28, 1885, RAC.

89. EJ to JDR, June 8, 1886, RAC.

90. S. E. Vassar to EJ, December 14, 1886, EJ Papers, ABHS. Vassar, pastor of the South Baptist Church in Newark, New Jersey, felt that it was an imposition to be asked to sell shares for the Judson Memorial Church, which his congregants regarded as a "local" project. Judson, on the other hand, maintained that it was the responsibility of American Christians to keep downtown urban churches afloat.

91. EJ to JDR, November 6, 1886, RAC.

92. S. E. Vassar to EJ, December 14, 1886, and I. I. Yates to EJ, June 5, 1906, EJ Papers, ABHS. Also, EJ to JDR, March 5, 1889; May 4, 1889, RAC.

93. EJ to JDR, March 5, 1889, RAC.

94. EJ to JDR, January 22, 1892, RAC.

95. EJ to JDR, November 9, 1887, RAC.

96. Ibid.

97. EJ to JDR, February 11, 1888, RAC.

98. JDR to EJ, February 16, 1888, RAC.

99. EJ to JDR, February 17, 1888, RAC.

100. EJ to JDR, March [n.d.], 1887, RAC.

101. Adoniram Brown Judson to JDR, February 19, 1888, RAC.

102. It is unclear as to why or when Judson's conception of the residence changed. It never was an apartment exclusively for young men. When he spoke of a "young men's building," he did not mean to pro-

vide free residence. From the start, he envisioned the residential complex as income producing.

103. EJ to JDR, December 8, 1888, RAC.

104. Ibid.

105. EJ to JDR, March 5, 1889; March 12, 1889, RAC.

106. EJ to JDR, March 16, 1889, RAC.

107. Ibid.

108. EJ to JDR, February 12, 1890, RAC.

109. EJ to JDR, May 4, 1889, RAC.

110. EJ to JDR, July 30, 1890, RAC.

111. The two churches under consideration by Judson were the MacDougal Street Baptist Church and the East Church. EJ to JDR, April 24, 1891; September 8, 1891, RAC.

112. EJ to JDR, April 24, 1891, RAC.

113. EJ to JDR, September 8, 1891, RAC.

114. Ibid.

115. EJ to JDR, February 12, 1890, RAC.

116. Ibid.

117. EJ to JDR, Jr., April 13, 1906, RFA.

118. EJ to JDR, November 9, 1893, RAC.

119. Ibid.

120. JDR to EJ, November 15, 1893, RAC.

121. Gates, pp. 114–20; Nevins, p. 193. By 1902, Rockefeller had given $10 million to the University of Chicago.

122. Gates, p. 159.

123. Ibid., p. 101.

124. Ibid., p. 162. Gates allowed that Rockefeller also had a "private list" of individuals to whom he gave Christmas and annual gifts. Gates "was rarely consulted" on any of these individual cases which he considered rather unimportant compared to the standardized giving that he supervised.

125. EJ to JDR, April 13, 1906, RFA.

126. JDR to Adoniram Brown Judson, July 6, 1904, RFA.

127. JDR, Jr., to EJ, October 2, 1906, RFA. In a letter dated May 25, 1906, Rockefeller, Jr., told Gates that the Memorial Church debt "will have to be taken care of some time, and it might be more embarrassing after Dr. Judson's death than now." This statement probably indicates that Rockefeller, Jr., and Gates were already sensitive to the financial difficulties of this church and its pastor.

128. EJ to JDR, September 21, 1906, RFA.

129. EJ to F. T. Gates, October 26, 1906, RFA.

130. EJ to F. T. Gates, October 26, 1906, November 5, 1906; F. T. Gates to EJ, October 31, 1906, November 2, 1906; F. T. Gates to JDR, November 1, 1906; JDR to F. T. Gates, November 2, 1906, RFA.

131. F. T. Gates to EJ, October 31, 1906, RFA.
132. F. T. Gates to EJ, November 2, 1906, RFA.
133. EJ to F. T. Gates, November 5, 1906, RFA.
134. F. T. Gates to EJ, November 2, 1906, RFA.
135. F. T. Gates to JDR, November 5, 1906, RFA.
136. EJ to F. T. Gates, November 5, 1906, RFA.
137. EJ to JDR, November 3, 1910, RFA.
138. F. T. Gates to JDR, November 7, 1910, RAC.
139. EJ to JDR, November 3, 1910, RFA.
140. F. T. Gates to JDR, November 17, 1910, RFA.
141. JDR, Jr., to F. T. Gates, November 4, 1910, RFA.
142. F. T. Gates to EJ, November 3, 1897, RFA.
143. F. T. Gates to EJ, March 15, 1906, RFA.
144. F. T. Gates to EJ, March 25, 1906, RFA.
145. In 1898 and 1899 Judson had been offered the presidencies of both Brown and Colgate Universities. In 1903, he held the chair of Homiletics at the University of Chicago and in 1905 lectured at Union Theological Seminary.
146. Memo, F. T. Gates to JDR, October [n.d.], 1908, RFA.
147. Ibid.
148. F. T. Gates to JDR, November 17, 1910, RFA.
149. Memo, F. T. Gates to JDR, October [n.d.], 1908, RFA.
150. EJ to JDR, November 26, 1910, RFA.
151. William Henry Hays to JDR, June 20, 1913, RFA. Edward Judson did serve as president of the New York City Baptist Mission Society. In July 1913, Rockefeller agreed to take on one-third of the added expenses of the New York Baptist City Mission Society incurred because of the transfer of the Memorial Church. In effect, the Rockefellers continued to support Judson's *magnum opus*.
152. See Robert Weibe, *The Search for Order,* 1877–1902 (New York, 1967).
153. EJ to JDR, November 20, 1911, RAC.
154. Memo, JDR, Jr., December 4, 1913, RFA.
155. E. L. Ballard to JDR, Jr., December 18, 1913, RFA.
156. EJ to JDR, Jr., February 16, 1914, RFA.
157. JDR, Jr., to [the] Misses Judson, October 24, 1914, RFA.
158. EJ to JDR, December 25, 1912, RFA.
159. EJ, *Church and the People*, p. 4.

AFTERWORD

1. The First Great Awakening is the name that is generally given to the New England religious revival of the 1740s. The term Second Great Awakening usually represents the popular evangelicalism that swept

New England, the Middle Atlantic states, and the western and southern frontiers in the period 1790–1850. A less common designation, the Third Great Awakening, is sometimes used to represent the surge of urban revivalism that swept large cities in the last decades of the nineteenth century.

2. *Time* (December 26, 1977), p. 53.
3. In 1979, Campus Crusade for Christ (CCC) employed 9,000 staff members. Information from a phone interview with Pat Pearce, Field Ministry Division, CCC.
4. George Gallup, Jr., "U.S. in Early Stages of Religious Revival," *Journal of Current Social Issues* (Spring 1977), pp. 50–52.
5. See Christopher Lasch, *The Culture of Narcissism: American life in an age of diminishing expectations* (New York, 1979).
6. Archibald D. Hart, *Feeling Free* (Old Tappan, N.J., 1979), John Dobbert, *Give Yourself a Chance* (Old Tappan, N.J., 1979); Cyvette Guerra, *The Joy Robbers* (San Luis Obispo, Ca., 1979).
7. Richard Quebedeaux, *The Worldly Evangelicals* (New York, 1978), p. 68; *Time* (December 26, 1977), p. 54.
8. *Publishers Weekly (PW)*, 215:7 (February 12, 1979), p. 78. For religious views of this phenomenon, see Ben Armstrong, *The Electric Church* (Nashville, 1979), and Fulton J. Sheen, *The Electric Christian* (New York, 1979).
9. Ibid., p. 12. "The Christian Revival," *The Saturday Evening Post (SEP)* (April 1979), p. 40. It should be noted that Christian book sales are actually higher than the CBA figure; some thirty-five percent of Christian bookstores do not belong to the CBA.
10. *New York Times* (November 26, 1978), p. 24.
11. *PW*, pp. 2–3.
12. *SEP*, pp. 40, 136.
13. Quebedeaux (see n. 7 above) uses this term to distinguish politically and socially conservative evangelicals from what he identifies as "a new generation of evangelical Christians" who "repudiate and disown" the traditional conservatism of the movement. See Richard Quebedeaux, *The Young Evangelicals* (New York, 1974) for a description of what he calls the evangelical left.
14. See Linda Gordon and Allen Hunter, "Sex, Family and the New Left: Anti-Feminism as a Political Force," *Radical America* XI:VI (November 1977-February 1978), pp. 9–17. Gordon's and Hunter's analysis deals primarily with the antisexual and antifeminist elements of "white ethnics," primarily Catholics.
15. "The New Housewife Blues," *Time* (March 14, 1977), p. 63.
16. Ed Hindson, "The Total Family," *Faith Aflame* 4:1 (January-February 1979), p. 12.
17. Ibid.
18. Maude Aimee Humbard Letter, May 1979. This letter followed on the

heels of her husband's public announcement that the family would remain in the United States, rather than travel, in 1979. In America,
which is "like Nineveh then," Humbard plans "to share the message
of God's love with American families . . . to help strengthen families
across our nation . . . to help repair broken hearts and heal sick relationships." *The Answer*, pp. 2–4. The message America needs, says
Humbard, is that "You Are Loved." Consequently, his 1979 work re-
volves around that theme, which also forms a stylish, contemporary
logo on all of his recent publications.

19. The following members of the U.S. Congress participated in the
Falwell rally: Senators Jesse Helm (North Carolina), Harry Byrd (Virginia), Paul Laxalt (Nevada), Gordon Humphrey (New Hampshire),
and John Warner (Virginia); Congressman George Hansen (Idaho),
Robert Dornan (California), and Tom Kindness (Ohio).

Bibliography

I. Works by the Judsons

Boardman, George Dana. "Address to the First Baptist Church at Malden, Massachusetts on the Occasion of the Judson Centennial, 1888." *Judson Centennial Services*. N.p., 1888.
_____. *Epiphanies of the Risen Lord*. New York, 1879.
_____. *Ethics of the Body*. Philadelphia, 1903.
_____. *The Church (Ecclesia)*. New York, 1901.
_____. *The Divine Man, from the Nativity to the Temptation*. New York, 1887.
_____. *The Kingdom (Basilica)*. New York, 1899.
_____. *Studies in the Creative Week*. New York, 1875.
_____. *Studies in the Mountain Instruction*. New York, 1881.
Judson, Abby Ann. *A Happy Year; or Fifty Two Letters to the Banner of Light*. Newark, 1899.

_____. *Development of Mediumship of Terrestrial Magnetism*. Minneapolis, 1891.

_____. *From Night to Morn; or An Appeal to the Baptist Church*. Norwich, Conn., 1894.

_____. *The Bridge between Two Worlds*. Minneapolis, 1894.

_____. *Why She Became a Spiritualist: Twelve Lectures delivered before the Minneapolis Association of Spiritualists*. Minneapolis, 1891.

Judson, Adoniram. *A Cry from Burmah. A Letter from Adoniram Judson to Rev. Mr. Grow of Connecticut, March 4, 1831*. N.p., n.d.

_____. *A Letter Addressed to the Female Members of the Christian Church in the United States of America*. New Haven, 1832.

_____. *Christian Baptism, A Sermon Preached in the Lal Bazar Chapel, Calcutta, September 27, 1812*. Boston, 1817.

_____. *Elements of English Grammar*. Boston, 1808.

_____. *The Threefold Cord. Written by a Missionary in Burmah*. Philadelphia, n.d.

_____. *The Young Lady's Arithmetic: A Complete Mercantile System for the Use of Young Persons, More Especially the Fair Sex*. Boston, 1808.

Judson, Adoniram, Sr. *A Sermon Preached in the New Meeting House, Plymouth, December 22, 1802 in Memory of the Landing of Our Ancestors*. Boston, 1803.

Judson, Ann Hasseltine. *A Particular Relation of the American Baptist Mission to the Burman Empire. In a Series of letters addressed to Joseph Butterworth, Esq., M.P., London*. Washington City, 1823.

A Little Book of Judson Verse: From the writings of Sarah Boardman Judson and Fanny Forester. Chicago, 1908.

Judson, Edward. "The Church in Its Social Aspect." *Annals of the American Academy of Political and Social Science*, XXX (July-December 1907).

_____. *The Christian and the People*. Boston, 1886.

_____. *The Church and Children*. Philadelphia, n.d.

_____. *The Church and the People*. Chicago, 1886.

_____. *The Institutional Church: A Primer in Pastoral Theology*. New York, 1899.

_____. *The Life of Adoniram Judson*. New York, 1883.

_____. "Worship God by Giving Money." *Baptist Home Mission Monthly*, XIX (January 1897).

Judson, Emily Chubbuck [Fanny Forester]. *Alderbrook*. Boston, 1847.

_____. *Allen Lucas; The Self Made Man*. Utica, 1843.

_____. *An Olio of Domestic Verse*. New York, 1852.

_____. *Charles Linn; or How to Observe the Golden Rule*. New York, 1841.

_____. *Lilias Fane, and Other Tales*. Boston, 1846.

_____. *Memoir of Sarah B. Judson*. New York, 1848.

_____. *My Two Sisters: A Sketch from Memory*. Boston, 1853.

_____. *The Great Secret; or, How to Be Happy.* New York, 1842.

_____. *The Kathayan Slave and Other Papers Connected with Missionary Life.* Boston, 1853.

_____. *Trippings in Author-Land.* New York, 1846.

II. PRIMARY AND SECONDARY SOURCES DEALING SPECIFICALLY WITH
THE JUDSONS

Allen, Jonathan. *Sermon Delivered at Haverhill, February 5, 1812 on the Occasion of Two Young Ladies Being About to Embark as the Wives of Rev. Messieurs Judson and Newell, going as Missionaries to India.* Haverhill, 1812.

Alvord, Reed. "Fanny Forester." *The Upstate Monthly* (October-November, 1942).

Anderson, Courtney. *To the Golden Shore: The Life of Adoniram Judson.* Boston, 1956.

Babcock, Rufus. *A Discourse Commemorative of the Life and Labors of the Rev. Adoniram Judson.* New York, 1851.

Bailey, Faith Coxe. *Adoniram Judson, Missionary to Burma.* Chicago, 1955.

Boardman Papers, American Baptist Historical Society, Rochester, New York.

Batten, Jennie Rowena. *Golden Foot: The Story of the Judsons of Burma.* London, 1956.

Bruce, James Manning. *In Memoriam: Edward Judson. A Sermon Preached in the Memorial Baptist Church, Washington Square, New York City, November 1, 1914.* New York, 1915.

Carver, W. O. "The Significance of Adoniram Judson." *Baptist Review and Expositor* X (October 1913).

Clement, J. *Memoir of Adoniram Judson: Being a Sketch of His Life and Missionary Labors.* Auburn, 1851.

Chubbuck Family Papers, File #1837, State Historical Society of Wisconsin, Archives Division.

Conant, Hannah C. *The Earnest Man or the Character and Labors of Adoniram Judson.* Boston, 1856.

Cushman, Robert Woodward. *Grace and Apostleship: Illustrated in the Life of Judson. A Discourse delivered before the Maryland Union Association, May 5, 1851.* Philadelphia, n.d.

Dowling, John, ed. *The Judson Offering, intended as a Token of Christian Sympathy with the Living, and a Memento of Christian Affection for the Dead.* New York, 1846.

Eddy, Daniel C. *A Sketch of Adoniram Judson: The Burman Apostle.* Lowell, 1851.

———. *The Three Mrs. Judsons, and other daughters of the Cross.* Boston, 1859.

Floram, Philip. "Fanny Forester: A Critical Estimate of Her Prose and Poetry." Unpublished M.A. thesis, Department of English, St. Bernardine of Siena College, Loudonville, New York, 1953.

Gillette, Abram Dunn. "Adoniram Judson." *Christian Souvenir* I (December 1846).

———. *A Sketch of the Labors, Sufferings and Death of the Rev. Adoniram Judson, D.D.* Philadelphia, 1851.

Grahame, Nigel B. *Judson of Burma, the story of a man who faced torture and death with unflinching Courage . . . retold for boys and girls.* New York, 1924.

Gray, Edward Harkness. *The Christian Hero of the Nineteenth Century.* Cambridge, 1852.

Grose, Edward, and Haggard, Fred P., eds. *The Judson Centennial, 1814–1914.* Philadelphia, 1914.

L.J.H. "Fanny Forester's Writings." *The Christian Examiner and Religious Miscellany* XLIII (May 1847).

Hague, William. *The Life and Character of Adoniram Judson. A Commemorative Discourse Delivered before the American Baptist Missionary Union, Boston, May 15, 1851.* Boston, 1851.

Hall, E. B. "Dr. Judson's Life and Labor." *The Christian Examiner and Religious Miscellany* LVI (January-March 1854).

Hartley, Cecil B. *The Three Mrs. Judsons, the Celebrated Female Missionaries.* Philadelphia, 1863.

Hill, James D. *The Immortal Seven: Judson and His Associates.* Philadelphia, 1913.

"Fanny Forester." *Hogg's Weekly Instructor* II (1848–49).

Hubbard, Ethel Daniels. *Ann of Ava.* New York, 1913.

Johnston, Julia Harriette. *The Life of Adoniram Judson.* New York, 1881.

Lewis, J. Nelson, ed. *Judson Centennial Services. A Compilation of the Addresses, Papers, and Remarks Given at These Services.* Malden, 1888.

Kendrick, Asahel Clark. *The Life and Letters of Mrs. Emily C. Judson.* New York, 1861.

Knowles, James D. *Memoir of Mrs. Ann H. Judson.* Boston, 1829.

Lloyd, Hinton S. "Adoniram Judson and the Institution at Hamilton." *Watchman Examiner* (January 29, 1914).

Marrat, Jabez. *The Apostle of Burma.* London, 1890.

[Middleditch, Robert.] *Burmah's Great Missionary. Records of the Life of Adoniram Judson.* New York, 1854.

Morrow, Honoré Willsie. *Splendor of God.* New York, 1929.

Morchaine, Janet Kerr. "George Dana Boardman: Propagandist for Peace." *Foundations* IX (April-June 1966).

Mortensen, Joseph Ide. "The Career of the Reverend George Dana Board-man." Unpublished Th.D. dissertation, Boston University School of Theology, 1966.

Murdock, John Nelson. *Our Missionary Pioneer. A Paper Read at the 74th Anniversary of the American Baptist Missionary Union at Washington, D.C., May 21, 1888.* N.p., n.d.

Nott, Samuel. *A Letter Addressed to Rev. Enoch Pond on the Insinuations and Charges Contained in His Reply to Mr. Judson's Sermon on Baptism.* Boston, 1819.

Page, Jesse. *Judson: The Hero of Burma. The Stirring Life of the First Missionary to the Burmese Told for Boys and Girls.* New York, 1915.

Percy, Laura Helen. *Adoniram Judson: Apostle of Burma.* Anderson, Ind., 1926.

Phinney, F. D., ed. *The Judson Centennial Celebrations in Burma, 1813–1913.* Rangoon, 1914.

Pond, Enoch. *Nott's Testimony in Favor of Judson. Examined in a Letter Addressed to Rev. Samuel Nott, late missionary to India.* Boston, 1819.

Porter, Edward G. *Address at Bradford Academy, March 26, 1884, on presentation of the portrait of Ann Hasseltine Judson. . . .* Haverhill, 1884.

Richards, William C. *The Apostle of Burma. A Missionary Epic in Commemoration of the Centennial of the Birth of Adoniram Judson.* Boston, 1889.

Robinson, Vergil E. *The Judsons of Burma.* Washington, 1966.

Sears, Charles Hatch. *Edward Judson: Interpreter of God.* Philadelphia, 1917.

Simmons, Dawn Langley. *Golden Boats from Burma: The Life of Ann Hasseltine Judson.* Philadelphia, 1961.

Statistical Sketch of Dr. Judson's Missionary Life. New York, 1846.

Vail, A. L. "The Mysterious Library that Helped Judson." *The Journal and Messenger* LXXXIII (February 19, 1914).

Walter, George W. "Fanny Forester Herself." *Mid-York Weekly* (Hamilton, N.Y., May 1951).

Warburton, Stacy R. *Eastward! The Story of Adoniram Judson.* New York, 1937.

Wayland, Francis. *A Memoir of the Life and Labors of the Rev. Adoniram Judson.* Boston, 1853.

Willson, Arabella Stuart. *The Lives of Mrs. Ann H. Judson and Mrs. Sarah B. Judson with a Biographical Sketch of Mrs. Emily C. Judson. Missionaries to Burma.* Auburn, 1854.

Wyeth, Walter. *Ann H. Judson: A Memorial.* Cincinnati, 1888.

———. *Emily C. Judson: A Memorial.* N.p., 1890.

———. *Sarah B. Judson: A Memorial.* Philadelphia, 1889.

Index